DONGRI ᴛᴏ DUBAI

DONGRI to DUBAI

SIX DECADES OF
THE MUMBAI MAFIA

S. HUSSAIN ZAIDI

LOTUS COLLECTION

ROLI BOOKS

Lotus Collection

© S. Hussain Zaidi, 2012

First published in April 2012
Third impression, June 2012
The views and opinions expressed in this book are the author's own and
the facts are as reported by him which have been verified to the extent
possible, and the publishers are not in any way liable for the same.

The Lotus Collection
An imprint of
Roli Books Pvt. Ltd
M-75, Greater Kailash II Market
New Delhi 110 048
Phone: ++91 (011) 4068 2000
Fax: ++91 (011) 2921 7185
E-mail: info@rolibooks.com; Website: www.rolibooks.com

Also at Bangalore, Chennai, & Mumbai

Layout: Sanjeev Mathpal
Production: Shaji Sahadevan

ISBN: 978-81-7436-894-2

Typeset in Perpetua by Roli Books Pvt. Ltd
and printed and bound in India by Nutech Print Services

Dedicated to my friends

Dr Shabeeb Rizvi
Chandramohan Puppala
Mir Rizwan Ali

Contents

Foreword

Ifirst met S. Hussain Zaidi in the winter of 1997, when I had just begun writing a novel about the Mumbai underworld. I desperately needed help, and was lucky enough to have a sister who knew Hussain through their shared profession of journalism. So I met up with him at the cheerfully-named Bahar restaurant in the Fort area of Mumbai. I asked questions, and Hussain told me stories about greed and corruption, about shooters and their targets, and despite the chill that passed over my skin, I was aware of a rising swell of optimism—this guy was really, really good.

I didn't know that day that S. Hussain Zaidi would become a friend, an extraordinary inside informant about matters relating to crime and punishment, and my guide into the underworld. But that is exactly what happened. Over the next few years, as I wrote my novel, Hussain generously shared with me his vast knowledge, his canny experience, and his host of contacts. I can say with certainty that I would not have been able to write my book without his ever-ready help and advice.

It makes me very happy that Hussain has finished his magnum opus, *Dongri to Dubai*, so that the general reader can now benefit from his expertise. This book does much more than narrate the saga of one man's rise, it brings alive the entire culture of crime that has grown and formed itself over the last half century in India. And as much as we like to distance ourselves by pretending that the underworld exists quite literally under us, beneath us, the truth—as Hussain shows—is that we mingle with it every day. The influence of organised crime reaches into the economy, our polity, and everyday life.

Yet, our knowledge of the intentions and operations of the players on all sides of the law is mostly a mixture of legend and conjecture. Our histories begin with a few names—Haji Mastan, Varadarajan, Karim Lala — imbued with dread, and continue with still others —Dawood, Chhota Rajan, Abu Salem—haloed with matinee glamour. What we have lacked is a narrative that provides both detail and perspective, that lays out the entire bloody saga of power-mongering, money, and murder. *Dongri to Dubai* is that necessary book, and more. It gives us an account that is vast in its scope and yet intimate in its understanding of motive and desire. Hussain moves us from the small gangs of early post-Independence India to the corporatising consolidations of the eighties and through the sanguine street wars of the nineties; we better comprehend our present, with its abiding undercurrent of terror, if we follow the tangled, stranger-than-fiction history that puts an Indian gangster in a safe-house in Karachi, with a daughter married to the son of a national celebrity, and his coffers enriched by the bootleg sales of Mumbai movies to Pakistanis.

Anthropologists like to use the phrase 'thick description' to describe an explanation of a behaviour that also includes and explains context, so that the behaviour becomes intelligible to an outsider. For most readers, I think, reading *Dongri to Dubai* will at first feel like a journey into an alien landscape with a trustworthy, experienced guide; by the end though Hussain has made us see, helped us to comprehend, and we recognise this terrain as our own world, and we understand—but don't necessarily forgive—its inhabitants.

I am grateful for this book. The work that Hussain does is exacting and sometimes dangerous. Reporting about these deadly intrigues and the human beings caught within them is not for the faint of heart; the web stretches from your corner paan-shop to the bleak heights on which the Great Game is played, and there are many casualties. We all profit from Hussain's intrepid investigations.

Vikram Chandra
Mumbai, December 2011

Preface

*D*ongri to Dubai: Six Decades of the Mumbai Mafia has been my most complex and difficult project since I took to reporting on crime way back in 1995. The biggest challenge by far has been chronicling the history of the Mumbai underworld and keeping it interesting for lay readers as well as choosing incidents that marked an epoch in the Mumbai mafia.

It was first suggested to me by a friend in 1997, when I was barely a couple of years into crime reporting, that I should try to write about the history of the Mumbai mafia; I was advised to replicate something like Joe Gould's *Secret*. At the time, I had not even heard of the book; to be honest, I felt it was too colossal a responsibility for someone who was still wet behind the ears.

But having put my ear to the ground for *Black Friday*, I felt ready for a bigger challenge. Initially, I set out to find out why so many Muslim youngsters from Mumbai were drawn to crime. Was it the aura of Dawood Ibrahim or was it economic compulsion that drew them? That was the question with which I started. And somewhere along the way, I ended up doing what my friend had asked me to do initially.

When I set off on the story from Dongri, the metaphor was not lost on my friends. Am I guilty of linking members of a particular religion with crime? Unlike in the US, where exhaustive studies have been conducted on race and crime and their correlation, if any, there has been no serious debate or study on the causes that made Muslims prone to following a life of crime in the last fifty years.

When I say Dongri, it is not just the area that starts from Mandvi near Zakaria Masjid but from Crawford Market to the end of JJ Hospital, covering Null Bazaar, Umerkhadi, Chor Bazaar, Kamathipura, and all the interweaving cloth and retail markets and masjids.

Tracing the history of Mumbai, historian and researcher Sharada Dwivedi writes that the area was once a flatland and Dongri was a hill; there used to be a Portuguese fort here that the British took over and fortified. But before the British started reclaiming the land, the fort area was a low-lying area below the rocky heights of Dongri, which provided easy access to the sea. Muslim settlers are known to have lived in the higher lands near the present day Chakala Market, and in Dongri, from as far back as the fourteenth century.

The eastern part of Bombay[1] island was predominantly Muslim dominated for a long time, and remains so even today. After the seven islands were linked, Dongri got a life of its own. The chaos around it happened gradually; with access to the markets, commerce thrived and so did the population. Traffic is a mess, the pavements have been taken over by hawkers, pedestrians spill onto the streets, and the place is always bustling with activity. To the west of Dongri is the Chor Bazaar (literally meaning 'thieves' market') where you can get everything from old wardrobes discarded by Parsi households to antiques, gramophones, and other curios.

Long before Dawood changed the way Dongri is perceived today, others who had walked the hall of fame and notoriety in the Dongri area were Chinka Dada, Ibrahim Dada, Haji Mastan, Karim Lala, and Baashu Dada.

In those days, the easiest crime was to accost late night travellers and relieve them of their valuables. The art of pickpocketing was yet to be learnt and perfected. But the wielding of the shiny blade of a knife, sword, or chopper was enough to send shivers down the spine of the peace-loving residents of Bombay, as it was known back then. Every little crime was reported with flourish by the British journalists. One of them, Alfred W. Davis alias Gunman, who reported on crime for the *Blitz*, was a legend. A reporter who flowered under his tutelage was Usman Gani Muqaddam. Usman was known for his diligent news gathering and investigative skills. After extensive interviews with Usman Gani and other veteran crime reporters and my own research, I gathered that Dongri had always been the epicentre of crime in Mumbai.

In the first fortnight of 1947, the city witnessed a spate of crimes. the *Times of India* reported four incidents. On 1 January 1947, stray knife attacks were reported at Lalbaug, Agripada, and Dongri. The police arrested nine people and launched a drive to nab the culprits involved. Within days on 8 January, the Anti-Corruption Bureau seized 400 carving knives from a flat on Marine Drive but could not arrest anybody. The same day, a social worker was stabbed in Parel. B.J. Deorukhkar, a municipal councillor, was also murdered, an incident that shocked the city and raised an alarm.

Even before the cops could take a breather, there was another incident, but this time, they showed amazing alacrity. On 11 January, the police arrested two Pathans who had looted a bank within ninety minutes of the crime being committed. The robbers had entered a bank in south Bombay and decamped with the booty in a waiting car. The car, bearing the registration number BMX 1221 (they had covered the license plate on the back of the car with a red cloth) was making a getaway at full speed when a constable with the Esplanade Police Station, now known as the Azad Maidan Police Station, intercepted it and hauled them to the police station, where they were arrested. Ah, the power of the constabulary! Once upon a time, the constables were the backbone of the police force in Mumbai.

In the next couple of days, on 14 January, the police busted a gang of racketeers operating at the parcel booking office at Victoria Terminus (now called Chhatrapati Shivaji Terminus). The members of the gang would approach people and ask for money, assuring in return that their parcels would reach their destination earlier than via the usual route. Needless to say, the parcels never reached. Those arrested were identified as Nazir Abdul Kader, Sayed Bashir Nazir, and Fakhruddin Kaderbhai.

Most criminals from in and around Dongri became increasingly emboldened in their modus operandi as their crimes went undetected. Others from the area joined the fray when they realised that it was a chance to make easy money with very little chance of being caught. Thus, the boys from Dongri began making their mark in the crimedom.

But Dongri gained notoriety with Dawood Ibrahim; nobody took Dongri to Dubai like he did. This book traces the eventful journey of Dawood's predecessors, but most importantly, it follows Dawood's trail too, the life of a boy from Dongri who made crime very fashionable; the boy from Dongri who flew out of the coop but refused to leave India behind, who took refuge in an enemy country but continue to play his games here. The boy from Dongri who became a don from Dubai.

Endnote

1   The name of the city 'Bombay' was changed to 'Mumbai' in 1995. So the city is referred to as 'Bombay' in the book for the time period till 1995.

Introduction: Up, Close, and Personal

In the nineties two things happened in India that changed the fortunes of the mafia in Mumbai. When I was writing about the Mumbai mafia back then, it had been a decade since Dawood had left its shores. Three years earlier Dawood had emerged as a key player in the serial blasts of Mumbai in March 1993. It was also at this time that Prime Minister P.V. Narasimha Rao woke up to release the country from the grip of the Licence Raj and ushered in the liberalisation of the Indian economy. When the Indian perestroika happened, it released a flood of economic opportunities and the first to smell the potential profit was the mafia, by then already entangled with Bollywood.

Suddenly there were so many real estate opportunities. There was talk of mill land sales. At the time, the many mills in Bombay were closing down fast, which meant that there was a whole lot of land in the real estate business to play around with. The only surviving mafia don at the time in Mumbai, Arun Gawli, spent most of his time behind bars. Ashwin Naik was absconding and Dawood was still in remote control mode in Dubai. His brother Anees Ibrahim was more active on the ground. And then there was the breakaway Abu Salem. Chhota Rajan had broken off with Dawood and anointed himself a Hindu don. Both were baying for each other's blood and in the intermediate period were busy bumping off each other's business associates in broad daylight. If it was the now defunct East West Airlines chief Thakiyuddin Wahid one day then it was builder Om Prakash Kukreja another day. The Mumbai police were blushing at the horrific body count. One police commissioner even recommended using hockey sticks for the public to defend itself. It was a great time to be a crime reporter.

Although I had missed out on the earlier generation that saw Dawood actually emerge as a don, I was there for the part of the action that resulted in the meltdown of the Mumbai mafia. As I wrote their stories, taking swipes at them, describing their hidden dens and their networks, their interests, their women, their colourful lives, their hold over Bollywood and real estate deal-meddling, I met with the dons themselves to hear their stories firsthand and set them down. So there was a meeting with Arun Gawli, the don from Dagdi Chawl in south Mumbai at the Harsul Central jail in Aurangabad. I spoke to Chhota Rajan, who was spitting fire at Dawood, his one-time friend and benefactor, who was holed away in southeast Asia; then I spoke to Dawood's Man Friday Chhota Shakeel and, of course, Abu Salem and Ashwin Naik. As a crime reporter, however, my repertoire would not be complete until I had interviewed the one man who had left the shores of Mumbai but still held sway over his city from afar.

By then, of course, everybody was writing about Dawood but access to him had trickled away. Although Dawood had given interviews to journalists before 1993, he had simply vanished off the media radar after 1995. Dawood had just relocated to Karachi at this time and was virtually inaccessible on the phone.

I decided to take the second best option. I began working on Shakeel's Mumbai network: his hawala operators, gang managers, and other contacts. Within a few months, I was one of the first journalists to crack a hotline to Chhota Shakeel.

Eventually I asked Chhota Shakeel to set up an interview with Dawood. Soon after, T-Series music baron Gulshan Kumar was killed by Abu Salem, who was by then operating on his own. But Chhota Shakeel did not want any part of the blame to fall on Dawood, as his boss was not responsible for Kumar's death, Salem was. So finally Dawood Ibrahim did agree to an interview. The terms for the interview were set: I would publish Dawood's interview without any distortion and I would not contact the man who had led me to Dawood any more. A big price to pay.

This is how it was to work. My instructions were to wait patiently; Dawood would contact me whenever it suited him. For a long time after that, there was no beep on my pager from my source. Then *Outlook* magazine ran a story on how Dawood was public enemy number one. This hit him badly—so much that he sent his men to attack the *Outlook* office. The office was badly vandalized although nobody was hurt.

Within a couple of days, my pager beeped and I was asked to call on a local number. I was in a rickshaw passing through Kalina so I got off and called from a local restaurant. I was asked to wait for a couple of minutes, and soon after I received a call at the number I had just used.

The caller spoke in a very polite manner. His phone manner was perfect, enough to put a well-bred Lucknowi to shame. I was amused, thinking to myself that the don had done well for himself and hired some really cultured phone attendants. I switched to my own repertoire of chaste Urdu and asked, '*Janab, aap ka isme geraami* [pray what's your good name]?'

I was utterly taken aback when he said, '*Main Dawood bol raha hoon, aap mujh se baat karna chahte the.* [This is Dawood speaking. I believe you wished to speak with me.]'

We spoke for fifteen minutes, during which he painstakingly tried to explain how he was not public enemy number one and wondered how his name had unnecessarily been dragged into the serial bomb blasts case. I said, 'Okay, I want to record this. Can you give me an exhaustive interview?'

The interview was to be conducted over the phone and via fax. If he did not like a question on the phone, I was not to repeat it on the fax. I agreed.

He gave me a date and time and the number of a PCO, where I was supposed to wait. On the appointed day, he called exactly at the designated time, 10:40 pm IST. The interview lasted for fifty minutes.

I called my editor, Meenal Baghel at the *Indian Express* afterwards. She sounded pleased, as she usually did, with my big stories. She gave me a compliment too: 'You have reached the stature of Ritu Sarin [a top-notch reporter in the Delhi bureau of the *Indian Express*].' This was a scoop that was to go down in reporting history; also the first time Dawood had given an interview after he had gone into exile.

Here is the gist of the interview, which appeared on the front page of the *Indian Express* in September 1997.

'Film industry shouldn't be afraid of me'

AFTER a long silence of over four years, India's most wanted underworld don, Dawood Ibrahim Kaskar, spoke to S HUSSAIN ZAIDI recently. Speaking on the telephone for over 45 minutes from an undisclosed location, Dawood skirted questions about Pakistan's ISI and denied he had engineered the serial blasts in Mumbai. Excerpts from the interview, sans comment:

In which part of the globe are you now?

I don't have any problem visiting any part of the world, except India where false and politically motivated cases await me.

But there are reports that you are holed up in Karachi and that your movements are watched by Pakistan's Inter-Services Intelligence [ISI]...

Hmmmm. How do I know who is watching me? They never tell you, do they?

There are reports that you have invested heavily in real estate in Karachi, that you are at present involved in constructing a few shopping plazas there?

What? This is absolute nonsense.

What do you think of that country?

Pakistan is an Islamic country and the next door neighbour of India. But, I don't have much knowledge about it.

Have you retired from your gang activities? Who controls your gang now?

Except for my short stint with the underworld in Mumbai, I was never engaged in any gang activity. So where is the question of my being involved with them now?

Any comments on your flourishing extortion rackets and your expanding drug empire?

Nonsense. I have never extorted money from anybody. These are baseless charges.

And your drug business?

Zaidi *saheb*, because I respect you, I pardon such an irreverent line of questioning. I was never into the drug business. In fact, I don't even associate myself with those who are in this business. I hate this stuff and also hate those who deal in it.

Is it not true that among your men, Ejaz Pathan is executing drug deals for you?

Rubbish! Ejaz Pathan is not my man. He does not do any business for me.

Then how come there are so many charges against you?

As you know, I am not in India at the moment. Which civilised nation would ever allow an expatriate to engage in drugs business in their land? Despite the Indian law enforcement agencies' perpetual hatred for me and my family they have not been able to frame even a false drug case against me. The recent offensive has been launched against me with political motives. But the people behind this malicious propaganda cannot deceive the international anti-narcotic agencies.

Do you still consider yourself to be a patriotic Indian?

How do you think one feels about the country of his birth, where his family and mother still live? Not only was I born and raised in India, innumerable people in that country know that I am their 'bhai'.

Then why did you engineer bomb blasts killing more than 300 people?

The bomb blasts were a conspiracy to distance me from the people who loved me. As I have stated earlier, I had nothing to do with the Bombay blasts. Every day I see the blasts being mentioned in one newspaper or the other, but I have rarely seen newspapers condemning the people who orchestrated the demolition of the Babri Masjid and forced 140 million Indian Muslims to reassess their future in this country.

OK. But tell me, why are you threatening and killing the film industry people?

This is absurd. I would like to tell the film world that there is no need to be afraid of me. Also, those who terrorize them in my name are not my people.

Who are your friends in the film industry?
I have shared an excellent relationship, based on mutual respect, with a number of film personalities, though in the present climate of suspicion I would not like to name them.

Were you aware of Gulshan Kumar's killing?
Only after Reuters filed the story from Mumbai.

Is it true that Abu Salem carried out the killing without informing you?
I don't know what you are talking about. The press and the Mumbai police should talk to the people who have publicly claimed to have full knowledge about the killers. These important people are ready to unravel the whole mystery. The police must now stop blaming me for every death in Mumbai. Thank God I was not around in 1947; otherwise I would have been blamed for the Partition.

Are you financing films?
No.

What do you think about Nadeem? Is he innocent or guilty?
I don't know Nadeem. To the best of my memory I have never met him. Somebody should ask the police to stop chasing shadows.

What do you think of Mumbai police? Do you approve of encounter killings?
Mumbai police is degenerating. Once the most respected police set-ups in the country, it is now framing false cases and getting innocent people killed in fake encounters. It is fast losing the respect of Mumbaiites.

Which political party you are close to?
To tell you very frankly, before the Babri Masjid demolition I used to have pretty liberal political views and had held two different national political parties in very high esteem. After the Babri mosque demolition I have developed this rigid political opinion that the Muslims of India must only associate with the Muslim league.

What do you think of Gawli and Rajan?
Who?

Arun Gawli and Chhota Rajan, your rivals, who are after your life.

My views about them are similar to that of an average Mumbaiite. For me they are street hoodlums. As regards their challenge, elephants don't react to barking dogs.

Are you supporting Ashwin Naik?

No.

Do you like being addressed as a don... do you miss a common man's life with your wife and children?

I am a businessman not a don. As regards my family life, I am quite happy and don't miss anything.

Have you ever thought of coming back to India?

Several times. Once the government of India withdraws false cases against me, my friends and family members, I will catch the first flight to Mumbai. I will then go and offer my prayers of thanks at the Jama Masjid.

As it turned out this was Dawood's last published interview. After this, he might have spoken to journalists but he never allowed them to publish the conversation as an interview. During the several conversations I had with him, I found him to be an intelligent, witty, and softspoken man. He displayed a cool, baseline temperament that did not spike at any point during the conversation. He showed no trace of arrogance or power as a don but kept dropping hints and clues of his well-informed network within the police department and his own intelligence network.

Dawood did not like any kind of aspersion to be cast against himself, any negative image of himself to be painted. He hated the way in which the *Outlook* article portrayed him as traitor. He wanted to be the Don. For, he was the boy from Dongri, the man who managed to outdo Haji Mastan, Karim Lala, and Bashu Dada and, of course, the giant Pathans. He became numero uno through his skill and a certain amount of luck. What follows is the tale of all these men and the empires they built.

PART I

1

The Big D

Power flows from the barrel of a gun. Ask Dawood Hasan Ibrahim Kaskar: he is not just an attestation to this power, he is living testimony to its omnipresence. India's mafia export to the world, now living in hiding somewhere in Pakistan, underworld leader Dawood Ibrahim is the most wanted man on the planet. When Dawood, leader of the infamous criminal outfit D Company, was dubbed a global terrorist by the US Treasury Department in 2004, there were no furrows in the brows of his henchmen, spread all over the globe. They said the United States had reaffirmed the numero uno status of their boss who, according to them, believes from the depth of his twisted heart that he is on par with the President of the United States

And so for many years, Dawood would name all his villas 'The White House'. He had one in Dubai until 1994, and when he shifted base to Karachi, his new headquarters became The White House; and there was another White House in London. Like the original White House incumbent, Dawood juggles deals with several countries—the difference being that most of the people he deals with are the shadowy ones who fuel the black economy of most countries. Wanted by India for various crimes including masterminding the 1993 Bombay serial bombings in which 257 people died and over 700 others were wounded, Dawood is also suspected of having provided logistical support for the 26/11 terrorist attack in the city.

In the years after he left Indian shores in 1986, the ganglord kept pining for his home country and made many attempts to stage a comeback. So while in enforced exile in Dubai, Dawood would recreate India in Dubai or Sharjah, by getting Bollywood stars to dance to his tunes or cricketers to do his bidding in his adopted country of residence.

Dawood had managed a pleasant lifestyle, a home away from home. But he would frequently send feelers about his wish to return to India through some politicians whom he was close to; it would be stonewalled, he would try again, and so on.

Then the March 1993 serial bomb blasts happened and Dawood realised that he had to finally cut the umbilical cord. Named as one of the accused, Dawood understood that he had no hopes of ever returning to his motherland. His rise to international fame began after 1992; until then he was chiefly involved in real estate; gold, silver, and electronics smuggling; and drug trafficking.

Dawood loved Mumbai and was the quintessential Mumbai boy, sharing with the city its zeal for living and ability to persist in the face of adversity. On the other hand, Pakistan beckoned and it was offering him refuge, a new name, a new identity, a new passport, a new life, if not much else. There was a catch of course; he would be a pawn in their hands. But then he was Dawood Ibrahim, he would change Pakistan and make the country dance to *his* tunes, he thought. Since he held the purse strings, this would not be a problem. So, leaving his beloved Mumbai behind, he chose to cross borders.

And so began Dawood's new journey with India's arch enemy, Pakistan. In the last forty years, two people have changed the equations between India and Pakistan; one is Dawood Ibrahim and the other was former president of Pakistan General Zia-ul-Haq. If Zial-ul-Haq got Salafi Islam to Kashmir and changed the Sufi Kashmiris of India by giving more impetus to militancy in Kashmir, Dawood Ibrahim has soured the relations between the two countries to the point of no return.

The situation has become a standing joke. The Indian government has been shrilly seeking custody of Ibrahim, and Pakistan, with a straight face, has been denying that he is on their soil. But he manages to be Pakistan's trump card, to be used against India every once in a while. Both countries are aware that Dawood holds the key to the peace process between India and Pakistan.

In Karachi, Dawood initially lived in a Clifton neighbourhood bungalow, his local White House. But when he had a son called Moin, after having had three daughters in a row (Mahrooq, Mahreen, and Mazia), he built a sprawling mansion called Moin Palace in the same neighbourhood, in celebration of a long-awaited male heir. Moin Palace is the most guarded villa in the area today, with a huge posse of Karachi Rangers on round the clock vigil. The house boasts opulent Swarovski crystal showpieces, has a waterfall, a temperature controlled swimming pool, a tennis court, a billiard court, and a jogging track. His special guests are housed in Moin Palace while other less important ones are accommodated in a guesthouse in the vicinity of the Palace.

Obviously, Dawood lives life king size. His dapper suits are from Savile Row, London. A collector of timepieces, he wears exclusive Patek Philippe wristwatches and sometimes Cartier diamond studded ones, all worth lakhs of rupees. He smokes Treasurer cigarettes and wears Maserati sunglasses, sports shoes from Bally and signs with a diamond-studded pen that must be worth more than 5 lakh rupees. Dawood has a fleet of cars, but moves about in a black bomb-proof Mercedes. When he is on the move a cordon of Pak Rangers escorts him, putting the security of the Pakistani president to shame.

But all the wealth in the world cannot guarantee you a good night's sleep. Dawood is an insomniac; he drags himself home only in the wee hours of the day if he has not brought the party home already. He sleeps during the day and works in the evening. He often throws lavish *mujras* (dance recitals) for Pakistani politicians and bureaucrats, a former caretaker prime minister of Pakistan included.

Those who have met him at his villa say that various chief ministers of Pakistani provinces were found queuing for an audience with him in his waiting hall. Even those who were made to wait for hours at a stretch did not murmur a word in protest though; one meeting with the don could change their fortunes.

Dawood owns various properties scattered across Pakistan including the Khayabane Shamsheer area and the main avenue of Shah Rahe Faisal in Karachi and Madina Market in Lahore. He also has a home in Orkazai near Peshawar. Starlets from Pakistan receive his special attention and are more than willing to entertain him.

Despite being in Pakistan, he still calls the shots in India. Until some time back, Indian movie moguls and gutkha barons asked him to arbitrate disputes. And in Mumbai, many businesses—from real estate to airlines—carry the invisible Dawood logo. In that sense, he has not let go of Mumbai. He operates several real estate projects and companies in Mumbai via remote control. The police and politicians from India are still in touch with the don; many policemen in Mumbai have in fact lost their jobs after they were exposed as having links with his gang.

Dawood is 5 foot 11 inches with a menacing gaze. So what makes the man tick? He has presence; there is the way he talks, a kind of charm with a convincing quality about it; our very own Al Pacino.

Born on 26 December 1955, Dawood is now 56 years old. His look has undergone a sea change—he has lost a lot of hair and he does not sport a thick moustache anymore due to the constant threats on his life and its easy recognisability; it had earlier earned him the nickname of 'Mucchad' in the Mumbai underworld. Affluence and age have increased his waistline and the paunch is visible though not overly offending. For a man of 56, he looks fit.

The boss of the D Company is a billionaire many times over and it is said that his parallel economy keeps Pakistan afloat. It is also said that he bailed out Pakistan's Central Bank during a crisis in 2000. His net worth is allegedly more than 6 billion rupees.

Dawood's mafia connections are extensive and his business interests span many countries including India, Nepal, Pakistan, Thailand, South Africa, Indonesia, Malaysia, United Kingdom, the United Arab Emirates, Singapore, Sri Lanka, Germany, and France, and areas such as 'franchises' in the fields of drug trafficking and gambling dens.

In Karachi, Dawood Ibrahim is the uncrowned king, controlling the city's gun running business, the stock exchange, the parallel credit system business, and many real estate holdings in the city. He trades in the Karachi bourse and in the *hundi* (hawala) system. He has invested heavily in the Sehgal Group and is very close to Javed Miandad, son-in-law of one of the Sehgal brothers. Dawood has also married his daughter Mahrukh to Javed Miandad's son, Junaid.

He has thirteen aliases, one of them being Sheikh Dawood Hassan. In Pakistan, this is his identity. Some of them also call him David or Bhai. In Mumbai or Delhi, when he used to call friends, the person who made the call for him introduced him as Haji Sahab or Amir Sahab.

The D Company has many businesses in Mumbai and, it is believed, carries out billions of dollars of operations in Mumbai alone, much of it in Bollywood and real estate. Dawood is believed to control much of the hawala system, which is a very commonly used unofficial route for transferring money and remittances outside the purview of official agencies. Its turnover is much bigger than Western Union and Moneygram put together.

Dawood is the ultimate twenty-first century businessman: ruthless with his competitors but generous to those who are loyal. He knows how to manipulate relationships with his cadre, the mafia, the terrorist networks, and with the bigwigs in the Pakistan government and the ISI.

Strange that a man with so much talent and potential ended up being an antelope on the savannah, a prisoner of another country, a pawn, one that is being played by both Pakistan and many other countries including the USA, who are aware of his activities in Pakistan. Strange that the man who had the guts to take on the might of the humongous Pathan syndicate has botched his chances for a life. Dawood has managed to turn the tide in his favour on several occasions in the past. It is said that now, he is deliberately lying low.

In retrospect, perhaps Dawood's status as a fugitive and an outlaw beyond the reach of the Indian legal system suits many back home in India. Empires built with his money would collapse and many skeletons would tumble out of the closet if he was ever brought back home. The powers that be would rather have Dawood Ibrahim stuck in Pakistan. And so the cult of Dawood will be perpetuated. Movies with his trademark moustache and the cigar tucked in between his lips will continue to be made, and Dawood will be discussed between India and Pakistan forever. The man, of course, will forever be elusive; the real Dawood may remain a myth. This book is an attempt to understand what is known of him and his world.

2

In the Beginning: Bombay 1950–1960

Even in the fifties, people from all over India were drawn to Bombay like a moth to the flame. The city had earned a reputation for its nurturing abilities, in the way it welcomes in all newcomers who get the opportunity to grow in their lives. It never seemed short of resources and, despite the influx, it was growing in affluence, power, and importance. Like in New York of yore, which drew the masses into its embrace, poor youth from all parts of the country were landing in Bombay by the droves. From the north, boys from India's more rural states like Uttar Pradesh and Madhya Pradesh began descending on the city. There were few Biharis though, because until then, the Biharis regarded Calcutta (present day Kolkata) as the golden bowl and refused to look beyond the eastern capital of the country. Uttar Pradesh residents however, were sharp enough to figure out the difference between Calcutta and Mumbai. After all, Calcutta was more of a socialist set-up, where new enterprises would find it difficult to flourish, unlike in Mumbai. Also, Mumbai has always been the financial capital of the country, and has always been known as the land of opportunity. Escaping a life limited to ploughing their fields, these north Indians rooted for Mumbai hands down. The boys were mainly from Allahabad, Kanpur, Rampur, and Jaunpur in UP. At the time, the population of south Mumbai was pegged at a meagre two lakh.

The north Indian migrants began living in ghettos of their own, divided on the basis of the cities and villages back home. But slowly the boys realised that without education they could not make much headway in the city of gold; thus a few frustrated youth turned towards the task of acquiring easy money. As Napoleon Hill said, necessity may be the mother of invention but it is also the father of crime.

In those days, the easiest crime to perpetrate was accosting late night travellers or families and relieving them of their valuables. The art of picking pockets was yet to be learnt and perfected. Wielding a shiny blade of a knife, sword, or chopper was enough to send shivers down the spine of peace-loving citizens of Mumbai. The criminals were emboldened when a few crimes went undetected; it was regarded as the success of their modus operandi. And soon, other players entered the fray.

According to records maintained at the Byculla Police Station in south Bombay, Nanhe Khan, who hailed from Allahabad, was the first history-sheeter, who threatened people with a long knife and robbed them of valuables.

Soon, sometime in the fifties, other natives of Allahabad joined hands with Nanhe Khan and the group came to be christened the 'Allahabadi gang'. Nanhe Khan found lieutenants in Wahab Pehelwan and Chinka Dada. Moreover, Chinka Dada was technologically savvy and possessed something his boss never even dreamt of; two country-made revolvers at the either side, tucked in his belt.

Byculla was regarded as the epicentre of criminal activities at the time. Even in those days, Byculla residents were either Christians or Muslims. The Byculla Police Station divided the stronghold of two communities: the left hand side, that is the east side, which comprised the Byculla zoo and railway station, was the Christian dominion, while the right side, which includes the present day Sankli Street stretching till Byculla station west on one side and Nagpada on the other, was predominantly Muslim.

You cannot have a gang without an adversary gang. While Byculla don Nanhe Khan and Wahab Pehelwan were busy getting their names permanently embedded in the pages of police rosters, three Christian brothers from the Christian portion of Byculla were giving them sleepless nights. The brothers leading the Johnny gang were known as Bada Johnny, Chhota Johnny, and Chikna Johnny; the youngest was fair and good looking, hence the epithet 'Chikna' Johnny. The Allahabadi gang and the Johnny gang often engaged in skirmishes and a miniature turf war soon broke out between them.

But when the gang graduated from street-level crime to drug trafficking with the Pathans, they left behind a void in the Byculla area which soon turned into more turf wars between two budding gangs in the area: the Kanpuri gang and the Rampuri gang. These two gangs, however, could never make it big because they lacked the required chutzpah; the police and the Criminal Investigation Department (CID) soon neutralised them with quick arrests and an intensive crackdown. The Rampuri gang— before beating a hasty retreat from the Mumbai crime scene—left behind a relic: a long foldable knife with sharp edges on one side. The knife could be folded and hidden in the trouser pockets and it was meant to be thrust in the rib cage to savagely tear apart the innards of the stomach from one end to another. This lethal knife became known as 'Rampuri Chaaku'. And to date, the Rampuri Chaaku is the first weapon of the neophyte gangster in Mumbai.

None of these turf wars had ever turned very ugly or communal. Eventually, though, in the late fifties, the Johnny gang was sucked into communal frenzy in its engagement with another group—Ibrahim Dada's gang. After the Allahabadi gang bowed out of petty crime, the new incumbent, Ibrahim Dada managed to fend off other gangs on the rise by the sheer force of his charisma. Rival gangs like Kanpuri, Jaunpuri, and Rampuri had few educated young people in their ranks whereas Ibrahim Dada was the first matriculate amongst them, a well-dressed gangster who could speak English.

Popular gangster lore has it that when Ibrahim Dada had gone to the American Consulate at Peddar Road to meet a friend at the consulate he met the receptionist, Maria. Fair Maria could not resist the raw appeal of the tall, robust, and brawny Ibrahim. It was love at first sight. Soon Maria began visiting Ibrahim at his residence on Sankli Street.

When Bada Johnny's spies informed him of the budding love affair between Maria and Ibrahim, Johnny Dada was furious. He accosted Ibrahim once and warned him, '*Tum ek Christian ladki ko lekar kyun bahar jate ho* [why do you go out with a Christian girl]? Stop seeing that girl at once.' Ibrahim remained unruffled and in reply began singing the popular Bollywood song from the blockbuster of those days, Dilip Kumar-Madhubala starrer *Mughal-e-Azam*, *Jab pyar kiya to darna kya, pyar kiya koi chori nahin ki, ghut-ghut kar yon marna kya* [Why fear when you're in love. You have loved and not committed a crime, so why hide?]). It left Johnny fuming and helpless. He tried to scare Maria off by invoking religious sentiments, but to no avail.

Soon Ibrahim and Maria were married and the girl embraced Islam. This enraged Johnny Dada, who saw their union and subsequent conversion as a personal humiliation. This behaviour eventually led to his downfall because until then, Mumbai's crime lords had never allowed communal feelings to interfere with business.

Muslim boys began deserting Johnny's gang and joined ranks with Ibrahim's, weakening the older gang's muscle power and clout. Johnny's reputation took another beating when his agents and pimps, some of whom were Muslim, refused to pay up his share of their spoils to Johnny and sought refuge, instead, with Ibrahim Dada.

Johnny decided to take matters in his own hands. One day when Ibrahim was alone, he cornered him with a group of his hoodlums near Bombay Central station, and assaulted him with lathis, iron rods, and knives. Ibrahim was severely battered at first but soon summoned his reserves of strength and rallied, attacking Johnny and his men. Though they all escaped eventually, some of them were injured grievously.

Ibrahim decided to teach Johnny a lesson. He cornered Johnny in the Kamathipura area one day and challenged him to a one-on-one dual. Ibrahim beat his adversary mercilessly, humiliating him, and leaving him on the verge of death. His retaliation was finally effected: Johnny then disappeared from the scene.

Both his brothers also met an equally tragic end. Chhota Johnny used to terrorise the shopkeepers and loot their cash boxes at the end of the day. The hapless shopkeepers, mere traders by profession, could not summon enough strength or resources to retaliate. But, the story goes, a Bohra shopkeeper decided to take care of Chhota Johnny at last, even if it meant losing his life in the process. The shopkeeper devised a crude, makeshift weapon by fitting nails on the end of a stick. Chhota

Johnny had become so careless in his confidence that unlike others of his ilk he did not even carry any weapons on his person, and when he staggered in, inebriated, the shopkeeper assaulted him mercilessly. He continued to hit him until Chhota Johnny collapsed on the ground in a pool of blood; witnesses recall that he continued to hit him long after he was dead. Fellow traders were surprised; Bohras are Gujarati Muslims, essentially a trader community found in all corners of the world plying their trade peacefully, simple businessmen who rarely turn violent. But something in the man had broken, it was evident. The shopkeeper was booked for manslaughter but the police made a weak case against him and let him off.

Chikna Johnny, the Casanova of the family, became the ringleader of his own fledgling gang. His story ended when he failed to return from a picnic with his girls. He had gone to the Gorai beach with some girlfriends and drowned while swimming. With even the runt of the family gone, the gang ceased to exist and its members switched loyalties and merged with other gangs like the Jaunpuri gang, the Kashmiri gang, and some other stray ones.

Meanwhile, Ibrahim Dada was arrested on murder charges in another case and convicted. He was sentenced to life imprisonment. Maria continued to live in his house at Sankli Street and gave birth to his son. With Ibrahim Dada behind bars, Johnny Dada doing the disappearing act, and the neutralisation of other gangs, the star of the Allahabadi gang of Nanhe Khan was on the rise again. The gang had grown in size, numbers, clout and money, and came into focus.

Kamathipura, incidentally, has attracted gangsters for business as much as for pleasure. The red-light district housed a Kashmiri betting club run by one Sumitlal Shah who was the personal secretary of Habib Kashmiri, head of the Kashmiri gang. Ahmad Kashmiri, Ayyub Lala, and Feroz Lala too were part of the gang that operated out of Kamathipura.

Ayyub, incidentally, was also a police informant, much to the chagrin of his gang members. Once a fight ensued between him and Habib with the latter reprimanding him for telling on the other gangs. Ayyub on his part, was justifying that he did so only to remain in the good books of the cops. However, no consolation would placate Habib and they soon split their gangs.

What followed was a constant battle for one-upmanship that resulted in Ahmad kidnapping Ayyub's lover and Ayyub retaliating by having Ahmad killed. While much of the gang's time was spent dealing with internal rivalry, elsewhere in Bombay, legendary gangsters were gaining their hold on the city.

Bombay's Midas

M astan Haider Mirza was born on 1 March 1926 into a farmer's family in Panankulum, a small village 20 kilometres away from Cuddalore, Tamil Nadu. Mastan's father, Haider Mirza, was a hardworking but impoverished farmer who moved to Bombay with his son after miserably failing to make ends meet in his hometown. Arriving in 1934, they tried their hand at various odd jobs, finally managing to set up a small mechanic shop where they repaired cycles and two-wheelers in Bengalipura, near Crawford Market. The father-son duo laboured hard from eight in the morning till late in the night. But 8-year-old Mastan soon realised that even after all this toil, he could only make a meagre 5 rupees a day.

As he walked home to his basti from Crawford Market, he would often walk past the grandiose southern Bombay area of Grant Road, which housed those marvellous theatres, Alfred and Novelty. Every time he noticed a huge, sparkling car whizz past him or walked by the plush Malabar Hill bungalows, he would look down at his dirty soiled hands and wonder if a day would come when he would be able to own these cars and bungalows. This, more than anything else, stirred a certain feverish desire in him to think of ways and means to become bigger, richer and more powerful. But uneducated and unskilled, with the additional burden of supporting his family, Mastan could see only a bleak road ahead of him.

When the boy turned 18, he boldly decided to quit the cycle repairing business for good to try his hand at something else. Mastan's father Haider was a very religious man and had always taught him to be honest and industrious. While allowing him to join the workers at the Bombay docks, he reminded Mastan that he had brought him up right and that he would not be around forever to supervise him all the time; hence Mastan must refrain from stealing, fighting, and using dishonest means to better himself.

In 1944, Mastan joined the Bombay dock as a coolie. His job was to unload huge boxes and containers of ships coming from Eden, Dubai, Hong Kong, and other cities. Bombay was not such a large dock at that time but it was still bustling with activity.

As India won its freedom in 1947, Mastan completed three years as a coolie, at the Mazagon docks in Bombay. Mastan, in those three years, saw that the British used to charge import duty and that there was a good margin to be made if this import duty could be evaded. In those days, Philips transistors and imported watches were hugely popular in Bombay.

Mastan realised that if the goods were never passed through custom, there would be no question of duty, and so, he could instead make a quick buck by passing this evasion on to the owners. And if he helped the owners evade customs duty, they would give him a cut, which, taken into account the numerous goods passing through the customs, turned into quite a substantial amount of money for Mastan. To him, this was really not a question of honesty. He believed customs duty was a British legacy and could be justifiably evaded.

Mastan knew that if he could manage to import these transistors and watches without paying import duty, he could make a small fortune for himself, which would supplement his salary of 15 rupees per month. While he thought out this devious scheme, he serendipitously met a man named Shaikh Mohammed Al Ghalib, an Arab by descent. Ghalib was also looking for someone young and energetic who was willing to support him in his illegal activity of evading import duty.

At the time, smuggling was not a full-fledged activity and people were not yet aware of the massive amounts of money they could make in the business. The only smuggling operations that existed consisted of small-timers trying to bring in imported goods in permissible quantities, which back then consisted of such prize catches as six watches, two gold biscuits, four Philips transistors, and so on.

Ghalib explained to Mastan that it would be easy for him to stash a couple of gold biscuits in his headband, a few watches in his underwear, or a couple of transistors in his turban, as he was a coolie and worked on the ground. Mastan asked him what he would get in return for the work. Ghalib promised him a good reward. Both struck up a good rapport and decided to work together.

Within months, Mastan realised that his measly salary of 15 rupees had now become 50 rupees. He began to enjoy his work with Ghalib and soon became known as the Arab's blue-eyed boy. He was now a coolie to watch out for. Importantly, his reputation and the fact that he enjoyed special treatment by an influential and affluent Arab caught the attention of local hoodlums.

One such dada or local goon was Sher Khan Pathan, who at the time used to have his way at the Mazgaon dock. These were the days when there was no unionism at the dock. He would extort money from coolies and anyone who refused to pay would be beaten up by Pathan and his men.

Mastan witnessed this day in and day out. He wondered why someone like Pathan who did not belong to the docks and was not even a coolie or a government servant should be allowed to come to the docks and threaten and extort money from hard working coolies. Enterprising lad that he was, he decided to take on Khan.

Mastan gathered a couple of other strong people, sat with them, and told them that Sher Khan Pathan was also a human being like them. If Sher Khan could beat them up with his own hands, they had the stronger hands of labour: they were tougher and used to hard work. If their strength could collectively be channelled to beat up Pathan and his goons, the coolies could ensure that their community was relieved of the goons.

Next Friday, when Pathan came for his weekly round of extortion, he realised that ten people were missing from the huge queue. Before he could get a grip of the situation, Mastan and ten of his men attacked Pathan and four of his cronies. Pathan had his Rampuri knife and *guptis* (stiletto) and Mastan and his people had lathis and rods. Pathan had only four men, while Mastan had ten. Despite the Pathan's *guptis* and rampuris, Mastan managed to overpower him. Finally, a bleeding and battered Pathan and his acolytes had to run for their lives. This occasion of triumph further added to Mastan's fame and growing clout within the coolie community.

And Ghalib's admiration and respect for Mastan grew and he started giving him a percentage of his profit, rather than tipping him. Mastan became Ghalib's 10 per cent partner and the Arab began to teach him how gold was to be valued and tested, as well as how it should be imported or sold off in local markets.

Soon after, in 1950, Morarji Desai, the chief minister of Bombay presidency, imposed prohibition of liquor and other contraband in the state. With such imposition in place, the mafia had a brilliant opportunity to increase their profits—provide the illegal goods not available to interested customers at exorbitant prices.

This was the time when Ghalib and Mastan came into their full form. Within months of the imposition, they started raking in money. Mastan bought himself a bicycle. Soon, he managed to buy a house of his own. He became the leader of the coolies in the early fifties, but his joy did not last long. Ghalib was arrested by the police and customs authorities for smuggling and evasion of duty, and Mastan's dreams of success were shattered prematurely.

A legendary tale is told about Mastan's rise after the years of Ghalib's arrest. Mastan, who at the time of Ghalib's arrest had just taken delivery of a box of gold biscuits on behalf of Ghalib, toyed with the idea of disposing of the box and decamping with the money. The thought of whether he should use the money to get more material from Eden or whether he should leave the box intact for Ghalib to return tormented him for a while. Finally, his father's lessons showed him the path to take. Tempted as he was, Mastan did not embezzle the money. The box remained in his house—hidden and untouched.

Ghalib had been sentenced to three years imprisonment. Mastan returned to his life of helping small-time coolies and smugglers for these three years. Ghalib, after he served his sentence returned a broken man. In those three years, he had suffered huge losses fighting his case. His family was also in trouble. He was contemplating investing in horses for the derby, or starting a hotel or even relocating to Dubai, which was his hometown. He could not make up his mind, on which would be the best option.

For weeks Ghalib remained confused and he tried to sell off his property to support his lifestyle. It was in this confused state of affairs, that he met his old employee one day. Mastan caught hold of Ghalib's hand and took him to a small house in the Madanpura ghetto, where Mastan showed him the wooden crate that had remained unopened for three years. It was very discreetly hidden below heaps of dirty clothes.

'Alhamdolillah, glory to God, it is incredible. How did you manage to hide it for three years?' Ghalib exclaimed, his eyes popping with disbelief as he stared at the crate brimming with sparkling gold biscuits. 'Thieves or government officials will always look for valuables in well-protected trunks carefully secured with a lock. They would never think of checking a carelessly abandoned crate beneath a pile of dirty clothes,' Mastan explained with a triumphant smile. 'Why didn't you take this gold for yourself and disappear from the city? Nobody would have missed you. You would have been a rich man, *Bambai ka baadshah* [emperor of Bombay]!' Ghalib screwed up his eyes, still trying to understand through the incredulity in his brain. 'My father always taught me that I could escape everyone, but I would never escape the Creator. I believe I can still become *bambai ka baadshah* someday,' Mastan replied quietly.

The words, spoken with faith and confidence, brought tears to Ghalib's eyes. He realised that in a world plagued by distrust and deception, there were still men, albeit very, very few, who were trustworthy and honest despite the strongest temptations. 'I will accept this only on one condition. We shall both share it equally and become partners,' Ghalib proposed in a rush of gratitude.

Mastan smiled. 'There is nothing else that I would love more at this moment then to be your friend and partner for life,' he said, and held out his hand.

The two partners shook hands.

It is a known fact in the world of business and crime that gold in any form could have impurities, but the yellow metal in its biscuit form is regarded to be in its purest. It was a crate full of these yellow biscuits that changed Mastan's life and made him an overnight millionaire.

In 1955, Mastan was richer by 5 lakh rupees. He did not need to be a coolie or a dockworker any more. He immediately quit his job and decided to take up smuggling as his full-time business. He, along with Ghalib, came up with a scheme of importing gold. Ghalib had already told Mastan that they were now 50 per cent partners in the business. Ghalib went to Eden, Dubai, and other African countries and started sending gold, wristwatches, and other valuables to Bombay.

Mastan, by this show of 'honesty', had become quite popular in the smuggling community. His clout had grown and he was growing richer.

In 1956, Mastan came in touch with Sukur Narayan Bakhiya, a resident of Daman and also the biggest smuggler in Gujarat. Bakhiya and Mastan also became partners and they divided certain territories among themselves. Mastan used to handle the Bombay port and Bakhiya used to handle the Daman port. The smuggled items would come to Daman port from UAE and to Bombay from Eden. Bakhiya's consignment was taken care of by Mastan.

Mastan recognised early on in life that money alone was not enough to remain powerful in the city. He also needed muscle power if he wanted to establish his supremacy across Bombay. And it is in search of this muscle power that Mastan is later found forging friendships with two of the most renowned musclemen in the city—the unlettered but influential Pathan Karim Lala and the don of central Bombay, Varadarajan Mudaliar alias Vardha bhai.

4

Madrasi Mobster

On a scorching afternoon, an industrious young boy from Tamil Nadu was working very hard at the famous Victoria Terminus as the sun shone down relentlessly. Around the same time that Mastan was struggling for his livelihood at the Bombay Port Trust in the dockyards of Bombay, Varadarajan Mudaliar, another coolie, was trying to make a living at the landmark railway terminus.

Both of them were oblivious to the fact that their destinies would be closely intertwined with the other and that their lives would be entrenched in a similarly heady mix of crime, money, and power.

One story in particular precedes the 'Madrasi mobster' ('Madrasi' is a colloquial north Indian term for a south Indian), alias *kala babu*. He is said to have changed an institution, and put in its place, another: this was the only time in the history of Bombay's crime that the ubiquitous cutting chai made way for a cold, dark beverage called *kaala paani*, across police stations in the city. The fizzy liquid was substituted for chai because of this singular coolie. According to stories from the time, at many police stations across the central belt of Bombay, the *chaiwallah* (tea-vendor) who brought his daily quota of tea several times a day in chipped glasses would walk in with glasses filled with the fizzy cola instead. The *chaiwallah* would leave this drink only on the tables of the senior officials in the police station and walk away without charging any money for the drink. In what seemed like an unwritten law, junior officials would immediately clear the room, people who had come to register complaints would be told to empty the premises, and the senior officials would put all other work on hold. The black liquid was a message sent to the officials that *kala babu*, was on his way to the police station. A policeman, who did not wish to be named, says, 'Those days, it was his way of saying: I am coming to meet you. Make necessary arrangements. He had the whole force serving him.' Till date, there is no one who ran the mafia the way *kala babu* did; and his biggest trump card was that he knew people's weakness, especially that of the system. He was always heard saying, 'Keep people's bellies full and balls empty'.

If the anecdote has any truth in it, it is certainly further evidence of a phenomenal rags-to-riches story. For this *kala babu* who started his life in the city at the Victoria Terminus station as a coolie went on to become one of the most powerful Hindu dons to rule over the city.

Varadarajan Muniswami Mudaliar was born into a feudal Mudaliar family with scarce means in the small town of Vellore, in Tamil Nadu. It was 1926 and he had begun working when he was just 7 years old as an errand boy at a photography studio at Mount Road in Madras (present day Chennai). He never completed his studies, but was the only boy who could read and write in English and Tamil in his family.

With nothing but a sheer force of aspiration, Varadarajan moved to the city of dreams and settled into one of the lanes adjoining the then Victoria Terminus. As much as his hard-working nature brought him under the radar of his employers, his name became synonymous with a person with a heart as large as the nameless crowd that he passed every day in the crowded station. The lore of his 'large-heartedness' was exemplified in the fact that when he finished his hard day's work, he went to the dargah to offer *niyaz* (sacred food) to the devotees.

Varda used to visit the 260-year-old shrine of Bismillah Shah Baba, which was located just behind the main concourse of the long-distance terminus at VT. Starting off with a small amount of food for the poor every day, he began organising food for them at a massive scale as he flourished.

Even as he progressed in his life—from a simple errand boy to a porter and eventually to a notorious figure in Bombay—the dargah continued to receive food from the Mudaliar household and he continued to rub shoulders with the people with whom he started out his life—the porters. 'He believed that he owed the dargah his dues. That was the first roof for him in Bombay,' says his doting daughter Gomathy. Till today, his family has maintained the tradition of giving *niyaz* every year in June, where over 10,000 people are fed.

The police circles however refute the good Samaritan history. The policemen only recall incidents that involved words like 'theft' and 'mitigator' when it came to his generosity. The police had never documented that he was a helpful type; for them Varda was only a crook. The positive aspect of his character was, however, highlighted in two movies, *Nayakan*, starring Kamal Hasan, and *Dayavan*, starring Vinod Khanna.

The innocent boy from Vellore with nothing on his side but sheer drive became a man much before his time in the hard and rough lanes of Bombay. His circle of friends went beyond the porters that he worked with every day to include local thieves and he was quick to learn easier means of making money through these friends. The daily toil may have earned him only a few annas and lots of abuse from passengers, but this new route also offered him a circle of friends that was bound by solidarity in an otherwise lonely city.

When Morarji Desai imposed the prohibition of liquor and other contraband in the state in 1952, the ban, especially of liquor, only provided licence to a growing illicit liquor trade. This trade required brawn and this proved to be the first turning point in the life of Varadarajan Mudaliar.

His local network brought him closer to goons who were already engaged in this trade. A policeman who had once caught Varda in the thick of the night recalls, 'He was a glib talker. It is that attribute of his which made him dearer to the liquor mafia. They needed men who could talk and get the work done. Varda had that in him. He could convince anyone that he was right. Even if he had just killed an army, he could legitimise it.' It took him just a few days to set up base at Antop Hill in central Bombay. It was this area that was going to turn Varda into Varda Bhai. The little locality witnessed the metamorphosis of the naïve Tamilian boy in his late twenties into the enigmatic outlaw.

The geography of Dharavi, Sion, Koliwada, and Antop Hill was the greatest advantage for the illicit liquor trade with nothing but hutments everywhere. In fact, even the police found it difficult to enter and patrol the area. The poorest people along with illegal migrants had their address in Antop Hill and Dharavi in those days. Like a local policeman narrates, 'It was a matter of pride to be on a police chargesheet those days for people living in this area. Each boasted of FIRs as one would about awards. Men would be ridiculed if they were caught in silly offences.' The area was dotted with small huts where local liquor was illicitly produced. With the help of the local network and bribes to the police, the trade made way to bars in Bombay. Varadarajan started gaining entry into the trade when it was still in its early days.

The area was mostly occupied by non-Brahmin Tamilians who operated and maintained the *bhattis* (furnace) in *khaadis* (marsh lands). The number of *bhattis* ran into hundreds, with each one having a capacity of making around 120 litres of concentrated hooch each night.

The police files detailing Varadarajan's trade said that he was the only one to plough the profits back into the trade as he looked at a much bigger canvas unlike the locals who were complacent with an area under them. He used his 'south Indian card' to his advantage and started creating pockets of mini Tamil Nadu by recruiting people into the illicit trade. He also identified similar pockets across central Bombay and even moved the production of illicit network to Sion-Koliwada, Dharavi, Chembur, Matunga, and some other areas to create a stronger, tighter network. The word regarding Varadarajan's tenacity spread and those who came from Tamil Nadu for work invariably ended meeting Varadarajan and settling in this highly lucrative trade.

The logistics of work those days were very nominal. The trade, mostly active after midnight, would consist of a few who knew how to mix liquor, and another set of people who provided the security cover and kept vigil. The next set-up was of foot soldiers who, along with retired cops, worked in the nights round the week to provide liquor to many small shops across the city, especially close to the access points of the city.

The journalist Pradeep Shinde who covered the trade very closely, once observed, 'The entire kingdom of Varda Bhai rested on the distribution and collection of illicit hooch.' 'The concentrated liquid', one of his reports states, 'was filled in tubes of truck tyres, which are piled up in the deserted roads of Dharavi and taken over by the "wheelmen" or distributors. These carriers, ironically are by and large from the ranks of retired or suspended police personnel who have switched sides because of the lure of money. These are transported in gunny-bags, car trunks and other innocuous places.

'In Bombay, it is easy to identify these carrier vehicles—the rear seats are invariably missing to provide more storage place. In areas which are called "*garam* sections" [hot spots], meaning areas that were devoid of friendly police protection and had the risk of meeting a hostile cop party, an escort vehicle was provided. Its function was to intercept police vehicles which would suddenly be blocked by a car whose ignition had conveniently failed.' Witnessing this intricate yet simple web of transportation, the upper ranks of policemen soon realised that the trade had became a big menace. And slowly but surely, Varda Bhai was transforming from just another illicit liquor producer into a big don.

The dawn of Varda's power came when his men could get anyone a ration card, illegal electricity, and water supply and make them a Bombay citizen faster than the local administration. People started pouring into the city in groups, especially from southern India—Karnataka, Tamil Nadu, Andhra Pradesh, Kerala—and with each day the slums lined across the central region began to grow. It would not be an exaggeration to say that Varadarajan, in a small way, had much to do in making Dharavi the biggest slum space in Asia. Such was the allure of his might, that people started working blindly for him. Press reports during the sixties peg his trade of illicit liquor to around 12 crore rupees a year. In those years, that was a huge footprint considering the clandestine nature of the trade.

The aura of his power had engulfed not only his trade but also the psyche of the people around him. An Antop Hill Police Station diary entry records a very sketchy detail about a man from Uttar Pradesh who went missing. He lived with his wife and two children at one of the first floor corridor-houses in Antop Hill. Every night, when Varadarajan's men would gather to make liquor, the noise from the vessels would disturb his sleep so much that he complained to the local police, who poignantly chose to turn a deaf ear to it. When news of his complaint reached Varda's men, it so vexed them that they simply just decided to shut him up 'forever' when he came down to yell at them one night. His name is still registered under the missing list at the Antop Hill Police Station records. However, as was widely reported in several newspapers at the time, his wife had another story to tell: she was adamant that the police was very handsomely paid to keep mum about the whole incident, she left the city soon after.

Varda, however, knew too well that he needed to be very far-sighted in his approach in handling the network that chose to function under his name. While he handicapped the intelligence network—as bribes ensured that the informers in the backstreets were kept satisfied—he also ensured that the other end was well oiled. A news report published during the sixties did not shy away from stating on record that 'constables on the hooch beat made quite a sum. The rate for police protection for the *addas* [where hooch was sold in public] was Rs 5,000 per *adda*. Each police station had on an average 75 to 130 *addas* in its area. For the owners of the *addas*, the monthly turnover in just one suburban area with five *addas* is around Rs 50,000 per month'. The economics worked at 10 rupees per glass for diluted hooch, which means anywhere around 1 crore rupees a month.

He also divided his work area-wise, and let individuals from each local area handle their own business, making the areas more work-efficient while completely eliminating ego hassles. This only furthered healthy competition in upping returns, ensuring no individual or group encroached upon the other's designated area and distribution network. To maintain the smooth running of his business, he had two trusted lieutenants to look after migrants from Tamil Nadu—Thomas Kurien known as Khaja Bhai and Mohinder Singh Vig known as Bada Soma.

It was not long before Varda slowly edged out rivals in the trade to the point of achieving a complete monopoly. It was also during these early days that he started getting cheap migrant labour into the city. Slowly, his men started grabbing government land and allocating space to the new entrants for a price and with that, south Indians began to dot the cotton mill-dominated central Bombay of Dadar, Sion Matunga, Dharavi, and Wadala.

Along with the hugely successful hooch trade, there was another trade that Varadarajan's profits started to control—prostitution. Although Varda was never directly involved, he was aware that his men were pouring profits into this very vicious trade. As a former assistant commissioner of police observes, 'He never stopped his men from letting the prostitution trade grow. That is where we would like to believe that he was equally involved.' It was a very unique system, where eunuchs were given the reins of the flesh trade. And with a society that treated them with disdain, the eunuchs felt indebted to Varda Bhai's system that put them in a position of power.

Innocent girls were brought from poverty-stricken areas in Karnataka and Tamil Nadu and were left in the care of eunuchs for a few days. The eunuchs would follow a certain initiation system whereby initially they would lure the girls with the money they would earn by selling themselves. If their sweet talk did not work, force would be applied. Houses in Antop Hill and Dharavi became hotspots for this flesh trade and though Varda Bhai was never seen at the forefront of the business, he certainly was a benefactor of the trade.

Varda's clout had increased ten-fold, but in the sixties, smuggling was still considered the 'real innings'. The big share of the pie was still in gold smuggling with the business tilted to the side of Muslim dons who had the right contacts in Arabia. One of these was Haji Mastan.

5

Tamil Alliance

Over the years, Haji Mastan's financial state had gone up remarkably. But the burning ambition to achieve more still remained. So, once when in the course of conversation his collaborator Bakhiya told him that he should first consider becoming *Bambai ka Baadshah* before venturing towards Gujarat, Mastan was badly stung. To the up and coming smuggler, such a blatant dismissal was a slap in the face. He made up his mind to take over the city but he knew he could not accomplish this alone. He needed the help of powerful musclemen to reach where he wanted to. Varda seemed to be the perfect man for the job. For, while Varda was a don based in central Bombay, he had the clout to get things done all across the city. His men like Nandu Satam could pull things off in the farthest coasts of Versova, Vasai, Virar, and even Palghar.

Mastan was waiting for an opportunity to befriend Varda. What followed was a strange twist of fate: it would seem as though destiny had conspired to get these two men together.

Varda was arrested for stealing antennae from the customs dock area. The consignment was meant for a top politician in the Union ministry.

Initially, customs officers and the cops remained clueless about the mastermind behind the theft. However, a tip-off led them to pick up Varda from his den in Dharavi.

The captured Varda was told by the police that if he refused to tell them the whereabouts of the consignment they would be forced to unleash the third degree on him, as it was their neck on the line.

According to this possibly apocryphal story, as Varda was mulling over the threat in the night in the loneliness of the Azad Maidan lockup, he saw an affluent looking man, dressed in a white suit approaching him. The man was smoking a 555 cigarette and exuded a certain calmness. The man walked up to the iron bars, and not a single one of the cops on duty stopped him. Years of smuggling had made several customs officials Mastan's friends and put them on his payroll; he had assured them that he would retrieve their consignment tactfully and that Varda must not be tortured.

In the history of the Bombay Mafiosi, Mastan and Varda were the only two Tamilian dons. But ironically, the two were as different as chalk and cheese. While Mastan was known for his suave ways, Varda exuded the aura of a ruthless ruffian. Mastan walked very close to Varda and surprised him by greeting him in Tamil. 'Vanakkam thalaivar,' he said.

Varda was taken aback for a moment—both with the greeting in Tamil and the choice of words. 'Thalaivar' is a term of respect used to refer to the 'chief'. No one had even spoken to Varda in a civil manner ever since he had been dumped in jail. So the irony of the greeting appeared starker. Of course it was being used partly because Mastan was using their common language so the policemen would not understand what they were saying; as he had a business offer for Varda, he could not take the risk of the police smelling an unholy alliance.

After striking up a conversation and developing a rapport with Varda, Mastan came straight to business, 'Return the antennae to them and I will ensure that you make a lot more money.' Varda was stunned. He could never imagine Mastan being the spokesperson for the customs and the police. Belligerent at this apparent presumptuousness, he replied brusquely, 'What if I say I don't have it and even if I do I don't want to part with it?'

Mastan remained calm and composed as he spoke, 'If you presume it will be my loss, then you are mistaken. I deal in gold and silver. I don't touch such low value stuff that you will have to sell in Chor Bazaar. I am making an offer to you which no wise man can refuse. Return the antennae and be my partner in the gold business.'

Varda was surprised again. Mastan had said so much in such few words. He not only derided Varda and made his suspicions look small, he had also demonstrated his own stature and offered him a partnership in his business. At this juncture, Haji Mastan was the moneyed guy, the man with the pull, whereas Varda was still to make an indelible mark anywhere. So, when Mastan proposed the alliance, it was an offer Varda could not refuse.

'What will you benefit from this?' asked Varda. 'I want to make friends with you as I want to use your muscle power and clout in the city,' replied Mastan.

Varda, who had seen enough struggle in his life, must have thought that this was his only chance of walking away from certain torture and humiliation. He agreed to Mastan's offer and disclosed where he had hidden his stolen consignment. Policemen in the lock-up still remember that strong handshake of two very different looking men—one in a sophisticated suit and polished boots smoking an expensive cigarette and the other in a white vest, *veshti* (dhoti), and slippers.

Customs officials got their consignment and saved their jobs, Mastan got his partner to help him achieve his new-found dreams. Customs officials kept their word with Mastan and released Varda.

✠

As Varda returned to his den, people assumed he would be in a nasty mood and would unleash a bout of terror to show he still ruled the roost. His men thought he would be eager to prove that his detention should not be misconstrued as a sign of his waning power. Instead, Varda returned a happier man. He immediately called for a celebration. Even his close aides were a bit baffled at this strange behaviour. What also surprised them was the fact that Varda had actually agreed to return the consignment of antennae to the customs officials. It was nothing but a loss of face and revenue. But instead of displaying his foul temper, Varda ordered a public feast for his people.

They did not know that Varda had stooped to conquer. He might have lost the consignment, but he had struck a bigger deal. He had always wanted an alliance with the Muslim mafia, but he had managed to get a partnership on a platter without having to work for it at all.

Earlier, at the jail, Mastan and Varda had struck up the deal, simply by a few well chosen words in Tamil, and mostly through eye contact, the perfect tacit contract. After his release, Varda spent another week or two laying low, assimilating the fact that he, a small time crook, was now muscleman for the powerful, rising Haji Mastan.

Varda knew he could never penetrate into the smuggling trade, as the margins and the territory already came marked. This was closest to the profitable smuggling business. A shrewd Varda saw an opportunity in stealing legally imported goods and passing them off as smuggled goods. For this he had to tap his operatives at the Bombay Port Trust Docks. Crime Branch officials who probed the matter during the late sixties realised that the networks were made based on Varda's contacts during his days as a porter. It was a very clandestine and calculated scam that took shape. Cheap migrant labour from Thirunelveli found work in the docks and soon many networks were formed and strengthened.

The cartel took roots as a nexus was formed between the labourers, the customs officials, and officers at the Bombay Port Trust, through Varda's calculated shrewdness. Over a period of time a pattern emerged: once the goods were unloaded at the docks, in the fifty-three sheds of around 30,000 square feet, cargo would miraculously get transformed into 'missing cargo'.

The goods would be scattered around the docks by labourers who were recruited by Varda. The goods would then be classified as cases of wrong delivery, missing goods, misplaced goods, short landing, and everything else that could go wrong in the transporter's books. The importer would file a missing complaint and get insurance for the value lost, and the goods would come under the custody of Varda, who along with the importer would share the insurance amount and release the cargo to the importer for half the price. Initially, importers complained of the crime, but when they realised that they could get the cargo at half the price by giving a share of the insurance to Varda, even they fell in.

The insurance companies, who were the only losers in the game, later realised that the 'missing' goods were first spread across the docks. So they became more alert to ensure that such thefts do not occur.

To counter this, Varda came up with a completely new strategy. The 'missing' goods, spread across the docks would lie there until the insurance companies would despair, and pay off the importers. Meanwhile, the authorities at the port trust and the customs were paid off handsomely by Varda. They would keep the goods in their places until the insurance companies lost interest, and would then, after a pre-designated period, release them as 'unclaimed'. Varda would then waltz in, right under everybody's nose, and make away with the goods.

A policeman from the Crime Branch, said, 'Even the Muslim dons lacked this kind of shrewdness. The system was very calculated and showed the extent to which Varda could have his way. Even with crores of rupees at stake, there was no bloodshed, nobody lost his head, since Varda was intelligent enough to know how to plug every level right from the steamship agents who got to know if the cargo was worth stealing to the last leg, where the importer was willing to part with his share.'

Illicit liquor, eunuch-run prostitution, dock theft, and pushing the highly vulnerable south Indian migrant population into criminal activities: all of this was slowly transforming Varda Bhai into somewhat of a philanthropist slumlord. To law enforcers, of course, he remained a merciless mobster surrounded by 'Madrasi minions'.

Varda had the pulse of the crowd. He was always available at his house, where people crowded around him with their problems. The police at that time said that if anybody ever needed Varda's protection in the city, the easiest and perhaps the only way to tug at his heartstrings was a good tragic story of struggle. The swelling crowd and settlers in pockets like Dharavi, Chembur, Matunga, Antop Hill, Koliwada, and far suburbs made for a strong vote bank. This did not go unnoticed at the annual celebration at Matunga's Ganesh pandal which was organised by Varda. Being a religious man, Varda began spending lavishly on the Ganesh pandals outside Matunga station. With his stature, grew the size and opulence of the pandal. Many celebrities would come to the pandal to pray. It is rumoured that even Jaya Bachchan had prayed here for the life of her superstar husband Amitabh, when he was injured during the filming of the movie *Coolie*.

Police officials recall how smooth a talker Varda was. They recollect instances when his men, who habitually dodged the police, would come and surrender willingly at his behest. 'He kept both sides of the rung happy. He would keep a tab on each of his soldiers. The minute he knew that the accused was wanted at the lower rungs, he would negotiate with the police and get the accused in front of them. Once inside, the accused was confident that he would be bailed out. In turn, once his men were inside the jail, they would start the second rung of recruitment for Varda,' says a senior police official adding, 'there was a designated hotel at Sion Koliwada where so-called surrenders took place.' 'The maximum number of arrests has taken place at this hotel over cutting *chai* and bun maska on the table than out on the field,' says veteran crime journalist, Pradeep Shinde.

✠

After striking his alliance with Varda and greasing more palms of customs officials, Mastan's beliefs in the right collaborations and connections grew manifold. Also, Mastan concluded that as his ill-gotten empire was growing, he had to be wary of cops. He realised that if he wanted to play it safe, he had to befriend some policemen and politicians. Then, Mastan became aware that while foreign gold was popular in Bombay, silver from Bombay was in great demand abroad. He started importing gold from Africa and the Middle East and starting selling silver bricks known as *chandi ki eente* to countries from where he was importing gold.

As Mastan's empire was growing tremendously, it became almost impossible for him to supervise each and every operation, so he enlisted the help of a man called Yusuf Patel. Yusuf Patel was Mastan's acolyte and considered Mastan his mentor. While learning the tricks of the trade from Mastan, his fortunes grew. Yusuf knew that the silver bricks that Mastan sent abroad were considered of the purest quality and even had a 'brand' name: 'Mastan ki Chaandi'. His honesty in the business had earned him his credibility.

Mastan, who had dreams of owning a bungalow and a fleet of foreign cars, now finally saw them take shape. He had a palatial house in Malabar

Hill and several cars at his disposal. After marrying Sabiha Bi from Madras, Mastan had three daughters, Kamarunissa, Mehrunissa, and Shamshad.

On the business front, Mastan was now known to be the most affluent don in the city, and was growing from strength to strength. He began to use other ports like Chembur, Versova, and the Thane creek. And by the early seventies, Varda in central Bombay, Haji Mastan in the south and west, and the final member of their triumvirate, a Pathan called Karim Lala who provided the muscle, formed the most formidable alliance of smugglers and dons in Bombay. When they were mentioned together, they inspired awe in the youth and other small or aspiring dons.

6

Pathan Power

No one, not even his family, knew exactly when Karim Lala arrived in Bombay. What is known is that it was approximately in the thirties. Mumbai was known even then for its cosmopolitan identity and inclusive character. Nepalese, Burmese, Ceylonese, and *Kabuliwallahs* (Pathans) visited the city and made it their home because they saw more opportunities for business and personal advancement in Bombay than they ever saw in cities like Kabul, Kathmandu, or Colombo.

Abdul Karim Khan alias Karim Lala, a towering Pathan—almost 7 feet tall— came to Bombay from Peshawar with dreams in his eyes. Unlike his mentor Khan Abdul Ghaffar Khan, whom he followed into the country, he was not drawn to India's freedom struggle. Despite being a bonafide member of the Pakhtoon Jirga-e Hind, he did not participate in the movement. Instead, he was drawn to the city of Bombay—a city of myriad hues, which was very different from his motherland, with its mountains and wilderness. He fell in love with the city and decided to call it his own.

Karim Khan, like several others, had come to Bombay in search of fortune. He wanted to achieve here what he could not achieve in Peshawar. He rented a place in south Bombay, in Baida Gully near Grant Road station. Uneducated and unskilled, Karim Khan decided to be self-employed, as he could not think of any other way to earn a decent living.

He started off by establishing a gambling den — euphemistically known as a 'social club'—on the street he lived in. The club was frequented by all kinds of people—paupers and those with deep pockets; those who could afford to lose money and those who struggled to survive; daily wage labourers and middle-class men. Heavy losers borrowed money from Khan or his men to buy groceries or other necessities. When Khan noticed that this was becoming a trend, he decided to put an end to it by asking the borrowers to pay him interest on the 10th of every month for the borrowed sum. This discouraged some but others remained undaunted. Khan noticed that his cash box swelled on the tenth of every month, despite the interest, and encouraged by this, he decided to become a moneylender or *lala*. Thus, Karim Khan came to be known as Karim 'Lala'.

Karim Lala was not the only Pathan who lent money and lived off the interest. His brother, Abdul Rahim Khan alias Rahim Lala, also ran a social club near Jail Road in Dongri. There were other Pathans who did not own gambling dens but were affluent enough to lend money. Life started looking up for the sizeable Pathan community in the city.

Over a period of time, Karim Lala's gambling den became a hotspot for crime. Violence, brawls, and mugging became routine. This brought him into contact with the local police and subsequently with Crime Branch officials. But Karim Lala managed to bribe his way out of legal entanglements. Slowly and gradually he began to grow in stature and clout. Some began to refer to him in grander terms as Karim Dada. Following their tribal tradition the Pathans, who had begun to crowd around Karim Lala, looked up to him as their leader. In return, he would bail them out of tricky situations, from time to time involving himself in their concerns.

Soon Karim Lala became a household name in south Bombay and unwittingly became part of what is referred to as *matter patana* or *kholi khali karana*. *Matter patana* meant resolving an ongoing dispute by becoming an arbitrator between the two parties, while *kholi khali karana* meant evicting the occupant of a house by force. This informal arbitration, truth be told, was much smoother than the court cases and resultant verdicts were treated with more respect than those that had the seal of the court.

Karim Lala developed a formidable reputation for himself as a mediator. It started off with his getting involved in the concerns of friends and their own friends, but gradually the Pathan became the choicest arbiter in any kind of dispute in south Bombay. Soon, he realised he was raking in good money because of this weekly arbitration, which took place on the terrace of his building on Sundays.

At this point, his cronies like Murad Khan and Yaqub Khan decided to diversify into eviction. South Bombay had the maximum number of houses on the *pagdi* system, in those days. *Pagdi* technically means turban, but in this context it means that the tenant has placed his *pagdi* or honour in the hands of the owner, and which he will get back once he vacates the house. In the business, this *pagdi* system meant that once an individual gave the money to the owner, he or she would have complete right over the property. In the sixties and seventies, even 500 sq feet tenements were given out for a nominal amount of 5,000 to 10,000 rupees. At times, the rooms were given out for 9 to 99 years in a lease as low as 20,000 rupees. So when after a couple of years, the seller regretted giving out the room for such a meagre amount, he expected more money, which the occupant might not agree to pay, later in the day. There were also several instances when the lease period was completed, but the occupant was not budging or shelling out more money. In cases like these, the landlord or the tenant made use of the services of Karim Lala and his minions.

Karim Lala realised that he could make more money out of this than through lending money, waiting for the 10th of every month. As this new business thrived, he took on such a fearsome aura that several properties were evicted just by mention of his name. No sooner did the landlord say, *'Ab toh Lala ko bulana padega* [now Lala needs to be called]', the occupant, whether in the right or wrong, would vacate the house.

It was now several years after Indian Independence and the Pathans had now settled in comfortably. Khan had become the uncrowned leader of the Pathans in the city. His exact age was not known, but in the early fifties, the Pathans threw a huge party for his fiftieth birthday.

Karim Lala had now graduated from starched Pathani suits to white safari suits. He had a flamboyant lifestyle. He sported dark glasses and was almost always seen smoking expensive cigars and pipes. On his 50th birthday, one of his sycophants gifted him an expensive walking stick. Initially, Karim Lala had frowned at the gift saying he was still strong and fit enough to walk around without the help of a stick. But when several of his aides suggested this would only add to the strength of his personality, Karim Lala readily agreed. After this, he could be seen walking with his fancy new present at all major gatherings.

The stick began to accompany the man everywhere. If he went to the mosque and got up for ablutions, leaving the stick behind, even if the mosque got crammed and crowded, no one would dare to move the stick aside or occupy Karim Lala's prayer spot. Likewise, in any social gathering, if he made a trip to the washroom and left his stick behind, resting on a sofa, no one would dare to come and sit on the sofa. There was much talk of the stick and the awe it commanded amongst ordinary mortals. Remarkably, Karim Lala enjoyed this new height of power without having entailed bloodshed or effort.

Landlords like Chaman Singh Mewawala and Abdul Qureishi who had become regulars in Lala's *baithaks* (gatherings) realised that every time they contracted Lala for an eviction, they had to dole out a sizeable amount to him and his goons. So, in order to cut down on expenses, they sought to use solely the symbol of his power and pay a fraction of what they had to otherwise pay him.

Between the two of them they devised a plan to obtain his consent so that he would not know the actual reason behind the proposal. Catching him when he was in a good mood one morning, they began. As Lala had been running into rough weather with the cops and CID and they were making a file on him, they suggested he should abstain from physically leading eviction assaults and even avoid sending his Man Fridays.

'*Phir kholi kaisa khali karega* [then how will the eviction happen]?' Lala asked with sincere concern. '*Hamari khopdi mein ek kamaal ka idea hain, jisse saanp bhi mar jayega aur lathi bhi nahin tootega* [we have the perfect strategy in place, which will ensure that the snake will be killed and the rod will not be broken],' the landlords replied. Lala looked at them incredulously.

Whenever they wanted to evict a house, Lala's men now left only his stick at the desired site, as an ominous symbol. It always seemed to work, they found. Many tenants would almost immediately evict the house and leave the fear-inspiring stick behind.

Nobody before this had commanded such clout. This not only added to Lala's fearsome reputation but also caught the attention of Haji Mastan. Mastan had always wanted a man who could pull off tricky things for him without violence. He sent a message to Karim Lala for a meeting. Karim Lala had heard a lot about Mastan but had never met him earlier.

They both met during Friday prayers at Grant Road mosque and proceeded to Taher Manzil, Karim Lala's Baida Gully residence for lunch. For religious Muslims, lunch after Friday prayers should be sumptuous and rich. Karim Lala had laid down a scrumptious feast for Mastan. Both of them immediately struck a rapport over the meal, laughing and talking like old friends. After the meal, it was time to move to weightier issues.

'Khan, saab,' Mastan said, addressing Karim Lala, 'it has been great talking to you like friends, but now, I have a business proposition for you.' Karim Lala had been waiting for just such an opening, and he leaned forward, interested. 'Of course, Mastan bhai, tell me. What do you have in mind?' he asked.

Mastan slowly sipped some water before he started to talk, 'As you know, I have quite a lucrative business going at the docks. But I am in need of some manpower, people who know what they are doing. I was wondering if you would be interested in providing me with men.' Karim Lala's eyes gleamed. 'You intrigue me, Mastan bhai. But tell me, what would my men have to do?' he enquired.

Mastan replied, 'Nothing too dangerous. I have a lot of goods coming in at the docks at Bombay Port Trust. They need to be unloaded quickly and efficiently, taken and stored in a warehouse, and then, transported out. Your men will have to give their protection to me and my men, for the goods at the docks and the warehouses, until they are sold off. That's all.' Mastan knew that if he pitched it like this, the up and coming Karim Lala would be assured that there would not be much danger involved.

Karim Lala sat back and folded his arms across his chest, brow furrowed as he thought about Mastan's proposition. After a minute, he asked, 'I see. Will there be any violence involved?'

Mastan smiled. He knew he had Karim Lala hooked. 'Khan saab, if your men are around, there isn't a soul who will dare intrude or interrupt us. So there won't really be much violence involved.'

'Well then, it sounds pretty doable. But what do I get out of this, Mastan bhai?'

'Well, Khan saab, I can't promise you a fixed cut, but our shares will depend upon the value of the goods that we unload. So, how about we decide on our shares on a consignment basis?'

Mastan knew this was the tricky part, but he knew, almost as a certainty, that in the end Karim would not be able to resist.

A short silence prevailed, in which Mastan watched the man sitting across him think furiously. Finally, Karim Lala released a deep breath, looked up, and, with a smile, offered his hand. Mastan took it, and shook hands. This sealed one of the deadliest deals of the time in the Bombay underworld, Mastan would be the brains, and Karim Lala would provide the brawns. Finally, Karim Lala had skyrocketed into the big league.

This newfound alliance presented a headache for the cops. Mastan was a well-connected smuggler and Karim Lala, a ruthless muscleman: a most unholy alliance. As Mastan's political connections were well oiled, they knew they could not touch him; they decided to try to clip Lala's wings.

In a very concerted attempt, cops unleashed a crackdown on Karim Lala and his brother Rahim's gambling dens. At times their hotel managers were picked up, detained and subjected to relentless questioning. Baida Gully began to see frequent visits from the police. Strangely, these police officers came bragging about what they could do to Karim Lala because of his involvement in mediation and eviction deals. But after all their histrionics and hard talk, they left tamely, pockets full of *bakshish* (bribe). Once in a while Karim Lala was also summoned to the CID office. Threats were issued that he would be produced in front of the then Deputy Commissioner of Police Huzur Ahmed Khan, but the moment he put his hands in his pocket and brought out wads of notes, they became as docile as donation seekers from charity organisations.

The only policeman the Karim Lala respected was Head Constable, Havaldar Ibrahim Kaskar. Ibrahim had never ever asked him for money and never displayed any sort of deference towards him. In fact, despite his being a constable, Ibrahim chose to admonish him in the strongest terms.

They had known each other for several years and Ibrahim exhorted him to close down his gambling dens and his business of lending money on interest, as both businesses were considered haram in Islam and thus the money earned qualified as unlawful and ill-gotten.

Karim Lala was astonished at Ibrahim's devoutness and bluntness in the face of a notorious don. Ibrahim was a pauper and was struggling to make both ends meet, yet he did not want to accept money from him and preferred to survive on a meagre salary of 75 rupees a month. Karim Lala had never felt such a sense of respect for anyone else in his life—he almost venerated Ibrahim. Despite the head constable being younger to him by a decade or more, Lala began to call him Ibrahim Bhai.

7

The Original Don: Baashu

The three men lurking near the state-run JJ Hospital in Teli Mohalla looked so menacing that passers-by instinctively crossed the road to avoid them. Khalid Pehelwan, Raheem Pehelwan, and Lal Khan were massively built by Indian standards. They had earned the title 'Pehelwan', or wrestler, by toiling at their boss' gym. Their effort showed in the biceps that bulged under their taut skin.

While the trio flexed their muscles and others scurried past, a gleaming black Mercedes Benz glided into view; the kind that was later popularised as the customary ride of innumerable reel dons. The gritty neighbourhood of Teli Mohalla seemed transformed by the moment. In the early seventies, people saw few Mercs cruise the streets of Bombay. They were beyond the means of all but a handful of people, and Ahmed Khan alias Don or Baashu Dada belonged to that exclusive club. He was the vain owner of not one, but two of these expensive status symbols.

When the car pulled in close to his office, Baashu Dada's minions stood to attention. According to his closest aides, Baashu Dada was unlettered and incapable of even signing his own name. Despite this, he wielded absolute power over his fiefdom of Dongri in the seventies.

The don stepped out, clad in a pair of jeans and a T-shirt, his well-built frame matching those of his acolytes. Baashu Dada never wore full-sleeved shirts. He liked to show off his body builder's biceps and sinewy forearms. He wanted to show that he was as strong as he was shrewd.

Today, as Baashu Dada walked up to his henchmen, he threw down the gauntlet at once. 'What kind of fucking pehelwans are you?' he thundered. 'Can you do a hundred push-ups without a break?'

Khalid and Raheem's ability had never been questioned with such contempt and that too by Baashu Dada. They had little choice but to prove themselves.

'Of course, I can do a 100 dips,' Rahim replied, trying to salvage his wounded pride.

'Go on, do it!' Baashu egged him on, 'Khalid, you join him too!'

Teli Mohalla was abuzz. A small crowd gathered to watch the two wrestlers in their exertions. Both took up their positions, palms outstretched, hips raised, and legs extended, only their toes touching the ground.

The countdown began: one… two… three… four… five… .

Baashu Dada joined the battle of the biceps, slipping into position easily. The crowd's excitement went up a notch.

By the twentieth push-up, Khalid and Raheem were panting. But Baashu Dada, who had been quietly keeping pace, showed no signs of flagging. When they crossed seventy, the going got even tougher. With each passing number, Rahim found it more and more difficult to rise. When he hit eighty-seven, he could not do it anymore. He flopped to the ground, his face kissing the dirt.

Khalid managed three more dips. He was determined not to collapse in a heap like Rahim. He also did not want to lose when he was so close. Unable to rise and too spent to dip again, he suddenly froze, mid-position, sweat pouring from his creased forehead. His heavyset body trembled with the effort.

By now, Baashu Dada had become the centre of attention. He had cruised past ninety and was well on his way to a century. But instead of stopping at 100, he continued with astonishing speed. His breathing got heavy when he crossed 110, but he never once slowed down. When he finally stopped at 120, his T-shirt was drenched with sweat, but he rose to his feet and gave both his bodyguards a big smile. He had proven his point. He did not exchange any words, but ordered three glasses of badam sherbet.

Badam sherbet (a sweet, refreshing concoction made of milk and almonds) was the favourite drink of Muslim bodybuilders of yesteryears. For men like Khalid and Raheem, it symbolised a reward for their hard labour.

The two men from Uttar Pradesh worked out at Baashu Dada's Teli Mohalla headquarters, which doubled up as a gym. Huge mirrors lined the walls of this room, while an assortment of pulleys, dumbbells, and barbells were strewn on the floor.

It was from this den that Baashu Dada surveyed his smuggling universe and lorded over Dongri, the toughest territory in the city. One of the top smugglers of his time, Baashu dealt in gold and silver.

The police steered clear of Baashu Dada, as he was the most powerful don in the area. In fact, the local policemen regularly sought his help in solving cases. Baashu's contacts in the city helped them nab pickpockets, bicycle thieves, violent criminals, and underground casino operators.

Baashu Dada's helpful gestures did not go unrewarded. When the customs department or the Directorate of Revenue Intelligence implicated him in a smuggling case, policemen from the Dongri Police Station or the Yellow Gate Police Station found themselves in a tricky situation.

To save face, they would ostensibly mount raids on Baashu Dada's premises. The police jeep would park at the corner of the NU Kitab Ghar at the JJ Junction. An officer, accompanied by a lone constable, would get out of the jeep, take off his cap and walk towards Baashu's evening *baithak*. The don would not budge an inch from his seat, barely acknowledging the policeman's presence. And the officer would greet him humbly and sit on a chair, if he was offered one.

Sometimes, the don would treat these men in uniform to badam sherbet. At other times, he would ask them to leave, no questions asked. Even the policemen of Bombay, who had the reputation of being India's toughest, were forced to comply—if not grovel—in front of Baashu. Once a starving slum dweller, Baashu Dada had scaled dizzying heights.

Baashu landed in Bombay in the post-Independence years of poverty and despair. A young boy barely in his teens, he spent days searching for food in the south Bombay areas of Null Bazaar, Khetwadi, and Grant Road. Although he made some money as a cycle mechanic and errand boy at a scrap shop, he went hungry more often than not. One day, in a desperate bid for survival, Baashu snatched a leather bag from a Marwari businessman outside Shalimar Talkies and ran for his life. When the businessman raised an alarm, a mob started chasing him. At the Null Bazaar junction, a police constable nabbed him and confiscated the bag, which was stuffed with wads of currency.

As punishment, Baashu was sent to the Dongri Remand Home, the city's biggest penitentiary for juvenile offenders. At the age of 15, he had to work like a hardened convict, lifting heavy barrels of water and gunny bags. It was in the throes of such strenuous work that Baashu began to pay attention to the interesting ways his body was changing, his friend Shaikh Abdul Rahim alias Rahim Chacha recalls. The initial fancy he took to bodybuilding turned into an obsession. With his expanding pectorals and bulging biceps, he became a force to reckon with inside the remand home; the inmates and even the wardens became wary of his volatile temper and physical prowess.

Legend has it that Baashu once slapped a cook for serving him less food. The enraged cook retaliated by hitting him with an iron rod, which Baashu twisted out of shape with ease. The astonished eyewitnesses, who had never seen such a display of brute strength, grew increasingly deferential to Baashu.

The administration, which had initially sought to punish him for this act of intimidation, let it pass as the lad was only few months short of 18, the age of release from the remand home.

Once released, Baashu joined the ranks of unemployed youth in the city. But not for long. Before his release, he had chalked out a plan of action. For, inside the remand home he had met a couple of teenage criminals who showed him how to make a quick buck.

Swiftly, he assembled a band of equally daring boys who were itching to make some money. The newly founded gang waited outside the Bombay dock at Masjid Bunder and clambered atop trucks carrying imported fabrics and electronic items. By the time the truck reached the city, Baashu and his gang managed to steal enough goods to earn themselves several thousand rupees at Mohatta Market. These exploits earned the intrepid Baashu an early nickname: *godi ka chuha* (dock rat).

The profits he made off this scam were sufficient to afford Baashu a luxurious lifestyle. But soon enough, he got bored of this risky small-time business. He turned his eye to direct smuggling. In the very first consignment of Rolex and Rado watches he smuggled in, he managed a windfall profit. Within months, the young man made it to the top league, joining Haji Mastan and his fellow don Bakhiya. He began driving fancy cars and bought flats in plush Malabar Hill, in addition to several other properties in Bombay and a few in Hyderabad. Secretly, though, Baashu was quite disdainful of Mastan and Bakhiya. He was a self-made man, who saw to all the nitty-gritty himself, and consequently, never thought highly of anyone who would make others do all the dirty work for them.

One quality remained unchanged despite his meteoric rise: his obsession with bodybuilding. This extended to his collective use of force; unlike other smugglers like Haji Mastan, who had to hire muscle from Karim Lala or Varda, Baashu always used his own muscle and men to conduct his business.

Baashu, like most dons, hated the system and treated the police machinery with disdain—something no other don before or after him managed so effortlessly, perhaps. Among the members of his coterie, however, was the retired head constable, Ibrahim Kaskar, so revered by Karim Lala. Baashu was a master puppeteer who manipulated and used several retired and serving cops. Ibrahim was one of these, a former head constable. Under the guise of friendship, Baashu would often make use of Ibrahim and his knowledge of the system to get his smuggled goods cleared by customs. But despite all the contempt he displayed when it came to the police force, he showed deference towards Ibrahim bhai. Baashu genuinely liked the man for his honesty and integrity. He often told Ibrahim bhai, '*Agar aap police mein na hote toh aap mere saath hote* [if you weren't with the police, you would work for me].' And known for his bluntness, Ibrahim Bhai would retort, 'God forbid, I'd never have to see a day like that'.

An offended Baashu decided he needed to crush Ibrahim Bhai's pride. Nobody had the guts to snub him the way Ibrahim Bhai did.

Baashu found out that Ibrahim Bhai, for all his popularity and the respect accorded him by society, was close only to a handful of people. One of these friends was a small-time racketeer called Abdul Rahim, with whom Ibrahim had grown up. A short puny man, Rahim was used to selling off smuggled goods from Mastan or Baashu to big markets and in sales hubs like Mohatta Market and Manish Market, earning a commission on the sales.

Rahim was well-known in smuggling circles and Ibrahim Bhai often got him out of tricky situations. Rahim and Ibrahim Bhai were childhood friends and were known for being thicker than blood brothers. Bashu learnt that Rahim did not have a steady income. Rahim was the type who was flush if he had just handled a smuggling consignment and then went through a lean patch subsequently, once a lull hit.

Baashu summoned him and asked him to work for a fixed salary of 500 rupees as his manager. For Rahim, it was a princely sum and he lost no time in accepting the offer. But there was a rider—'Baashu bhai, *dost bana kar rakhenge to dosti mein jaan de sakta hoon, lekin ghulami nahin karoonga* [Baashu bhai, treat me like a friend and I'll give up my life for you, but I won't be your slave],' Rahim told him.

Something about Rahim immediately endeared him to Baashu and they both began working together. Although Baashu had hired Rahim to get Ibrahim bhai on his payroll, he soon realised that Rahim himself was a versatile man. Rahim increased his profits manifold with his sharp business acumen. Soon Rahim became indispensable to Baashu and an integral part of his think-tank.

With changing circumstances, almost everyone forgot that Baashu wanted Ibrahim to pay obeisance to him. But destiny has an indelible memory.

8

The Star Called David

Ibrahim Kaskar's family was originally from the village of Mumka in Ratnagiri district in Maharashtra. Ibrahim's father Hasan Kaskar owned a small hair cutting salon called the Naaz Hair Cutting Saloon at Char Null in Dongri. Ibrahim had three brothers, Ahmed, Mehmood, and Ismail. All of them were based in Khed village near Ratnagiri. Ibrahim alone had made his home in Bombay and a name for himself though the Kaskars were poor, the constable was well-known in the Dongri area. There were few head constables from the Muslim community, and in those times, head constables were considered more powerful than even the Deputy Commissioner of Police (DCP).

By then, Haji Mastan and Karim Lala were established and ruling the roost. However, one man who could always enter their darbar was Ibrahim Kaskar. This speaks volumes about his clout and the respect that he commanded in those circles. Even though he used to work for Mastan and earned remuneration for his services, they still looked upon him as their friend.

After Karim Lala's example, everyone had begun to address the man fondly as Ibrahim Bhai. Whenever there was a social or family dispute in the area, whether between brothers regarding property or between couples or between two businessmen, Ibrahim bBhai was always summoned to play the role of mediator. Inevitably, these issues were resolved after his intervention. And aside from settling local disputes, the man was also ever-willing to help the poor. He was known to offer food, shelter, clothes, and even money to those who needed them, from orphans to destitutes to the unlucky. He would even borrow money from the dons to help out someone when he himself did not have the resources.

But the same Ibrahim Bhai who yielded such clout and exuded such authority in the area would rise to his feet with genuine reverence each time he saw anyone who claimed to be a Sayyed Muslim. Although there is no caste hierarchy in Islam, Sayyed Muslims are considered superior by pedigree as they are said to have descended from Prophet Mohammad. It was this deep reverence towards Sayyeds that presented opportunity to many unscrupulous people who wanted to take advantage of Ibrahim bhai's religiosity.

Regarded as a resourceful cop in CID, Kaskar had, in a career spanning over two decades, built up a formidable reputation in the police. In the early sixties, Yusuf havildar, Adam havildar, and Ibrahim Kaskar formed a powerful group of constables in Dongri and used to make criminals quiver. Their methods of interrogation, using both psychological and physical torture, were so effective that the thugs used to say, 'Yahan deewaren bhi bolti hai [even the walls will confess their crimes].'

Kaskar was a constable at several different police stations like Colaba, Mahim, Malabar Hill, as well as the traffic police HQ and retired around 1967 with his final posting at the Crime Branch. At the time, there was only one Crime Branch stationed in the commissioner's headquarters: an elite squad made up of competent people. How ironic that the same room Ibrahim bhai was once saluted in later became the backdrop for discussions around the rise of the most dreaded gangster of the era — his very own son.

Kaskar lived with his wife Amina and a two-year-old son, Sabir in a small, nondescript 10 x 10 square feet house in Temkar Mohalla, a far-flung corner of south Bombay. It was here that his infamous second son was born on 26 December 1955.

Despite his already having been a father, the news of the birth of second son made Ibrahim ecstatic. Posted with the Malabar Hill traffic police at the time, he was manning the roads when he was given the good news: his wife Amina *bi* had delivered. He immediately sought leave from his superiors and rushed to his wife's side. As he looked at the infant, he recollected that only a couple of months ago, Nirale Shah Baba, a seer whom they all revered deeply, had predicted that he would have six sons, and that his second born would be powerful, famous, and wealthy.

Ibrahim Kaskar was a very religious, pious man. When he looked at his son and thought of the power and wealth the seer had predicted, he could not conceive of any other name but Dawood. And thus Constable Ibrahim Kaskar's second son came to be christened Dawood Ibrahim Kaskar.

The Holy Quran and the Old Testament of the Bible both hold references to Dawood (or David), as a highly venerable and powerful prophet of God. Dawood was also a king who ruled all the creations of God including animals and birds. According to Muslim folklore, Dawood was strong enough to bend an iron rod by a mere touch of his hand. The biblical Dawood also had a sweet voice—such that when he sang the Psalms, even birds would stop to listen to him, mesmerised by the sonorous voice.

When he named his son Dawood, Ibrahim hoped his son would reach the heights of glory, fame, and wealth predicted for him, and that the magical effect of this most apt of names would rub off on the boy.

Karim Lala, Pathan of Peshawar, was the first to receive news of Dawood's birth outside the Kaskar clan. In fact, it is said that as Kaskar could not afford a *walima* (a feast organised on the birth of a son), Karim Lala hosted a lavish feast on behalf of his dear friend, Ibrahim Bhai.

Fortunately, no clairvoyant attended the feast, or else they might have warned Karim Lala that instead of celebrating the birth of his friend's son so generously, he might do well to mourn the birth of his future nemesis.

9

The *Baap* of Dons

Ibrahim believed in the old world ideology wherefore children are regarded as the bounty of Allah. Thus Ibrahim's family kept growing at a steady pace. After Dawood, Amina gave birth to five more sons: Anees, Noora, Iqbal, Mustaqeem, and Humayun. They also had four daughters Zaitun, Haseena, Farhana, and Mumtaz. Her eldest were Saeeda. It was quite a struggle to survive, trying to subsist and raise twelve children with a meagre salary. Stories from that time tell of how the Kaskar children starved most of the time. After they had their morning meal, which comprised tea and a piece of bread (known as *brun pav*), the next meal was dinner late at night.

Most of the time, the family did not have anything to eat through the day. But in spite of the abject conditions they lived in, Ibrahim wanted his children to have a good education. He got Dawood enrolled in Ahmed Sailor High School, a prominent English-medium school at Nagpada, while his brothers were sent to municipality schools and sisters to Urdu-medium schools. Dawood's father also ensured that his second son, intended for great things, was involved in extracurricular activities. He enrolled him in the RSP (Road Safety Patrol) team where he was given traffic training. Until the sixth grade, things went smoothly and Dawood did not play hooky.

But one day, Ibrahim and a few of his colleagues lost their jobs. It was never clear as to what exactly precipitated the crisis, but it was widely suspected the blow had been dealt because the policemen had not cracked a particularly high-profile murder case in 1966. Subsequently placed under suspension with his colleagues, Ibrahim could not believe his fate. The family was virtually on the brink of starvation.

Education now seemed a distant dream. Perhaps life would have taken a different turn for Dawood if he could have continued his education. But the family's deteriorating financial circumstances forced him to drop out. Dawood was thus 10 years old when he bid farewell to formal education.

One man who was deeply disturbed by this development was Ibrahim Kaskar's senior, ACP Dastagir Burhan Malgi. He insisted Dawood should continue his education at any cost, but Ibrahim Kaskar had no choice. From the summer of 1966, Dawood was one happy boy. He did not have to go to school, study, or complete his homework. He did not have to undergo the RSP training his father had put him through. And most importantly, he had all the free time in the world to do what he wanted—hang out in the area with other boys his age.

The boy started spending time with the street urchins in the Dongri and JJ area, much to the chagrin of his parents. At other times, he was found in the huge sprawling precincts of the JJ Hospital where he played cricket. He loved the game, patronising it even when he was on the run from the law, much later. Another favourite hangout was the JJ Square, where he played with other Muslim boys.

In the meanwhile, Ibrahim was busy with a new kind of work; he had begun doing various odd jobs to feed his family. He was forced to run certain errands for Baashu Dada, even—petty jobs like running around with files to the clerks of the customs department and Bombay Port Trust officials. But he remained honest and despite temptations and enticement from friends like Rahim, he did not succumb to the temptations of a life of crime. He could not, however, keep a check on his sons, especially Sabir and Dawood.

Soon, Dawood's family had to give up their house in Temkar Mohalla and shift to Musafirkhana, Pakhmodia Street, a stone's throw away (at the time, called Bohri Mohalla). The Kaskars had barely shifted when Dawood made his presence felt in the area as the local goon. The Bohra community bore the brunt of the activities of the budding gang of thugs. Musafirkhana became the unofficial headquarters for the budding Dawood gang.

Despite all the religious teachings and education imparted by his parents, Dawood was drawn to crime and power and he was hungry to earn lots of money. Even before his teens, he had begun to indulge in street crime like petty theft, chain snatching, beating up people, pickpocketing, and extorting money from shopkeepers.

Dawood was just 14 years old when he committed his first crime. He snatched money from a man who was counting cash on the road and ran away with it. The victim managed to trace Ibrahim and complained to him. A furious Ibrahim got hold of his son and gave him a proper thrashing. This kept Dawood and his minions under check for a few days, but not for long. The boy soon returned to his wayward behaviour.

Dawood's menace, clout, and propensity to cause mischief were soon common knowledge in the area. Whenever his father heard of his crimes, he was doubly embarrassed and enraged; both as a cop and as a father. However Ibrahim, who was transferred to the Crime Branch, was swarmed with work in his new posting and did not have the time to constantly discipline and watch over his troublemaker son. When he was not working, he was caught up in endless rounds of community work. But he never failed to haul up Dawood when he heard of his misdeeds, losing count of the number of times he had beaten the boy black and blue.

Dawood was very much in awe of his father, and yet he listened to no one other than his mother. There would be long spells when father and son would not be on talking terms: Ibrahim because he thought Dawood was a stigma to his name, and Dawood, sulking for having been pulled up. However, during these spells, his mother would never haul him up as his father did, but instead would remain a friend to him. So, the two would never not communicate. When it came to hooliganism, though, he would not listen even to his mother. 'Beta, this is not right for you. Look, your dad is a policeman and your activities will ruin his reputation', she would gently reprimand him. And each time, a noncommittal '*dekhoonga maa*', was the budding don's refrain.

Dawood could not resist being what he was. He loved the power that came by means of terrorising people and he wanted to earn pots of money by any means. Although poor and lacking the monetary resources, he longed to see his brothers in fine clothing and sisters and mother laden with jewellery. It was Dawood who called the shots and took major decisions regarding household expenses whenever these were needed. Amina always reserved her remonstrations for Dawood, directing her words to him because she knew that the others simply followed suit. Even Sabir, older to Dawood, was content playing second fiddle to him. The boy who would one day be the uncrowned king of the underworld lived a pauper's childhood; therein, perhaps, lies the key to his greed and ruthlessness.

As was bound to happen with so much spare time on his hands, Dawood had crossed paths with ubiquitous local goons, by this time. He had heard about the power of the Allahabadi and the Kashmiri gangs, but the gang that Dawood really admired and wanted to be a part of was the Pathan gang.

In the meanwhile, a huge influx of Muslim youths from Ratnagiri to Mumbai had come about, particularly from Dawood's village Mumka. They all invariably converged around Dongri. Ibrahim had become the pivot for most of the milling Konkani Muslims who landed in the city in the late sixties and early seventies. A small cluster of Konkani boys fell in with Sabir, Dawood, and his brothers. Ali Abdulla Antulay, later called Ali bhai, was one of these many boys new to the city. By the early seventies, the teenaged Dawood had become a ringleader of a small gang of boys, consisting of his brothers Sabir and Anees, his cousin, Ali, and others like Ayyub and Rashid.

The Bohras were a well-to-do community with established businesses that stretched right from the Khada Parsi junction to Claire Road in Nagpada, parts of Agripada, and Musafirkhana. They owned glass houses, eateries, and travel and tourism operations and were relatively the most prosperous of the lot in the area. Being peaceloving people, they shied away from confrontation and open fighting. When Dawood or his boys tried to extort money from them, they preferred giving away the money to creating a scene or worse, risking bodily harm. In this way, Dawood's impertinence grew unchecked. After a while, he did not have to personally go to extort money—the gang members did the job for him, providing the muscle for his operations. All the boys, sometimes a motley crew of three or four, and at others, a gang of over ten, looked up to him as their leader, and with the title came perks such as a crew of willing boys working under him and reporting to him directly. In this manner, until 1972-73, Dawood was involved in extortion.

Dawood always wanted to get to the next level and he was no different as a young lad. Gradually the gang graduated to conning people. They set up a shop in Mohatta Market selling imported watches. One or two boys would walk the streets outside the shop and look for prospective targets. Finally, when they saw a potential victim approaching, they slid up to him quietly and showed him a watch in a case—'Rado *ghadi*—*5,000 ka maal 2,000 mein. Andar aa jao, baat karenge* [A 5,000 rupees-worth Rado watch, only for 2,000 rupees. Come in, we can negotiate.]'. Saying this, they would lure the catch inside the shop. Once inside they would allow the man to bargain and finally close the deal at about 1,200-1,500 rupees. They would then take the watch in to be wrapped and packed, and replace the watch with a stone. They called this act '*palti maarna*'. Emerging, they would tell the man, '*Yeh leke jaao. Idhar mat kholna. Koi dekhega toh problem ho jaayegi* [take this with you, but do not open it here because if someone sees it there might be a problem].' The man would unwittingly take it and walk away. Once a little away from the shop, he would open the box and discover the con. If he returned to the shop, the boys would deny everything with impunity. It was a cheeky and calculated little con game, and Dawood pulled it off.

Sometimes, the odd Parsi gentleman would lodge a complaint with Pydhonie Police Station. If the police came looking for them, they would decamp for days and sometimes even months to their villages. These little games served as a huge confidence-building exercise for Dawood and the rest of the gang, and they slowly but surely began to believe that they could pull off anything in this city.

10

Of Young Turks

Back in 1972, Bombay was made up of several constituencies and unlike the apathy between neighbours today, people knew everyone who lived in their neighbourhood. They knew, in particular, who the *galli ka dada* (local goon) was and which politician was thick with him. Baashu Dada was a well-known name in Teli Mohalla. Nobody dared cross his path in his backyard. One flex of his muscles, nursed carefully by the litres and litres of badam sherbet he downed during his daily *baithaks*, was enough to frighten away even the most fearless.

Baashu Dada always held his *baithaks* in the afternoon when he deigned to step out of his den into his lair just outside. Surrounded by his henchmen and soothsayers, he reigned over his principality with the sceptre of fear and terror. On one such day, he rolled into Teli Mohalla in his swanky Mercedes-Benz. The car drew to a halt and Baashu lay one foot encased in a shiny white shoe on the ground, then the other, and swung gracefully out of the car. For a man of his size, his movements were amazingly lithe and graceful. Rashid came running to greet Dada and immediately fell to his knees in front of him. He was not paying some form of medieval obeisance to Baashu, only tying a shoelace that had had the audacity to come undone on one of those spotless white shoes. Baashu never bowed before anyone, not even to tie his laces. The arrogance that gave rise to such behaviour is irksome. Baashu's people quaked and curtseyed and bent over two times to accommodate his every wish, request, and demand.

On that day, there was a football match being played, part of a month-long tournament. Cricket was not the popular game as it is today among dons. His men, the Pathans, were staunch fans of football and all their activities ceased for the ninety minutes that the game ensued. In Baashu's *baithak*, this event acquired an almost festive air. In those days, the only way to be tuned in to the match was through the radio. So accordingly, on the day of the match, everything was set to just the right mood for Dada to enjoy the match. The radio was tuned to the right frequency, the charpoy laid out, the badam sherbet cooled to just the right temperature.

But there was a problem that had to be dealt with at the earliest and the unpleasant job of dealing with this problem lay with Rashid. He creased and uncreased his brow trying to portray a measure of composure, failing miserably.

The Maharashtra Assembly elections were around the corner. The Umarkhadi constituency was Baashu's home territory and he liked to keep it that way. However, things were not looking good this time round.

'Dada,' Rashid finally spoke up.

Baashu looked up in mild amusement at the quiver in Rashid's voice.

'Dada, *election aa rahe hain* [the elections are just round the corner],' Rashid murmured.

Baashu stretched his back and leant on the charpoy. Rashid dropped the bomb, '*Maulana bohot ekdi dikha raha hai* [Maulana is acting a bit too smart].' Finally it was out of his system!

Rashid's declaration made Baashu sit up. The Maulana he was referring to was Maulana Zia-ud-din Bukhari, a respected leader of the local Muslim community. The Maulana had always enjoyed Baashu's support, until now. Baashu had one very simple rule with politics—the winner of the seat in his constituency was simply the one who gave him more respect and more money.

He sat back in his charpoy in contemplation. No one was allowed to believe he was greater than Baashu. And God help the one who disturbs

Baashu while he is listening to his match commentary, Rashid thought, as he waited.

In an ominous half whisper, Baashu replied at last, '*Phir Maulana ko haarna hoga* [then the Maulana will have to lose]!'

Rashid breathed out a sigh of relief. The worst had passed, he thought.

✠

That same month, Maulana Zia-ud-din Bukhari lost the Maharashtra State Legislative Assembly Elections of 1972 to the candidate nominated by the Muslim League. He knew whose doing it was and he was not at all happy, of course. Baashu had beaten him at his game. He had pushed the Muslim League into nominating another candidate, Noor Mohammad, in his place and backed Noor Mohammad to win the election.

The Maulana put his wiles to use and thought up a two-step action plan to win back his good favour and pride. One morning, he went to Ibrahim Kaskar's home with a unique proposal. After the requisite niceties were exchanged, he sprang his idea on the unsuspecting Ibrahim.

'*Ibrahim bhai, ek khayal aaya mere zehen mein,* he began, '*hamare ladkein yun dinbhar awaaragardiyon mein masruf rehte hain. Kyun na unse kuch tamiri kaam karayein.* [I have an idea. Our local boys are idling away their time through the day. Why not enlist them for more honourable purposes?]'

Ibrahim replied politely, '*Ji main samjha nahi Maulana sahib* [I'm not too sure I understand what you're saying].'

'*Kyun na naujawanon ki ek anjuman banayi jaayi* [why don't we gather the boys for a cause]?' the Maulana continued.

Ibrahim agreed, saying, '*Jee Maulana, jaisa aap theek samjhe. Hamari qaum ke naujawanon ko sahi raasta dikhana aapki buzurgi hai. Mere betein toh aapki khidmat mein hamesha haazir hai* [as you wish Maulana, my sons will always be available to you].'

The Maulana left Ibrahim's house very pleased. Next, he filed an appeal in the Bombay High Court alleging that the elections had been won by the MUL through unfair means.

Ibrahim brought his sons together and informed them of the Maulana's plan. 'Maulana's suggestion is almost like a firman of god for me. You all should join his *jammaat* and work hard to improve your community,' said Ibrahim. They were all excited at the thought of the youth of the neighbourhood uniting under one banner. And once the idea had Ibrahim's approval, all the families in the neighbourhood were keen to have their sons participate. It was decided that the group be called 'Young Party', appropriately. They began with activities like decorating the neighbourhood for festivals and organising rallies. Then, the Maulana's idea caught the fancy of the neighbourhood and the numbers of the Young Party swelled to mammoth proportions.

However, there was a setback; the Bombay High Court dismissed the Maulana's plea. The Maulana took his appeal to the Supreme Court but the apex court too upheld the decision of the High Court. Dejected and disappointed, the Maulana then withdrew from all further activities of the Young Party and gradually faded away from public involvement with electioneering in the area.

But in the meanwhile, the Young Party's popularity had given rise to another idea in the mind of young Dawood. Canny as ever, he saw this as a golden opportunity to showcase his leadership skills and influence the other youth to do his bidding.

Pakhmodia Street and Musafirkhana earned another leader with the loss of one. There was now a board at the beginning of the street proclaiming it as the territory of the Young Party, one that was led by the formidable Dawood Ibrahim Kaskar.

✠

Dawood was going past Kedy company, a high-rise in Nagpada, on his motorbike when he saw Karim Siddiqui's nephew rushing towards him. The youth, a very close friend of Dawood's, was severely bruised. He stopped Dawood and said to him, '*Hamid ne phir mujhe peeta Dawood bhai* [Hamid thrashed me again, Dawood bhai]!' Dawood was enraged. The brothers Hamid and Majid were annoying him to no end. Hamid, a brawny Pathan who believed he could take on anybody and Majid, a drug addict who was wasting away in the by-lanes of Dongri, were flies Dawood could have swatted away long ago, but for Baashu Dada, who enlisted their services. And no matter what, Dawood still had respect for Dada; not because of any of his personal attributes but because of the mutual respect between Ibrahim Kaskar and Baashu. Nevertheless, it was time to put Hamid in his place. He asked Siddiqui to get on his bike and they sped off towards Hamid's home.

Face-to-face with Hamid, Dawood could not control his temper at Hamid's behaviour.

'*Behanchod, tu bahot bada shaana ho gaya hai kya bambai ka* [sisterfucker, you've become too big for your boots]!' he roared.

'*Nahin* Dawood bhai, *kuchch ghalat fehmi hui hai* [no, Dawood bhai, there seems to have been a misunderstanding],' Hamid quivered.

'*Ek baat sun le, Baashu Dada ka moonh dekh kar maine tujhe baksh diya, nahin toh tera kheema banake rakh deta* [now remember one thing: I've spared you all this while only because of Baashu Dada, else I surely would made mincemeat of you],' Dawood thundered.

Hamid had seen his death in Dawood's eyes. He knew very well that he would have been dead meat but for Baashu's name, a veritable suit of armour for him.

Fuming at his inability to do anything to Hamid, Dawood stormed out. Meanwhile, Hamid started thinking quickly. He knew that sooner or later the news would reach Baashu's ears. Wouldn't it be better if he, Hamid, was the source? With all this and more on his mind, he went to Baashu's darbar. Baashu was trying to enjoy what was left of one of the tournament's matches. He was already annoyed by the Maulana's uppity behaviour and now here was Hamid.

'*Dada, Dawood ne aapko maa-behen ki gaali di* [Dada, Dawood hurled some rather tasteless abuses at you]!' Hamid exclaimed.

An enraged Baashu, unable to bear the idea that someone could have the temerity to insult him, let alone a young boy on the rise, rose from his charpoy immediately. He asked for Ibrahim, Rahim, and Sabir to be summoned to the *baithak*. His football match had now completely gone for a toss!

Ibrahim, Rahim, and Sabir, still a lad, came, and stood in front of Baashu, surrounded by the don's men.

'*Dawood ne mujhe maa-behen ki gaali di Ibrahim. Sambhalo apne chhokre ko* [Dawood has abused me Ibrahim, you better keep a check on your son]!' Baashu raged.

'*Galti ho gayi hogi ladke se Dada. Maaf kar dijiye* [he's made a mistake Dada, please forgive him],' Rahim ventured.

'*Galti* [mistake]!" the don bellowed.

Addressing Sabir he said, '*Jab tere baap ke paas tum log ko khilane ke bhi paise nahi the tab maine sahara diya. Aur ab tum log sab saale behenchod log, usi thaali ko gaali deta hai! Tum logon ne mere ehsaanon ka yeh sila diya hain, is tarah namakharaami karke* [I helped your father when he had nothing to feed you all. And today, you people bite the hand that feeds you]!'

'*Dafa ho jao yahan se* [get lost]!' he said, with a wave of his hand.

Ibrahim and Sabir walked out clutching what little dignity remained while Rahim stood where he was. The word *ehsaan* (favour) and *namakharaami* (disloyalty) kept ringing in the ears of the father and son.

'*Aapko chhote ladke ko aisa nahi bolna chahiye tha Dada* [Dada, you shouldn't have spoken to the little boy like that],' Rahim reasoned.

'*Chhota ladka? Usike chhote bhai ne meri maa-behen ka naam apni gandi zubaan se nikala aur main kya tamasha dekhta rahun? Nahi Rahim!* [Little boy? The little boy's younger brother abused me and you expect me to be a mute spectator? No Rahim!]' Baashu raged.

Sabir, meanwhile, returned home and began to sob. While it was well-known that the family of fourteen often faced difficulty in getting by, because of Ibrahim's popularity in the neighbourhood no one had ever spoken a word in public about it. Now the fact that Baashu had insulted his father to this extent was unbearable to Sabir, and he could not control his tears. Ibrahim himself maintained a stunned silence and a stoic face. Dawood heard of the series of events from Sabir and his blood boiled. He could not bear to see his father and brother insulted and dishonoured like this by another man. Vowing revenge, he vowed to bring the empire and the pride of Baashu Dada crashing down.

11

David Versus Goliath

D awood's presence in Dongri was growing increasingly powerful. A mere lad, he had already surprised people with his adeptness and ability to plan meticulously with a sharp mind. The Young Party was also gaining fame and their activities did not stop at the Eid-e-Milad processions they had begun with. They were now notorious for extortion. Along with Hanif Kutta and Sayed Razi alias Rajji, they extorted money from all and sundry under the pretext of meeting expenses for weddings and funerals in poor families. The moneyed would be asked to 'contribute' to the wedding coffers or funeral expenses of the poor, or else face Dawood's ire. Playing partly on the emotions of the people and partly on their fear, Dawood and his pals created the perfect con strategy.

The Young Party, of course, had been created to further the aims of Maulana Zia-ud-Din Bukhari. However, not only was Bukhari no more involved with the Young Party, but the party itself had become a front for criminal activities, albeit of a non-violent nature. It was around this time, circa 1974, that Ibrahim Kaskar and Sabir were humiliated by Baashu. The problem that faced the young Dawood was very grave. He truly loved his father and brother. No matter his general impunity, where his father and brother were concerned, he was generally with his head bowed in their presence out of fondness and respect. Baashu, a mere goon, had shamed both of them and even listed all the favours he had done for Ibrahim over the years. The more Dawood thought about it, the more he regarded it a faulty assessment.

He knew how much Baashu owed his father. A lot of Baashu's smuggled goods had been released with the assistance of Ibrahim Kaskar. When Baashu's goods would get caught in the docks, Ibrahim would be away for days, wheeling and dealing and peddling favours to get it released. His father had helped Baashu make his millions to buy his Mercedes and custom-made white shoes while he gave Dawood's family a mere pittance from time to time. And in exchange for that small amount of money that changed hands, he had insulted Dawood's family. This was absolutely unacceptable.

Rahim chacha tried to console Dawood and coax him into calming down, 'Gussa achi baat nahi. Chalke Baashu bhai ki galat fehmi door karo. [Anger is not good. Let's go to Baashu and clear this misunderstanding.]' But his sermons were falling on deaf ears. There was no way Dawood was going to see anyone else's way. He knew that Baashu would have to go. In the quiet manner that was somehow also menacing, Dawood retorted, 'Baashu Dada ko yeh baat badi mehengi padegi [Baashu will have to pay for this].' At these ominous words, Rahim chacha's blood froze.

✠

The Juma Namaaz had just finished and it was a hot 2 pm on Friday. Baashu Dada offered his prayers in a masjid near Mastaan Talao. Dawood and his gang were waiting for Baashu. Hanif Kutta, Rajji, Sultan, Abu Bakr, and Sabir were with him. Sabir was against the idea of attacking Baashu, fearing reprisal, and he had told Dawood as much. But Dawood had made up his mind. They were all standing together near Pir Khan Street, a little ahead of JJ Square, waiting for Baashu to emerge through the archway.

It was not a very long wait because Dawood had planned the operation to its finest detail. They saw Baashu appear on schedule, accompanied by his *pehelwans* (musclemen). Responding to a cue from Dawood, the gang began throwing soda water bottles and used electric bulbs at the don. Soda water bottles as weapons? Now that was a first! The gang continued to throw bottles incessantly, even hitting some passers-by.

If those around were shocked, Baashu was stunned. Firstly, absolutely nobody attacks Baashu Dada and to add salt to injury, soda water bottles were a belittling choice of weapons. This was the first time an incident like this had taken place, but in the riots that broke out in the following years, bottles came to be commonly used.

As he got over the initial shock, Baashu regained his composure and decided to take on Dawood singlehandedly, in man-to-man combat. Baashu knew that Dawood was no match for him and Dawood himself was not ignorant of this. He had even anticipated that Baashu would try something like this. So he began to target Baashu specifically, before it came to this pass. He rained bottle after bottle on Baashu while his boys took on the other *pehelwans*.

Finally, one of the *pehelwans* managed to pull the black Mercedes out of its parking slot. Baashu and Umar Pehelwan were seriously injured by this time, and as Baashu saw the car coming towards him, he realised it made sense to retreat when they were so seriously set back. The don and his pehelwans scrambled into the car, some of them even getting in through the windows as the car picked up speed, in their desperation to get away.

Dawood and his boys continued with their bottles-and-bulbs attack. Even as the gangsters retreated, the boys managed to shatter the car's rear window and tail lights, and made huge, satisfying dents in the luxury car's shiny exterior.

As the car drove away, the boys began to celebrate their unheard of victory. But Dawood had other things on his mind. He was not satisfied. He was not done with Baashu. Not done with teaching him a lesson and not yet done with his revenge.

Picking up their motorcycles, the gang went to Temkar Mohalla where Baashu's darbar and *akhada* were erected to massage his ego.

The traditional *akhada* is a big ring-like space surrounded by mirrors where people can pump iron, jest, duel, and keep fit. Baashu's *akhada* had a speciality. A place of pride in the *akhada* was given to the *badam* sherbet-making machine. Dawood took to the walls with a hockey stick. He shattered the mirrors brutally, remembering how Baashu had humiliated his family. Together, the young Dawood and his gang destroyed the entire *akhada*; the mirrors, the furniture, the equipment, and even the sherbet-making machine. It broke the spine of Baashu Dada.

Unable to face himself after this episode, Baashu withdrew from public life. The *akhada* was an integral part of Baashu and his aura, and when it was utterly destroyed, he was finished. And when luck turns, even the oldest and most faithful servant seeks greener pastures. Why would Baashu's case be any different? Soon after this incident, Baashu was detained by the Bombay Police under the National Security Act (NSA), entailing a year-long detention without bail. The charge of Teli Mohalla was handed over to Khalid *pehelwan*. This was an opportunity for what was soon to become a signature Dawood move; Khalid, despite being Baashu's right-hand man, had been treated as just another minion in Baashu's fiefdom. Dawood moved fast to earn the loyalty of Baashu's Man Friday. He made sure to impress upon Khalid that he did not bear any enmity or rancour towards him, and would be glad if Khalid joined him. So, with one swift move, Dawood effectively emasculated Baashu and brought an end to his reign.

After this, even after he returned from jail, Baashu refused to meet anybody and never again did he set foot in Temkar Mohalla. He divided his time between his houses in Hyderabad and Walkeshwar and was rarely heard of again.

12

The First Blood

A couple of years later, when Dawood Ibrahim heard that Bombay's reigning Gold King, Haji Mastan Mirza, had got some Pathans to beat up two of his cronies, he was seething with revenge. Nobody knew exactly why Mastan decided to beat up Abu Bakr and Ejaz, but he had now strayed into Dawood's territory. He wanted to get even with Mastan, who he thought had garnered enough glory by smuggling gold and silver. Resting on the laurels of Mastan was the 'Madrasi', Varda bhai. Dawood knew that Mastan was not a man of action; he had never done anything to assert his might in the city. He believed that such a man had no right or authority to rule over the city. And Dawood had had enough of his photographs being splashed in the newspapers while attending various film mahurats. Bollywood was obsessed with Mastan and sought to epitomise him in forthcoming movies.

This just was not right to Dawood's mind. So, while a seemingly harmless group of boys and men were caught up in a heated discussion on 4 December 1974, one of them, young Dawood Ibrahim, was masterminding the gangster's downfall.

After toppling the might of Baashu and staking his claim as the big boss of Dongri, Dawood felt he could do just about anything in Bombay and get away with it. Offence is the best form of defence and the best way to take revenge is to hit where it hurts most. For Mastan, money was everything. So, Dawood decided to get even with Mastan by stealing a chunk of his black money. On that December morning, the group had received intelligence from their local spy network; in mafia parlance, 'tip mili'. The tip-off was that some *angadia* was going to carry 5 lakh rupees belonging to Mastan from an office in Masjid Bunder to his house at Malabar Hill.

Angadias in Bombay are unofficial money carriers, acting like a local form of Western Union, and generally hail from the Marwari community. It was spontaneously decided to deny Mastan this much of his precious cash as compensation for all the beatings and torture meted out to their two dear friends for no rhyme or reason. For the Dongri youth, this was a matter of prestige, as they felt obliged to avenge their friends' beatings. Also, the two were part of Dawood's gang, and were his friends. Out of a sense of loyalty for his boys, Dawood could not simply turn away and ignore the whole episode. Back in those days, 5 lakh was a huge amount. These young men had never seen so much money earlier. While they were a bit nervous about the plan, there was also a certain complacency; they had heard that the *angadias* were foolish enough to carry this kind of money around unescorted.

Dawood and his band of cronies decided to strike when the *angadia* left from Masjid Bunder and moved towards the Carnac Bunder Bridge. As Musafirkhana was the area where Dawood ruled the roost, he knew the area like the back of his hand. He also knew how he could intercept vehicles, trap the money, and disappear in a crowd without the cops or anybody else getting wind of him.

He gathered seven boys around him, including Abu Bakr, Yusuf Khan, Ejaz Jinki, Aziz Driver, Abdul Muttalib, Sayyed Sultan, and Sher Khan. Among these seven, the latter two were his favourites.

Sayyed Sultan Ayubi had strong shoulders, bulging biceps, and a powerful body. The 20-year-old had just been voted as Mr Bombay and was vying for the top title at the body-building competition that would begin as part of Mr India in the following year. In the seventies, muscular men were a rarity. Even the popular Hindi films of the time sported clean-cut, chocolate-faced heroes like Rajesh Khanna and Jitendra. So when Ayubi graduated from Mr Bombay to Mr Maharashtra to Mr India, he managed to remain consistently in the news with pictures of his awe-inspiring torso. Legend has it that when he strolled on the Marine Drive promenade in south Bombay, women were beguiled by his very broad shoulders. The other, Sher Khan Pathan aka Sher Singh, was well-known for his loud, bone-chilling voice, which inspired great fear in people.

Dawood at the time was barely out of his teens and had just acquired a moustache. He had developed all the traits of a typical Dongri lad; the lingo, the chicanery, the know-it-all attitude, yet he was regarded as a greenhorn in the underworld, as he did not have the kind of money that Baashu or Haji Mastan did, and everyone thought of him simply as a wannabe don.

Carnac Bunder area lies at the periphery of Bombay's three big markets Mohatta Market, Manish Market, and Crawford Market, a legacy of the colonial era. The entire area was at the time a hub for all the wholesale and retail markets for all agricultural produce. The place was a madhouse as all the traders and long distance trucks offloaded their goods here. It was always teeming with handcarts, porters carrying gunny bags or trunks on their shoulder, cabs moving in and out of the market with goods laden either in their boot or on their overhead carrier space. There was an air of urgency with the hectic activity ongoing everywhere.

The amateur robbers had seen a lot of movies and wanted to make a reproduction of their meticulous planning and preparation. So, two men were stationed theatrically at the Carnac Bunder Bridge while two men were standing near Musafirkhana, to efficiently seal off both the entry and exit points of the cab. The men were armed with iron rods, sticks, and choppers. The remaining lads were supposed to intercept the cab. These men were carrying choppers, knives, and country-made revolver called katta. Somehow, by sheer coincidence or simply bad planning, the major players like Ayubi, Abu Bakr, Hanif, and others were either stationed on the bridge or left behind and by default Dawood got pushed to the forefront. Perhaps it was destiny or his own bravado, but he ended up leading the team of seven men who, willy-nilly, were in charge of intercepting the cab. The moment the cab came out of the narrow lane of Dana Bunder and moved out towards the road that connected with Carnac Bunder towards the market, they would spring into action.

Around 2 pm, as the cab drew out from the road below the Carnac Bunder Bridge that links Crawford Market to P. D'Mello Road, the informant pointed out the vehicle, implying that this was the car carrying the cash. Surprisingly, the taxi had two Marwari-looking men seated in the passenger seat and an escort in the front seat next to the driver. As it slowly made its way from the bridge towards the route that led to Mohammed Ali Road, the seven men positioned to attack ran towards the cab at once, their arsenal ready and drawn.

No instructions were given and there was no coordination at all between the team members. The whole gang of seven men had swung into action in the most haphazard manner. The first strike was made by Sher Khan, who took the handcart and rammed it against the cab, bringing it to a screeching halt. Even before the Marwaris or the driver could comprehend anything, Sher Pathan the body builder opened the driver's door and threatened the driver, instructing him not to move.

The sight of seven men surrounding them was a menacing one for the Marwari businessmen. The weapons froze their blood. Dawood was the first one to speak. He asked them not to make noise or do anything foolhardy that could endanger their lives. '*Agar halak se awaz nikli, to zindagi bhar nahi niklegi, kyunke main tumhare gardan kat lunga* [if I hear your voice emerge from your throat, it'll never make a sound again, because I'll slit it],' he said, steely and calmly.

The final act belonged to Dawood, who opened the door of the passenger's seat, looked at the Marwari seth with fire in his eyes and asked, '*Maal kaha hai* [where is the money]?' The menacing tone and the icy glare of the lanky 19-year-old sent shivers down the spines of the Marwari seths. Both stared at each other, speechless. The time they were wasting in indecisive fear made Dawood impatient. He slapped one of them, hard enough to make his spectacles fall to his lap, and said, '*Mere paas zyada waqt nahi hai tumhare saath baat karne ko* [I don't have much time to talk to you]!'

With that he grabbed the bag that the seth had on him and opened it. '*Aur kaha hai* [where is the rest]?' he asked. The seth, with a trembling hand, pointed towards the boot of the car. Dawood waved to Ejaz, who went and lifted the hood. There, he found a small black box, locked and sealed.

Now that Dawood had both the bags, he did not waste any time. He immediately signalled to his boys to move and all of them disappeared on foot from the scene of the robbery, leaving behind two seths and a cab driver, shaken and stunned in their seats. When the Marwaris finally got over their shock, they decided to approach the police. At the Pydhonie Police Station, they registered a complaint, CR No. 725/74, under the section of dacoity and armed robbery.

Dawood and his men did not realise they had committed the biggest bank robbery of the decade. This was the first time such an audacious robbery had taken place, executed by seven inexperienced men who had by luck carried off their feat.

At the time, Dawood was three weeks shy of his 19 th birthday. What he did not know was that he had actually robbed money that belonged to the Metropolitan Cooperative Bank, not Haji Mastan. The amount looted on that day was 4, 75, 000 rupees and it immediately brought the whole focus of the crime on one youth, Dawood Ibrahim. He was front-page news in the city the next day.

Ibrahim Kaskar was speechless when he heard of his son's temerity. After being suspended Ibrahim had resigned, and was let go unofficially from the elite Crime Branch of the Bombay police only a few years ago, but was still highly respected in police circles. In the predominantly Muslim stronghold of Dongri, Ibrahim's *baithak* was the first place people went to if they had a problem. It was privy to everything—from people discussing their choking lavatory drain to the excitement of the elopement of lovers or cases of police harassment. When Dawood and Sabir picked fights on the streets or indulged in other misdeeds, Ibrahim felt small but ignored them, while putting their delinquency down to the passion of youth. But this incident threatened to destroy his hard-earned respect and reputation.

That evening, out of shame and embarrassment, Ibrahim did not even go down to his *baithak*. He did not have the courage to face people and their queries about Dawood. He was reminded of the seer's prediction about his second born, who would be known for his success and power. His son had indeed found power, but he had, in the process, defamed him. Ibrahim had to hide his face even from his friends.

In the meanwhile, the Bombay police were at the boys' heels and while the other members of the gang were caught without much effort by the police, the Kaskar brothers, Dawood and Sabir, proved elusive. The day after the daring robbery, a constable knocked at Ibrahim Bhai's house and asked him to see the officer at the Crime Branch. Ibrahim, who was squatting on the ground, thumped his hand on the floor, all the while cursing himself. He was expecting this. It is not known what transpired behind the closed doors of the Crime Branch, but Ibrahim's friends say he was very grim and had resolved to drag his sons to the police station, allowing the law to take its own course.

Ibrahim had his own network of friends and well-wishers and he worked all of them to trace the duo. They had not come home for two days. After days of intensive search and pursuit, finally the enraged father heard his sons were hiding at a friend's house in Byculla. He picked them up and brought them back to their house. As they stood with their heads bowed, their mother Amina raving and ranting, he went to the loft and opened an old steel cupboard. He came down bearing a thick leather belt that he had worn proudly as the Head Constable of the Crime Branch. When he came down, his sons looked at him with fear, dreading what was to come. But they dared not move an inch.

Neighbours still recall the hammering that Dawood and Sabir were subjected to, for a whole day and night. They screamed and the entire neighbourhood trembled at the brutal punishment. Ibrahim belted both incessantly, so much so that the skin on their backs peeled and bled; both of them were reduced to a heap, lying in a corner of the room. Ibrahim finally stopped when he was overpowered by his friends and they snatched the belt from his hand.

Still, this father did not relent. Even before Amina could offer them food or water, Ibrahim dragged his sons out of the house, put them in a cab and took them to the Crime Branch. He threw his sons at the feet of the officers and folded his hands as he wept. Before leaving the Crime Branch, Ibrahim apologised profusely to the officers and asked them to forgive him and his sons for their disgraceful act. When the

Crime Branch officers looked at Dawood and Sabir, witnessing their pathetic plight and Ibrahim's sincerity, they spared the boys their own stock of blows.

This was the first case of a severe reprisal that came most naturally to Dawood. This incident, this one shot of adrenalin and the 15 minutes of fame that followed, is perhaps the event that gave birth to the man who would one day become Dawood Ibrahim, the don.

13

A Seed is Sown

A warm breeze braced with the crispness of January swept through the congested by-lanes of Dongri. Here the quaint old building of Dongri Police Station had stood for decades like a lone sentinel in one of the most infamous neighbourhoods of Bombay. Senior Police Inspector Ranbeer Likha sat at his desk.

Normally, he was lulled into drowsiness by the regular monotony of trains crossing Sandhurst Road and the domestic sounds emanating from Smith House, just outside Sandhurst Road station. But on this particular afternoon, Senior Police Inspector Likha had other things on his mind. He was listening to the patient voice of Head Constable Dilip Mane registering the complaint of a bakery worker who had been beaten up within an inch of his life for delaying the payment of the monthly instalment of his loan to the local Pathan, Asif Khan. It was the third such complaint being registered that afternoon.

Likha was silently seething at the sheer audacity of the Pathans, who engineered their machinations in plain sight of both civilians and police. Ordinary citizens, workers, and even traders were harassed by Pathans either for extortion because of property disputes or failure to return a

Pathan's interest on his money. This was his second stint at Dongri Police Station and the menace had only escalated since 1960.

As he mulled over the situation, he suddenly realised there might be a way out. He called Constable Gogte and asked him to make a visit to Musafirkhana at Pakmodia Street and ask Ibrahim Kaskar to visit him at his convenience.

Ibrahim might have retired as a mere Head Constable in the Crime Branch but his clout in the area was much more than that of a DCP or prominent social worker. And Ibrahim on his part was ever willing to help the needy and destitute, or his own department whenever they needed his services.

Ibrahim Bhai entered the police station and took his seat opposite Likha. It was Likha who seemed more in awe of the person who came in, rather than the other way round.

A concerned Likha got to the point quickly. *'Ibrahim bhai, yeh kya ho raha hai? Karim miyan se baat karo. Kuch karna padega. Pathanon ki harkatein hadh se bahar hain ab!* [Ibrahim Bhai, why is this happening these days? Please speak with Karim Lala. Something needs to be done. The Pathans' antics are clearly going out of hand!]'

Ibrahim Kaskar shuffled anxiously as he sat before the visibly upset senior officer and tried to reassure him, saying, *'Sahab, main baat karta hun Karim bhai se. Pehle bhi kahan hai maine unse, woh bahut qaedey ke aadmi hain... woh meri baat kabhi nahin taalte... yeh doosre log hain jo unki bhi nahin soonte hain, main kuch karta hun... jo ban sake.* [I will speak with him. He is a good man. He will listen to me. Unfortunately there are some in his group who don't even listen to him.]'

A reassured Likha exhaled, knowing all would be well again. Everyone knew how well-respected Ibrahim was in his community and that he had considerable clout even amongst the much-feared Pathans. While the rest of the police ranks quaked at the mention of dealing with the Pathans, the dignified Ibrahim Kaskar quietly enjoyed mutual respect even with the Pathan mafia.

The Pathan mafia were at the height of their rule over the city. Their sheer power and hold over the community ensured they stayed protected and camouflaged within it. They knew that as long as they could maintain that aura of menacing evil that mafia legends are made of, they would be on top. For them the government, authority, police, law of the land, and such things did not matter. What mattered was power and money. As Karim Lala often said, '*Duniya ko mutthi mein rakhna seekho, haath kholo sirf paisa lene ke liye.* [Learn to clench the world in your fist. Open your palm only when you have to receive money.]'

Likha knew Ibrahim was a man who could be held to his word, if he said that the Pathans' behaviour would be kept in control. A mere remark to Ibrahim had several times in the past shown tangible results in terms of the period of peace that ensued, and these periods had often been timed perfectly to pacify the administration. This was, of course, the same administration which raised questions about the inaction of the police or its brutality at different times, depending largely on their stand in the Legislative Assembly.

This time, however, Ibrahim seemed to be losing his touch. Several afternoons came and went and there seemed no end to the Pathan menace. They had in fact become even more adamant and set on misbehaving. Once, Hamid Khan Pathan was summoned to Dongri. Hamid Khan was a monster at six and a half feet and his gait sent people around him scurrying, for fear of getting in his way. Amir Zada, Alamzeb, and their brothers were also slowly gaining notoriety in the area and inspiring similar fear.

Hamid Khan, for example, stormed into the police station and smashed a huge table at the station house office with his bare hands; lifting the massive table above his head, he then crushed it by dropping it to the floor. The whole posse of cops, including constables and officers, were reduced to gibbering spectators.

Likha realised that Ibrahim's conferences with Karim Khan were not bearing the desired results. He dreaded that the situation was going to get out of hand if something drastic was not done, and done soon. He was after all in charge of his pack and his jurisdiction, and he was doing a very bad job of managing both, at the moment. It would not be long before someone else noticed and made him the scapegoat. As he sat there, however, twisting his mind into knots, the doors swung and Iqbal Natiq breezed in.

Mohammad Iqbal Natiq, then 35 years old, is the rare overnight success story of a self-made Bombay journalist. He edited and published an Urdu weekly called *Raazdaar* (The Confidante).

Journalism in India or Bombay was still in its infancy, at this time. However, the city never had a shortage of tabloids and newspapers serving a particular segment, region or an area. After working as a freelance journalist and columnist in established papers, Natiq launched his own paper from Dongri in 1969 at the age of 26, as was the tradition for aspiring young reporters like him.

In two years, Natiq managed to turn around his life, going from struggling journalist to successful newspaper owner and editor. From owning his own press to driving a spanking new white Ambassador, Natiq began to rise, rubbing shoulders with the elite.

'In fact, my father provided so much luxury to us that despite being a six-year-old at the time, I could never travel in anything but his car, and would refuse to wear plastic slippers,' recounts his 35-year-old commerce graduate son, Parvez Natiq, who is a successful professional photographer in the city today.

Raazdaar, which is a dismissible rag by any judgement, was a typical tabloid known for sensationalism and its habit of exposing local bigwigs. Operating from his first floor small house in the BIT Chawls near JJ Hospital, Natiq had managed to strike a good rapport with local cops and instil fear in the minds of the goons of the area; it was the language they spoke.

Natiq could enter any senior cop's office unannounced and could recklessly write about any mafia biggie, thus acquiring the reputation of a righteous journalist who did not fear anyone, not even death.

One man who openly admired him and proudly proclaimed his friendship with him was Dawood. '*Bande mein dum hain* [this guy has some substance]', he used to tell his friends. Both Natiq and Dawood hailed from Ratnagiri, but more resilient a bond than their common native place was the intrinsic chutzpah they both had. Natiq looked at Dawood as an underdog pitted against the mighty Goliaths of the time, comprising money bags like Baashu Dada and Haji Mastan and the cunning Karim Lala, Amirzada, and Alamzeb, both budding warlords in the Pathan syndicate.

Natiq was a frequent visitor in the darbar of Likha, in keeping with the long time motto of crime reporters: to be where the action is. On this visit, he took one look at Likha and saw all was not well. Not that it was to be expected; after all, Dongri was not Pleasantville. But what could make Likha look as especially perturbed as he did today?

A few mandatory pleasantries later, Iqbal asked, '*Kya baat hai saab? Aap ki badli kaa order nikla hain ya kuch aur baat hain?* [What's the matter? You've been issued a transfer order or something?]'

Likha replied with the ferocity of a man plagued by an issue, '*Yahan kuch alag hota hai kya kabhi? Yeh behanchod Pathanon ne dimaag ki maa chod daali hain. Ye sale jaanwar Pathan kisiko peet dete hain ye aapas mein ladhte hain! Naak mein dam kar diya hai saalon ne!* [Does anything different ever happen here? Either the Pathans trouble someone else, or they're fighting amongst themselves. I'm so tired of them!]'

Iqbal gave a lopsided smile and reclined in his chair. His expression spoke more about his take on the issue than his tongue chose to. Almost like a quip, he said, 'Sahab, *Sholay.*'

'*Sholay?!* Dimaag ghar par chod aaye kya Iqbal? [*Sholay*? Have you lost your mind, Iqbal?]' Likha replied, more confused than ever.

Iqbal's smile morphed from humorous to mysterious. '*Loha lohe ko kaatta hai* [you use iron to combat iron].' he said.

The famous line that the handicapped Thakur Baldev Singh of *Sholay* had told the cop in the film had become so famous that whenever repeated, it conveyed its meaning in its perfect sense.

Understanding dawned. Sceptically, he asked, '*Magar in Pathanon se kaun uljhega* [but who will deal with the Pathans]?'

Iqbal spoke with authority, '*Hai ek ladka,* Dawood Ibrahim Kaskar [there is a boy, Dawood Ibrahim Kaskar].'

Likha recoiled at the name. '*Tumhara matlab hai... Ibrahim bhai ka chokra... na baba na* [You mean Ibrahim's son? No way!]...' he trailed off.

Iqbal nodded and rose to leave. As a parting shot to the already reeling Likha, he said, '*Mohalle mein sab ko pata hai, bahut himmat hai usme* [everybody in the locality knows that the boy is courageous].'

Now it was Likha's turn to recline and contemplate. Yes, Ibrahim Kaskar's son was a neighbourhood ruffian, a small-time hood, that much he knew, although this thought in itself was hard to digest. But to contemplate actually trying to use him as a pawn to uproot the Pathans? How on earth would he outwit and neutralise the Pathans? He was only a chit of a boy after all. Barely in his twenties and he had all the characteristics and trappings of a street fighter.

Dramatic dialogues from blockbusters were all very well, he thought, but Iqbal must have been out of his mind to even suggest such a thing. This was not reel life, where the underdog rookie upstages the reigning don. This was real life, where there was the reality of his age and position to consider. And the staid Ibrahim Kaskar's son at that! Outrageous, Likha thought! Almost laughable! He dismissed it and went back to the game of ping pong ricocheting in his mind before Iqbal had entered.

'Boys upstaging dons,' he sniggered. He sighed. 'Crime reporters and their imagination, never a combination to be taken seriously.'

Days passed and Likha remained gloomy over the deterioration of the law and order situation in his jurisdiction. Then, one day a small encounter scripted the destiny of both the cops and the crime bosses.

It had been an idyllic morning thus far, unmarred by anything unpleasant. As Likha was on a routine patrol, his jeep turned from Khada Parsi junction towards JJ Hospital. Soon he realised he was stuck in a massive traffic jam; the vehicles were honking and there was no way that his police jeep could inch forward. Furious, he jumped out and charged towards the source of the jam. He spotted a small group of people collected on the roadside, obviously enjoying some kind of spectacle. The crowd parted when they spotted a three star officer approaching in angry mode. What Likha saw made him speechless.

A Pathan was bleeding profusely from his head and mouth and a youth, his shirt torn, was hitting him left, right, and centre. 'Now I have to break up these measly fights too', he thought at first, resigned. But then he saw the boy; barely 20 years old, short in stature, and beating up a taller, stouter Pathan. The sight amazed him. Although Likha had no love lost for the Pathans, he actually felt sympathy for this man, who must have lost a lot of blood and self-esteem. Curious, he pulled the boy away by the scruff of his shirt and asked, '*Aye, kya naam hai tera* [hey, what's your name]?'

The boy stared right back into his eyes and replied, 'Dawood. Dawood Ibrahim Kaskar. *Policewale ka bachcha hun main!* [I'm the son of a cop]!'

Senior Police Inspector Ranbeer Likha froze. One word rang in his ears like a prophecy. '*Sholay!*' An idea took root in his mind.

Swiftly, he pulled him out of the crowd and shooed bystanders away. He felt invincible, as though he was riding on the most incredible luck ever. He could not think of anything other than the brilliant idea that had been planted in his head by Natiq and that he now knew would reach fruition by means of this boy in front of him.

Trying to collect himself, he asked Dawood, '*Chal gaadi mein baith* [let's go sit in the car].'

Dawood eyed him quizzically and sat in the jeep quietly, but with an air of composure far beyond his years, calling another lad nearby and telling him, '*Aye ghar pe bol thoda late ho jayega* [inform them at home that I'll be a little late today].'

'*Pathanon se ladhne ka bahut shauq hai tujhe* [you like to fight with Pathans]?' Likha asked, sitting next to him.

'*Shauq nahin sahib, zaroorat hain. Ladenge nahin toh mit jayenge* [it's not that I like to, if we don't fight, we'll perish],' Dawood tried to explain.

'*Aisa kuch kyon nahin karte joh tumhaari ladaee hamare kaam aa sake* [why don't you do something that makes your fight with the Pathans aid us as well]?' Likha asked, tentatively.

'*Aisa kaise ho sakta hain, sahib* [how is that possible]?' Dawood said, curiously.

'*Wohi jo tu kar raha hain... qanoon haath mein liye bagair qanoon ki madad karo. Pathanon ko apne qabu mein kar lo. Tum mera yeh kaam karo. Baaki main sambhal lunga* [Continue to do what you're doing, but instead of taking the law in your hands, you can do it with the law by your side. Defeat the Pathans for me and I will handle the rest],' Likha replied fiercely.

It was then that the balance of power shifted in Dawood's mind; the baton passed from Likha to Dawood. Instead of being Likha's main man, Likha would now be his main man. Such was the thinking of Dawood. So, the foundation of a new rule was laid, and at last, a don was officially born.

The police jeep had now slowed down and was about to turn left to move towards the Noorbaug junction for Dongri Police Station.

'*Theek hain saab gaadi roko, mera ghar aagaya... sochkar bolta hoon* [Ok, sir stop the car as my house has come. I'll think about this and get back to you],' said Dawood. Likha was taken aback at the casual way in which the boy was addressing a senior police officer. The jeep halted at the intersection of the JJ Hospital. Dawood waved at Likha and crossed the road, heading home.

14

Beginning of the Bloodshed

Iqbal Natiq had an inherent dislike of the Pathans and their reprobate ways. For Dawood, Natiq was an embodiment of courage, one who lived correctly amongst the Pathans like Amirzada, Alamzeb, Ayub Lala, and Saeed Batla, who had a wayward way of life. He even defied them and consistently exposed their misdeeds. But Natiq failed to draw a line between bravery and recklessness. At last, his fight to unmask the truth took him too far.

Now, Dawood was Natiq's main source for most of his stories. Dawood's boys used to collect street level intelligence and paan shop gossip and pass it onto Natiq, who made headlines of these meaty tales. Most of the time, the stories were unverified plants but Natiq trusted Dawood enough to take the risk. He was never sued though he faced some subtle threats and hostility from the Pathans who held *baithaks* in the BIT compound.

With the police and the press on his side, Dawood was no more an underdog. Riding on the crest of invincibility, Dawood thought of testing waters for himself. He knew that until he toppled Baashu Dada from power, Baashu had been known as a kingmaker. Whichever party he supported won hands down and whomever he deserted could never win. Maulana Bukhari's case was a classic example of Baashu's clout and power. And Dawood wanted to see if he could wield clout and power like Baashu did. Thus Dawood proposed the idea to Natiq of contesting the Lok Sabha elections.

Political aspirations should never be based on presumptions. True, he was a fantastic journalist and a known name in the circles, and this could make him a favourite for the common man. Natiq, however, made the mistake of assuming these under the delusion that he could win the election. He filed his nominations as an independent candidate for the sixth Lok Sabha elections in 1977.

Dawood thought that through his boys he would give Natiq the necessary support and ensure that he managed to win. This was a useful litmus test for the wannabe don.

Inevitably, however, Natiq lost the elections badly and could manage only 800 votes. Rajada Ratansingh Gokuldas of Bhartiya Lok Dal won comfortably.

Unfazed with Natiq's loss, Dawood became certain he was still far from his desired peak of power. He now had to work harder to get there sooner. Natiq was a first timer; it was but natural that he might not perform so well, he convinced his candidate. The next time, the victory would be his, an explanation Natiq readily bought.But Natiq's cup of woes had begun to brim. For the Pathans had decided he was a party pooper, following his actions after their gruesome killing of a man and the rape of his newlywed wife at Chawla Guest House, Ibrahim Rahimtullah Road.

It so happened that the Pathans used to hide their smuggled goods in the vicinity of the guesthouse. Ayub Lala and Saeed spotted the couple who were staying at the guesthouse on one of their errands. One night, they barged into their room and gangraped the woman for no other reason but sheer lust, and then killed her husband to leave no witnesses.

People were not willing to disclose the names of the killers, but Natiq went ahead and reported the whole story, disclosing everything. The cops managed to crack the case and arrested Ayub Lala and Batla as well as their aides, including Saeed.

After spending months in jail, the criminals got bail and returned to their base at Carrom Club in the BIT compound. They were plotting to eliminate Natiq but somehow were not able to summon enough audacity to kill him. After all, they had just got bail.

Nonetheless, they began making threats to Natiq. They tried to ransack his small editorial office. Natiq lodged a complaint at the Dongri Police Station, saying that the Carrom Club had become a den for several anti-social activities and the cops subsequently raided the club and shut it down—a major victory for Natiq and the last straw for the Pathans.

On the fateful night of 17 August 1977 around 3:30 am, after Natiq had gone to sleep, he was woken by a persistent knocking at his door. A sleepy Natiq opened the door and found Saeed standing on the door.

'Bhai has called you,' Saeed said. 'Bhai' here referred to Amirzada.

'What the hell! Have you seen the time? I cannot come now. I will meet him tomorrow,' Natiq replied.

'No, he wants to see you now,' Saeed insisted.

'Are you crazy? My wife is alone at home, I cannot leave her like that and go,' Natiq tried to reason with him.

'Iqbal bhai, Bhai is in a very angry mood. If you meet him now you will be able to ward off the trouble lightly. If you provoke him by defiance, it may prove very costly to you,' Saeed said, indicating by the menace in his tone that they were willing to drag him out from his house to the Bhai's den if need be.

A reluctant Natiq realised there was no point in arguing with them anymore. He might as well just go talk to the Bhai, to simplify the issue.

Natiq's 22-year-old wife Zaheda was new to the city. She was worried and a vague premonition gripped her heart; she wanted to dissuade her husband from going out at that hour. But Natiq was sure that they would not go as far as to actually kill him, and somehow consoled her, and left with Saeed and Ayub. They crossed the road and sat in the car, which was parked outside the petrol pump just outside the BIT compound.

No sooner did Natiq enter the car than he was greeted with a volley of expletives. Taken aback, Natiq tried to get out of the car immediately, but by then the car had begun gaining speed. Ayub and Saeed also slapped him hard. The attack came totally unexpected to Natiq, and he could not bear the humiliation as tears welled up in his eyes.

Despite Natiq's protests, the car kept running and halted only at the Kadar building at Grant Road, which housed the office of Amirzada. Natiq was subjected to further humiliation and violence in this office.

'*Dawood ke kutte, bahut hoshiyari karta hain* [Dawood's dog, you think you're being very smart]!'

A thin and wiry Natiq was reduced to a punching bag; blows and kicks were showered on him brutally. Then Saeed, who had been waiting to exact revenge for all the hardship he had encountered in prison following Natiq's articles, brought out a chopper and inflicted several serious injuries. Natiq began to bleed profusely and lost consciousness. The goons again bundled him into the car and took him all the way to Mahim, where the half dead Natiq was dumped at an isolated spot near the Mahim creek.

Lying in a heap of faeces, urine, and other filth near the massive gutter of Mahim, Natiq regained consciousness to the brightness of a shining afternoon sun. He had no clue how many hours he had been lying in that state. But he was aware that he had lost a lot of blood; life was slowly draining out of him. No strength left, he felt his limbs had turned to lead. But Natiq knew that if he was to remain alive, he would have to make a grand effort. Since he could not stand, he began to crawl on his hands and his knees and somehow got to the road, where two men and a traffic cop spotted him, fortunately.

They immediately put him in a cab and rushed him to the JJ Hospital, where his family was informed. Dawood too was given news of the assault, and came running to meet his friend. A weak Natiq gave a statement to the police officers in the Dongri Police Station, and other revealing details to his friend Dawood. Likha himself had come to talk to Natiq, and he stood by as the man spoke.

Dawood blamed himself for Natiq's plight, in a sense, and he was to feel even worse. Despite the best efforts of the doctors, Natiq did not survive; after two days of an excruciating battle in the Intensive Care Unit (ICU), he succumbed to his injuries. Dawood, Sabir, and their boys were furious at the Pathans' beastly behaviour and felt beaten by them. Natiq had, after all, been a bulwark against the Pathans.

Dawood had not known bereavement earlier. This was the first such instance where someone who was so dear to him—a dear friend and almost a brother—had been so brutally killed. He vowed to take revenge in such a way that the Pathans would never dream of ending up on his wrong side. Revenge was the only way to salvage pride. Standing on the freshly made, flower-laden grave of Iqbal Natiq, Dawood swore revenge,. 'Iqbal Bhai, *main kasam khaata hoon, jis tarah unlogon ne tumko maara hain, us hi tarah main bhi unko maaroonga* [I promise to avenge your death in the same torturous manner they killed you].' Officer Likha, standing next to Dawood, kept a hand on the 22-year-old avenger's shoulder and assured him all support.

The chroniclers of the Bombay mafia debated for decades whether it was the killing of reporter Iqbal Natiq that was the great watershed. For until then, the 22-year-old Dawood had never tried his hand at killing or bloodshed. Natiq's murder opened a bloodletting spree in Bombay.

15

The Executioner

It was 1977. Death loomed like a dark mist that seemed to engulf Dawood's every sense, tinged with a sense of deception. Dawood's only promise of deliverance from the vagaries of fury and the hollowness he felt inside was vengeance. Every single Pathan in Bombay was abhorrent to him.

It had been only around a year since Baashu Dada had been repressed and isolated from the kingdom of the Bombay mafia, discredited, but this accolade felt inadequate in the face of the void left by Iqbal's death. Khalid Pehelwan, who had earlier been Baashu's right-hand man, now approached Dawood to place before him his brutal, instinctive and biased form of expression of solidarity towards a man he had grown to respect after Baashu Dada's decline.

Khalid was an austere, self-made man, inclined towards incisive precision in all he did. He had been Baashu's right-hand man for a long while and his status as a serious player in the mafia was formidable. After Baashu's ousting, his admiration for the way Dawood had fortified his status within Bombay had grown tremendously. Khalid had far-reaching influence and assessing the power that Dawood himself had come into, he deemed it honourable to collaborate with Dawood. He offered him his services.

Khalid and his posse had already earned a name for themselves. His notoriety was catapulted to greater heights when a heist he had masterminded and taken part in, targeting a diamond merchant in Grant Road, resulted in the arrest of most of his men, while Khalid himself walked away unscathed. After all, he was the mastermind, who had to be, by default, elusive, unlike the smaller fry.

Dawood's notion of Khalid's personal courage and a primitive sense of authority gave him an idea of how he could help him discredit his opposition. He brought Khalid on board. In turn, Khalid decided to become the symbol of Dawood's fight against the Pathans. He knew that at this point Dawood had nothing on his mind but to wipe out the Pathans' empire in Dongri. The ending of this vendetta had almost become Dawood's right as well as a necessity, to quell anyone who sought to oppose him.

Two men had had a bigger hand in the business of Iqbal's murder, Saeed Baatla and Ayub Lala, and Dawood had no intention of sparing these two Pathans. Khalid, in his bid to prove his loyalty and detonate the drama that was to unfurl, promised Dawood that he would personally ensure the two were punished. Thus the campaign of extermination had begun.

By this time, word had gotten around all over Bombay that Dawood was on the lookout for Ayub and Baatla. Knowing they were on Dawood's hitlist, and definitely with a bounty on their heads, the two men went underground. Their every move was discretely handled; a maze of secrets played out as they maintained a difficult safety. But theirs was not an impenetrable group, and it was not long before Khalid caught on.

An informant told him that Ayub Lala was visiting a bar at Girgaum Chowpatty. He wasted no time in heading out straight for the bar with his men in tow. Now, while Khalid was a sturdy, well-built wrestler, Ayub Lala was a well-built man himself. But Khalid was a man driven by the motives of a grand revenge that he had to enact to prove his loyalty, while Ayub was already weakened. He had already displayed his cowardice when he chose to escape Dawood.

Transfixed by Khalid's sudden entrance, Ayub knew that the sinister gleam in Khalid's eyes held nothing but sadistic intentions for him. Ayub and his men struggled to put up a stiff resistance, but the sheer strength of

Khalid and his men seemed to overpower even the considerable might of his men. Mercilessly, they beat up Ayub and his group of gangsters.

Khalid dragged Ayub all the way to Dongri market. Not satisfied with the moans of Ayub after his beating, Khalid took his knife out and slowly but surely started to slice into Ayub's ankles, leaving him at the mercy of his arms to drag himself forward in a hopeless, desperate bid to get away from the inhuman torture he was being subjected to.

As the veins of his ankles trickled blood onto the road he lay on, Khalid gently grabbed Ayub's hand and slowly cut into his wrists, the veins spurting blood across his own face. Ayub's hoarse cry for help went unheard and the stream of blood grew into a pool of futility. Profusely bleeding and unable to move, Ayub Lala succumbed to his wounds on the street.

News of this inhuman killing sent shock waves across the city, reverberating into the depths of the Bombay mafia. Dawood was mighty pleased. The killing had effected evidence of his status. But with moral perversion comes venomous prejudices. In any case, the political might of Dawood's mafiadom had come into its own.

A few months after Ayub's murder, the alcoholic Saeed Baatla headed out to a country liquor bar in Dongri. He had earned the name 'Baatla' because of his excessive drinking and his huge pot belly. Baatla was a distorted version of *baatli*, which means bottle in Bombay slang. Saeed Baatla was a crude, frivolous man who engaged in the deep vulgarities of a man with too much fondness for drink. He was known, for example, for molesting women on the street.

Tipped off, Khalid and his men headed out to the little bar to hunt down Baatla. Patience exhausted, this time Dawood accompanied them to witness and be a part of the execution. Cruelty was becoming, increasingly, Dawood's forte.

Dawood, Khalid, and their men found an almost drunk Baatla at the bar. Caught off guard and thwarted by liquor, Baatla had no time to react as one blow after the other landed on his chubby frame. If he was even capable of thought at that point, Baatla was left with none as the men threw him around the bar, wreaking severe damage to his face and body. As onlookers scattered from the bar, Baatla lay gasping for breath. Desperately, he tried to writhe free. Suddenly, he felt two men grab his arms and drag him to the same table he had been sitting on. As the men laid his hands on the table, he saw a knife flashing in the light of a low-hanging light bulb, out of the corner of his swollen eyes. Khalid approached the table, a strange expression on his face.

As Baatla lifted his beaten head, the only sound he heard was a clean crunch that went all the way through to the table and a screeching pain that ran through his body into his head, from the end of his palm. He had just lost a finger. Khalid proceeded to cut off Baatla's fingers one by one, savouring each moment before moving on to the next. As the bones crushed under the blade and blood gushed across the table, Khalid never completely severed each digit, instead letting it hang by a piece of skin as Baatla knelt on the floor of the bar, grimacing in agony. This incredulous craft, that of sick pleasure, seemed only to please Dawood and the men around him at the bar.

As tears of pain scored down his shocked face, Baatla somehow managed to slip out and darted towards the door. He bolted out of the bar and towards the Dongri Police Station, which loomed close; as though fate had placed it there for him. Screaming in anguish, Baatla gave himself up to the police, confessing his every crime. Even in his intoxicated state, Baatla knew that he would be safer with the police than out on the streets. Dawood and his men had pursued Baatla for a while but when he entered the police station, they let off their chase, knowing there was no way out for him either way.

Baatla spent fourteen years in jail after this incident. And Dawood asked Khalid Pehelwan to move into Musafirkhana, the headquarters of the D Gang. Dawood had underscored his point—made it loud and bloody clear. He had just begun to arrive into his element and the first stage of his dominance in the Bombay mafia was ushered in with the advent of Khalid Pehelwan.

16

The Emergency

The Research and Analysis Wing (RAW), India's premier spy agency, was constituted in 1962 at the end of the war with China. The idea was to improve India's intelligence abroad, because during the hostilities against the Chinese there was a total failure of intelligence. Biju Patnaik gave a helping hand in the initial stages because he had earned a reputation of 'working well behind the enemy line' when, many years ago, during Dutch rule over Indonesia, he had himself flown a plane to Jakarta to rescue Sukarno, the then head of Indonesia's national movement.

RAW was directly under the Prime Minister's secretariat. Indira Gandhi was the first prime minister to use it for political intelligence within the country. Its advantage was its compactness and the personnel, who were chosen either for their brilliant academic record or for their relationship with a dependable top civil or police officer. RAW had built up dossiers on government opponents, on critics within the Congress party, businessmen, bureaucrats, and journalists. Preparing lists of opponents was no problem; RAW had everything ready in its files.

It was during a meeting between the then Maharashtra Chief Minister V.P. Naik and Prime Minister Indira Gandhi that it was concluded that the mafia could not be controlled by intelligence or prohibition; but rather by tougher laws, which showed no leniency. As the mafia had become a big menace in Gujarat and Bombay, two of the most flourishing regions in the country, it became imperative for the Central Government to act.

And thus began promulgation and implementation of tougher laws which until then were unprecedented. The Maintenance of Internal Security Act (MISA) had been amended in 1974 to authorise the government to detain or arrest individuals without producing charges before a court of law. However, when this law was passed, the government had given its assurance to the Opposition in Parliament that MISA would not be used to detain political opponents. The MISA was originally constituted in 1971 and since then had undergone several amendments.

One of the points that Indira Gandhi raked up as a 20-point programme was special legislation for confiscation of smugglers' properties. Gandhi also said that MISA would be used to catch smugglers. Indeed, their operations were worldwide while their headquarters were in Dubai. Banks and insurance companies had opened their offices there to finance as well as cover the risks involved in smuggling. An elaborate network of transport by sea, land, and air had been built. The long coastline from Gujarat to Kerala was dotted with marked points where smuggled goods were received and then transported to numerous consumer centres in the country.

Madras was a hub for smugglers while Bangalore (present day Bengaluru) provided a safe retreat for them to meet and compare notes. They had their own godowns, markets, and code of conduct. There was a direct link between smugglers and black money operators.

As the government went on overdrive against the smugglers, criminals, and black marketeers on a war footing, it decided to tighten the grip on the country further and declared a state of Emergency on 26 June 1975. One gain of the Emergency was stabilisation of the prices of essential goods. Schools, shops, trains, and buses showed the effects of discipline. And effectively, the mafia was underground for nineteen months during the period of Emergency.

On the political front, the killing of Shaikh Mujibur Rahman, the president of the newly-formed Bangladesh and most of his family in cold blood on 14 August, caused ripples in New Delhi. Neither RAW nor any other intelligence service had had the faintest clue beforehand. They had failed Gandhi once again. In fact, from that day on, Sanjay, her son and confidant, began to call RAW the 'Relatives of Wives Association'; there were too many 'relations' of top RAW officials within the organisation. Gandhi expressed to the RAW chief Ramji Kao her unhappiness over the lack of prior intelligence reports on Bangladesh. What worried her was that if the intelligence could fail her in Bangladesh, it could fail her in India as well. Emergency, though imposed for political reasons and with the ambition to sustain supremacy in Parliament, had crippled the Indian media and deprived a common man his basic rights. To the Bombay mafia, it in fact dealt a death blow.

For the first time, on the floors of Parliament, the names of Bombay smugglers Haji Mastan, Yusuf Patel, and Sukur Bakhia were mentioned. And this was enough for the government machinery to swing into action.

Mastan, who was already under detention under MISA for ninety days since 17 September to 19 December 1974, could not even rally round to plan his next move as the government slapped on him charges under yet another law: Conservation of Foreign Exchange and Prevention of Smuggling Act (COFEPOSA). Mastan, despite hiring the best criminal lawyers like Ram Jethmalani, had to spend the entire period of the Emergency in jail.

An ordinance was issued on 1 July 1975 under which persons detained under the COFEPOSA need no longer be given grounds for detention. Whatever Indira Gandhi's political compulsions might have been for imposing Emergency, it became an era of ruthless enforcement against the smugglers. A good deal of black money was unearthed and a number of traders were held under MISA for 'economic offences'.

Arthur Road Jail in Bombay, Thane Central Prison, the Yeravada Jail in Pune, Harsul Jail in Kolhapur were all packed to their capacity, with most of the criminals, smugglers, economic offenders, goondas, and black marketers rounded up and thrown behind bars.

If Mastan was detained under MISA and COFEPOSA, others like Varadarajan, Karim Lala, Dawood Ibrahim, the Pathans, Rama Naik, and Arun Gawli were picked up under the National Security Act (NSA) and imprisoned. In a way this brought all those gangsters together, men who had had no formal introduction or interaction earlier. For instance, Naik and Varda struck a rapport and became so thick that they began discussing how to handle the Vasai and Virar jetties for smuggling, a plan they eventually managed to execute after their release.

The then Police Commissioner S.V. Tankiwala, appointed police chief barely weeks after the Emergency was imposed, in one of his reports to the Union Home Ministry wrote: 'The anti-smuggling drive made the business of smuggling goods not only hazardous but also expensive. As many as 288 smugglers, including their top men like Haji Mastan and Yusuf Patel, were detained and the property of 177 smugglers was attached.'

However, people like Haji Mastan and Karim Lala, who ended up spending almost two years behind bars realised that they had reached a dead end. They felt that they were fighting a losing battle against the government and it seemed that they might end up in jail for a lifetime unless they assured the government that they would not indulge in any illegal activities anymore.

After the Emergency was lifted and the Janata Party came to power in 1977, Mastan and Karim Lala both implored Jaiprakash Narayan to intervene with the then Prime Minister Morarji Desai to show compassion towards them. Both of them had filed affidavits and under oath gave promises to the government that they would not get involved in any illegal activity again. The Desai dispensation accepted their plea and finally they were released from detention.

Subsequently, other gangsters like Dawood, his brother Sabir, Gawli, Naik, and other criminals filed bail applications in court, and as the charges against them were not as serious and not backed by substantial evidence, they managed to procure bail from a court of law.

17

Mill Worker-Turned-Don

It was twilight one winter night in 1977, just after the Emergency. A huge crowd had gathered outside the shop. Angry voices of outraged people could be heard from within. The crowd outside spoke in muted tones, hushed voices, and staged whispers, not sure whether to believe the rumour that was spreading. People were saying Parasnath Pandey was dead, not killed! In his own den at that. This could not be. Who could possibly have mustered the nerve to commit such an act?

On walking into the small dingy shop, you could see the broken, bloodied body of Pandey. All over the room were strewn the remains of all the trappings of his earthly power. Blood and gore were the only leftovers of his arrogance. Who could be responsible for this outrageous act?

Pandey's *matka* table was broken in two pieces. The last vestige of Pandey's power had been destroyed. The same table that plotted and predicted the downfall of many families, killed so many futures, was now destroyed. Everyone knew of Pandey's clout and the fact that someone murdered him would mean that the killers were either rookies or the big guns. The question was, which one of them would prove more dangerous?

The history of the mafia in Bombay is dotted with challenges and fraught with stories of boys who grew to become giants. It was common practice to see young upstarts challenging the old brigade and eventually replacing them. Pandey was no different. Just a few months before his death, the Lambi Cement chawl in Byculla where he propagated his trade had witnessed the emergence of some new heroes.

A trio, an informal association of Kundan Dubey, Parasnath Pandey, and Mohan Sarmalkar that came to be called the Byculla Company grew together in the bylanes of Byculla. Any extortion, killing, or operating gambling dens were carried out by these three, the notorious Byculla Company. While this was not uncommon in the streets of Byculla, it was how they were going to use their relationship that ultimately made them different.

Soon, a man from Maharashtra called Rama Naik dared to dream. Amidst the predominantly north Indian majority monopolising the *matka* business, he opened his own *matka* and liquor den. It was his first open challenge to the Byculla Company. The swords were drawn. While Dubey and Pandey owned *matka* dens, Sarmalkar was involved in the liquor business and collected *haftas* (protection money paid to dons) from the locals—in fact, he was rumoured to be associated with murders that happened on the 'S' Bridge in Byculla. Naik sought to show his own power in this field.

With Dubey, Naik had another axe to grind. Kundan Dubey had killed Umakant Naik because one of his brothers, Arvind, had been in love with Pushpa, Dubey's sister. With Pandey, the uncrowned king of the *matka* business, it was pure business. A fiefdom can never have two kings and one must topple the other to reign supreme and thus it had become necessary to kill Pandey. But Naik was not going solo in all his work. There were two others—Babu Reshim and Arun Gulab Ahir alias Arun Gawli. The latter would go on to become Dawood's biggest detractor of the time.

Arun Gulab Ahir was Rama Naik's senior in school. They went to the same Municipal School in Bakri Adda in Byculla. Rama, however, dropped out of the school in the seventh standard. They maintained their alliance, and what was surprising was that though Gawli was the older boy, Rama Naik was the dominant one of the two and the decision-maker. Gawli looked up in deference to him and held his judgment in high regard.

Arun came from very humble beginnings. If there was a die that cast future dons, it seemed to have missed him. The Gawli family belonged to Khandwa in Madhya Pradesh, and came from the traditional clan of shepherds or *gawlis*, thus lending them their titular surname, Gawli.

He had four brothers and two sisters. His father Gulab worked with Simplex mills and his mother was also a mill hand. His first job was at a mill too. He found employment with the Shakti Mills in Mahalakshmi when he was only a little more than 20 years old. Lacking special skills, he later drifted to the dye-casting department at Godrej and Boyce, Vikhroli. In fact this was where he first tasted blood, by scoring a victory over his first opponent Bala Mapankar, a representative of the Shiv Sena in the union, who was upstaged by Gawli. He then moved on to Crompton Greaves Ltd. in Kanjur Marg. This is where he began to spend time with Rama Naik and Bablya Sawant. This is also the time when he encountered Sadashiv Pavle alias Sada Mama, who later went on to become the second-in-command in Gawli's gang.

Babu Reshim was the leader of the canteen workers of the Mazgaon docks. He lived in the same region that Rama and Gawli operated from and gravitated towards them. The two continued to be involved in skirmishes regularly with the various factions operating in Byculla, and the turning point in their lives came with the arrival of the Emergency. In 1975, Rama Naik was arrested under MISA. While in jail, he made contact with Varadarajan Mudaliar alias Varda Bhai, and they got along so well that Naik felt bold enough to recommend an alliance to Varda Bhai. He told him, 'Kuch kaam ho toh bolo [let me know if there's any work that is to be done].'

Varda on the other hand was impressed by this boy. Rama Naik was not exceptional to look at in terms of size, but the conviction with which he spoke convinced an individual of his competency. From the look he had in his eyes, no one would ever doubt that the work assigned to him would be completed with authority and finesse. And as the kings of yore used to honour and shower maestros with their largesse, so did Varda. He began recommending Rama, Arun, and Babu to everyone as competent persons. Thus under the able aegis of Rama Naik, the alliance gained in strength and public opinion.

But where things stood at that point, Rama Naik, Arun Gawli, and Babu Reshim had cemented their position with the murder of Pandey.

Closing a number of *matka* businesses, they had broken the back of the *matka* and liquor trade—a task that the police and state had not managed to accomplish.

Following the murder of Pandey, Gawli was detained under the NSA. But surprisingly, he was released within a month of custody. Those were treacherous times. Dissenters languished in jails for months and here a known local criminal had been released within a month. Surely there was something to this, thought the locals of Byculla. Everyone thought it was his clout and his power as a don that got him out of custody early. Gawli, of course, made no bones about exploiting this misconception to his advantage. He strutted around, knowing fully well that his power had nothing to do with his release. As soon as he came back to Dagdi Chawl, he built a minaret in the area and had a board nailed to it that would herald a new time. The board said 'B.R.A. Company', 'B' for Babu Reshim, 'R' for Rama Naik, and 'A' for Arun Gawli.

His power and influence increased several fold post his return from jail. He decided it was now time to find his lieutenant and partner, someone who would hold fort in his home and keep his hearth warm. He found such a person in Zubeida Mujawar, who lived in the same area as Gawli. She belonged to Wadgaon in Pune. Zubeida's marriage had already been arranged with a boy from within the Muslim community but when Arun Gawli asked the family of Zubeida Mujawar, they could not refuse and so there was a match.

Rama Naik and Babu Reshim, however, opposed the alliance on communal grounds. They could not believe that Arun Gawli was marrying a Muslim girl, but he remained adamant and insisted on marrying Zubeida. After the marriage was solemnised, elaborate rituals were conducted to 'convert' Zubeida to Hinduism. In an attempt to wipe out her Muslim identity, her name was changed from Zubeida to Asha. He had truly found an ally in her, as she often held the fort while he was in and out of prison.

18

Pathan Menace

Karim Lala and Jangrez Khan were good friends; Lala came from Peshawar and Jangrez had his roots in Swat village in Afghanistan. Lala had managed to amass a huge fortune and began to have clout in south Mumbai by this time. His friendship with Mastan made him a stronger ganglord in every manner. It was the early seventies.

This alliance and the rise of Lala, a Pathan by origin, had bolstered the arrogance and nonchalance of the Pathan gang. They had heard the stories of the valour of their ancestors, the famous warrior Pathans of old, and how for the sake of honour, they would go to any length and defy even the kings of their time. This mindfulness of ancient legend had made the Pathans totally heedless of the law of the modern land. Street brawls, violence, eviction of tenants, smashing shops, and breaking bones in public had become routine for them. The Pathan menace was growing unabated and the cops seemed to be totally clueless when it came to controlling this multi-headed hydra, which dealt with everything from extortions to hits to helping settle disputes.

One of these disputes was that between Haji Mastan and his long-time partner Yusuf Patel. Finally, Mastan decided to teach him a lesson and declared a contract on him. The *supari* was given to the Pathan mafia.

The term *supari* comes from an old story of kings and warriors. It means 'betel nut' in Hindi. According to folklore, the King of Mahim province in Bombay, Bhim, who was also the chieftain of his Mahemi tribe, used an interesting ritual when he was deciding how and who to assign a difficult task. He would call for a general meeting at his Mahim fort and huge pandals were erected. Select warriors and bravemen would be asked to participate in the royal feast. Once the feast was over and the warrior tribesmen were satiated, a huge *thal* (plate) was placed right in the middle of the gathering. The *thal* had betel leaves, *suparis*, and some other herbs.

Then the commander-in-chief announced the king's predicament and put forth the challenge. According to this ritual, whoever volunteered to accept the task would rise and partake of a betel leaf and betel nut from the thali. This gesture is considered the giving and accepting of *supari*. Afterwards, the commander-in-chief would walk over with a small bottle containing *surma* (eyeliner) in his hands, and applied the eyeliner on the brave man's eyes, declaring him a *soorma* (a gallant man). Much after the king died and the Mahim fort was reduced to ruins, this idea of *supari* remained in the lingo of the Bombay mafia though for a different reason. *Supari* now refers to a hit job.

The first ever major *supari* in the history of Mumbai mafia was that of Yusuf Patel, announced by Haji Mastan in 1969. It carried a staggering sum of 10,000 rupees and was given to two Pakistanis with Pashtoon origins.

In keeping with the recklessness of Pathani traditions, the two burly Pathans, chose a crowded spot at Minara Masjid, one of the most picturesque and beautiful mosques in the city, which displays a dazzling illumination during the sacred month of Ramzan. Muslims avoid violence, bloodshed, and such unpleasant activities during the holy month. However, these two Pathans disregarded even the sanctity of the Islamic month and decided to take the hit at Yusuf Patel in the crowded area of the masjid.

The old residents of Minara Masjid will still never forget the night of 22 November 1969 and the gruesome incident that took place after midnight and continued into the early hours of 23 November.

Minara Masjid is located in a predominantly Memon locality. The area is milling with happy-looking Muslims gorging on food starting early in the evening. Here, spirituality was not sought in day-long fasting and abstinence, but rather in the few hours of break that allowed them to have meals. The atmosphere is one of festivity. Small gatherings of people cluster in corners, chatting. Around the precincts of the mosque, Patel had occupied one such corner and was holding his *baithak*, thronged by his acolytes and bodyguards.

Two huge Pathans in their characteristic white Pathani suits appeared, surveying the area with a determined gaze. They identified Patel, who was at the helm of the small gathering, and decided to walk on and take their shot upon their return.

However, one of Patel's bodyguards picked up on their presence, noticing their stealth and atypical manner. They looked as if they did not belong, yet they were not curious while looking at his boss. Something was amiss. The bodyguard whispered in the ears of Patel. Patel nodded and assured his man he would leave after their discussion was concluded. But the man did not have this much time at his disposal. Within moments, the two Pathans came charging up with their British made guns and opened fire. The alert bodyguard flung himself on his boss, while a stunned Patel was thrown on the ground.

The others pounced on the assailants. Pandemonium erupted in the area which only moments ago had borne an air of celebration. The Pakistanis thought their bullets had hit Patel, as they saw him bleeding and began to make their escape. However, the alert Memons, who believed Yusuf Patel was their own, surrounded the assailant duo from all sides. The well-built Pathans put up a fight but the enraged mob overpowered them and handed them over to the police. Patel had sustained two bullet injuries, luckily on his arms, but his plucky bodyguard had died. The Crime Branch subsequently arrested Haji Mastan, Karim Lala, and eleven others.

Even as the Bombay police were racking their brains over how to tackle this Pathan menace, the Pathan branch of the Special Branch (SB-I) got a tip-off that Ayub Khan Lala had been sighted in the city.

Special Branch or SB is the intelligence wing of the Bombay police. It was established in the Victorian era and the British police machinery made better use of the SB than Indian police bosses, many hold; the British believed in prevention more than the cure. For the Indian police, however, the Crime

Branch or Crime Investigation Department was more important. The credo was simple: controlling crime was important and most intelligence inputs were hogwash. Thus the SB was neglected and reduced to a mere clerical or administrative wing of the city police, which registers the influx of foreign visitors and keeps tabs on illegal immigrants in Bombay.

Ayub was one of the most influential, notorious, cunning, treacherous, and elusive Pathans the Bombay police had dealt with. He was a person known to lose his temper at the slightest provocation and resort to violence, in fact, once, he had sliced open a man's torso just because he had called him a 'pagal Pathan'. He was also so slippery that whenever he surfaced, the cops were sure a violent trail was likely to follow. He had been summoned by Karim Lala, who had decided to put an end to the warring smugglers in the city; Mastan and Patel. The smugglers decided not only to put an end to their enmity but also to rid themselves of someone who had long been their bête noire.

Not many journalists dared to write against the mafia in those days. However, M.P. Iyer, a veteran crime reporter driven by reckless idealism, persistently wrote about the mafia and made their life increasingly uncomfortable. His articles in the Press Trust of India (PTI) exposed all sections of the crime syndicate. Iyer was unsparing of Mastan, Karim Lala, Yusuf Patel, and the other reigning dons of the time. Finally, the henchmen of these dons got together and decided to silence the daring reporter.

The *supari* was given to Ayub Khan Lala. Ayub thought the best way to get rid of Iyer would be to silence him in such a manner that none of the mafia dons would be suspected of putting a hit on his head.

Iyer was fond of driving a white Ambassador and was reluctant to hail a cab even when his car was giving him trouble. Ayub put his henchmen on the job to keep a tab on Iyer's movements. They reported that Iyer was planning a trip to Pune and was likely to travel by road in his Ambassador. The day Iyer was supposed to begin the journey, Ayub sent a mechanic to ensure his car would lose control after a bit, which would lead to an accident on the treacherous Ghats of the Mumbai-Pune highway.

An unsuspecting Iyer fell prey to Ayub's Machiavellian machinations. The moment he accelerated, when he got to Panvel, an exurb of Bombay, his car sped out of control. Iyer crashed against a tree, dying on the spot due to head injuries.

In 1970, Iyer became the first ever journalist 'silenced' by the mafia. (Forty-one years after his killing, the mafia, this time at the behest of Chhota Rajan, according to the police, shot to death noted crime reporter Jyotirmoy Dey in broad daylight in Powai.) The Bombay police got wind of the incident only after everything was over and they were left with nothing but the paperwork. They realised the Pathans were going berserk.

Around this time, although no one can be sure how and when it started, Hindi movies began a derisive depiction of the Mumbai police. Cops were shown reaching the spot only in the end, after all the action; just to handcuff the criminals or to make the *panchnama* (the spot report of the crime). There was no way the Pathans could be tamed or controlled and Bollywood was sounding this message loud and clear.

19

Mastan's Masterstroke: The Truce

In the upmarket Warden Road area in Bombay, the rich live in a different stratosphere. Perched on these once-upon-a-time hills, the elevated stretch from Haji Ali to Napeansea Road curried favour with the then British governor of Mumbai, at his majestic residence at the foot of Malabar Hill. After Independence and the formation of the state of Maharashtra, the governor of Maharashtra then enjoyed the run of the vast expanse of wooded forest facing the sea.

That a mafia don like Haji Mastan managed to get himself an address in this snooty neighbourhood spoke volumes of his clout in the sixties. The Baitul Suroor bungalow was a modest building, and Mastan also managed to carve a one-room outhouse in glass for himself at the back of the house.

On a particularly wet evening in July 1980, a group of visitors were seated in the well-furnished drawing room of the bungalow, fitted with purple upholstery. The scene had the look of a cordial afternoon visit, but nothing could deflect the tension in the air. Mastan was pacing around the room puffing away at his trademark 555 imported cigarette. He was clad in his usual attire: sparkling white shirt teamed with white trousers and white shoes. The meeting had been called hastily at the behest of the don himself. He was considered something of a legend having managed to cock a snook at the police and the administration at the time.

This was not an ordinary assemblage of gangsters. The hackles raised by the presence of two warring factions of the mafia in the same enclosed space electrified the air. This was unheard of in the history of Bombay's Mafiosi: rival members of the mafia never sat across each other at a table. Even now, it seemed they were ready to fly at each other's throats.

For the first time, Haji Mastan had managed to get across to the Pathans and the former underdogs, Dawood-Sabir Ibrahim's gang, in an attempt to broker peace. Mastan's friend Karim Lala, considered the chief of the Pathan gang, was present along with Majid Kalia, Hussain Somji, Dilip Aziz, Hanif Mohtaram, and, of course, the ubiquitous Jenabai Daruwali, the only woman who walked the fine line between the mafia and the police in those days. Adorned with gold jewellery, she was a curious lady to whom every gangster in Bombay went for advice. Haji Mastan addressed her as Jena Ben (sister) while Dawood called her Jena Maasi (aunt).

Pathan gangsters like Amirzada, Alamzeb, Shehzada, and Samad Khan were also present, and so was Dawood Ibrahim, now in his mid-twenties, Sabir, and their brother Anees.

Bombay's streets were littered with corpses and the police were baying for the blood of gangsters—any gangster. The violent skirmishes between the Pathans and the Dawood-Sabir gang had become a cause for concern for the stalwarts of the Mumbai underworld. Mastan and Karim Lala had not only been suffering sleepless nights, they were also growing increasingly worried at the bloodshed. The killing of any Pathan affected Karim Lala, while any hit taken by the Dawood-Sabir gang forced the cops to launch a crackdown on the Pathans. After all, Dawood was the darling of the Bombay police. Then, there was Ibrahim Kaskar, patriarch and Crime Branch cop, and personal friend of both Mastan and Karim Lala. Ibrahim, absent today, was in turmoil; his sons were taking the bull by the horns and the bloodletting could consume all of them. Mastan spoke firmly, as he stood looking at all those who were present in the room. He said, 'Bloodshed is bad for any business, especially ours, because for our government it is not even worth a stray dog's piss. We are all Muslims; and believe in the same religion, as opposed to our hostile government.

Why make them happy by our infighting and dog fights on the streets of Bombay?' Using their common religion, he strove for a common chord.

'Mastan chacha, we never initiate any attack. We know they are from our *qaum* (community) and in a way our brothers, but we cannot tolerate it if someone wants to fuck us royally,' Sabir interjected.

'You are jealous of our clout. The mighty Pathans have ruled Bombay for decades. You are just not able to digest our supremacy,' Amirzada replied.

'Supremacy, my ass! Had not the elders intervened, we could have decided the matter once and for all in a matter of days. It is because I respect Karim chacha and his family that I have swallowed my pride so far, but for how long?' Dawood barely restrained his anger.

'How about deciding it right now, here in this room?' Amirzada said, gesturing towards the others, who lost no time in heeding his call. The Pathans stood menacingly in unison, ready to face Dawood's challenge.

The atmosphere in the room had swiftly turned dangerous. Dawood, of course, remained seated nonchalantly, seemingly unperturbed by the turn of events. Only his hot-headed brother Sabir seemed ready to accept the challenge, and rose even as his brother laid a hand on him to keep him from making a fool of himself.

All eyes were set on Sabir, who looked at Dawood. In turn, Dawood quietly rose from his chair. He walked to the corner where Mastan stood, increasingly aware of the possibility of potential bloodshed in his house. Mastan was still holding his cigarette; Dawood took it from his hand, quietly. Then he walked towards the centre table where the ashtray was kept. Instead of stubbing it in the ashtray, he simply took the burning end of the cigarette in his palm and crushed it to ashes.

In a calm, measured tone, he addressed the meeting. 'We know how to handle the fire and when to crush it with bare fingers. We don't need any provocation or challenge. It is not a lack of courage but the veneration of our elders that has held us back so far. We can hurt ourselves but not their prestige,' Dawood said, scoring a point over his adversaries. For the first time, the world saw the young Dawood mature enough to refrain from being provoked by the violent Pathans at a meeting called for truce.

A hush of admiration fell over the room, at the guile of his speech and the delivery of his powerful rhetoric. Amirzada and Alamzeb were bristling with anger but they had just been smoothly disgraced and did not want their foolhardiness on display again. They stood there for a while, seething, then sat down without a word.

Dawood was now matching his gaze with that of everyone in the room.

'*Beta, yeh sab khatam karo* [boy, let's get over with all this],' Karim Lala said in his gruff, Pathani-accented Hindi.

Mastan, who had not uttered a word beyond his opening speech, interjected at last, 'I think we should resolve our differences and for the sake of Allah and the Koran take an oath that we shall refrain from targeting each other anymore. We will abstain from bloodshed.'

Dawood and Sabir nodded. Karim Lala and Ibrahim gave smiles of encouragement. Rahim chacha got up and asked one of the boys to lift the Koran from the corner table and place it in the middle of the mahogany table kept in the centre of the room.

'Let us take an oath,' Rahim said.

Dawood and Sabir were among the first to place their hands on the Koran, followed by others present in the room. They all muttered something to the effect that they would henceforth try to live peacefully and abstain from violence.

Thus, a historic peace pact was engineered by Mastan, far from Dongri. The truce was intended to ensure that the Pathans and the Sabir gang gave up the power struggle and bloodshed. They would demarcate their respective turfs in the city and refrain from violating the pact. With the pact in place, it was time for celebration. Tea and biscuits were served and there was even some lighthearted banter.

For Mastan it was a major victory. And Karim Lala and Ibrahim Kaskar were greatly relieved at the prospect of safety and security for their boys. For two men—Amir and Alamzeb—in the room, the pact meant they could marshal their forces and catch their rivals off guard. For two other men, Dawood and Sabir, the pact was something they were seriously applying their mind to, though they were wary. The underlying thread that connects and defines the underworld in Bombay is the agenda beneath all its actions. The ability of those few men to think beyond the here and now under all circumstances set them apart.

Of course, Mastan himself had his own agenda in arranging this meeting. For a very long time he had coveted a plot of land on Belassis Road near Mumbai Central. This plot belonged to a group of Gujarati Muslims from the Banaskantha district in Gujarat, a tribe called the Chilias. The Chilias are a particularly fierce tribe, committed to protecting themselves and their properties. As Mastan was known all over the city as an all-money-no-muscle don, he had not taken them on, till now. But the alliance he created between the Pathans and Dawood ensured that the plot of land that he had so far only made several unsuccessful bids to win, would be his. He knew that the combined strength of the Pathans and Dawood could put him in a position of ultimate power and the fact that he had played this messiah-like role in bringing about this understanding between the two gangs put him in a position to leverage them.

Soon after the truce, he let them in on the problem he was facing at Belassis Road. The Pathans and Dawood's gang proceeded to meet the tenants and coax them to vacate the land. There was fighting on the battleground for a while; the Chilias fought valiantly. But they could not withstand the joint might of the two gangs and finally lost their land. Mastan then went on to build a tall, multi-storied building on the plot and name it, gloriously, Mastan Apartments.

20

Dawood's Smuggling Business

Dawood was now riding high. Only 25 years old, he had been adjudged important enough by the enormously powerful Haji Mastan to be included in a meeting with the other powerful gangs of the time. He had committed successful robberies; he had managed to avenge his friend against the reigning gangsters of his time, the Pathans (Amirzada, Alamzeb, and Samad Khan); he had shown that he could not be taken for granted. He had even managed to get senior cops dancing to his tune, something that the Pathans had never managed to do despite a reign of thirty years or so.

But now, after a peace pact with the Pathans, Dawood became a bit complacent and stopped watching his back. To him, the covenant of non-violence by taking an oath on the holy Koran was sacrosanct, and he assumed that nobody would have the temerity to violate it. Now his one-point programme was to expand his business and fill his coffers. With Khalid Pehelwan's chutzpah and his brains, Dawood's financial stock began looking north. From Bombay to Daman, electronic goods to silver and gold, Dawood had it all covered. And soon he found himself making inroads to Gujarat. Emboldened and brazened by his success and mettle,

Dawood's business mushroomed all along the Western coast. Khalid Pehelwan had taught him well. Being a part of the smuggling racket and the right-hand man of Baashu, he was already in the trade for over a decade, and taught these to Dawood. Through all of this, he continued to stay in Musafirkhana, which was a veritable fortress, and almost impenetrable to outside attacks.

Dawood had begun making trips to Dubai, hobnobbing with the sheikhs of Dubai. He was fascinated by the opulence and affluence of the Gulf megacity. His quality of life and the people he kept company with had now improved; from street-level riffraff to millionaire Arab sheikhs.

Dawood now cemented his position as the ultimate man to be dealing with. This status drew, in part, from his ever-growing clout over the Bombay police and its Crime Branch.

As Dawood arrived at the shores of Gujarat, he knew well that Alamzeb and Amirzada had already set up base there. Abdul Latif Khan was heading their Gujarat operations. But shrewd as Dawood was, the only man he wanted to outsmart and break was Sukur Narayan Bakhiya, the single largest gold smuggler in the country. Haji Mastan had earlier tried to outdo Sukur's business but had miserably failed to do so.

When Sukur and the Pathan gang learned of Dawood's foray into Gujarat, they tried to edge his business out, but there was nothing much they could try against a man who had already long established himself in the business of smuggled goods, courtesy Khalid.

Dawood's current status was further strengthened when he moved from the coasts to the airports of Bombay. The devious modus operandi of the gang while smuggling gold from Dubai was appropriately called *Kachra Peti* line (garbage line).

His men would board the Bombay-bound plane from Dubai, storing gold biscuits in innocuous boxes in the guise of mithai boxes. Before the person got to the customs officials when the plane landed in Bombay, he would signal the sweeper in the area by making eye contact and nodding and then dump the box into the garbage bin. The sweeper would immediately take this valuable bit of trash out of the airport with the rest of the bin's contents. He would then hand over the smuggled gold to Dawood's men. The sweeper would get a commission every time he picked up a box.

It was a strategically executed plan, its ears close to the ground as was the case with all of Dawood's schemes. Unfortunately, somebody had already tipped off the authorities this time, and Indian customs officials swooped down on airport maintenance within minutes. The police retrieved gold biscuits worth 25 lakh rupees from the Santa Cruz airport. This was after interrogating every person employed with the airport authority. When they finally caught the sweepers who had had a hand in the smuggling, the men confessed that they did not know anything except that all the boxes were for Dawood bhai.

And very soon, Dawood was arrested under Conservation of Foreign Exchange and Prevention of Smuggling Act (CoFEPOSA). For the first time in his life as a don, circa 1980, he was being legally detained for smuggling. But on his climb up to great monetary and muscle power, Dawood had begun to cultivate men in the government machinery. He managed to buy off witnesses and work over the papers, and was acquitted of all charges in 1983.

Emboldened and raring to take back his position as Bombay mafia's numero uno, Dawood went on a vengeful quest of self-assertion. The Pathan gang seemed like distant folklore, as waves of Dawood's new campaigns sent ripples all over Bombay's underworld. He had found his calling and the edge he had always sought over the Pathan gang, and intensified his activities, and kept trying new ways to carry out his old schemes. All the while, he was also on the lookout for the Trojan horse in his outfit.

Soon, Dawood's men invented new ways of smuggling using the cavities of human bodies that the X-ray machines of those days failed to detect. They began hiding gold pieces in the rectum and named it the 'godown line' or 'underground line'. Passengers were called carriers and in addition to return airfare and a week's stay in Dubai, they were paid a satisfactory amount of what was relatively easy money. People began to queue up to become carriers and the business flourished. Residents of Bombay no. 3 and Bombay no. 9 (to use Bombay police lingo for areas like Bhendi bazaar, Imam Baada road, Sandhurst Road), in south Bombay became rich by making few trips to Dubai. Of course, if carriers could rake in money in huge amounts, Dawood and his men stood to gain much more.

Bombay became too small, and he had to now look for other avenues, mostly opportunities in Dubai to invest his monies. The Dawood–Sabir syndicate had not only become flush with cash but also clout and connections in the Middle Eastern countries.

The human tendency is to become oblivious to other issues in life when the coffers are filling. Dawood got busy counting cash and stashing his ill-begotten money. Unfortunately, Dawood lowered his guard towards his one-time nemesis, the Pathans, who were watching each and every move of their arch rival. They were witnessing the rapid strides forward that the don and his brother Sabir were making.

There was a distinct difference between the smuggling business of the Pathans and that of the Dawood-Sabir gang. While the Pathans had more or less remained the landing agents or distributors on the coasts of Gujarat, Diu and Daman, Dawood had managed to transcend these lower level operations. He negotiated deals with Arabs directly, fixed prices, and oversaw all operations till the final bit of execution. This benefited him in two ways: his profit margins soared and this gave him a centralised grip over operations. His business grew manifold.

The Pathans could never penetrate the market in such a manner. Despite their best efforts and huge risks they could only incur losses and never managed to break even in the high stakes business of smuggling. They simply did not have the resources, or contacts, and acute business acumen of Dawood and Khalid Pehelwan.

Dawood not only had a sharp mind in the form of Khalid but also growing connections in the police force, something which the Pathans could never manage to approach in terms of tenacity and canny strategising. The frustrations of defeat, losses in business, and their rivals' unstoppable success had fuelled the fire of jealousy and rancour among the Pathans. They now realised that the famous truce at Mastan's bungalow had been enacted only to fill his coffers and give Dawood time of around a year and a half to grow in Bombay and Dubai. It had done nothing for their own business.

Amirzada and Alamzeb also thought Dawood was meant to give them a hand in business and treat them as partners, as part of the goodwill inferred in that pact, sharing the spoils with him. However, they felt that Dawood had given them a royal ignore, thereby becoming, in their eyes, the first one to violate the holy pact.

The Pathans got together and began plotting what they did best—violence and bloodshed. As they believed Khalid was a mere manager, they did not accord him much importance. They had to get one of the two brothers, Sabir or Dawood. Or why not both of them? This would effectively destroy the whole of the Dawood-Sabir syndicate.

21

A Don in Love

She was the spitting image of yesteryear starlet Leena Chandavarkar. Voluptuous, with a perfect round face and charming dimples, the charms of Sujata Kaur could be resisted by few men. Dawood proved no exception. He was besotted with her, though they were an odd pair. She was a Punjabi *kudi*, while he was a local lout.

But if they did not look good together as a couple, they more than made up for it with a potent chemistry, one that made married couples blush. It all began with Dawood's shop in Musafirkhana in south Bombay. Sujata lived nearby and every time she passed by Manish Market on her way to the shops, Dawood never missed a chance to catch a glimpse of this tall, lithe beauty. Of all the girls that walked that route, this woman was a class apart. Dawood began tailing her, until she became aware of him. He then began wooing her. He tried everything that someone of his standing could do, from meeting at bus stops to waiting hours for the love of his life.

Sujata could not resist Dawood's charms and after a few furtive meetings, she was inexorably drawn to him. In the next two years, the couple were inseparable. Sujata was the only person who could vouch for the fact that there was another side to Dawood. Most people only saw the violent and brutal man that was Dawood Ibrahim, but Sujata saw and experienced his tender, loving, romantic side.

It was around this time that Sujata's parents heard of her dating Dawood. Her father was furious. First, Dawood was a Muslim and then a hoodlum to boot. In no time, he got her engaged to a boy from their community. To make matters worse for Dawood, he confined Sujata to their home, banning her from even stepping out of the door.

When Dawood heard about this, he became furious and stormed over to Sujata's residence, brandishing a Rampuri knife. Seething with resentment and anger at her father's actions, Dawood hammered on Sujata's door.

Sujata's father opened the door diffidently to face a raging bull. Dawood threatened him, adding, 'Let her choose whom she wants to marry.'

The entire neighbourhood gathered, in the meanwhile, to witness the family's moment of trial. 'My daughter can exercise her choice but she will be an orphan if she marries you. My wife and I will jump off this building if she doesn't leave you,' Kaur informed him calmly. Caught in a dilemma, Sujata, who was weeping inconsolably along with her mother, decided she could not upset her parents. She looked at Dawood and firmly said, 'We cannot be together. I don't want to marry you.'

For a moment, Dawood was dumbstruck. He wanted to hit out at Sujata, drag her down the building by force, and make her pay. But that was a fleeting thought. Dawood was wise enough to know that you cannot force anybody to love you. What he did not understand was the pain, the hot, searing pain that was stabbing at his heart as if he had been just shot. Not even in the savage world he inhabited, where violence was a byword, did such pain exist.

A numb and distraught Dawood walked down the steps of Sujata's residence. 'The bitch turned against me,' he kept muttering.

Soon after the break up in 1983, Dawood was melancholic, mournful because of his failed love. He was often heard humming that famous song from 1966 Dilip Kumar starrer, *Dil Diya Dard Liya*, *'Guzre hain aaj ishq mein, hum uss maqam se, nafrat si ho gayi hain mohabbat ke naam se* [today, I have passed that stage in love where I cannot bear the name of love]. '

He had never been a diehard romantic, but Sujata had turned him into one. And now, a year from his involvement with her, he was back to being a misogynist. He decided women were not worth adoring; they should be just treated as an object of lust, and nothing beyond that.

Dawood's friends suggested he drink away his pain but he refused to hit the bottle. When they tried to set him up with women in their circle with the intention of helping him get over his grief, he always turned down their offers and foiled their efforts. He had decided not to love any woman with this intensity, never fall in love at all. But then Mehjabeen happened, and all his resolutions were turned to dust.

22

Ageing Dons

Mastan had managed to achieve almost everything in life: money, power, clout, respectability, popularity, and whatever else that matters in life.

He had managed to get his three daughters, Qamrunnisa, Mehrunnisa, and Shamshad, married into good households and as a father he was satisfied with his filial responsibilities. However, he longed for a son who could have succeeded him and immortalised his name. Mastan often looked at Ibrahim Bhai and felt envy at the way the Almighty had blessed him; so many children and six of them sons.

When a man is getting older, he becomes both more devout and desperate. Mastan had become highly religious and apparently philanthropic as well. He made a trip to Mecca and Medina again. Nobody knows how many times he had accomplished Hajj, but with his newfound faith in God, he added a prefix of Haji to his name. He was now known as Haji Mastan Mirza. Muslims normally do this to show the world they have made a trip to the Holy Kaaba, and have in a way repented and given up all the vices in their lives. The prefix is also cited as evidence of credibility and probity.

Mastan had also begun making supplications for a son at the shrines of all the revered saints. He began visiting all the religious shrines in the city and across the country, giving charity and feeding the poor and asking everyone to pray for him to get a son.

His devotion went to a new level when he got interested in Muslim social movies, which focus on religious messages for the family. Mastan saw that films were a powerful medium; and that the masses react to movies more than anything else. So, he became interested in producing these films. The seventies and early eighties subsequently witnessed a spate of Muslim social movies like *Mere Gharib Nawaz, Niaz aur Namaz, Bismillah Ki Barkat, Awliyae-Hind, Dayare-Madina,* and scores of other movies.

In the course of meeting film personalities, Mastan encountered Veena Sharma alias Sona. She was touted as a Madhubala lookalike, and Mastan, like the youth of his time, dreamt of marrying Madhubala, the most beautiful screen diva of Bollywood since the inception of the film industry. They say there will be none like her ever again, but when Sona appeared on celluloid in the late seventies and early eighties in Muslim social movies, some thought she bore a striking resemblance to Madhubala.

Mastan lost no time in sending her a marriage proposal, which she readily accepted. He was a powerful producer, and she a struggling starlet, so the union was almost pre-ordained. He bought a palatial bungalow for her in Juhu and moved in with her. Soon he began flaunting her at public functions. He ensured that he was photographed with Dilip Kumar and Saira Banu with his new wife in town, at all the major dos. Mastan cherished these photographs, often showing Dilip Kumar and Mastan together, and adorned the walls of his bungalow with them. Soon, he gained the reputation of a socialite, and talk of his smuggling activities and offences became history.

In hindsight, it seems like this was Mastan's ploy for shedding his dark image and going legit. He had always craved respectability and some position in society. The Muslims of Bombay had had no respectable reformist leader in the community who could hold sway in the community, till now. So, Mastan decided to take over the mantle of the community's leadership. Unfortunately, the masses were not wise enough to resist his attempt to fill the void at the top.

Mastan, who was invited to all respectable gatherings and given a significant spot on the dais of these functions, played to the gallery at times and made inflammatory speeches. The Special Branch (SB)-I of the police, which always went sniffing around occasions like these, realised that Mastan's emergence could mean trouble. This was duly reported to the top bosses at the Mantralaya.

During the communal riots of 1984, when the government began a crackdown on anti-social elements, the police top bosses decided to detain all mafia head honchos. Senior Police Inspector Madhukar Zende, who had quite a reputation, picked up Mastan and Karim Lala and charged them under the National Security Act (NSA). Mastan was actually in hiding at his Juhu bungalow, but Zende managed to drag him out of it and hauled him to the Crime Branch. Subsequently, Zende raided the Taher Manzil at Grant Road residence of Karim Lala and took him to the police headquarters.

The Police Commissioner Julio Ribeiro, who had heard much about Mastan and his ill-gotten fame, was shocked to see him when Zende produced the smuggler. What he saw was a puny, frail, wiry little man. Zende would not forget the way his police chief reacted: 'Is *this* Mastan, that famous guy?'

Both Mastan and Karim Lala were convicted under NSA and had to serve several months in the Thane jail. Mastan felt thoroughly humiliated and chastened. All his wealth, money, and hobnobbing with Bollywood and politicians were of no avail. He wanted people who could stage *rasta rokos* (demonstrations) for him, a mob who could subjugate the authorities; hordes of supporters who would become a formidable force on his side, a source of power. After days of thinking and consultation with his think-tank, which also included his mastermind, his police informer and sounding board Jenabai, he came up with a master plan. Why not bring the Dalits and Muslims together? Both of them are downtrodden and oppressed groups of people, he thought, and both have an axe to grind with the system, as Dalits and Muslims both feel the government has been unfair to them. A joint platform as a united force would also be an answer to the Shiv Sena's muscle. In fact, they would emerge stronger than Bal Thackeray's Shiv Sainiks, dreamt Mastan.

After meeting with several Dalit group leaders, one of the senior leaders and intellectuals, Jogendra Kawade, gave his support to Mastan's brainchild. Thus came into existence Dalit-Muslim Suraksha Mahasangh (DMSM), in 1985. Despite good coverage in the print media, the party failed to make its presence felt, however; even in the face of Mastan's best efforts to fund and promote the party, it could never rise to become a force to reckon with.

All the smuggling cases against Mastan had now been disposed of. He now devoted his time between politics and real estate. Karim Lala followed suit and decided to reform himself as well, focusing on his hotel business and disassociating himself from any kind of criminal activity. Baashu Dada had in the meanwhile migrated to Hyderabad and vowed never to return to Bombay.

The only one who was still active, still nursing his ambitions to become numero uno in the Bombay mafia, was Dawood Ibrahim.

23

Death of a Brother, Birth of a Gang War

Popular Hindi film songs rent the air as girls, dressed in their gaudiest finery, hung about the long verandahs of Congress House in south Bombay. The address was a misnomer. Once upon a time, stalwarts of the Indian National Congress who spearheaded the freedom movement in India had set up base at Congress House. But those were nobler days. By the seventies, it had become a whorehouse where nautch girls, called *mujrewallis* in the local lingo, entertained clients àla *Pakeezah*. Some of the nautch girls were good singers and nimble with their feet, but over the years, the place had disintegrated into a proper prostitution joint where men came up to pick up the finest piece of flesh they could find. Unlike their counterparts in Kamathipura and Falkland Road, sex workers from Congress House catered to a richer clientele. So while the place looked tawdry, it did not wear the desolation and desperation of Kamathipura. It had the unkempt look of a whorehouse but the girls were classier and prettier, and wore fragrant *mogra*, but the scent of sin could not be masked.

The girls lived in tiny, water-tight compartments with equally small dreams. They had no siblings and family; their fellow workers, pimps, customers, and the madams who stood guard over them doubled up as this. Most of them lived and died in the same place. Some of them had managed to put their children in boarding schools, where they were being educated unaware of their mothers' dark secrets.

In this vast cauldron of sex and sin, lived Nanda and Chitra, two women in their late twenties. Both were friends and had been forced into prostitution at a tender age. They had lost their parents in infancy and their relatives had dumped them at Congress House for a few hundred rupees. They were raped in the initial years, before finally coming to terms with their destiny and getting some small measure of control over it.

Now, a prostitute will give pleasure to over twenty to twenty-five men in a span of twenty-four hours but she will always cherish sex with one particular man. Sex with the chosen one is never be treated as a chore, for she chooses her beau as the man's interest in her is not confined to her body or face. For Chitra, Sabir was one such customer.

Sabir was only in his second year of marriage when Chitra happened to him. Chitra was no head turner, but she was charming and good looking, and most importantly, she lavished attention on the curly-haired Sabir. He was a poet at heart, showering her with Urdu ghazals and *shayari* (poetry) which actually made her blush.

Sabir had married for love, and his wife Shahnaaz was quite a good looking woman. Although she was seeing a Pathan before marriage and was known as *Lala ki Lali*, Sabir wooed her and eventually convinced her to marry him. Dawood had never liked the idea of his brother marrying someone else's girlfriend but he loved his brother and had given in to Sabir's wishes. Within the first year of their marriage, Shahnaaz bore Sabir a son, Shiraz, and then Shahnaaz conceived again. It was then that Sabir was drawn towards Chitra, who made time for him and returned romance back to his life. Not that he stopped loving or caring for Shahnaaz, but she was heavily pregnant and sex with her ballooning person did not appeal to him.

With his new paramour, he went to watch movies, where Chitra did things to him that never even happened in the movies. They ate bhelpuri at Chowpatty, dined in expensive restaurants, and drove around in their car on the streets of Bombay.

Chitra enjoyed Sabir's company and the luxury that money could buy. He was a divinely prescribed antidote for her otherwise bitter life; life in Congress House was depressing and Sabir's presence made her forget it for a while. Her meetings with Sabir barely lasted for a couple of hours, as he had his family and business and he was always in a rush. But whenever he dropped her off at Congress House, she was left feeling overwhelmed. She could not help but confide in her friend Nanda about her passionate encounters with him. For example, she said, one day Sabir had bought a cone of ice cream from the Chowpatty seaface and dumped the whole thing on her face before licking off the cream in full view of the public, even as Chitra shrieked in horror and delight.

Nanda envied Chitra though she never told her as much. Nanda wanted a man like Sabir; there were no fairytale endings in their lives, but a lover could help alleviate the pain of the life she lived. As Chitra kept filling Nanda with stories of her blossoming love life, Nanda lapsed into depression. And then one fine day, a tall, handsome Pathan walked into her life.

Amirzada befriended Nanda with a purpose. But Nanda, in her hunger for a real lover, failed to see through his designs. Amirzada had learnt of Sabir's interest in Chitra and knew that she was the key to Sabir. When he learnt that Chitra was completely smitten with Sabir, he latched on to her friend Nanda. Amirzada's entrance into Nanda's life filled a long pending void in her life, as he wooed her in just the manner she imagined Sabir had romanced Chitra. The red light area lives up to its image; nothing lies hidden here for long. In no time, Sabir learnt about Nanda's relationship with Amirzada. But even though Amirzada was a former foe, he thought the past was well behind them.

In the meanwhile, Amirzada began to keep tabs on Sabir's movements through Nanda. One evening, he called Nanda and told her he wanted to spend a night with her. Nanda was elated, but then she thought of her best friend Chitra. Lately, Chitra had been quiet; Nanda had not seen Sabir visiting her for a long time. Mindful of Chitra's pensiveness, Nanda asked Amirzada if she could bring Chitra along. When Chitra overheard Nanda's conversation, she immediately interjected, saying she would not be able to make it as Sabir was visiting her at night and they had planned to go out. Unwittingly, Nanda relayed the information to Amirzada. The Pathan did something Nanda did not figure out until the next day; he told her he could not make it and slammed the phone down. Nanda was left holding the phone, surprised and disappointed.

As there are restrictions on timings at Congress House, clients and visitors cannot stay in after 12:30 am. So, whenever Sabir was late visiting Chitra, he took her out on a long ride. This particular night, on 12 February 1981, at around 1 am, the two left in his white Premier Padmini Fiat.

That night, he had just returned from Shahnaaz's periodic medical checkup—she was in her seventh month—when he had got a call from Chitra, who told him that she was missing him. Sabir left immediately, telling Shahnaaz he would be back in the morning. For Shahnaaz this was now routine. Sabir kept disappearing, night after night, on flimsy pretexts. They fought bitterly over his absence, but Sabir failed to pay heed and stormed out, every time, just as he had this night.

As Sabir's car exited Kamathipura and took a sharp left on Tardeo to emerge on Haji Ali shrine's intersection, he checked the rearview mirror out of habit. There, he saw a flower-bedecked Ambassador following them closely. A newly-married couple, he thought and smiled. It was past midnight, and Chitra, sitting beside him in the car, was in a mischievous mood, putting him, in turn, in the mood for love.

Suddenly, Sabir's attention was drawn to the fuel meter. He cursed under his breath and looked around for a petrol pump to refuel his vehicle. After several failed turns, he remembered that there was a gas station at Prabhadevi a few kilometres away. He just hoped his car would pull through the four to five kilometre distance.

Suddenly, he noticed that the wedding party was still following his car. Were they going to the suburbs? What were they doing while he kept zipping in and out of smaller roads looking for gas?

The flower-bedecked car was, in fact, his cortege. There was no bride or groom in it, only agents of death who were stalking him. They were actually following a well-laid plan, hatched the same evening. The car had Mamoor Khan at the wheel, Amirzada, Alamzeb, Manohar Surve alias Manya Surve, and others. They were carrying assault guns, rifles, pistols, swords, and choppers. Surve used to devour James Hadley Chase paperbacks, and he was the one who outlined the plan to finish off Sabir that night. The trick of decorating the car with flowers and giving it a celebratory look, even, was Surve's. The pursuers knew they would have to intercept Sabir at some point after tailing him for a while, and the flowers would allow them access to him without his getting suspicious.

Sabir spotted the Servo Care petrol pump at Prabhadevi and drove his car in. As he rammed on the brakes, his heart went wild, thumping away with alarm and fear as he saw the white Ambassador screeching to a halt behind his car. He asked Chitra to get off, at once, and groped for his gun. But Sabir was seconds too late.

Five armed men jumped out of the white Ambassador and surrounded Sabir's car. Slowly one of them opened the car's passenger's door and extricated Chitra, who was quaking with fear, her face ashen. Sabir's limbs were frozen, his throat dry; even as blood rushed into his brains, everything seemed to blur.

Guns began to spew fire then, shattering the windscreen and piercing Sabir's body. The gangster's screams of pain and agony lasted only a few seconds, so powerful was the assault. Years later the gas station attendants and the neighbourhood would recall in horror the cold-blooded killing and the endless screams of a woman. No one could keep a count of the number of bullets fired on Sabir that night, but the autopsy recorded a total of nine bullets extracted from his body, and nineteen from various cavities in the car seats, carpet and metallic frame of the vehicle.

As Sabir slumped, his forehead on the steering wheel, one of the killers whipped out a rampuri knife and slit his wrist. By then Sabir was beyond any pain or sensation, however. Blood simply gushed out of his wounds like a river in spate. Even his expensive white leather shoes were soaked and softened.

The slaying of Sabir went down in the Bombay police annals as one of the most violent and brutal mafia killings the city had ever witnessed. One of its witnesses drew a parallel with the mythological Abhimanyu in the battle of Mahabharat, surrounded in stealth and killed without being allowed a proper defence.

The victorious band of killers got into their Ambassador and headed back towards town immediately afterwards. Within 15 minutes they had reached JJ Square and veered onto Pakmodia Street. It was pitch dark and the denizens of Dawood's fiefdom lay fast asleep when their car halted outside the imposing wrought iron gate of Musafirkhana. The five gunmen, ready to finish off the Dawood group's upper echelon, got out of the car muttering *'Aaj iska kissa bhi tamam kar dete hain* [let's finish him off today itself].'

The high of shooting Sabir had led them to feel invincible. They began to mindlessly fire at the iron gate, without targeting any particular person or place. The silence of the night was shattered with the hail of bullets. Suddenly, the assailants realised they had emptied their gun, and hastily began to reload. But someone from inside Musafirkhana sprung a surprise on them; a volley of bullets was fired from within the gates. The killers ducked for cover, looking at each other in surprise. They had never expected retaliatory fire at this hour of the night.

The gunman was Khalid Pehelwan, who was firing from the first floor from behind a pillar. Khalid had been awake since the time Sabir had left. The moment he saw the Ambassador coming to a screeching halt, he had grabbed a gun.

The Khans were a bit rattled at this rallying. They decided to leave as they had already won a major victory that night; this assault was only a bonus. By then, Dawood and his men had taken their positions and were ready to launch their onslaught. When they saw the Ambassador backing off, they started firing, bullets hitting the boot and the bonnet and breaking its glass windows. Speeding off, the Pathans somehow managed a safe passage.

The gunfire had woken Musafirkhana and the gang members were now assembled outside the gate. Dawood noticed that one key man was missing—his brother Sabir. Dawood's first fear was that he had taken a hit from one of the bullets. But Khalid, who was the hero of the night, told him that Sabir had left a while ago to visit Chitra. A strange foreboding took over Dawood. Where was his brother? Sabir lay, of course, lifeless in a pool of his own blood.

Henceforth, the Dawood-Sabir gang was officially rechristened the Dawood gang. The death of Sabir changed two things: Dawood Ibrahim and Bombay's mafia. Neither would ever be the same again. Bombay's mafia opened a new chapter of blood and gore; revenge and broad daylight killings; fresh recruits and new gangs; big money and drugs. Dawood not only turned vengeful but intensely motivated and driven, propelling him out of the small league in the Bombay pool and pushing him into the big sea of crime.

24

Dawood's Coronation

When Sabir's body was brought into Musafirkhana, the neighbourhood was reeling with the cries of Dawood's mother and four sisters. Ibrahim, though, was utterly silent in his shock as he gazed at this eldest son's bullet-ridden body. The *janazah* (coffin) of Sabir was laden with flowers and the whole street was heavy, under a pall of gloom.

Dawood was shattered. The killing of Sabir was like killing off half his own existence. He had no clue how and why it had happened. He had been crying the whole night and had not been able to reconcile himself with the fact that his brother was no more. But he had to take charge of his emotions; he had to complete the last rites and he was the only one who could take care of his family. All his brothers were rallying around him, but in tears.

Karim Lala, Haji Mastan, and even Baashu Dada who, respectively, may not have liked Dawood or had had a tiff with him, had come for the funeral rites and offered their condolences to Ibrahim Kaskar, and Dawood himself. In the midst of his grief, Dawood took note of the visitors who had come for his brother's funeral. This scene was to stay in his memory for a long time; Dawood would use it to know who was on his side and who were his enemies.

The final rites were performed on Sabir and he was given ghusl, the final bath given to a dead body. He was borne away in the coffin, draped in a sheet which bore the holy names, and a huge crowd followed the funeral procession. It wound its way from Musafirkhana on foot and went to the Bada Kabrastan at Marine Lines, Chandanwadi.

Sabir was buried and the police had to call in extra forces to ensure there were no law and order problems. Shops were closed, if not out of reverence for Sabir, then out of fear of violence. The entire area around Pydhonie, JJ Marg, Dongri, Teli Mohalla, Musafirkhana, Bori Mohalla, Bhendi Bazaar, and Mandvi was closed. This was the killing of a gang leader, and that too the brother of Dawood Ibrahim: a major, unprecedented event. Everyone, from the dons to the cops was on tenterhooks about the repercussions of this tragedy.

After burying his brother, Dawood returned home and went through the last rites of the dead, at the same time trying to plan his next move. He had, of course, figured out who was behind his brother's killing. As he sat with his brothers and his cronies, Anees, Jind-ul Haq, Ranjeet, Khalid Pehelwan, and others, there was only one thing on his mind; he wanted revenge, not through the Indian judicial system but death for Amirzada, his way.

The retaliation would not only settle the score and avenge his brother's death, it would also send a necessary message to the world; that he was not to be challenged. The harder Dawood thought, however, the tougher he found it was to think straight. He was confused and with each passing day he was getting madder and madder.

At the same time, his father and his friend Karim Lala, as well as others, were of the opinion that Dawood should give up the thought of revenge. A shattered Ibrahim Kaskar even met the then Chief Minister A.R. Antulay for expeditious investigation into the case and arrest of the killers. The Kaskars were hopeful of the chief minister's intervention not only because he was a Muslim, but because he hailed from the Konkan region. But nothing happened.

And though Dawood knew that Amirzada and Alamzeb were involved in the killing, he did not know where they were. The cops too were hunting for them, but Dawood wanted to beat the cops to Amirzada and finish him off for good.

After many months of chase, the cops finally managed to arrest Amirzada. But this did not satisfy Dawood. He wanted revenge, even if the man was behind bars. Dawood felt that courts could never give justice to the people. He realised that it was quite possible that the lone eyewitness, Chitra, could be bought or intimidated. Due to the lack of circumstantial evidence, Amirzada might well walk free. Even if the lower courts convicted him, he could go to the higher courts and then to the Supreme Court, where he was likely to be released. Years would pass and Dawood would remain indebted to the soul of his slain brother Sabir. In his own eyes too, he would be a weakling who could not avenge his brother's death.

Finally it was suggested to him that he should outsource Amirzada's killing. In this way, he would not only stay clear of the murder but also ensure that the man who killed his brother did not live. Lots of names were thought of, including those of some foreign killers; some even from the Italian mafia. But he could not really decide on the person who would avenge his brother's death.

There was a brave man called Rajan Nair, someone soon suggested, in the north-eastern suburbs. He could arrange for the killing of Amirzada even if he were in jail. And since Nair lived in the far eastern suburbs of the city, nobody would be able to connect him to Dawood, achieving the purpose of taking revenge without it being traced back to him. Convinced, a bloodthirsty Dawood decided to give this lead a chance and asked for a meeting to be arranged.

25

Mumbai's Hadley Chase

'*Madarchod! Policewala bhadwa log!* [Motherfuckers! You cops are all idiots!]' Manya screamed.

Sub-inspector Tambat stared down at the bleeding 37-year-old man that he and his squad had been hunting for the last two months.

'*Gaddari kiya mere saath* [I have been betrayed]!' Manya snarled before coughing up blood and spitting it at Tambat and his three fellow policemen in the sedan that was racing towards the Lokmanya Tilak Municipal General Hospital, also known as the Sion Hospital. In his final moments, the gangster, infamous for his violent ways and bitter hatred for the police, seemed to be spewing his venomous loathing at the system that he claimed was responsible for making him the criminal that he was.

The car hurtled towards the hospital, as the policemen kept up their efforts to save the man that they had just shot six times. The victim of Mumbai's first encounter kept up his tirade against the police till the last bloody hiccup took away his life. At Sion Hospital, he was declared dead before admission.

The man was Manohar Surve, aka Manya Surve, one of the most feared gangsters of Bombay, who eluded the police for over a decade, before being shot to death in the city's first encounter.

Manya Surve had always claimed that he had been wronged by the police and his older brother Bhargav Surve, and he maintained his stand to the very end. Bhargav was in the illicit liquor business, and was always addressed as Bhargav Dada. With time, he began to take his 'Dada' tag seriously, and started working as a recovery agent for businessmen and financiers.

In 1969, Manya was named as an accomplice in a case against Bhargav, in which a businessman from Prabhadevi was beaten to death with hockey sticks and bamboo shoots for not returning the 50,000 rupees that he had taken from a financier. The death of the businessman created outrage among the entire businessmen's community in the Dadar-Prabhadevi area, and they all went on strike for three days, bringing the bustling commercial area to a standstill. The police, realising the seriousness of the situation, acted swiftly.

When Manya was arrested, he claimed innocence and to protest the 'injustice', went on to stage a hunger strike at the Yerawada Central Jail, where he was lodged after being convicted. He was subsequently admitted to Sasoon Hospital after he developed severe health problems.

On 24 November 1979, Manya's close friends Bajirao 'Bajya' Patil and Sheikh Munir visited him at the hospital. There, they threw powdered chilly into the eyes of the policemen guarding Manya, who promptly jumped out of his bed and fled.

A BA grad from Kirti College, Manya had a somewhat unique trait among his fellow gangsters—he was an ardent fan of James Hadley Chase. So much so that before almost every heist, robbery, or murder, he would spend hours working out the details of the job, using ideas and material from the books. From bank heist to orchestrating hits to actually carrying out murders, every single aspect of the job would be meticulously planned by him.

After his escape, it was time to move on, and establish himself as a name to be feared. Manya went on to build a gang of ten to twelve men, with Sheikh and Bajirao as his two chief lieutenants. Over the next two years, he terrorised the people of Bombay with the most violent crimes that the city had ever witnessed. He robbed banks, held people to ransom, and brutally assaulted those who dared to oppose him. Even his own friends were not safe from his rage.

Ashok Mastakar and Papi Patil were two such victims. On separate occasions, Manya asked them for money, a steady supply of which he always needed as he was constantly on the run. Both of them refused, with brutal consequences.

One evening in 1979, Manya strolled into a gymnasium in Mahim. The gym was just beginning to fill up. Every eye was on Manya as he walked in, then in his early 30s, wearing a tight chequered T-shirt and baggy trousers with biceps and forearms bulging.

In those days, such a physique was not a frequent sight, and the people inside watched appreciatively as Manya strode in confidently, and stopped and looked around. Everybody expected him to walk over to the weights and start pumping iron; they were all waiting to watch that physique in action.

Nobody was prepared for what was going to happen next, though.

Manya cast his eye around until he spotted Patil, who too had noticed the gangster stroll in. Manya walked up to him and stood looking at the anxious man for a moment, eyes locked in a ferocious battle. Then he reached into his pocket, calmly pulled out a revolver, took aim, and without batting an eye, shot Patil's legs, blowing both his kneecaps out. Then, as calm as ever, almost as if nothing had happened, he looked around at the others, cowering in the corners, and walked out. It was more than a minute before the stunned people could move and rush to help Patil who lay on the floor, bleeding and groaning.

Mastakar too was dealt with equally brutally and mercilessly. Manya, along with Sheikh and Bajirao, forced their way into his house and savagely assaulted him. His daughter, being held at knifepoint, was made to watch the brutality as it unfolded. Manya then threw acid over Mastakar's face, disfiguring him horribly, before leaving.

Mastakar later gave evidence against Manya, and his courage earned him a place on Manya's hitlist. However, Manya was killed before he could get to Mastakar. The attacks on Mastakar and Patil are significant as both were good friends of Manya's before he was arrested. Manya was apparently so close to Patil that he had eaten at the latter's house on several occasions. Apparently, 'no' was something that Manya refused to accept from anybody, no matter who he or she was; anyone who said no to Manya automatically became an enemy.

Manya's temper was observed on several other occasions, when he was particularly brutal against people who resisted or opposed him. On one occasion, Manya and Sheikh lay in wait for a businessman outside a Dena Bank branch in Prabhadevi. Just as he was leaving the bank with a bag containing 2 lakh rupees in cash — a significant amount in those days — the duo walked up to him, shoved their guns into his face and demanded that he hand over the bag. Instead of complying, the businessman threw the bag into the bank. Enraged, Manya, and following his lead, Sheikh, pumped bullets into the businessman, barged into the bank, picked up the bag, and walked away with the money. Manya's gang later staged a daring heist in Matunga, and robbed an Ambassador of 7 lakh rupees that was being taken to a bank.

Manya's hitlist also included Police Inspector Ashok Dabholkar (name changed) from the Dadar Police Station, who had arrested him in 1969. After escaping from police custody, Manya went to Dabholkar's residence in the Worli police colony while the policeman was at work and told his family that he was going to finish Dabholkar. He also made several threats to Dabholkar over the phone. So dire were the threats that after his retirement, Dabholkar dyed his greying hair black and grew a beard in the hope that he would not be recognised by Manya.

Legend has it that Manya was the master strategist in the Sabir Ibrahim Kaskar killing. At the time, Manya's name, like many other dreaded gangsters, had already become a surefire way to instill terror and fear into one and all, but his ability to strategise was by far what distinguished him from almost everyone of his tier.

This is what made the Pathan gang single him out to orchestrate a killing for them. They approached a suspicious Manya, known for his paranoia and his singular, universal mistrust for others. The offer, a mind boggling reward that left even Manya smacking his lips, was something that he could not refuse.

They say even Manya had an axe to grind and was on the lookout for an opportunity to bump off the Kaskar brothers, their power, and with it their fearsome reputation that was growing in leaps and bounds.

Almost every other gang, including the Pathans, was finding it difficult to check the burgeoning power of the Dawood-Sabir gang. This is what the Pathans wanted to do, and where Manya came in.

Manya realised that the only way to ensure the downfall of Dawood and Sabir was to divide and rule, in other words, to separate the one from the other, and take them out singly. Again, he fell back on his Headley Chase novels, and came up with a novel idea. Much planning and strategising later, Manya and a gang of Pathans were ready for the Kaskars.

Sabir did not suspect a thing when, on one of his frequent night-time visits to the prostitute Chitra, he saw a wedding car pull up behind him. Black-tinted windows and adorned with flowers and silk, it was like any other wedding car. Sabir dismissed it from his mind, dreaming of the delights of the flesh that he would soon experience.

Armed with machine guns and pistols, the gang of Pathans and Manya followed Sabir discreetly, knowing that they would never be suspected. The Pathans followed Manya's instructions to the letter, and choosing the correct, pre-assigned moment near a petrol pump at Prabhadevi, riddled Sabir's car with bullets, leaving Sabir to bleed to death.

Dawood was always known to be unforgiving. He decided to avenge his brother's killing and eliminate each and every person involved in the murder. He had no personal enmity with Manya, and so, he could not fathom why Manya should have gotten involved in the ongoing vendetta between the Pathans and the Kaskars. But Manya will have to pay for this, Dawood swore.

Meanwhile, the police themselves were shaken with Manya's unabated run of violence. After a string of murders, violent robberies, and kidnappings, the then Police Commissioner Julio Ribeiro formed a special squad of policemen to hunt down Manya late in 1981. The squad included Senior Police Inspector Isaac Samson; Inspector Yashwant Bhide; and Sub-inspectors Raja Tambat, Sanjay Parande, and Ishaq Bagwan. Officers of the squad visited all the places where Manya had committed crimes and spoke to several of his victims, including Mastakar and Patil. They also visited some of Manya's associates in jail, where a couple of them promised to inform on Manya's movements if the police helped them get out of jail. The squad then arranged for some lawyers, who helped these informants get out on bail.

The constant evading of the law had instilled into Manya a tendency to be ever ready for a confrontation. In fact, Dombivali residents recall that he used to move around with a bag of hand bombs, the way people carry chickoos in their plastic bags. No one ever dared to cross his path. He never went anywhere without arming himself with a gun, a dagger, and a bottle of acid, something which no other gangster was ever known to do. He trusted no one and in order to avoid being caught, he did not keep even his aides fully informed of his movements.

But finally, it was the love of a woman that proved to be his Achilles' heel. The police hit squad, which was on Manya's tail for two months, hit pay dirt on 11 January 1982, when they learnt that Manya would be meeting his girlfriend near the Ambedkar College in Wadala and taking her to Navi Mumbai. He was in a relationship with a woman from his locality, and she had been living with her parents after her husband died.

The squad immediately swung into action and set about laying a trap. One team was dispatched to Sector 17 in Navi Mumbai, to lie in wait for Manya in case he managed to escape from the police's clutches from Ambedkar College. Meanwhile, Tambat, Bagwan, and Parande, all in their mid-20s at the time, donned jeans and T-shirts and started loitering outside the college posing as students, while two older officers lay in wait posing as professors. All of them had guns concealed in cavities cut out in the pages of thick books. The cavities were a couple of inches larger than the guns, to enable the cops to draw them quickly when the action began.

Things began to heat up when Manya's girlfriend arrived and stood waiting at the bus stop outside the college. The cops' informant, through signals, informed them that she was the woman who would be meeting Manya, and the cops discreetly stationed themselves around her.

At around 10:45 am, Manya approached in a taxi, which drove past the bus stop and stopped several feet ahead. Oblivious to the trap, Manya got out and started back walking towards his girlfriend, right past Tambat and his 'college-mates'.

Bhide recognised Manya first, and signalled to the others, who immediately moved in, surrounded the gangster with weapons drawn and called out the warning: '*Manya Surve, thamb! Aamhi police aahot* [stop, Manya Surve, we are policemen]!'

With a snarl on his lips, Manya drew a Mauser pistol from under his shirt and pointed it at Tambat and Bagwan, who were directly in front of him. Both cops dove for cover behind parked vehicles as Manya opened fire. In retaliation, Tambat and Bagwan each shot Manya thrice.

Even six bullets in his torso could not subdue the lean, muscular criminal, who had hated the police with all his being ever since his arrest. Manya reached inside his sock for the bottle of acid that he always kept with him. However, he was overpowered and disarmed.

The police had already kept several private vehicles on standby outside the college, and Manya was carried into one of them, spitting up blood and curses. He died before he reached the hospital. Tambat, along with Sub-inspector Bagwan, were later awarded the president's police medal for gallantry.

Manya's arrest in 1969 and the encounter were the only two times when he actually came face-to-face with the police. He had managed to give even Ribeiro's special squad the slip on three to four occasions.

Manya's aide Sheikh was killed in an encounter, also by Bagwan and Tambat, shortly thereafter, and Bajirao was arrested. He now lives in Matunga and is believed to be reformed. However, one mystery has never been unravelled till date. How did the police know the exact location and time of Manya, who was known to be obsessively secretive about his movements? Some say his woman betrayed him. Newspapers reported that he was supposed to pick up a prostitute who was actually a decoy set up by the police, and he walked into the trap completely unaware. The prostitute was said to have been pressurised by the police to trap Manya; her name was never disclosed. There is also a strong suspicion among a section of the police that it was actually Dawood who had kept a watch on Manya for days and finally tipped the police off about his visit to Wadala. Some even believe that the mysterious woman was working at Dawood's behest, and knowing Dawood and his way of using the police machinery, this actually seems highly believable. In fact, *Current*, which was the most widely read weekly in those days, said as much in their spot report on Manya killing on 23 January 1982, 'The shooting of Manya has acquired an aura of mystery. Whatever actually happened on that day, the fact remains that both the cops and the public have heaved a sigh of relief (*Current*, 23 January 1982, Manya Shot Dead).'

26

The Fallout

Khalid Pehelwan had gotten himself inducted into the two-storey building on Mohammad Ali Road—Musafirkhana. Dawood had deemed him loyal and trustworthy enough to live with him and his brothers, and after the death of Sabir in February 1981, they both became closer; almost like blood brothers. Khalid was an intelligent man with a sharp eye for detail. He realised that there was more money to be earned than the meagre amounts collected from extortion or the petty money made from cheating and robbing people.

Dawood had made several trips to Dubai and established contacts with the sheikhs, but could not establish a strong base in the Gulf region. Also the *Kachra Peti* line and other means of smuggling gold was not that revenue oriented. Khalid began exploring ways and means to ensure they could enhance their turnover by smuggling big time, instead of making small-time profits. He was looking for opportunities to try and generate bigger profit margins through larger turnovers.

The idea was simple—while smuggling through air there were limitations in terms of volume, but by sea the cargo could be much bigger. They just had to ensure they dodged the customs cleverly.

Dawood was very interested in the idea but had no experience on this front. However, Khalid assured him this campaign would succeed, and laid out his plans before him. Small fisherman boats would set out to the high seas or the coast lines of Raigad and Alibaug. He said that they could use the jetties of Srivardhan and Mhasla. These small boats could meet the steamers or ships with the smuggled cargo of gold or silver, which would get to Indian waters. The fishermen's boats would then ply the cargo back onto the shores across the coast of Maharashtra and the Union Territory of Daman. It would take an estimated four hours for the barges to get to the Indian coasts, thereby avoiding coastguards and customs.

After a couple of successful test runs, Dawood began to see the ingenuity of Khalid's ideas. Musafirkhana had now expanded as the smuggling centre of Dawood's gang, and this foray into smuggling increased Dawood's stature as a don.

However, most of the smuggling business was handled by Khalid Pehelwan, while Dawood handled the distribution business. When he was not involved in the distribution and marketing, he looked after the extortion business. Having grown up on the streets of Bombay, Dawood was not suave when it came to interacting with Arab Sheikhs, which came with the territory of dealing in smuggled gold and silver. He was not aware of the finer nuances of the smuggling business either. The bigger money, rich businessman and sheikhs, were being handled by a more polished and intelligible Khalid, who spoke Arabic.

It was not long before Dawood began to feel sidelined by Khalid. Khalid orchestrated the entire campaign of landings along the Bombay coastlines to Daman. While Dawood sat in his office behind his desk, Khalid was busy entertaining Arab sheikhs and brokering deals. In a business where complexes develop as quickly as alliances are dishonoured, Dawood's impassive, less involved take on this aspect of business strengthened Khalid's position as a leader. Susceptible to gossip, Dawood began to listen to his flunkies when they spoke of how Khalid was becoming too big for his own boots and how Dawood would soon be only his minion and nothing else. This disconcerted Dawood greatly. He needed to be the boss and decided to speak to Khalid about it.

Although Khalid tried to explain his position and how the business was always about the gang, he knew only too well that a rift had already grown. This presented a huge dilemma for Khalid, but his nobility would not allow his relationship to sour. He had developed his partnership and friendship with Dawood for over seven years, but knew that the growing discomfort between them was straining these ties. Finally, a few months after Sabir's death, he decided to part amicably and slowly withdraw from the gang. Planning to retire with his wife and child, he bought himself a bungalow in Karol Bagh in New Delhi. Dawood heard about this but did not discourage him.

As Khalid was contemplating an amicable departure, Dawood went to seek the advice of police informer and bootlegger Jenabai Daruwalli. Dawood wanted advice regarding Khalid and the growing pains of his insecurity. He did not want any sort of enmity with Khalid since he had brought his own people into Dawood's life and his gang.

Jenabhai did not say much, only stating that she would sort this out for Dawood. She only wanted a small piece of information—the next landing of the smuggled goods.

Once the landing took place and cartons of gold and silver were brought into the office at Musafirkhana, Dawood called on Jenabai and told her that the consignment would be lying in the office for a day or two before dealers and customers showed up and took them away.

That very day, customs officials closed in on Musafirkhana and clamped down on the office. While most of the people who were involved managed to escape customs' clutches, the smuggled goods of gold and silver were all seized and taken away.

Khalid Pehelwan was aghast. No one knew about the consignment and its dealing and placement in the office save Dawood and he. Appalled by Dawood's treachery, he could not, however prove that Dawood had deceived him. While his growing distrust in Dawood left Khalid with little to say to him, he did not want any violence within the gang. He resolved to leave but not before fortifying the gang. In spite of their personal tug-of-war, Khalid was loyalist to the core, especially because after taking him over from Baashu Dada, Dawood had shown a lot of trust in him. Besides, the underworld is a one-way street. Practically speaking, if Khalid sabotaged the gang in any way, they would come after him eventually. This way, he could protect himself from Dawood's ire, and at the same time protect himself if rival gangsters came after him.

He looked around at his men and thought to himself, why not have non-Muslim members as well? His rationale stemmed from the fact that Dawood's arch rivals—the Pathans — were also a Muslim gang. Both gangs were vying to be on the right side of Allah and be the righteous gang. So, people were changing sides from here to there without flinching; loyalty was less binding as religion bound them both.

Khalid realised that if the gang had non-Muslim members, they would not change sides once they pledged their undying loyalty to the gang. Moreover, while the Pathans were originally Afghans, Dawood had the advantage of being a Maharashtrian. Locals would definitely have an affinity towards him more than the Pathans. Playing on all these sensibilities, Khalid began working on strengthening ties with other gangsters who had so far shied away from the gang on the assumption that it was only for Muslims.

Khalid, being an old timer within the Bombay circle, roped in a number of emerging Maharashtrian dons including the BRA gang comprising Rama Naik, Arun Gawli, and Babu Reshim, who more than willingly joined the gang. This also drew other Hindu boys to the gang like Sunil Sawant alias Sautya, Manish Lala, and Anil Parab.

This was a big boost to the gang's ranks, and realising his work was done, Khalid Pehelwan left for England to the Isle of Man, where grocer-turned-drug-baron Iqbal Mirchi had offered him a partnership in his drug business. He later moved to Dubai, where he eventually settled down. In the future, he would meet Dawood fleetingly at parties and such, but the two never shared the kind of bond that they had had earlier.

In the meantime, Dawood grew stronger with the passing of each day. In 1981, Dr Datta Samant had called for a mill strike. This strike had escalated the joblessness and unemployment among Maharashtrian youth in central Bombay. Lack of job opportunities forced these youths towards the world of crime, and these young Maharashtrian boys had begun to gravitate towards the Dawood and Gawli gangs.

There were more and more non-Muslim members being inducted now, and Dawood's gang had a greater outreach than any other gang in Bombay.

He now had two Rajans in his gang—South Indian Bada Rajan and Maharashtrian Chhota Rajan—and two Shakeels—Shakeel Lamboo because of his height and Chhota Shakeel. Apart from the Hindu dons that Khalid had inducted, Danny, Sanjay Raggad, and Sharad Shetty were all reaching out to other gangs. The Muslim criterion previously requisite for those who wanted to be in Dawood's gang was forgotten, waning into the dusk of the Middle Eastern shores.

Khalid, the architect of the secular gang model, bid adieu to Dawood and his insecurities and chose to retire from the active mafia life. This was perhaps the only split in the mafia that took place without any violence and bloodshed. Perhaps that is why Dawood continues to harbour the guilt of being unfair to Khalid—the man who was instrumental in elevating him to lofty heights.

27

Mafia's Bollywood Debut

The white Fiat came to a screeching halt. Even before Mushir Alam could understand what was happening, three men came out of the Ambassador which had just intercepted his car, rushed towards him, and dragged him out. At a busy Worli intersection in broad daylight, Mushir could not believe that he was being kidnapped by men brandishing swords, a chopper and a gun in their hands. It was later learnt that the men were part of the most dreaded organised syndicate of the time——Amirzada, Alamzeb, Abdul Latif, and Shehzad Khan.

Even before Mushir could raise a word of protest or raise an alarm for help, he was bundled into the rear seat of the white Ambassador whose engine was still running and the driver behind the wheel was warily looking outside. The men forced him to sit in the middle and two of them sat on either side of him, while the other one sat in front. Mushir was blindfolded with a strip of white cloth and the kidnappers left the car behind on the road and escaped. Bombay's biggest kidnapping so far was over in a matter of less than a minute. The Bollywood mogul, Mushir Alam of Mushir-Riaz fame was abducted within yards from his office. Mushir-Riaz were known for making films with Dilip Kumar and they had shot to fame with movies like *Safar, Bairaag,* and the latest blockbuster *Shakti* starring Dilip Kumar and Amitabh Bachchan. Such an incident had never happened in Bombay.

On that fateful day, as usual Mushir had left his office M.R. Productions at Filmistan building in Worli at around 4:30 pm. He had an appointment in south Bombay. He had barely gone a few yards on the Annie Besant Road when he was ambushed.

What Mushir did not know was that he was being tailed by the white Ambassador soon after he had left the office. The car driver kept irritating him by coming dangerously close instead of keeping a safe distance. Only once he had an uncomfortable feeling about the car but he had promptly brushed that aside. But his heart leaped to his mouth when he saw the Ambassador suddenly swerve towards a side and abruptly brake in front of him. Mushir almost rammed into the Ambassador. Before he could give vent to his anger and scream his lungs out, the men shoved him into their car and took him to an unknown location.

Mushir grimaced with discomfort and tried to raise his head and peep through the slit that was left between his nose and corner of the eye. Abdul Latif, one of his tormentors, saw him peering furtively from the hood and pushed him down to the floor of the car.

The movie magnate Mushir was lying at the feet of the thugs. But he realised soon that they would not kill him but extract some money out of him. Mushir was trying to catch some glimpses of the place that he was being taken to. Suddenly, he caught a major rush of colour which he soon realised was a poster of *Sholay*. Mushir realised that he was somewhere close to a hoarding of the film. Little did he know that this would be a vital clue in tracing the whereabouts of his kidnappers. After ten minutes of further driving, the car halted and all of them trooped out. Mushir was helped out of the car.

'Watch your step, there is a plank ahead', someone instructed Mushir as he was nudged to move forward. Mushir raised his foot higher, climbed the plank. 'There are stairs ahead, be careful', he was instructed again. Mushir began climbing what seemed like wooden stairs as he held on to the wooden railings. He felt disoriented. Ironically, he never had any such scenes in his movies either. When he reached a landing, he was asked to turn and walk towards his left. As he was walking, he heard a chorus of children reciting some Quranic verses. Mushir had the sense of being in a building which was thickly populated. The realisation comforted him that he was not in some isolated spot. He was ushered into a room and the blinds were removed from his eyes. The first thing he saw was the photograph of the Prophet Mohammad's green tomb of Masjid Nabavi in the holy city of Madina.

The next few hours were very painful and intolerable for him. They threatened, abused, and slapped Mushir. They all looked serious and menacing. Mushir learnt that they were well aware about the business that *Shakti* had made.

'*Hamein sirf pacchis lakh chahiye* [we want only Rs 25 lakhs]', said Amirzada in a very polite manner and in a tone that suggested that Mushir owed him a lot but he was being considerate in demanding such a paltry amount. Mushir was forced to make a call to his brother-in-law and partner, Mohammad Riaz, and ask him to get whatever liquid cash he could organise and keep it ready to be delivered at a place which would be told to him. Obviously, he was not supposed to seek any kind of help from anyone, including the police. Riaz agreed and in the evening at around 9 pm, Riaz and Harish Sugandh delivered 2.80 lakh rupees in cash, which was what he could put together in the short time, to Amirzada and Alamzeb. Mushir was reunited with Riaz and a nightmare had ended.

28

Pathan in Patharwali Building

Sub-inspector Ishaq Bagwan had just joined the Crime Branch. He had been in service for over half a dozen years now, being an officer from the 1974 batch. But he was restless and wanted to do something soon. He was still reeling with anger over the way Sabir had been shot dead at a petrol pump by the Pathans and the Crime Branch could not make much headway except for the intelligence that the Pathans, namely, Amirzada and Alamzeb, had killed him. For Bagwan, this was a blatant assault on the pride of the police machinery. The Crime Branch was known as DCB CID, Detection of Crime Branch, Criminal Investigation Department and Bagwan was faced with a fresh challenge; the latest kidnapping.

Film producer Mushir Ahmed and his brother-in-law-Riaz Ahmed were big names in Bollywood. The daylight abduction of Mushir at the crowded junction of Worli seaface was a major blemish on the reputation of the Bombay cops. Not only did the intelligence of the police network fail, they remained totally clueless about the entire incident and the payment of ransom money, until thespian Dilip Kumar himself strode to the Crime Branch headquarters and met senior police inspector Madhukar Zende to register the filmmaker's abduction.

Dilip Kumar, along with Mushir, had visited the police headquarters and met Police Commissioner Julio Ribeiro. He apprised him of the whole incident and Ribeiro immediately summoned Zende to his office, assigning the case to him. Zende subsequently spoke to both the actor and filmmaker and respectfully escorted them to the Crime Branch, so he could take down their statement and launch the investigation. Bagwan was inducted into the investigating team and he sat in on the statements of Mushir and Dilip Kumar.

Mushir gave a description of the whole incident; how his car had been intercepted and he was bundled into another Ambassador and blindfolded, then taken to the first floor of a building and thrown in an office-like place. Looking for some kind of clue, Zende and Bagwan tried to coax some details out of Mushir. As a filmmaker, Mushir was always alert to details, and as he recalled the incidents of that day, he gave some very vital clues to the cops. For example, he had managed to see through a slit in his blindfold a huge poster of the film *Sholay*, while he was being driven through the city. After he saw the giant poster, the car took approximately 10-12 minutes to reach its destination. Once he was dragged out, he stepped on a wooden plank on a small platform which led to a flight of wooden stairs. As he was made to walk down a corridor, he heard a chorus of kids reciting Koranic verses, giving an indication of a madrassa on the same floor.

Bagwan meticulously took down details in his diary, but his mind had already begun working: 'A theatre with a giant poster of Sholay... After that a car drive of 10-12 minutes... An old wooden style building... A chorus of Madrassa kids...'

Immediately, he alerted all his informants and began working on his intelligence network in the city. At the time, Bagwan was known to be the most resourceful cop in town. As he sat, immersed in a file, he got a call on his direct line. Moving swiftly, he dashed towards the phone before any of his colleagues could.

'Bagwan sahab, *salam alaikum* [greetings],' a voice said.

Bagwan replied, '*Haan bol, kidhar tha itna din* [yes, tell me, where have you been all these days]?'

It was Baagwan's informant, Badruddin, known as Badr. Bagwan chided him for not keeping in touch. He was pushing him to help provide leads for an 'opening in this case'. In police terminology, opening a case means solving a crime or detecting a felony.

Badr said, '*Sahab, ek khabar hai, ek pata likho* [Saheb, write down this address]. That filmmaker Mushir was kept in Kadar building in Kamathipura, which houses the office of Alamzeb.'

'*Pakki khabar hai, ya...* [are you sure, or...]?' asked Bagwan.

When a cop asks '*pakki khabar*', he actually intends to find out whether the news has been verified.

'*Sahab ek dum sau takka* [yes sir, one hundred per cent], 'Badr replied.

Bagwan lost no time in replacing the phone, asking the orderlies to get the raiding party ready and leaving the premises of the Crime Branch. Before leaving, he informed his senior Zende that he was off to Kamathipura. The sight of police vehicles patrolling the seedy bylanes of Kamathipura is common to its pimps and prostitutes, so no one really raises an eyebrow when they see cops here. They could be seeking *hafta* (protection money) or executing a small raid. But this was no single cop on a bike or just one police jeep. Here were two jeeps and a police van. The police party seemed to be prepared for any eventuality.

As the police fanned out over the fifth lane of Kamathipura and cordoned off the area, Bagwan himself barged into Kadar building, first floor office of Alamzeb's headquarters. The well-furnished, gaudily-decorated office was empty except for Salim. Salim was a new convert, earlier known as Saniya Bhangi (sweeper), and had converted after his marriage to a Muslim girl. He used to look after the upkeep of the office and did errands for Alamzeb-Amirzada.

Bagwan took Salim into his custody, driving him back to the Crime Branch. Salim was a tough nut to crack but as it is said among cops, *Is patharwali building mein pathar bhi boltein hain* (even the toughest nuts crack in this *patharwali* building in underworld parlance). Within hours, Salim had begun to sing. He admitted that this was the place where Mushir had been confined during his captivity. But he could not provide any leads to the cops on the Pathan duo's whereabouts.

He did say that Alamzeb's father would know. Bagwan immediately went to Ali building on Duncan Road, where Alamzeb's ageing father, Jangrez Khan, lived. Khan was placed under detention and finally, after realising his position, the old man cracked, giving the police an address where they could find Alamzeb.

A police team led by Zende sped to the Kalupura area of Ahmedabad. They had only two important leads from Saleem and Jangrez: a white Ambassador with number plate GUJ-7999 and a *matka* (gambling) den behind a hotel. Even as the cops were sweeping the area for a *matka* den in Dariyaganj area, they found the white Ambassador, on the move. The police party began to follow the car. As Amirzada exited the car, the police party sprang on him and arrested him. The police also seized a huge cache of weapons which included three rifles of .12 bore, fourteen revolvers of Chinese and German Mauser make of all kinds .38, .32, and .22 and 300 cartridges. The police had not only arrested a kingpin who had engineered a filmmaker's kidnapping, but they had also nabbed one of the culprits in the most sensational gang-war killing of the time.

29

Typewriter Thief: Rajan Nair

Jails are supposed to detain people and deter them from further crime. In India, however, jails serve a purpose entirely opposite to what the criminal justice system purports to achieve. Sometimes, innocent people are turned into hardened criminals; people who are imprisoned mistakenly come out of jails with a crooked bent of mind, starting to think that the only recourse in order to move ahead in life is to commit further crimes. There are plenty of these examples in the annals of history of the Bombay underworld. The story of Rajan Nair alias Bada Rajan is one of those.

In the mid-seventies, Rajan Nair was a small-time tailor in a readymade factory by the name of Hindustan Apparel in Thane. He was known to be very skilled. But after toiling fourteen hours a day, he could take home only 30 or 40 rupees. Despite working for five years, he realised that he could not even get a proper house in Bombay and was getting nowhere.

In the meanwhile, he was trying to court a girl. The girl was interested in Rajan and thought of him as a hard-working, honest man. But many a girl has the mistaken perception that she must be wooed by a flashy lifestyle. So, Rajan also wanted to lead a luxurious life and throw his weight around, to drown her with gifts and marry her and settle down.

But when he realised that his meagre salary would not be enough to woo his girlfriend the way he wanted to, he tried to moonlight in several odd jobs like waiting tables and running errands for offices, but he really could not do much with his limited skills.

One day, with his girlfriend's birthday approaching, Rajan became desperate. His salary was a long way off and when he asked for an advance, his bosses refused. Hopeless and despondent, Rajan decided he had no option but to steal. He stormed into the office and picked up the only valuable thing in sight—a typewriter. Rajan lifted the typewriter, put it in a gunnysack, and made off with it. He sold the typewriter in Bombay's Mutton Street, known as Chor Bazaar, and got a good 200 rupees for it; with this he could get a saree for his girlfriend.

Rajan soon realised typewriters were used in all offices in Bombay and that the better or more sophisticated they were, the more the money they fetched. He did not have big dreams. He could have spent a lifetime stealing typewriters and make money off them, in a small-time racket.

But his luck was not to last long. When the police went to Chor Bazaar as part of another case's investigations, they were told that all their typewriters were sold to them by a South Indian guy who came every week with two typewriters.

The cops kept a watch on this Chor Bazaar vendor for a few days. When Rajan Nair came by with his weekly two typewriters, he was arrested. The Bhoiwada police made a very strong case against him, and he was convicted and sent to prison for three years.

Rajan's life changed completely after the jail sentence. When he returned to his house in Ghatkopar, he decided to form a gang. Within months, the Golden Gang was created. The gang ran its empire in the north-eastern suburbs of Bombay which consisted of Ghatkopar, Chembur, Vikroli, Mankhurd, Bhandup, and the nearby areas.

They began with extorting money from shopkeepers, restaurant owners, taxi-drivers, rickshaw drivers, and others. Within a couple of years, Rajan became a formidable force and the Golden Gang became an entity. Rajan soon enlisted the services of a good man, Abdul Kunju. Kunju was a brilliant student of Anjum-e-Islam High School but he soon realised that his academic achievements would not be as rewarding as the support of Rajan *anna* (a South Indian term for big brother). He became a trusted aide and a right-hand man for Rajan, who in turn became increasingly dependent on Kunju.

Smarter than Rajan, Kunju soon capitalised on his talent for scheming. He soon developed a subsidiary gang of his own in the Shell Colony near Tilak Nagar and became a force within a force. After a while, he grew so strong that he challenged his own mentor, Rajan Nair. In doing so, he chose the time-honoured way of proving his mettle; he courted, won over, and eventually married Rajan's girlfriend, the very same woman who had supposedly inspired Rajan into taking up a life of crime.

Rajan was distraught and utterly humiliated. He fumed and fretted and swore a bloody revenge on Abdul Kunju. When Kunju was detained under the National Securities Act (NSA) in 1979, he saw his chance; his gang attacked Kunju's gang members and beat them up. Rajan also unsuccessfully attempted to abduct Kunju's wife, his old flame.

Kunju was helpless in jail and Rajan was slowly and effectively eroding his base. Kunju decided to take matters into his own hands. When he was being taken to Vikroli court, he threw chilli powder in the eyes of the policemen escorting him and escaped. After days of playing hide and seek with the police, when the matter cooled down, Kunju returned to Ghatkopar. Soon, he sent Rajan a message; he wanted to meet him now.

Rajan and Kunju did not want a direct confrontation at this time, so the feuding stopped for the moment. Both of them waited for an opportunity to hit out at each other, when time would give them an advantage over their opponent.

When Dawood, who had become a notorious underworld figure by then, met Bada Rajan at Musafirkhana to speak of avenging his brother's death, the former typewriter thief was in awe of him. Rajan had visited Musafirkhana only with a couple of Dawood's close cronies, who included his most favoured protégé Chhota Rajan. It was then that the two Rajans were exposed to the clout and power of Muslim mafia in the city.

Rajan Anna could never have imagined that a don like Dawood would need his services. During the course of several meetings, Dawood opened up and revealed the nature of his trauma to Rajan Anna in an unguarded moment.

It was never hard to understand Dawood's motivation to destroy the Pathan gang. They had done the unforgivable. Sabir's death was the death of a substantial portion of Dawood's emotions. He was living a nightmare. Facing his parents after the wanton murder of their eldest-born was something even Dawood could not do. He was seething; he had always looked straight into everyone's eyes and now he could not even face himself. He sought to calm himself down but here was only one thing he could do: kill Amirzada and Alamzeb.

He turned to Bada Rajan for solace, and the man, honoured to be trusted with this task, soothed him and told him not to worry. He took it upon himself to find a man for the job. As the don of Tilak Nagar in Chembur, he did not have to look very far. He shortlisted two local candidates for the job; one, a small-time offender called Philips Pandhrey and the other, a wastrel and loafer called David Devasayan Pardesi.

Pardesi was a 24-year-old good-for-nothing, without a job, family, or a life in general. He survived on alms or the odd job. Work as a means of living was an idea that did not seem to occur to him. Rajan's eye was on this drifter, as the man for the job. Bada Rajan concluded that as Pardesi was pretty much expendable, he would be the man to shoot Amirzada dead in Bombay city court.

30

Pardesi Kills Pathan

His heart was thumping loudly. His throat was parched, his breathing irregular. His legs were quivering and he felt as though he was going to collapse any minute. For Pardesi, everything was a blur, even if things were moving in slow motion. He was finding it difficult to focus and equally difficult to hold his gun.

The brief Pardesi had was clear: he was supposed to shoot Amirzada and then jump out of the window. Pardesi clearly had no reputation as a sharpshooter. In fact, he did not even know how to hold a gun. Moreover, the thought of killing someone in broad daylight in a courtroom was preposterous. No one could imagine that someone could pull out his gun and shoot a gangster dead, with the tight security in place. Court shootouts were unheard of in India in those days, it was a willing suspension of disbelief usually associated with Hollywood melodrama.

Rajan was fully aware that there was no way to escape the court after a shootout. He also knew that once the police got their hands on Pardesi, the story would end right there. Pardesi had no family, hence no one would come to collect the money, nor would he have to deal with a distraught mother or sister. And Pardesi would ensure that Amirzada was out of the way. He could not think of a more foolproof plan. Hence, Pardesi, expendable if inexperienced, was commissioned.

Pardesi had been taken to Ulva village in Uran. Ulva was a community of Konkani Muslims who regarded Dawood as one of their own. Its hills afforded seclusion and the shots of a practising shooter were likely to go unnoticed here. However Pardesi, in his trademark style, had not done anything constructive at the range. He had just fiddled around with the gun long enough to get used to the recoil. He lived off Dawood Ibrahim's money and rested most of the day, a life he was easily suited to. From time to time, Dawood Ibrahim would irritably enquire about the progress of the new trainee and Rajan would soothe him into silence. Dawood firmly believed Pardesi was no good and made his displeasure apparent on several occasions. However, Pardesi's utility still served to seal the deal. Pardesi was a marked man with numbered days, but he was blissfully unaware of it.

Finally, Rajan decided it was time. On 6 September 1983, David Pardesi was taken to the city court at the City Civil and Sessions Court. He was uneasy and sweaty. Wearing a loose shirt and trousers with his gun tucked in under his shirt, he walked around the courtroom ill at ease. The one thing that he did right was to evade attention. No one noticed the nondescript man walking around the courtroom. When the judge called for order and asked for Amirzada to be led into the courtroom. Pardesi took his revolver out.

He tried to adjust his position to get a clear shot but all he could see were the heads of policemen. He had been given strict orders to shoot to kill. Pardesi was supposed to jump out of the first floor window into the waiting jeep, after shooting. Rajan, his driver, Balaram Venugopal, and Ali Antulay were waiting below the courthouse to ensure that he did not end up in the policemen's hands.

Pardesi's mind was blank as he tried to take aim at Amirzada. The policemen in front of him moved and suddenly, he managed to focus on Amirzada's forehead, and fired. There was a dull boom in the courtroom and Amirzada collapsed, in the middle of his cordon. Pandemonium erupted in the courtroom as people ran in all directions and the police tried to contain the situation. For a few moments there was utter chaos and Pardesi turned to run. However, Sub-inspector Ishaq Bagwan had caught sight of him. He whipped out his gun and fired. He took aim at Pardesi's neck and got him. Pardesi was down—injured but not dead.

Bagwan rushed him to the nearby JJ Hospital. Meanwhile, Rajan's men waited long enough to ensure the target was dead and rushed off. They assumed that as Pardesi had been shot, he would die too. But Pardesi survived; his injuries were not fatal.

Pardesi made no show of bravado. He was not a gangster. He just wanted his nightmare to end. At the first suggestion of SI Bagwan, he turned into a police witness. He gave testimony against Rajan and Dawood, implicating both of them in the murder of Amirzada. Subsequently, Bada Rajan and Dawood Ibrahim were arrested. For Rajan, this had become a death warrant, as being a much smaller fry than Dawood, he did not enjoy the kind of protection as Dawood did, and could be bumped off easily once out of jail. For Dawood, it meant that Bombay was no longer safe for him.

Bagwan took Pardesi under his protection and helped him start life afresh. But once an enemy of Dawood, an enemy of Dawood forever. Dawood pursued him everywhere. Pardesi subsequently married and moved to Dubai, where he sold audio cassettes. But he was forced to flee from Dubai too, and returned to Bombay. Finally, after a few years, he was found dead under mysterious circumstances in a hotel in Bombay.

The way Dawood pursued Pardesi until the end is an example of how vindictive he could be. Pardesi had served his purpose yet he hounded him because he had let Dawood's name slip. Dawood never forgave or forgot even the smallest of betrayals.

31

Circle of Revenge

The Pathan syndicate was wild. They could not have imagined that a rookie could just walk into a courtroom and kill Amirzada in such a brazen manner. At the face of it, they presumed Pardesi belonged to Dawood's gang. But on the discovery that a small-time thug like Rajan Nair was behind the killing, they were more outraged than enraged.

They had to take revenge and they had to kill Rajan Nair, as a response to the murder of their brother. Initially, Alamzeb himself wanted to pull the trigger. But Karim Lala convinced him that if he tried doing such a thing in the courtroom, he would not survive, as this time the cops would be more alert.

For days, they schemed, but to no avail. Karim Lala was very fond of Amirzada; a Pathan baccha, a Pathan boy born in the same land as him. He could not jeopardise another clan member's life now. He decided that the best way to avenge the killing would be without putting another Pathan's life in danger. And the only way to go about this would be to hire an outsider.

The Pathans did not have to work too hard to identify the right candidate. Soon they found the man for the job: Abdul Kunju. He had, of course, been an arch-enemy of Rajan Nair's for a long time, as double incentive.

A message was dispatched to Kunju, summoning him to come and meet the Pathans in a hotel at Nana Chowk. When Alamzeb approached Kunju, he was delighted. Kunju had always wanted to kill Rajan and had been waiting for just such an opportunity and backing. With gangsters of the stature of the Pathans offering to join hands with him in killing Rajan, he was getting a great bargain.

Kunju was a brilliant planner. It was for this reason that he had managed to upstage his former mentor in many ways. He told Alamzeb, '*Bhai, apun Rajan ko courtroom mein-ich marenge. Jaise usne aapke bhai to mara* [Bhai, I will kill Rajan in the courtroom itself just the way he killed Amirzada].' This was the only way the cycle of revenge could be completed.

Kunju also pointed out there was no point in hiring a professional hitman, as whoever pulled the trigger was sure to be caught. The police could not afford to be caught napping a second time.

Kunju was confident that the task of locating a triggerman would be quite easy; Rajan had many enemies. They just had to locate one of them. Abdul Kunju personally launched a manhunt for someone who could kill Rajan Nair in court. After a couple of days of intensive search in the Ghatkopar area, Kunju and his men found a rickshaw driver called Chandrashekhar Safalika.

Safalika was a victim of Bada Rajan's high-handedness and his atrocities. He hated paying the monthly *hafta* of 10 rupees to Rajan and his men. Moreover, one of Rajan's men was constantly making indecent advances towards his younger sister. When Kunju's men offered him 50,000 rupees *supari* to kill Rajan, Safalika realised he could kill two birds with one strike. Not only would he be able to take revenge against his enemy, he would also earn some money for his family. With 50,000 rupees he could buy two or may be even three rickshaws, or leave behind a decent sum for his family if he died or got caught.

The plan was very cleverly hatched. Exactly twenty-four days after the Amirzada shootout, on 30 September 1983, one of the initial remand hearings for Rajan was taking place in the Esplanade Court in the Azad Maidan Police Station compound. This time the police were not taking any chances. There was heavy bandobast in and around the court. Anybody who entered the court was searched for weapons. The judge knew that Rajan Nair was going to be produced in the court that day though the police had not mentioned that in the *roznama*, the court register where daily proceedings are recorded. But Kunju also knew that Rajan would come. They had decided it had to be now or never.

The moment Rajan stepped into the courtroom, flanked by cops, the tension was palpable. Everyone in the courtroom stiffened. Lawyers held back, trying not to stand too close to Rajan. The policemen had their hands on the trigger, ready for any action, even if it felt silly to expect another courtroom shootout. But you never knew what the Bombay mafia would pull off next.

The tension had perhaps caught up with Rajan himself. He too seemed uneasy and did not look anything like his usual jovial self. Jumpy and constantly on edge, perhaps he was being haunted by that maxim: that those who live by a sword, die with a sword.

That brief court date ended uneventfully. Nothing happened. It was a kind of anticlimax. No assassin strolled up, no one emptied the contents of a revolver into his chest. No hitman could get at this target even from a nearby building. Rajan heaved a huge sigh of relief. The policemen were relieved too, thinking that this time they would not get any flak from their superiors.

The person no one noticed was a seaman moving around the courtroom premise, not having mustered enough courage to whip out his revolver and shoot. Yes, the naval officer was Chandrakant Safalika though the nameplate on his chest read S.S. Bilai. He kept walking around, looking for the right opportunity but nervousness and uncertainty kept getting to him. Rajan was a big don and all said and done, Safalika was an ordinary rickshaw driver. He had never imagined that he would be entrusted with the terrible opportunity of taking on Rajan Nair. The scene was later immortalised in Rahul Rawail's Hindi potboiler, the Sunny Deol-starrer *Arjun*. The scene I speak of was a straight lift from real life. A hitman dressed as a naval officer moves around nervously on the courtroom premises, trying to get a shot at a gangster produced in court.

Safalika, after a great deal of hesitation, finally decided it was do or die, egged on by the awareness of his sister's honour.

A small crowd passed by and lawyers watched with little interest as the police escorted Rajan Nair to the van. Suddenly the naval officer disentangled himself from the crowd and walked briskly towards Rajan. The police officer thought the officer was coming to give him a message. Nobody took him seriously until the time he whipped out a gun. Rajan was astounded; he could not believe a naval officer could do this to him. Safalika shot him point blank range.

Four bullets were shot at Rajan, who was wounded on his forehead, chest, neck, and face. He was bleeding profusely. The bullet also injured a constable who was with Rajan. For Rajan, it was too late to be rushed to the hospital. He slumped to the ground at once and died a few minutes later.

Once Safalika finished shooting, he dropped the gun to his side. He did not know what to do next. The police party was too aghast to decide what to do; the scene was a frozen tableau for a few moments. Finally, they realised they had to arrest Safalika, who had made no attempt to escape.

32

Rise of Chhota Rajan

The killing of Rajan Nair alias Bada Rajan marked the emergence of another Rajan—Rajendra Nikhalje alias Chhota Rajan. Chhota Rajan was a black marketeer at the Sahakar Cinema at Chembur. His father Sadashiv was a worker in Hoechst in Thane. Chhota Rajan has three brothers and two sisters, and the family is originally from Lonar village in Satara. After dropping out of school in Class 5, Rajan fell into bad company and joined a gang of boys led by Jagdish Sharma alias Gunga (meaning deaf).

And in 1979, immediately after the Emergency when the police had launched a crackdown on black marketeers of cinema tickets, a group of policemen had also started a lathi charge at Sahakar Cinema, during which Chhota Rajan had snatched a constable's lathi and attacked the police party. He had managed to seriously injure five cops and shot to infamous public attention soon after that.

All the major gangs in northeast Bombay wanted Chhota Rajan to join their gang. Slowly, rising through the ranks, he had joined the Bada Rajan's gang and with Kunju's betrayal had grown into his trusted aide. He knew that Bada Rajan always harboured a grudge against Kunju for stealing his girlfriend and knew that Rajan Anna wanted to settle scores with Kunju, but had never gotten an opportunity.

When he heard that Kunju had gotten Bada Rajan killed in the court, Chhota Rajan was livid. Kunju had underestimated the might of Rajan's men. The first thing that Chhota Rajan's men did in Ghatkopar was to enforce an impromptu bandh. In those days, parties like the Shiv Sena had not started organising bandhs and it was a concept almost pioneered by gangsters.

Once the bandh became effective, they began to hunt for Kunju, who had sought Alamzeb out for refuge. However, Alamzeb shooed him away. 'You should be able to protect yourself. Now get lost from here,' he reportedly told him.

So Kunju was running for his life and Chhota Rajan was chasing him like an apostle of death. Wherever Kunju went Chhota Rajan seemed to know where he was hiding. Kunju managed several times to escape just before the two of them came face-to-face. Chhota Rajan had taken charge of the gang by then and for him, finding Kunju and killing him had become a matter of prestige.

Finally, exhausted by the pressure and absolutely fed-up of running, Kunju did the only sensible thing left. On 9 October 1983 Kunju went to the Crime Branch and surrendered. He felt that he would be much safer in jail than outside. But Kunju was not 100 per cent correct. Chhota Rajan had spent enough years with the mafia and the police to know how to bribe officials and get work done. He pulled every possible string and paid every official who would accept money in his quest to nail Kunju.

Eventually, Kunju began to fear for his life even within the jail precincts. When Chhota Rajan heard that Kunju was supposed to be taken to Vikhroli court on 22 January 1984, he decided that this would be his best chance to ambush him. Kunju knew, of course, that Chhota Rajan was after him and that he might attack him.

For the mafia, the real challenge is not only to get revenge, but also to replicate their enemy's action while getting this revenge. Bada Rajan's killing of Amirzada could only be avenged by the killing of Bada Rajan inside the court premises. If he had got bail and had been killed outside, it would not have been revenge in the absolute sense for the Pathans. Similarly, for Chhota Rajan, killing Abdul Kunju while he was in custody was the only way of getting revenge. If Kunju managed to get out, then Rajan's vengeance would not be as effective. He wanted to kill Kunju on the court premises.

Kunju was well aware of this age old law of mafia revenge. He knew that his best option to evade Chhota Rajan's attack was to remain in judicial custody and out of the courts as long as he could. So on 22 January, while he was escorted to the court, Kunju bribed the constables who were to take him to the court and pleaded with them to allow him to use his own car rather than a police van. He promised them that he would not attempt escape. 'I don't want to die. If I escape, Chhota Rajan will kill me. I would rather stick with the police,' he reasoned with the police party. He also tried to tell them that in a police van, he would be more exposed while he would be less conspicuous in an Ambassador.

Kunju was wrong. After the hearing, as he was driven back in his car, the group noticed that the Ambassador was being followed by another car. Kunju could not believe his eyes; Chhota Rajan had been one step ahead of him. He was following the Ambassador instead of the police van. As Kunju was about to regain some control of the situation, his car stopped at a signal near Chembur. Just then the car pursuing him swerved alongside and its occupants started to fire at him indiscriminately.

Kunju ducked, as did the policemen. The idea was for Chhota Rajan's people to fire a hail of bullets and escape immediately without provoking the police party to fire back. So they opened a volley of bullets, and the moment the traffic began moving, they escaped. The firing party did not know that Kunju had managed to get only one bullet in his shoulder, and that one policeman had taken a hit too.

Kunju had survived again. After this attempt on his life, however, Kunju became paranoid. He began seeing Chhota Rajan's men everywhere. Policemen recall that even in jail he sometimes woke up covered in sweat and screaming with fear.

For months, nothing happened. The police thought that perhaps Chhota Rajan had given up. But Kunju was still unable to relax. He knew that Chhota Rajan would not give up until his honour was vindicated. He would be waiting for the next opportunity to present itself.

The Rajan Nair killing had been carried out in September 1983. But for months, Chhota Rajan had kept trailing Kunju, proving that the frenzy of wanting revenge never wanes. The next attempt on Kunju's life was on 25 April 1984 when Kunju was being taken to JJ Hospital by a police party for treatment of his shoulder. He had been going to JJ Hospital regularly and the police never expected any danger from the nurses, doctors, or patients.

Chhota Rajan's charisma and courage came from the fact that he almost always managed to surprise policemen. As the police party escorted Kunju to the doctor's cabin, a patient who was sitting outside the cabin on a bench stood up, threw off his plaster of Paris cast from his arm and took out a gun, letting loose a volley of bullets. Another patient was killed, but Kunju escaped with a wound on his shoulder. Kunju had managed to escape yet again, miraculously. But this move by Chhota Rajan had caught Dawood's attention.

Dawood liked Chhota Rajan's exploits and the way he had doggedly chased Kunju for months. He had heard about the boy while dealing with Bada Rajan in the matter of the Amirzada killing. And when he saw Chhota Rajan's persistence, his planning and execution, he thought that it would be worth working with the boy. In Dawood's mind, nothing happened without reason and no one was involved with his operations without a plan or an agenda justifying their place in it. Dawood had something in mind for Chhota Rajan.

Dawood invited Chhota Rajan to his gang headquarters in Musafirkhana and subsequently to join his gang. It is said that no mortal has ever refused the invitation of Dawood. Chhota Rajan was no different. And soon after he joined the Dawood gang, Chhota Rajan finally managed to get Kunju killed.

It was sometime in 1987, at a small maidan in Chembur. Kunju had not seen much of Chhota Rajan for a while, and was almost thinking that it was safe for him to venture out into the public again without fearing for his life every single second. Kunju and several of his men were playing cricket at the maidan, all of them dressed in white, just like professional cricketers of the time.

As the game progressed, all the men's minds were on the game, and nobody noticed some new people, wearing the same white uniforms, join the players. Before anyone could realise that something was about to happen, the newcomers pulled out knives, pistols, and choppers, and attacked Kunju. By the time Kunju's men rushed over to their boss, Rajan's men had literally slashed Kunju open and riddled him with bullets. All his men who rushed up were also attacked brutally, and died horrific deaths like Kunju.

It was all over in under a minute. And just like that, before anyone could raise an alarm, the attackers calmly walked away. Chhota Rajan got his man eventually.

33

Enfant Terrible: Samad Khan

October is considered the second summer in Bombay. The month marks the end of the monsoon and is the interim period before the beginning of winter. But these summer variations seemed to have no impact on the insatiable libido of Samad Khan the Pathan.

This particular evening, Shilpa Zhaveri was exhausted spending an entire day struggling to organise a good meal for her man. But the moment Samad stepped into her flat, food was the last thing on his mind. He reached for her and groped her, growling, 'First things first.' There was no chivalry, no tenderness, and no caresses. As far as Shilpa could recall, his kisses were more like bites.

Her clothes had been ripped apart with no glory in admiring her in her nudity. Pouncing on her naked body like a ferocious beast, Samad began biting her all over. Then Shilpa spat on him as they both stood there consumed by unabated passion by the act. She slowly licked her own saliva off his body, sending him into a delirium of ecstasy, as he did the same to her—spitting and devouring his own spit off her naked body as if that would bring her to the pinnacle of her orgasm.

Samad had sex with several Muslim girls but he found all of them to be coy and inhibited in bed. And while Samad liked Shilpa's boldness, she enjoyed his aggression. The couple seemed tailor-made for each other. Shilpa was a revelation, often stunning him with her natural flair to please him.

Oblivious to their outraged neighbours, their moans and screams echoed beyond the closed doors. They had no qualms, as they bared themselves for a no holds barred sex session. From the showers to the kitchen table where vessels and utensils were flung with as much fury as the abuses and the dirty expletives that Samad would hurl at Shilpa as he shoved her and himself into her in all their warped glory.

Finally Samad would carry her lithe body, still wrapped around him, and fling her onto the carpet in the drawing room where he would satiate himself with animal-like passion.

It was 4 October 1984. Bombay's streets were full of vibrant crowds, dancing and singing on the occasion of Dussehra, the day when Hindus celebrated the success of Ram over Ravan—and the victory of truth over evil.

People thronged the streets at Vallabhbhai Patel Road, and mindless of their surroundings, everyone was dancing in a mad frenzy. When Samad looked down from the seven-storied Sikka Nagar building, he could not help but reflect on the series of unexpected events that had unfurled that week.

There will be very few Pathans like him. Abdul Samad Abdul Rahim Khan was known for his irrepressible ruthlessness, insatiable lust, and brutality. So much so that even his own ilk—the Pathans—did not want to remain associated with him. Bombay's largest Urdu daily *Inquilab* had read a clear-cut proclamation from his uncle, Karim Khan alias Karim Lala: 'I have nothing to do with Samad Khan. Anyone dealing with him may do so at their own risk, I will not vouch for him in any manner. I refuse to take responsibility for any reference made to me during any transactions.'

Samad was enraged. With his primitive notion of honour, he felt betrayed. The old world loyalty of the Pathans meant nothing to him now. His uncle, who had always been a hero to him, had become a malevolent presence. Being a Pathan, his uncle could have kept the differences, if any, to himself, he thought. He had been publicly humiliated and this only corroborated the rift within the ranks of the Pathans.

What Samad did not know was that Lala had his reasons for this drastic action. Every time Samad committed a crime, Lala would be hauled to the police station, Crime Branch corridors, and subsequently to the courts and put through a lot of trouble in terms of interrogation and detention, which he was growing tired of. Samad's actions had disturbing implications and the only way to deal with it was to declare that he had nothing to do with him.

But, stoking his magnum ego, Samad Khan thought about how everything he had done so far, and believed that he had done it all on his own. He fancied himself as a lion. He had no need for his uncle's clutch to do anything. He remembered, proudly, the time he was given a *supari* to kill a businessman called Jain in July, the same year.

Samad had entered the hotel, his burly frame not quite blending with the more polished people loitering inside the lobby. Approaching the reception, he asked in a bellowing tone, '*Jain kaun se kamre mein hai* [which room is Jain in]?'

It is every hotel's policy against divulging room numbers of guests to anyone. The receptionist was about to refuse but something about this brawny man in his aggressive demeanour made him cringe in fear that he might be assaulted if he did not relent. '1921,' he found himself saying in heavily accented English, hoping that the Pathan might not follow. But room number 1921 had already registered in Samad's head as he quietly slipped out of the hotel lobby and waited for night to fall.

At night, he went to the hotel, did not even throw a glance anywhere and headed straight to the nineteenth floor with two other men. He knocked on the room 1921; a bespectacled man of very small frame opened the door. '*Tera naam Jain hai* [is your name Jain]?' asked Samad. Perhaps no one in his life would have referred to him in such a disrespectful manner.

The man behind the door was stunned and confused but it soon turned into fear, as he looked closer at the three men in front of him. The next moment Jain was knocked into the room with the blow of a fist on his face. The men brutally kicked and punched him on the face and all over his body as he lay on the floor squirming in pain. Then suddenly the blows stopped and he was dragged on to his feet. He was quickly stripped of all his clothes as he saw Samad light up a candle.

The men held up his hands as Samad drew the candle and whiffed it around Jain's face. He then dropped the hot wax onto a bewildered Jain's scrotum and all over his penis. As Jain screamed in extreme pain and anguish, Samad's face had eerily drawn into a wide grin.

Ironically, big hotel rooms are engineered in such a manner that no sound should escape the room premises. And even if they did, the hotel staff remained discreet under the presumption that the guest must be having a good time with his companion.

After a while of torture, Samad grew tired and quietly took a rope and strangled Jain. He let go of the rope and walked out, the grin never leaving his face. It had taken him about five blood curdling hours to complete the entire process.

But Samad, being the unscrupulous Pathan that he was, was not known for being meticulous about the finer details of the contract and executing them. He later realised the next day that the person he had killed was S.K. Jain, a tax macro executive, and not Ranvir Jain, on whom the *supari* had been issued. He was moved to remorse, not at the mistaken identity, but because he had not fulfilled his job.

Not one to let go, Samad set out to Hotel Sea Rock again the next day, and this time around, got the real target and killed him. With his exhilarating sense of machismo, Samad Khan had completed his campaign of extermination.

✠

Samad Khan single-handedly ruled the roost during his sentence between 1983 and 1984 in Arthur Road Jail, despite Dawood's men having had complete control over the jail previously. The jail was teeming with gangsters from various gangs, most of whom were Dawood's men. Despite this, Samad was calling the shots. He would threaten witnesses there and people would come to him for help; he had even managed to get the jail officials under his control. Samad had a colour television and a video cassette player installed in his cell. No other gangster had that kind of clout in the jail.

Apart from holding darbars, he was also demanding and extorting money during his incarceration. His dictatorial manner and evident power made people think that if he could unleash such extortion from within the confines of his jail cell, they would not want to deal with him at any point. Out of fear they would just shell out the money, and he played on this psychosis for a long time.

He fondly remembered the time when he, Kalia Anthony and Abdul Kunju decided to take care of two witnesses who had testified against him in the murder case of passport agent Raja Singh Thakur. Fully aware that the case in the session's court was entirely built on their testimony he wanted to silence them. They were Ghulam Hussain and Naseer Hussain, inherent reliable witnesses in the case. His logic bore him that if these two men turned hostile he would be able to change the ruling in his favour. And once their testimonies were changed, he could easily get bail in the case.

In that darbar, where Anthony, Kunju, and his other hang-arounds were sitting, he called on the two witnesses. The first thing he did was strip them of their clothes. Then he called a barber and he asked him to shave off the hair on their heads, their moustaches, beard, and eyebrows. Once their entire face was shaven off, he warned them that the next time the blade would not be shaving any hair but instead running along their throats and slitting their jugulars if they did not take heed of his warnings. He conveyed to them that if they did not do what he told them to, he would have them tortured and killed inside the jail without a single jail authority or anyone else coming to their rescue.

Albeit by intimidation, when the case came to the courts, Samad made bail and walked out of the jail. Still absorbed in his self-mortified thoughts, he thought about the time right after the Jain killings when he had proved his loyalty and love for his uncle when he surrendered to the police.

Once Ranvir Jain's killing was out in the open, the police were desperate to implicate Samad in the murder but he was absconding. So the cops picked up his uncle, Karim Lala from his flat near Novelty Cinema and detained him. They assured him that they would let him go only if Samad surrendered, well aware of Samad's loyalty and ties to his uncle.

The police knew that Lala was the only one who could get to Samad, so they even threatened that Karim Lala would be implicated in the case if they did not get Samad. This infuriated Lala and he conveyed a message to his friend Haji Mastan that Samad had better surrender to the police. Through various channels, Haji Mastan managed to convey the urgent message. He exhorted Samad to surrender for the sake of his old uncle and even conveyed that his bail would be arranged, that he would be out in no time.

Samad knew the only solution was to surrender, so he gave himself in, for love of his uncle. Arrested in July, he remained in prison for only two months. In September, he was released once again from Arthur Road Jail. And as always, the moment he got out, he wasted no time in throwing his weight around, creating havoc, and threatening people.

It was at this point that Lala was advised by Haji Mastan to break off all ties with Samad, if he wanted the cops off his back. So, seething with rage and self-indulged mania, Samad decided it was time he branched out on his own. He would do things on his own and be a ganglord himself. He did not need his uncle's help or his patronage.

As he brooded, a thought struck him. He considered clearing any bad feelings with Dawood, following his domination of his gang members while in prison, and his ties to the Pathans, so he had at least one less front to watch his back on. Samad arranged a meeting with Dawood and extended his hands tranquilly, proclaiming his friendship and loyalty and diffusing any enmity between them. He affiliated his loyalty to Dawood, proclaiming that whatever had happened between Alamzeb and Amirzada and the other Pathans had nothing to do with him and that he was not involved in the killing of Sabir. Hence Dawood should have no reason to hold any grudges against him.

Dawood, although taken aback and cautious, admired the man's courage and openness and respected the zeal and honesty with which Samad had approached him. Samad had won over Dawood when he had extended his hands. A certain level of friendship had been attained, even if temporarily. Knowing this, Samad went home a relieved man.

However, the very next day, when he was sitting in a bar, an informant told him that Dawood's younger brother Noora had been spreading malicious gossip about him. Apparently Noora had been abusing Samad and proclaiming that had he not been Lala's nephew, he would have been done away with a long time ago.

Fresh from the hurt of his uncle disowning him, and manically puffed up with his sense of his own might, Samad smarted at the insult. Samad's animal-like mentality had been openly challenged and his notoriety questioned. Being a Pathan, and anyway known for his brash, brutal ways, Samad could not fathom the thought that someone could actually question his independence and self-integrity. He immediately sought Noora out and attacked him that very day, following the day of his truce with Dawood. He single-handedly beat him up, leaving Noora severely injured. Samad smiled at how, in full view of Dawood's acolytes, he had beaten Noora black and blue and no one had come to his rescue. Had he not made friends with Dawood he would have killed Noora after putting him through Jain-like torture, Samad grinned with pleasure.

Surprisingly, Dawood did not retaliate immediately, which Samad took to mean that he had understood that Samad had been justified in his actions.

✠

So on 4 October 1984, as Samad left his apartment, he took a long puff on his cigarette, and realised his cigarette had already reached its end. He threw it off the balcony. He looked at people walking past in high spirits. Gazing into Shilpa's eyes before he departed, for some strange reason, his longing seemed to draw him to her in an almost repulsive way that was not sexual, but suggested his desire to stay. He wrenched his strong arms off Shilpa's finely manicured fingers, and left. As he pushed the button for elevator, a vague sense of foreboding engulfed him.

The elevator touched the ground and jerked him back out of his thoughts, a couple of minutes later. As he walked out of the elevator, he felt the presence of death. Samad Khan stood transfixed: Dawood and his brother Ali Antulay, Chhota Rajan, and Abdul Hamid stood before him, stonily silent. They all had guns cocked in their hands, and none of them seemed to be in the mood to talk.

Samad opened his mouth to say something but their guns began to spew bullets indiscriminately. As the firing died out and the dust settled, it was revealed that Samad's bodyguard and the housewife who happened to be in the lift with them had sustained multiple injuries. Samad's own body had nineteen bullets in it. He died on the spot.

Dawood spat on Samad's face, the bile rising in his mouth. What Samad had not realised was that his assault on Noora had infuriated Dawood. How could Samad attack his own brother when just the day before Dawood had been kind enough to put his grudges behind him and shaken the hands of one of his arch enemies?

Dawood surmised that the truce was actually Samad's unscrupulous cunning and that he would turn around and betray his trust. Dawood could not see beyond vengeance and payback for Samad's actions, and was paranoid that this pledge of friendship was just another excuse to disarm him. Dawood had always nurtured the desire to personally kill a Pathan but he could not lay hands on them thus far. Sabir's murder kept playing in his head. The day he visited Noora in the hospital, Dawood was consumed by a mindless rage. He had made his decision to kill Samad Khan and put an end to a very violent chapter in the Pathan gang; one where true repentance is comparatively rare.

Dawood's killing of Samad Khan was the last straw for the Bombay police. There were already a number of charges against him, and with the Samad killing, the police came after him in full force. In 1986, Dawood left Bombay for the last time.

34

Dawood's Better Half

While Dawood kept himself occupied with gang-building, he had totally shut the door on love after Sujata's humiliation. He spent much of his time reducing his rivals to pulp and forming a close coterie of trusted members.

One day as he sat in his favourite seat at the Gulshan-e-Iran restaurant near Manish Market, his mind drifted back to that crushing moment when Sujata chose her family over him. The thought 'how dare the bitch' reverberated in his mind. Unaware of the heartbreak, his acquaintance Mumtaz Khan—referred to by friends as 'Kaana' in a derogatory way because he was blind in one eye—walked over to Dawood's table.

Mumtaz owned a perfume shop in Manish Market and he went to speak to Dawood about some dirty work he wanted done. Manish Market's shop number 12 needed to be ripped apart and emptied out; in other words, Mumtaz, for his own reasons, wanted to get even with the owner of the shop. 'I know you can do it, Dawood,' he said.

Bubbling over with fury at the moment, Dawood was in the perfect state of mind for a task like this and promptly agreed. Upon arriving at Manish Market, his rage converted into a sort of fuel for violence and he began to tear the shop apart. Seeing him in such an angry mood, people lost the courage to confront him; they let him go about his job. Having thrown every little thing out of the store, Dawood pulled down the shutter with one arm.

Mumtaz was extremely pleased that his task had been undertaken and completed with such clinical precision, and following the shakedown of shop number 12 in Manish Market, Dawood became a regular visitor at Mumtaz's home. Over time, Mumtaz found himself very satisfied with Dawood's efficiency and hard work. So, he invited him over to his residence for a feast. As is the unwritten law in most countries across the world, business is never discussed at the dining table. Accordingly, Dawood and Mumtaz were having a lighter discussion over dinner, when it happened.

Dawood had never imagined he would meet someone quite as attractive as Sujata again. He never thought he would encounter someone who would fascinate him like she did. And yet, here he was unable to put a single morsel of food into his mouth, transfixed by the vision of beauty in front of him.

His hands and mouth betrayed him and refused to obey his brain. As soon as she walked out of the room, Dawood immediately inundated Mumtaz with questions. Was she, Dawood wondered, Mumtaz's daughter? As it turned out, the girl, Mehjabeen, was Mumtaz's sister-in-law and the daughter of Yusuf Kashmiri, a small-time businessman. Dawood was blown away by her beauty and soon began to date her. Mehjabeen, on her part, had heard tales of Dawood's bravery from her brother-in-law, and fell for him.

Soon, Dawood would pick up Mehjabeen regularly from her home and take her for a spin on his motorcycle. They would regularly make trips to the beach, where they would share a plate of bhel puri and a few tender moments in the sand among other couples. Sometimes, they would sit at Marine Drive and laugh as they were soaked with the ocean spray. They would then seek shelter in a nearby restaurant and sit there for hours over chai and biscuits, talking to each other like excited teenagers.

There were days when Dawood would take longer to finish his 'business' before meeting Mehjabeen for their daily outing. On those days, she would gaze wistfully out of the window and imagine him riding down the road on his motorcycle, fading away just before she could touch him. Until finally, that same vision of Dawood coming down the road was no figment of her imagination but a reality.

Sujata's memory was a thing of the past. Dawood was so besotted by Mehjabeen and the role she played in his life, that the hardened criminal had gotten over his big flame.

When Kashmiri saw what was happening, he was not happy. He promptly opposed the union, as any concerned father would. Dawood's tarnished reputation was by now well-known among the Muslims of south Mumbai. However, ostensibly he buckled when he was told about Dawood's father's impeccable record as a policeman and a respectable man in the community. He agreed to give Dawood his daughter Mehjabeen's hand in marriage.

35

Escape to Dubai

A half-smoked cigar lay burning on an ashtray. A pen had just been laid down, fresh from scribbling. Impressions on the soft leather chair drawn up to the desk had just begun to fade, returning the seat to its original shape. A window was open, the curtains fluttered from the soft warm breeze that blew into the room. Everything in the room pointed to a presence, missing only the actual human form. As policemen looked around baffled, the cops turned to the huge trunk that dominated the room and broke open each and every corner of the room.

The heavy odour of tobacco and smoke still hung in the air. The air conditioning in the room was running full blast, and the fragrance of Paco Rabanne still prevailed. It was certain that Dawood had just walked out of the room.

Sometime in 1986, a crack team of Crime Branch sleuths had stormed Musafirkhana, the headquarters of the D Company just before midnight. The officers were stunned at the eerie quiet in the two-storied dilapidated building, which was usually the hub of activity even in the wee hours of dawn. People never slept in this building, especially those on the ground floor which housed the opulent office of Dawood Ibrahim.

Today there was hardly anyone to be seen. Armed guards were posted at the gate, while other officers went about raiding each and every room in the building. Some were disturbed from sleep, others had to hurriedly abandon their love making. Residents were made to clear the room, while the policemen searched inside with ruthless meticulousness.

The policemen were on the lookout for Dawood. They sought to ferret him out. But he was nowhere. Fifteen days after Mehjabeen and Dawood tied the knot, the Mumbai police began their crackdown on Dawood and other members of the fledgling underworld of the time. There was no way he could stay on in Mumbai, Dawood had realised. The police had managed only to seize Dawood's cousin brothers and a number of his men, who were arrested from Musafirkhana, that same night. The crackdown was part of Police Commissioner D.S. Soman's express orders. Soman had issued an urgent search and seize warrant for the arrest of Dawood Ibrahim. The police chief had carefully chosen his team of officers to ensure that Dawood would not be alerted about his imminent arrest. Since the time Soman had taken over the reins of the city police, he had carried out a sustained campaign against the mafia. Soman had given a free hand to the Crime Branch officers. Police Inspector Madhukar Zende had ensured that all the top criminals were either thrown behind bars or made to recant. Giants like Mastan and Karim Lala had been made to respect the law. Dawood was the only gangster who was still running free.

Until now, Dawood had cleverly kept his cogs in the police machinery well-oiled. His moles always fulfilled their loyalties towards the don and tipped him off, usually giving him ample time to go underground and apply for anticipatory bail in court and evade arrest. Dawood had become too big for the Bombay police. In a way he had become Frankenstein's monster—a creation *of* the Bombay police. The cops in their short-sighted wisdom had decided to promote one outlaw to tackle other outlaws. They presumed that it would be easier to undermine one outlaw in the end rather than dealing with a bunch of them. As Dawood would be their minion, their own puppet, he could never go out of control, they assumed.

But Dawood outsmarted them. While the cops believed they were using Dawood to cut down top gangsters and dons to size, Dawood was actually using the cops to decimate his rivals. Nurtured by the police as their informer, Dawood had become the police's nemesis, one that had grown its own head.

From Bombay to Daman, electronic goods to silver and gold, Dawood had it all covered. Gujarat, which was earlier the stronghold of Pathans, had also been snatched away by Dawood. The Pathans' clout was considerably diminished in the neighbouring state. Dawood was Bombay's big man, partly due to its own police force.

In 1982, Dawood was arrested under COFEPOSA of the Customs Act. For the first time in his life as a don, Dawood was arrested for smuggling. When he had been arrested in 1977, it had been for a robbery and he was treated as a petty thief. The police called him several times and detained him at the Crime Branch lockup. But after the killing of Sabir and his phenomenal growth, the cops had become a bit more particular in making arrests.

Dawood was acquitted of all charges in 1983. His gang had reached its pinnacle of power in Bombay by this time, and violence erupted in flashes before the city's authority. He was able to wreak havoc easily, in this city so controlled by gangsters.Dawood was high on the most wanted list post Samad Khan's murder. Even his bail in earlier cases was cancelled so that he could be arrested in Samad Khan's murder case. But he was absconding.

Somehow, incredibly, Dawood had gotten a tip-off just in time, managing to escape minutes before the police party raided his headquarters. The police had been fooled, yet again. Soman was astonished when his men reported that Dawood had flown out of the coop. He could not believe that Dawood had such a well-entrenched network in the force. In a high level meeting the next day in the chamber of the police commissioner, further startling revelations were made.

'How did he get wind of the information that we were about to arrest him?' Soman asked.

'Sir, he had got a phone call just 10 minutes before we reached the door at Musafirkhana and he escaped,' said Sub-inspector Vinod Bhatt, checking the phone records. 'Who alerted him?' Soman was still incredulous, as the officers he had chosen were of impeccable character and integrity. Nobody knew at the time, but the Bombay police had made a grave mistake. When the small team was on Dawood's heels, the police commissioner sought the consent and instructions for the mission from a senior politician in Mantralaya. This politician told the police commissioner that he wanted Dawood to be brought in alive at any cost. Only later did the inner circle of officers realise that a leak must have occurred in the flow of information, which gave Dawood the last-minute warning he needed to escape just before the police arrived. If the cops did not leak the information, the only source could have been the politician.

'According to our information, he managed to reach the airport and catch a flight to Dubai,' said an officer.

'But we impounded his passport!' Soman said, in disbelief.

'Sir, his passport was in the custody of the Crime Branch and actually in the locker of officer Raja Tambat. We checked this morning and it is still sitting on its shelf,' said Bhatt, with a wry smile.

Dawood had managed to flee from Bombay and relocate to Dubai. He took a domestic flight to Delhi, and then a connecting flight to Dubai. He had bypassed their impounding of his passport and used another one to escape, with the cops at his doorstep. The boy who was born in Dongri may have escaped to Dubai, but his fiefdom continued to remain the same —Bombay.

PART II

1

Making of an Empire

In 1984, few Westerners could have located the city-state on a map, let alone speak authoritatively about the place and its people. Arabs, Iranians, Baluchis, East Africans, Pakistanis, and West Coast Indians, by contrast, had a deep historical acquaintance with Dubai. At the end of World War II, it was not much more than a coastal village which had survived largely on its wits as its only indigenous industry, pearl fishing, had been wiped out by the war and the Japanese development of cultured pearls. But in these barren years after pearls and before petrodollars, Dubai quietly resurrected its trading links across the Straits of Hormuz with Iran and across the Arabian Sea with Bombay. As both Iran and India pursued policies of severe protectionism to build up their domestic industries, Dubai's traders found they could exploit their own light taxation regime by importing all manner of material into Dubai and then exporting it to Iran and the subcontinent.

In terms of influence, Dubai's ruling Al Maktoum family ranked second only to the Al-Nahyans of Abu Dhabi. The discovery of huge oil reserves in the latter emirate proved godsend to Dubai, which was struggling to establish a form of stability, and the other five emirates that formed the new state of the United Arab Emirates (UAE) in 1973 after the British decided to withdraw all its forces east of Suez. At present rates of extraction, Abu Dhabi's oil will last for another 200 years. After less than half a century, the Al-Nahyan fortune (which is interchangeable with Abu Dhabi's capital reserves) is estimated to stand at around $500 billion, making the fortunes of Abramovich and the other Russian oligarchs look paltry in comparison.

Abu Dhabi has been generous in its subsidies to the six other emirates of the UAE, which have no comparable oil fields. But it is a measure of the perceptiveness of the Al Maktoum leadership in Dubai which as early as the seventies began preparing for a future when Abu Dhabi would no longer be content to underwrite the federal budget. Dubai has modest oil reserves, which still account for 15 per cent of the city-state's income, but these will dry up within the next decade. The Al Maktoums decided to diversify; probably spurred on by the traditionally competitive relationship with the Al-Nahyans. Thus they conceived the plan to build Jebel Ali port, with its sixty-six berths becoming the largest marine facility in the Middle East.

While critics scoffed at this grandiose project, the decision to create the new port and trading zone was quickly vindicated. In 1979, Dubai learned a valuable lesson from the Iranian Revolution and Soviet invasion of Afghanistan: frightened by the instability in their own countries, Iranian and Afghan traders moved to Dubai, bringing with them their business and bolstering Dubai's economy. With neither income nor sales tax, Dubai steadily developed a reputation of being a safe place in the Middle East to stash your money. Since then, the emirate has always boomed during a regional crisis.

This quality has enabled Dubai to attract leading figures from many industries over the past decade. Viktor Bout, renowned as the Merchant of Death in Africa and Central Asia, used to park his planes in Sharjah, Dubai's neighbouring emirate ten miles away, while he received his cheques for services rendered to warring factions through the Standard Chartered Bank branch there. Gangsters and their dark professions are therefore well represented in Dubai, in that they have always looked at and treated Dubai as a safe haven for their headquarters. But their individual stories are usually well-rehearsed elsewhere; the action takes place everywhere but Dubai. They also play cameo roles in a much bigger drama, which is the city itself.

Dubai is a microcosm of globalisation—85 per cent of its population are immigrants drawn from dozens of nations around the world. There are several *lingua francas*, each offering its own advantage—English for the Brave New World of Emirate futurism; Urdu/Hindi for those who trade in gold or drive taxis; Arabic for the Master Planners; Russian or Pushtu to buy or sell cars; and Chinese for the times ahead. The location is perfect, rendering it a haven of peace and stability in a notoriously unstable region where Asia, Europe, and Africa meet. Behind them, the immigrants leave Europe's weather and taxes, India's exhausting noise, or Africa's pain in exchange for a life in Dubai where they buy, sell, and chase the dollar. With no tax to pay, this is the rawest form of commerce and for those who hit pay dirt, the rewards are immense; as a result, you cannot get off the treadmill of wealth creation for a single minute.

The city also witnessed a huge growth in investment by Western companies seeking to get a slice of the market. Dubai could not countenance the imposition of rigorous controls on the import and export of money, which the United States was demanding at the time, as this would have confounded the city's unique selling point—'Bring your money to Dubai: No questions asked!'—and undermined the entire strategy of turning the place into the trading and financial pivot between Africa, Europe, and Asia. It naturally started to develop the largest money market. And there was no control over this whatsoever—you could take as much money out and bring as much in as you liked, whether in suitcases full of cash, converted into gold bars or diamonds, through one of the many banks founded to take advantage of this ever-growing flow, or through the *hawaldars* and *hundis*, the unlicensed money changers who are the mainstay of the informal financial economy on which the migrant labourers depend.

The development of Dubai began in the late sixties, especially after independence from Britain and the 1973 oil crisis, which triggered an influx of petrodollars for infrastructural development of the city. Dubai's own oil stocks were a small fraction of Abu Dhabi's, leading to an initial dependency on the neighbouring emirate. As a result, the ruling Al Maktoum family strove to find alternative revenue sources as a means of lessening this dependence on the al-Nahayans. From the outset, this inspired Dubai's historical role as a trading entrepôt on the Arabian Sea, linking the commerce of Iran with that of Karachi, Bombay, and the east coast of Africa. Dubai's relationship with Bombay had powerful political roots because the city was earlier administered during the Raj from the Bombay presidency.

The expat Western community had begun to grow soon after the opening of a modern airport in the late sixties. Like the Indian, Pakistani, and Iranian communities, they kept to themselves. Yet all communities had much closer relations with local Emiratis although they did not mix with each other much, even if it was to simply maintain a good rapport with those who were sheltering them. One does not bite the hand that feeds one. Communities did not live in the informally segregated areas that exist now. There were very few villas and most people lived in relatively small apartments. Furthermore, access to the ruling family was relatively easy. Prominent members of *all* communities had no problem paying a visit to Sheikh Rashid and in particular his younger family members, including his successor, the current ruler Sheikh Mohammed, known as Sheikh Mo. If there was an issue affecting a particular economic sector or a particular community, the family was open to frank discussions on the issues. Any Indian, Pakistani, or Irani having some clout in their country of origin, affluence, and connections could easily set up a meeting with Sheikh Rashid or his relatives and discuss business.

Dawood Ibrahim was aware of this when he and Khalid Pehelwan had started gold smuggling from Gujarat and subsequently from Bombay sometime in 1981. It was this accessibility and the growing business interests of the royal family that Dawood and his men decided to exploit.

Although Dubai's airport was modern by Middle Eastern standards, bureaucracy was slow, hopeless but in its own way endearing. There was no special treatment for any community — Indians, Westerners, Africans, Iranians were all treated the same way. Queuing for various permits and licences took hours and often met with frustration but the pace of life was extremely leisurely and nobody minded. Palestinians were in control of many aspects of the bureaucracy—the Emiratis were not yet interested in sinecure posts and this was convenient employment for the Palestinian diaspora. This also reinforced the lack of discrimination although it made for a very arbitrary process.

Till 1980, the number of Pakistani migrants to Dubai was very high, as their country was plagued by civil wars and their economy was in shambles. Also, being a Muslim helped with the already lenient authorities of Dubai. However, from the early eighties, the Indian community began to eclipse the Pakistani community in size and influence, although some of the older Pakistani families boasting greater commercial success were better able to integrate into Emirati society. Along with the Indians, the most important trading community were the Iranians who had migrated to Dubai in the first decade of the twentieth century to escape the high import tariffs imposed by the Persian government.

Then there was Mirdith, which lay about 6 to 7 km into the desert beyond the airport. The UAE government started to modernise the area in 1982 by erecting twenty-six houses and twenty-six condominiums in an area of some 20 square kilometres, and putting in a road network; clearly thinking ahead. Mirdith was the first upper-middle-class area shared by wealthy Westerners, Emiratis, and Indians, and it is now teeming with residents.

Dubai may be soulless, but a kind of honesty underpins its fantasy reality as a pleasure dome for the world's super-rich. Only two things rule here: the dollar and Sheikh Mo. Dubai may be a huge, undemocratic, money laundering centre in the Middle East but the country embraces free trade and globalisation, it is stable in a region renowned for violence, it has not relied on oil for its wealth but invented itself as a novel force in the Arab world. Furthermore, as long as the United States and Europe permit the existence of offshore banking centres, they remain guilty of hypocrisy. For organised crime, these are equally important instruments, offering flags of convenience, shell companies to disguise illegal activities and freedom from prying tax authorities. The only credible reason for their growth and success is the fact that many corporations in the 'illicit' economy use them for exactly the same reasons they are used in Dubai, especially tax evasion. Once a house or apartment is registered under an individual's name, he or she has successfully 'washed' the money and it can be reintroduced into the legitimate financial system anywhere in the world.

There was a new influx of south Asians in the seventies, fleeing persecution in various East African states, especially Uganda. There was at this time no significant Nepali or Sri Lankan population, which began to immigrate later, in the early nineties. The building boom required cheap (and often dispensable) labour and the rising living standards of Emirati families led to the growth of indentured servants from the dispossessed of South Asia and the Philippines.

The fall of communism and the deregulation of the international financial markets in the late eighties triggered a huge injection of cash into the global economy. Traders scanned the globe for the most profitable opportunities. The clients they represented sought out their services for a number of reasons: some were looking for maximum rates of return; a common motivation was tax avoidance; companies were also demonstrating their commitment to new markets; and then some investors wanted to launder their money to remove the stain of its criminal origins. The sums involved were vast.

An even greater change has been in the shopping culture. Dubai is now home to the largest shopping centres in the Middle East. One of its chief PR campaigns surrounds an annual shopping month which starts from mid January: a consumer orgy which attracts wealthy shoppers from all over the world. The most colourful and frenetic shopping area is the Old Gold *souk* (market). So successful was the trading in the eighties that they opened the New Gold *souk* as competition—both of them thrived, chiefly on the export market destined for Pakistan and India, and Pakistani and Indian traders built up huge empires during this period. The gold *souks* were close to the silk and spice *souks*, the former dominated by Indian and Pakistani traders, the latter by Iranians. The most fabulous wares could be purchased here for very little money, but by contrast any modern white goods, that is, anything purchased legally and legitimately, were difficult to get hold of and Westerners and Emiratis alike would travel as far as Singapore and Hong Kong to import their modern conveniences.

Sheikh Rashid was a moderniser from the outset. He was determined to encourage the rapid development of Dubai as a commercial centre. Even before the early eighties, he had overseen the construction of a modern road system straddling all of the Emirates. He introduced efficient roundabouts at an early stage and in the early eighties it was still possible to drive from one end of Dubai to the other in half an hour. This is extraordinary to conceive of if you have driven in Dubai today; the city flirts with permanent gridlock as hundreds of thousands of vehicles (among them countless Hummers and other SUVs, not to mention the occasional Bugatti Veyron) plough up and down the city's two major arterial roads all day.

If you descend one level from the glittering high-rise world of new Dubai, you come upon the middle men clustered around the harbour and *souk* in Deira. Here, the traders shift commodities in and out of the boats all day long; stacks of boxes three metres high appear to move of their own accord (in fact, they are borne by tiny Bengali, Sri Lankan, or Nepali men with limbs like twigs); there are hustlers with fake Rolexes, pirated DVDs, and counterfeit computers; the jewellery and gold merchants exhibit their nausea-inducing displays.

Propping up these two levels, that of the super-rich and that of the traders-who-never-rest, festers a swamp of inhuman conditions inhabited by labourers from the Indian subcontinent, Africa, the Philippines, and China. These workers are usually tucked neatly out of sight lest they spoil Dubai's clinical beauty. Sheikh Mo was intelligent enough to appreciate that the vision of whole battalions of these poorly nourished workers being moved from their squalid quarters, optimistically called labour camps, in trucks, like animals, to the construction sites where they toil 12 hours in the unbearable heat bore some unflattering historical comparisons. And so he ordered the open trucks be replaced with buses.

✠

As his flight descended and began taxiing on the runway, Dawood heaved a sigh of relief. He did not like travelling by air and had to fight off a vicious paranoia every time he took a flight. As he began walking on the tarmac towards the concourse of the Dubai international airport, Dawood had mixed feelings of elation and apprehension. He was certain that now he had to bid adieu to Bombay and its mean streets. Maybe for the time; maybe forever. Now he had to make Dubai his Dongri, his home. Dawood had been to Dubai twice earlier, but as a tourist and not as a prospective resident.

As he cleared immigration formalities and stepped into the air-conditioned interiors of a waiting Toyota, Dawood glanced at the vast desert plains in a new light. At first sight, they were utterly depressing. Wide, endless roads, bordered by scorching heat and sand with the relief of the occasional building—this was Dubai. A place which, for many Indians, was more important than their own homeland. Suddenly Dawood felt homesick, and began to miss Bombay. But he realised he could not afford to be daunted now. He had burnt his bridges for a reason. He would now make this his headquarters and run his empire from this desert city. In a way it was good that the country was growing; he would get to grow simultaneously.

Dawood's intrepid mind was at work. Known for having one of the sharpest minds in the world and more cunning than even Viktor Bout, Dawood had now begun to strategise. For the uninitiated, Bout is a Russian ganglord and arms dealer, who managed to dodge the long arm of the law until 2008 when the Thai police, following an Interpol Red Alert, detained him. The United States has since then wanted to extradite him but Bout has managed to resist their efforts. Dawood knew that there was no way Khalid would patch up with him, his first priority was to find a new chief executor of plans. He had to form a think tank and an executive committee.

Dawood wanted to dominate all the lucrative but legitimate businesses; at least in Dubai, he wanted to appear 'white' by investing in and endorsing all these businesses. Right from Bollywood to horse racing to the share market, he aimed to spread his tentacles everywhere. There was to be no megabucks business that was not controlled by his cartel. Horse racing and the film industry had fascinated him since his teenage years, but in Bombay he had been too busy toppling his rivals and playing hide-and-seek with the cops. In this country, he would not have to deal with the law and its enforcers because he would ensure they were on his side. In fact, he would ensure that the government would be on his side.

The car came to a stop, almost imperceptibly. The driver politely informed Dawood that he had reached. Dawood thought then that the car had glided in the same way as his flight earlier; not a single bump or pothole, no sound or jerk to remind him of the bad roads he was accustomed to. In Bombay, he could have never travelled this far with such ease.

Dawood looked at the plush bungalow in front of him, which one Sheikh Yusuf, Dawood's new smuggling partner who had already set up base in Dubai, had arranged for him to stay at until he managed to move into his permanent residence. Dawood compared this with the dilapidated building of his past, Temkar Mohalla and then Musafirkhana—broken railings, creaky stairs, dirty corners, stinking corridors.

This swanky bungalow, with colourful fountains beyond the patio, pristine lawns, a colourful canopy, liveried waiters, a huge wrought iron gate, a marbled portico, and granite flooring was a different world. In Bombay, even the state governor or the chief minister could not have this kind of royal lifestyle. Admiring the opulent bungalow for a moment, Dawood decided immediately that he would make a bungalow for himself which was even better than this. Here, he would entertain the rich and famous of Bombay and Dubai.

Returning to planning mode, he decided he had to get his core members to Dubai. He knew that he could not trust anyone new to think or take decisions. While his mind created his strategies, he needed hands to execute them. Within his first twenty-four hours, Dawood had placed scores of calls to Bombay. The recipients of these calls included several senior cops, some budding politicians, and a few of his trusted loyalists. While he thanked the politicos and police officers, to his men he had one common command: 'Wind up your business affairs and occupations and leave for Dubai'.

Thus began the exodus of Dawood's acolytes from Bombay. The first one to join him was his younger brother, Anees Ibrahim, followed by Anil Parab alias Wangya (meaning 'brinjal'; he was given this name because of his brinjal-like, short and rotund built). Sunil Sawant alias Sautya, Manish Lala, Ali Abdullah Antulay, and others began trooping into Dubai.

Dawood's two most trusted lieutenants took several months to disentangle themselves from their messy police cases and seemingly interminable businesses to pack their bags for Dubai. They were the two Chhotas—Chhota Rajan and Chhota Shakeel—and they managed to make it to Dubai only in 1987 and 1988 respectively. Rajan reached

Dubai earlier and because of his subservience, diligence, and readiness to accept any task, he became Dawood's right-hand man. Shakeel joined the growing empire later and though he also displayed the same slavishness towards Bhai (Dawood), he had to be content with playing second fiddle to Rajan.

Meanwhile, Dawood's self-importance reached such a peak that he bought a huge sprawling bungalow and named it The White House. Obviously, he did not deem himself any less important than the president of the United States of America.

2

Wiping Out Rivals

All eyes were on Dawood Ibrahim. He looked at everyone seated in front of him carefully, as if weighing the pros and cons before delivering a verdict that was likely to change the equations of the underworld.

Just then Chhota Rajan walked into the room with a phone, his face suffused with the relief of a man who seemed to have surmounted a major problem and now needed only to enable his boss to make a final call. But the moment he entered and saw everyone, he decided not to pass the cordless handset to Dawood. Instead, he whispered something to the effect of 'Bhai is busy now and will call later' into the receiver and tucked it away.

Rajan then started to scan the faces of every man seated in the room. There was Sharad Shetty alias Anna, a special friend of Dawood Bhai and the top honcho of Bhai's betting syndicate, while on the other side was Rama Naik, Bhai's friend from his early days of struggle in Dongri.

Rajan was aware that Anna and Rama were squabbling over a huge plot of land in Malad, the burgeoning western suburbs of Mumbai. The feuding had reached the brink of violence, both men ready to spill blood if needed. But as both of them were close to Dawood, they could not stake their claim on the piece of land or unleash their minions on each other until Bhai had given them clearance. After several long distance calls and much whining to the Big Boss, both decided to take the matter to him for arbitration as they believed in Dawood's sense of justice and fairness.

Their awe for the Big D was to increase; when Anna and Rama landed in Dubai, they were immediately checked into five-star hotels and provided with swanky, chauffeur-driven cars. Forgetting their enmity momentarily, they were utterly impressed with Dawood's clout in an alien new land.

Several meetings were held over the next couple of days. Sharad Anna maintained his men had spotted the plot first and that he had begun the initiative to take over the land earlier. For his part, Rama argued that as he had obliged the land owner in the past, he was more keen to do business with him, but as Sharad's men had threatened him, the land owner was terrified.

Dawood was quiet, a mute spectator to the rambling arguments of his two top aides, and asked only a few questions. Rajan realised that Bhai was tired of these tedious—and tortuous—hours of argument and explanation, and wanted to resolve the matter. He had probably been ready with a verdict a while ago. After a few years of close association with Dawood, Rajan had managed to develop a very accurate sense of the man's inclinations.

Finally, just when Rama and Anna had begun to raise their voices again, the whole room fell silent and Dawood, after a few pregnant moments, simply raised his hand; indicating that he did not want to hear anymore. Not making any effort to break the long uncomfortable silence, he instead lit a cigar, exhaling dark plumes of smoke. The whole gathering was now fraught with tension.

Dawood stood up and strolled towards the life-sized glass window that looked down on the busy streets and traffic of Deira Dubai. On the horizon, the sun was setting, spreading its redness across the azure sky. He turned and said, 'Rama, I think you should let Sharad Anna take up the land. And Anna, you should adequately compensate Rama.'

Total silence prevailed. No one dared to speak, anticipating that Dawood would elaborate, explaining why he had not ruled in Rama's favour. But Dawood did not utter another word. He moved towards the door, preparing to leave the room. Just then, Rama who had been boiling with rage but had managed to remain calm and composed till now, stood up and said, '*Bhai, yeh galat baat hai. Mera to nuksaan ho jayega. Aap nainsaafi kar rahe ho.* [Bhai, this is not correct. I'll face losses... this is unfair.]' Dawood did not reply, smoothly exiting out the door. Sharad got up at once and rushed after Dawood, while Rama flopped back onto the sofa. He looked at Rajan and muttered in Marathi: '*Mala he naahi jamnaar* [this is not going to work for me].' Rajan tried to placate Naik but he knew it was futile.

This was the day everyone realised Rama Naik would cease being an ally of the D Company. Rama was not only a mentor for gangster Arun Gawli but also commanded a lot of respect amongst the Mumbai mafia. He felt slighted not only because he had lost a business deal to a rival, but also at the way Dawood had treated him, behaving so brusquely and haughtily. It seemed clear that Sharad had already got an assurance from Dawood that the deal would be his.

A furious Rama, upon disembarking in Mumbai, decided to do the unimaginable: he decided to defy Dawood.

Now, Arun Gawli had warned him that since Dawood had moved to Dubai, he was not the same man. Dawood had become very dishonest and treacherous, and wanted to undermine the BRA Company. However, Naik had always felt that Gawli was too sceptical and suspicious of Dawood because he had refused to help him on a couple of occasions. But this time, Gawli had proved right on all counts: Dawood's treachery, his deliberate intentions to undermine the Gawli-Naik combine, and his partisanship.

However, Rama had decided not to abide by Dawood's diktat. He might be a Bhai but he was not in Mumbai anymore, and had no business meddling in disputes which could be resolved locally, was his logic.

Sharad Shetty was elated at Dawood's arbitration but he was also apprehensive of violent fallout. Shetty foresaw Rama would not let go of such a lucrative business deal so easily. And his fears proved justified when he heard from his boys that Rama had been in touch with the property owner and had made no signs of retreat.

At this time, Sharad was still enjoying Dawood's hospitality in Dubai; it was easy for him to go and plead his case, complaining of Naik's intransigence. Dawood heard out Anna's diatribe patiently, then made a very clichéd but significant pronouncement, '*Kuch na kuch karna padega* [we have got to do something].'

A hackneyed phrase normally used by helpless people in desperate circumstances. But, whenever people close to Dawood heard him say this, they understood that the Bhai had made up his mind to exercise the extreme option.

✠

Sub-inspector Rajendra Katdhare was the first man in his Brahmin family to join the police force in 1975. Katdhare had spent a dozen years of his career in mediocrity. Like everyone else, he was waiting for the one big break that would catapult him to the big league of famous officers.

His moment in the spotlight came roughly a decade later, but it was nothing like what he had expected. In the summer of 1987 Katdhare became famous—or rather infamous—overnight. He was in his office at the Nagpada Police Station in south Mumbai on 24 July when he received a call informing him about the whereabouts of Rama Naik. The intelligence implied that Naik was in a hair-cutting salon in Chembur, the northeastern suburb of the city. Katdhare lost no time in rushing towards the supplied location.

Ensuing events have remained a mystery till date. The media reported several stories and came up with various explanations as a background to the incident. Katdhare claimed that he had warned Naik to surrender, but the gangster had opened fire at him and tried to escape. Katdhare was forced to fire in self-defence, fatally injuring Naik.

Naik's death became the most sensational killing of its time. Katdhare had expected a reward for this mega hit. But the incident led to several inquiries, including a magisterial one against Katdhare, derailing his career. In fact, all of the Mumbai police force went under a dark cloud because of this one encounter, as several questions were raised, and none effectively answered.

The media speculated extensively and spread various versions of the incident. A columnist with the *Indian Express* even wrote that Dawood's uncle Ahmed Antulay and a shooter called Danny had killed Naik near Ludo Cinema in Juhu and handed over the body to Katdhare, who then claimed it as an encounter. Others reported that it was a fake encounter; Katdhare had gone to Chembur with the intention of killing Naik in cold blood. Reports claimed this that was no encounter but an extrajudicial killing executed at the behest of Dawood. Some even alleged Chembur was not under Katdhare's jurisdiction; if he was really so serious about netting a criminal, he could have informed the Chembur police who would have cordoned off the area and gotten Naik for him.

Never could Katdhare have imagined that one encounter could force his career to sink so terribly.

Katdhare might not have been able to celebrate his career's biggest break, but the White House in Dubai had erupted into party mode. Festive meals and drinks were served and lavish all-night parties were held. Sharad Shetty was overjoyed by the elimination of his arch rival. The lawns of the White House had become a favoured venue for Sharad Anna's parties. He was elated: he had managed to bag an over 50 crore rupees deal in Mumbai and the main obstacle in his path had been easily removed and in such a manner that no one could point an accusatory finger towards him.

As a matter of habit, Dawood remained secretive about his moves. But once in a while he is known to drop deliberate hints just to impress his aides and lieutenants. On the evening of their initial celebrations, Dawood was standing in front of a full-length mirror and trying to fix his black bow tie, cigar pressed between his lips. Next to him, Rajan was holding out his coat. As Dawood prepared to slip it on, he saw Sharad enter the room. Dawood smiled at him, and his grateful aide came up behind him and hugged him. They both then embraced, patting each other's backs.

Sharad Anna asked Dawood how he had managed to punish Naik for his temerity, knowing fully well that Dawood would not give him an elaborate reply. To which Dawood only smiled and said, 'Trade secrets.' Rajan and Dawood looked at each other, appreciating the significance of this trade secret more than Anna could.

It was widely speculated in police and mafia circles that Dawood had managed to arrange a tip-off for the Nagpada police about the whereabouts of absconding gangster Rama Naik. Normally, in the case of such anonymous tip-offs, the cops do not inquire about the identity of the informant but nevertheless try to follow up on their illicit intelligence.

At times, they manage to hit pay dirt thanks to such tip-offs, but often they are taken for a ride as mafia members also try to settle their scores and use the police for this purpose. In Rama's case, the Nagpada police heard of Naik's whereabouts from a *khabri* (informant) and passed on the intelligence to Sub-inspector Katdhare.

But it was not the first time a police encounter had created such controversy. Even earlier, such encounters had been attributed to Dawood, alleged to be the handiwork of his clever plots. One evening in July 1986 when Mehmood Khan alias Kaliya, so called because of his dark complexion, landed at the Sahar International Airport after his trip back from Dubai, he was ambushed by the police and killed in the ensuing encounter. His wife Ashraf later challenged this as a 'fake encounter'. Sub-inspector Emmanuel Amolik later claimed they had received intelligence that Kaliya was arriving from Dubai. As Kaliya was wanted in several cases of murder and assault, they had gone to arrest him; when warned to surrender, he tried to fire at them. However, even the most cynical of police officers found it hard to stomach that Kaliya, who had just landed from an international flight from Dubai, would be carrying a weapon in his pocket and had managed to pass through UAE security and Mumbai immigration unchecked.

Amolik's plea, that he had fired four bullets in self-defence, resulting in Mehmood's killing, did not hold much water before the judicial magistrate who presided over the inquiry following the petitions of Kaliya's wife.

Incidentally, the background of Kaliya's killings was more or less the same as that of Naik. A meeting between Dawood and his erstwhile foot soldier Kaliya did not go well, Kaliya told an unimpressed Dawood that he was quitting, the don had remained calm and allowed Kaliya to leave Dubai. But it was believed that the information of his arrival had been signalled to the police in this case as well.

It was decided that Kaliya would not set foot on Bhai's territory—Bombay—ever again. There was a message in Kaliya's killing; whoever dared to rebel against Dawood was dead. Dawood had just shifted his base to Dubai, and quelling small mutinies against his empire back in Bombay was par for the course.

Amolik was a veteran of fourteen encounters and most of his victims included enemies of Dawood Ibrahim. Apart from Kaliya, other prominent enemies of Dawood who were killed in alleged skirmishes with Amolik were Mannat Khan and Babban Koende. Koende had dared to oppose Ulhasnagar politician Pappu Kalani, who was allegedly close to Dawood. But Koende's killing proved too costly for Amolik, who was arrested and prosecuted.

Katdhare and Amolik bore the brunt for taking on the wanted men of the underworld, and Dawood's syndicate benefited immensely. Dawood's rivals and renegade men were being conveniently eliminated, and that too by the police.

3

Mafia's Most Daring Operation

Bombay is often spoken of as containing several cities within itself. Decade after decade, people created more and more satellites to the mainland of the city and yet another section of them created ghetto upon ghetto in the mainland. Such was the story of the Kanjarwada on Musa Killedar Street. Kanjarwada was located in a lane approximately half a kilometre away from Byculla railway station in central Bombay. It took its name from a large settlement of Kanjaris, a nomadic tribe said, by romantics and historians alike, to have originated from the brave Rajputs as well as the beautiful gypsies of India. Little wonder that the women of such a tribe should bewitch even a hardened criminal.

It was a bright, sunny morning when Babu Gopal Reshim, the B in the BRA gang, was traipsing up Musa Killedar Street. Full of himself and permanently high on his power, Reshim was surveying his area like a king surveying his subjects. Suddenly, his eyes fell upon a thing of ethereal beauty. Bathing in the open was a local Kanjari girl. The sunlight dappled on her skin as if taunting him to touch it. Her body swayed, trembling from time to time at the coldness of the water. It was not the first time Reshim had laid his sight on a beautiful woman, and he usually got what he wanted. Believing no woman could want to turn down his advances, he moved up to her and laid his hand upon her breast. The thing of beauty suddenly screamed like a banshee and Reshim recoiled, more in shock than from any waning in desire.

He watched, dumbstruck, as a group of men rushed towards him. One of them caught his collar and began to slap him relentlessly. Reshim snapped out of his stupor, and retaliated at last. He remembered who he was; Babu Reshim, master of all of the squalid splendour that was Byculla, not some small-time ruffian who could be roughed up by some local *chhokra* (lad). He caught hold of the young man and beat him up, as the others fell away. The boy turned away humiliated and Babu Reshim swaggered away, albeit slightly shaken up. Unknown to him, he had brewed a new storm in his wake.

The boy was Vijay Utekar Kanjari, a 26-year-old boy from the settlement. The idea of someone walking right into his neighbourhood and molesting a young girl sent waves of anger through him. To top it all, Reshim had raised his hand against him and beaten him in full public view and he had let it happen. It outraged him to think that a bully like Reshim had violated not only a woman from his community but also his own honour and pride.

Obsessed with the prospect of vengeance, Vijay was convinced he had to take action soon. As is the case with the youth of most minorities in this culturally confused city, Vijay was disgruntled about several things. He was the proverbial rebel without a cause, and now he had found a cause. He was already watching how Arun Gawli's men would extort, bully, and terrorise his tribe, and nursed a deep-rooted grouse against Gawli. On top of this, now, all his hatred amalgamated into that one face, that one name: Babu Gopal Reshim. He could only think of one thing, day in and day out: how do I eliminate Reshim? Vijay took up with Jayant Shetty and Appu Shetty, brothers of Shridhar Shetty, Gawli's rival in this area. The brothers supplied him with the resources he needed to tackle Reshim. Now all he needed was an opportunity.

Reshim, like most local goondas, had not graduated from the habit of frequenting local bars serving country liquor. He often went to several of these which dot the area around the Saat Rasta junction and B.J. Road. On one such occasion, Vijay, accompanied by Ravi Grover, stood in one of these cross-lanes and watched as Reshim sat inside accompanied by his goons. Each time he caught sight of Reshim laughing and making merry through the flimsy curtain at the entrance, he could hardly think amidst the noise of anger in his head. Finally, the blood rushed to his face and he could control himself no longer. He whipped out his country-made pistol and fired two shots at Reshim, screaming, '*Saaley! Tere maa ki...Aurat log pe nazar daalta hai... Idhar hi gaadh dega main tereko...* [You a******! Setting your dirty eyes on women, eh? I'll bury you on this spot...]'

Reshim took a while to realise what was happening and ducked for cover. Never in his wildest dreams had he imagined a boy like Vijay would pull a stunt like this. His company began to fire back, but under cover of their fire, Vijay had fled the spot. Seeing this, Reshim left too.

This debacle was yet another slap in Vijay's face. Reshim had escaped unharmed once more. But Vijay had learnt that he had to think ahead; he had to have a plan. He began racking his brain for ideas. Now Vijay was not just avenging with emotion but also with intent; the intent created by pure, unadulterated evil.

In the meanwhile, word of Vijay's exploits had reached the ears of Chhota Rajan. The harbinger of the news saw only the calm exterior of Rajan's face; no part of the plan formulating in his mind was betrayed. Reshim had been an annoyance and intrusion in this area for a while, to Rajan's mind. It was about time he was put in his place. And what better way than to use an unthinking chit of a boy whom no one would link to any other don? He decided to seek out Vijay Utekar for an audience.

Meanwhile, of his own initiative, Vijay was formulating a plan that was the mother of all plans. Babu Reshim had gotten into a brawl with Raja Karmerkar, another small-time goon from Byculla, in one of the country bars. The police were out for an arrest and they decided to take Reshim in for assault and grievous injury. Subsequently, Reshim was summoned to the Agripada Police Station. He had made a pact with the police that he should never be arrested in full public view nor dragged nor pushed into the van and in exchange, he would respond to any of their summons immediately; so he went quietly. Reshim was now booked under Section 307 of the IPC, attempt to murder, and imprisoned at the Jacob Circle police lock-up which is the common lock-up for the six police stations in the vicinity.

It is often quoted by the wise that when a man has nothing left to lose, his aim becomes an obsession which can only lead to achievement. There's nowhere to go but up when you hit rock bottom. Vijay Utekar was in a similar position. He was already on the wrong side of Gawli, and had even openly defied the don by taking up with his rivals. He had also failed in every attempt to kill Reshim, and was feeling helpless and humiliated.

Vijay Utekar heard that Reshim was at the Jacob Circle lock-up, and came up with the most inconceivable act of audacity. He finally met with Chhota Rajan, who pledged to support Vijay in entirety in any attempt on Reshim's life. But even he could not have imagined what Vijay had in his mind. On 5 March 1987, Vijay arrived at the Jacob Circle lock-up at 1:30 am with Jagdish Khandwal, Kishore Maheshkar, Ravi Grover, and Raju Shankar in tow. As he had no car of his own, he hired two taxis to take them there. One person was stationed outside to hold the two taxi drivers at gunpoint to ensure their escape. Initially, Vijay tried to convince the guard, policeman Uttam Garte, that he wanted to deliver liquor to Reshim but he refused. Vijay then retreated and hurled grenades at the gate, thus blowing it to bits.

All of them then stormed the jail and rushed towards cell number 1 on the ground floor of the lock-up, where Reshim had been detained. Vijay used the hammer he was carrying to break the lock of the cell. At first thinking someone was making a bid to break him out of prison, Reshim was horrified when he saw Vijay rush towards the door of the cell and savagely attack the lock. He backed up against the wall of the cell when Vijay fired. Three shots hit Reshim hard, at once, and he was dead before he hit the ground. Fury seized Vijay. It could not be! He could not allow Reshim to die such a quick, painless death. He took his hammer and began to attack Reshim's head till his skull turned to pulp, continuing long after it was possible for Reshim could feel the pain. All that remained of Reshim's head was a mash of brain mixed with bits of bone, splattered across the cold, stone floor of the cell.

The police officials at the scene were shell-shocked, rendered motionlessness. They later recalled Vijay shouting each time he raised the hammer, '*Mazha naav Vijay Utekar aahe* [my name is Vijay Utekar]!' It seemed as though each blow was to ensure Reshim learnt a lesson he would never forget though the man was long gone beyond the purview of mortal pain or comprehension.

Riding on the satisfaction of having been avenged, Vijay escaped from the prison with his accomplices. The two taxis outside served their purpose and the four vanished into the darkness of the night, but not into oblivion.

It was over within a few minutes. Senior Inspector Madhukar Zende, who was in charge of the Agripada Police Station, arrived at the lock-up and began to take down all details and make up a *panchnama* (report). Zende found five live bombs and some bullets in the lock-up. Police constable Ahire and others were sent to the JJ Hospital, as was the badly shattered corpse of Babu Reshim for a postmortem. Ahire succumbed to his injuries after a few hours. Witnesses, who included police constables and other détenus, identified two of the miscreants as Vijay and his accomplice Keshava.

The next morning, there was a huge uproar. Who would ever have imagined that a convict would be murdered so brutally inside a prison? The newspapers were full of outrage at Utekar's actions. The government immediately responded by setting up a commission to investigate the events of that night. As it always happens in the wake of such events, even the public was shaken out of its reverie and driven to censure. But even after this, there was no real action. As always, it seemed that the persons who took action were completely different from those who were elected to act. Moreover, Utekar had not killed someone known to be a saint; rather, he had helped rid the city of some scum.

But the police had not forgotten the insult; someone had challenged their absoluteness. After that day, Vijay Utekar was hunted like an animal and for him, no place was safe enough. Everywhere he went, the police were only two steps behind him. Now that the act had been committed, his former protectors and supporters were no longer ready to be associated with him for fear of being implicated. Every door closed in his face and Vijay Utekar was on his own, running for his life.

As Wu Ch'I, an official of the Ch'ing period, is known to have said: 'Now the field of battle is a land of standing corpses; those determined to die will live; those who hope to escape with their lives will die.' After having survived the storming of the prison, Vijay believed he was invincible and was actually under the illusion that he would come out standing. But his optimism was foolhardy. He was finally cornered at a hotel in Dadar in October that same year, by cops Vasant Dhoble and Kishore Phadnis, who disguised themselves as milkmen. They entered the hotel and as Vijay tried to flee, he was shot dead. A bag full of bombs was said to have been found in his possession.

The case that had shaken up the entire police administration had finally culminated with the encounter of Vijay Utekar. The police had gotten their way and eliminated him. It is uncommon for the police to rely on the judiciary for justice in these matters. Moreover, with Utekar it was personal. Not only had he broken into a prison, the last bastion of the police, but he had also killed an officer on duty. There was only one punishment for this crime: execution. Some rules never change.

Jagdish Khandwal, Kishore Maheshkar, Ravi Grover, and Raju Shankar were also eventually arrested. The case seemed to be an open and shut one. However, strangely, the case registered against Vijay Utekar and others was filed under sections 123 and 87; for murder and rioting. No action was taken to book them for storming a prison and attacking an undertrial or police officials for that matter. Of the four accomplices who were taken to court, Jagdish Khandwal was discharged from the case for lack of evidence and the remaining three were sentenced to life by the sessions court. However, on filing a subsequent appeal in the high court, all three were acquitted. Vijay Utekar was the only one who was martyred at the altar of Reshim's rival gangs. This story was to set a precedent in the history of gang war in the city.

Much later when the dust was beginning to settle, the *khabri* (information) network went into overdrive over the person who had played the most pivotal role in the entire incident, who had remained camouflaged: Dawood Ibrahim Kaskar. It was said that Dawood had arranged for the entire spectacle while coolly taking a backseat himself, enjoying the proceedings from afar. It is always in the squabble of the monkeys that the cat gets away.

A police dossier states, 'When the fact that Dawood had masterminded the killing of Babu Reshim came to light, the enmity between Dawood and Rama Naik/Arun Gawli groups increased.'

While the police could not substantiate this with evidence, the story soon broke. Everyone now knew of the treacherous nature of Dawood's machinations. He had used Vijay Utekar as a mere pawn in his bid to oust Babu Reshim, and he had succeeded.

Haji Mastan.
Photo courtesy: Press Trust of India.

Haji Mastan with his adopted son Sundar Shekhar (right).
Photo courtesy: Retired Assistant Commissioner of Mumbai Police (ACP), Ishaq Bagwan.

Karim Lala (left) Varadarajan Mudaliar (centre) with Jenabai Daruwali (right).

Amirzada   Alamzeb

Dawood Ibrahim with the Pathans after their truce in the eighties.
Photo courtesy: Retired Assistant Commissioner of Mumbai Police (ACP), Ishaq Bagwan.

Dawood Ibrahim in later years.
Photo courtesy: Press Trust of India.

Babu Reshim (above), Rama Naik (left), and Arun Gawli (right) of the BRA Gang.
Photo courtesy: Retired Assistant Commissioner of Mumbai Police (ACP), Ishaq Bagwan.

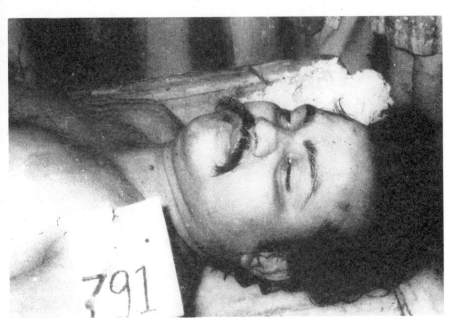

Dawood Ibrahim's elder brother Sabir after being killed on 12 February 1981.
Photo courtesy: Retired Assistant Commissioner of Mumbai Police (ACP), Ishaq Bagwan.

Dawood Ibrahim's younger brother Anees Ibrahim.
Photo courtesy: Press Trust of India.

Manya Surve, the mastermind behind Sabir's murder.

Photo courtesy: Retired Assistant Commissioner of Mumbai Police (ACP), Ishaq Bagwan.

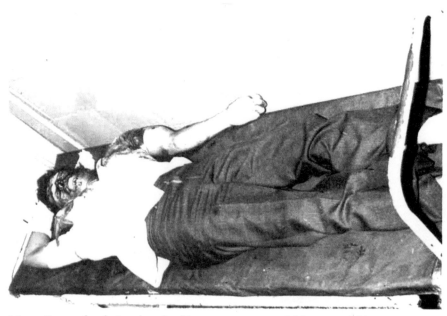

Manya Surve after being shot dead in an encounter on 23 January 1982.

Photo courtesy: Retired Assistant Commissioner of Mumbai Police (ACP), Ishaq Bagwan.

David Pardesi, the assassin of
Amirzada.
*Photo courtesy: Retired Assistant
Commissioner of Mumbai Police (ACP),
Ishaq Bagwan.*

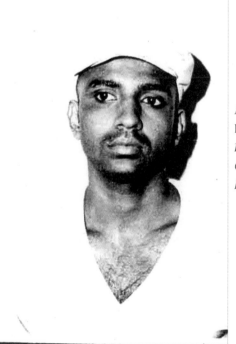

Abdul Kunju, the assassin of Bada
Rajan.
*Photo courtesy: Retired Assistant
Commissioner of Mumbai Police (ACP),
Ishaq Bagwan.*

Dawood Ibrahim with Chhota Rajan before they fell out.
Photo courtesy: MID-DAY.

Chhota Shakeel
Photo courtesy: Press Trust of India.

Chhota Shakeel, Sunil Sawant alias Sautya (left), and Abu Salem (right) are a few of the noted members of D Company.
Photo courtesy: Retired Assistant Commissioner of Mumbai Police (ACP), Ishaq Bagwan.

4

End of Dawood-Gawli Alliance

Unlike Babu Reshim's killing while in lock-up, Rama Naik's elimination could not be camouflaged as a police encounter. Arun Gawli had managed to see the strategic and systematic weakening of his gang by Dawood Ibrahim. Dawood, who claimed innocence in both killings, had obliterated the B and R of the infamous troika of BRA gang in two cruel strokes. Now, Gawli remained the only surviving member of the trio.

He began to regroup and strengthen his fledgling gang. Gawli's Maharashtrian boys had a presence in three pockets of the city: Kanjurmarg in the northeastern suburbs as Gawli had worked in a company there and had developed local contacts, Tulsiwadi in Tardeo and Dagdi Chawl, and Peon chawls in Byculla (in central Bombay), where he and his men—Ashok Joshi, Sada Pawle known as Sada Mama, Ganesh Tandel alias Vakil, Raju Mirashi, and Sunil Ghate—lived. At the time, Gawli's gang was the only one which boasted of two Christian sharpshooters, both of them known for their ruthlessness and slavish loyalty to Gawli: Raju Phillips and Paul Newman. Not the Hollywood actor, though, just your plain old Mumbaikar from Goa.

Gawli decided to zero in on Dawood's top confidantes in the city, those who still generated income for him. Soon, he pinpointed Satish Raje as one such trusted aide, a man who handled several major operations of the gang. It was certain that Raje's killing would cause a severe setback to Dawood's operations in the city. So, it was unanimously decided that Raje must die as a payback for Naik and an elaborate plan was hatched.

Raje was well aware of the fact that it was not an easy task to be Dawood's aide de camp in Bombay in his absence, seeing as his boss had left behind several groups of his bloodthirsty enemies. These deadly enemies included the Pathans and minions of Mastan. The threats of Bashu Dada and Abdul Kunju in the Chembur area were still not ruled out entirely since Dawood's relocation to Dubai. Moreover, he had become complacent and had been recklessly taking on his enemies. Raje inherited not only these ongoing rivalries but also a growing sense of insecurity from myriad gangs in the city.

Being a mafia man and one of Dawood's sharpshooters, Raje was intimate with the intricacies of mafia killings. Two shooters follow their quarry's car, halt it next to the car at a signal, point the gun, shoot mindlessly, and scurry off. This was the general modus operandi of most killings. Raje got himself a heavily fortified car with tinted black glasses and always sat in the middle of the rear seat with two bouncers on either side of him and one more in the front seat. He felt secure with this arrangement, but he forgot that security has failed many a target: even the president of the United States or Indian prime ministers can be killed if the killers are determined enough.

And these were determined men. Gawli and his men, which included Sada Pawle, Vijay Tandel, Paul Newman, Ganesh Vakil, and other boys from Dagdi Chawl, followed Raje from his den in Parel and decided to strike near Nagpada junction on 21 November 1988. When Raje's car reached the Mazgaon-Nagpada junction, two cars intercepted it. The plan was made with elaborate precision and with utmost care to complete the killing in less than a minute.

Before Raje's bouncers could get even a whiff of his assailants' plans, three hammers shattered the windowpanes of the car. Until then, hammers were not used in encounters in Bombay. Newman honed in on Raje, spotting him in between his bouncers, while others, as per instructions, kept the bouncers engaged. Nine bullets were pumped into Raje, leaving him dead on the spot along with his three bouncers.

The killing completely rattled Dawood. Not only had he lost his top man on home turf, Gawli had managed to kill a much-protected fox like Raje swiftly, reacting within months.

With this move, Gawli had declared war against Dawood. Now, he just could not be ignored. Dawood immediately assigned the task of avenging Raje's killing to his Man Friday, Rajan. Rajan's brief was clear: settle the score within a few days and cause greater damage to Gawli.

Rajan immediately began to scout for bigger wickets amongst the members of Gawli's gang. Finally, he zeroed in on Ashok Joshi, who was almost like an elder brother to Gawli. Rajan then bribed Joshi's driver Shyamsunder Nair, who tipped him off about Joshi's movements.

The trap was laid near the exurb of Panvel. Within fifteen days, Rajan activated his best shooters Sautya and Wangya.

It was a chilly night on 3 December 1988. Shyamsunder Nair smiled to himself as he drove his master, gangster Ashok Joshi, and three of his fellow gangsters towards Pune. While Joshi was engaged in conversation with the other occupants of the car, only Nair knew that a hit squad of fifteen men from Joshi's rival Dawood Ibrahim Kaskar's gang was on its way to intercept the vehicle.

The hit squad was led by Rajendra Nikhalje alias Chhota Rajan, who was still with Dawood at the time. He left his Tilak Nagar residence and was joined by Sautya, regarded by some as the Chhota Shakeel of the eighties. Sautya was armed with an AK-47 assault rifle and fifteen automatic handguns. Others joined the duo on the way, including Jayendra alias Bhai Thakur from Virar. The guns were distributed as the five cars sped towards Pune.

Nair had recently switched loyalties and had informed the rival camp of Joshi's plans to go to Pune that night. Wasting no time, Dawood, who had been aching to eliminate Joshi, ordered Rajan to ensure that Joshi was killed on the way.

The bloody face-off occurred near Panvel, where the attacking cars surrounded Joshi's car and the assailants jumped out. Joshi, who had for some time begun to suspect Nair, immediately recognised his treachery, drew his gun, and shot Nair through the head, cursing.

The shot elicited a volley of bullets from Rajan and his men, and Joshi's car was riddled with countless rounds. Blood and flesh splattered the interior of the car, and Joshi and his three henchmen were killed on the spot. Within seconds, Rajan sped away with his men as the car slowly fell apart, after having been hammered by their bullets.

With this killing, the battle lines were clearly drawn between two erstwhile friends, both wanting to prove their supremacy. The think tanks of both gangs began to plot each other's downfall, drawing up lists of probable targets.

And then began a violent and unabated chain of bloodletting. Hoteliers, financiers, gang sympathisers, financiers, and supporters on each side were eliminated with impunity. Bombay's police were reduced to mere spectators though a section of the top brass believed it was good that the gangsters were killing each other and thus reducing the number of outlawed people. What they did not realise was that the escalating law and order situation had rendered the common man vulnerable and the city unsafe. And as this spate of gang violence rocked the city, the mafia stooped to a new low and violated its own cardinal principles.

Family's blood is sacred and should never be spilled, howsoever bitter the animosity between the two warring groups, was a key tenet of mafia rule in Bombay. Family members who were part of the mafia gang were excluded from amnesty but the mafia never targeted those who were not involved in the murky business of organised crime.

Now, Dawood knew that Gawli did not have brains of his own. Earlier he had thrived on the cunningness of Rama Naik and Babu Reshim and when both of them had been killed, Gawli took Ashok Joshi as his mentor. After Joshi's killing, Gawli consulted his older brother, Papa Gawli. Gawli rarely left Dagdi Chawl but Papa Gawli walked on the street without reserve. Papa assumed that Dawood upheld the decree of mafia ethics and would not target him.

On 22 January 1990, Dawood's newly hired sharpshooter followed Papa Gawli to Sitladevi temple at Mahim and shot him dead. For the purveyors of death, a lifeless body is just another casualty. But Papa Gawli was a different ballgame. While Rama Naik's killing shattered Gawli, who lost a mentor, it was Papa Gawli's death that put him on a sticky wicket in his home turf.

Papa's killing paralysed the gang and its ringleader. Gawli was plagued by guilt, holding himself responsible for his brother's death and the deaths of those near to him, which lingered in his mourning.

Seizing the opportunity afforded by this lull, Dawood launched a full-scale attack against the Gawli gang. Gawli's top aides like Paul Newman were killed. Then Sunil Sawant stormed the Kanjur village with an AK-47 and killed six of Gawli's men in one single siege.

Gawli's silence and reclusion hit his gang hard. The morale of the gang plummeted, hitting the lowest point since its inception. At last, Gawli's men decided to retaliate and planned to eliminate someone who was not only considered close to Dawood, but was also regarded as a big hit for the gang.

The name suggested was that of Ibrahim Parkar. Parkar was Dawood's sister Hasina's husband. Of all his sisters, Dawood was closest to her. Ismail Ibrahim Parkar was the victim of the age-old adage—an eye for an eye. Parkar was chosen as his target.

Parkar, a junior film artist, also owned the Qadri hotel in Arab gully, Nagpada. On 26 July 1992, he was sitting at the cash register, going over the accounts and keeping an eye out for any young wannabe bhai who might think of causing trouble at the hotel. Men would drop in and talk to him at regular intervals and would be served tea while they discussed their business disputes. Parkar would listen carefully, ask questions, and try to settle their disputes.

Parkar stepped out of the hotel late in the afternoon, accompanied by his driver Salim Patel. He was standing outside the hotel when four men walked up to him rapidly. The men drew guns from under their shirts as they approached, fired at Parkar and Patel rapidly, and ran away.

Parkar collapsed amidst screams of alarm and cries for help from Patel. He was dead by the time he reached St George hospital, having succumbed to multiple injuries to his vital organs. News of his murder first reached his wife Hasina, and then her brother Dawood, who was in Dubai. Listening with boiling blood to the news on the phone, he issued orders that none of his men were to rest till the killers were hunted down.

The four shooters were identified as Shailesh Haldankar, Bipin Shere, Raju Batala, and Santosh Patil. A month later, Haldankar and Shere shot a Nagpada businessman dead and fled the scene. However, they made the mistake of returning to the area two days later, were recognised, and caught by residents of the area. They were arrested but were admitted to the JJ Hospital, due to the injuries they sustained while being beaten by the residents.

It took almost two years for Gawli to fully rally and retaliate, but they eventually affected a massive onslaught on Dawood's gang. It was now time for Dawood and his gang members to mourn. A pall of gloom had descended not only on the streets of Nagpada and Dongri but also extended to Dawood's hometown of Mumka in Ratnagiri and his headquarters in Dubai.

Parkar's killing brought the non-stop violence and bloodshed to a melancholy halt. But this hard-won peace was to prove transient.

5

Shootout at Lokhandwala

It was the morning of 16 November 1991. The Police Shield matches were in progress at the Hindu Gymkhana; the Police Gymkhana had not yet been built. S. Ramamurthy, the commissioner of Mumbai police, walked into the viewing stand. The officers clicked their heels together swiftly upon his approach. But he seemed to barely notice, appearing preoccupied. A chair was offered and he took a seat, still looking perturbed. Ramamurthy knew he did not have very long to prove himself. There were already whispers among the top cop circles that the bureaucracy was looking for his successor. Gang wars were at their peak, crime in the city was rising unbridled, and the Mumbai police was going through a rather embarrassing phase as a result. The weight of these concerns plagued Ramamurthy this morning.

Sub-inspector Iqbal Sheikh walked into the viewing gallery and saw Ramamurthy sitting there. He needed a word with him. Iqbal Sheikh, stocky, short, brawny-looking, was an authority on the Mumbai underworld at that time. He was known to have penetrated several mafia circles and had a considerable information network. When Ramamurthy rose to leave, he walked to his side and saluted him stiffly, saying as he accompanied him out, 'Sir, *aaj ek major operation hai* [Sir, there is a major operation today].' Ramamurthy looked at Sheikh, his face betraying a perceptible apprehensiveness. He opened his mouth to say something. Then he changed his mind and sped off in his car.

Sheikh turned on his heels and re-entered the gymkhana. His friend Atul Choudhary, captain of the Hindu Gymkhana team, looked at him and gestured to ask where he was going. Sheikh raised his forefinger and index finger, as if shooting an invisible bullet. Choudhury nodded and raised his thumb at Sheikh for good luck. Iqbal Sheikh collected his belongings and left. It was 10:45 am, and he was on his way to Lokhandwala, Andheri.

On Carter Road in Bandra, at the office of A.A. Khan, additional commissioner of police, north region, the members of the Anti-Terrorism Squad (ATS) were getting ready to leave. Inspectors M.A. Qavi, Pramod Rane, Ambadas Pote; sub-inspectors Jhunjharrao Gharal, Sunil Deshmukh, Jagdale, Iqbal Sheikh, Raja Mandge, and seven constables of the Local Arms Division prepared for what was to come. The ATS was a special squad that had been set up at Khan's insistence. In those days, the main role of the ATS was to fight the menace of the Khalistani terrorists and underworld gangsters; today, their ambit is far wider, including counter-intelligence measures against all kinds of terrorism as well as gathering and using intelligence.

A constable was dispatched to the storeroom to bring out the bulletproof vests. The constable came back reporting, *'Saheb, tala laga hai. Chabiwala constable aaya nahi.* [It's locked. The constable who has the key hasn't come in today.]' One of the inspectors commanded the man to break the lock and get the crucial vests. At last they found, five bulletproof vests for eight officers. When the vests were being distributed, Iqbal Sheikh said he would not need one, and upon hearing this, Gharal said, '*Mujhe bhi nahi chahiye* [I don't want one either].' With arms and ammunition collected, they prepared to set off. '*Chalo chalte hain Andheri Lokhandwala. Telephone number mil gaya hai!* [Come on, let's go to Andheri Lokhandwala. We've found the telephone number],' said Inspector Pramod Rane, as they charged out towards Andheri. It was 11:30 am.

The policemen had got a tip-off that Dilip Buwa, a ferocious sharpshooter of the Dawood Ibrahim gang directly under the command of Maya Dolas, there. Their team stopped at the RTO junction at Andheri and sent out a party consisting of Qavi, Rane, Pote, and Sunil Deshmukh and Iqbal Sheikh for a recce. The team arrived at the Apna Ghar complex in Swami Samarth Nagar, Lokhandwala, Andheri. The Apna Ghar complex consisted of four buildings: Rohini, Swati, Aditi, and Ashwini. Swati stood in the northwestern corner of the compound and had two wings, A & B. Flat number 5 was on the ground floor of the A wing. The policemen closed in.

Outside the flat sat two white Maruti Esteems. It was a well-known fact that Dilip Buwa drove a white Maruti Esteem. He was, in these days, so wanted by the police that he always left the keys in the ignition—just in case he needed to make a quick getaway.

The recce team surveyed the surroundings and returned to the rest of the team. Inspector Qavi drew a map of the area to work with. Flat number 5 was the only flat in the entire complex with two exits, so the police team decided to split up. The northern exit opened out near the staircase and the southern exit into the compound. One team, consisting of Qavi, Gharal, and Deshmukh, would enter through the southern entrance and the other team, consisting of Rane, Mandge, and Sheikh, would enter through the northern entrance. The remaining constables and officers were stationed in the compound.

Everyone in position, Qavi stormed through the door with his team. On the other side, Sheikh was standing with his ear to the door. At first, he heard what he later discovered were the dialogues of the Amitabh Bachchan starrer *Akela* playing, and then he heard gunfire. Rapid gunfire! The action had begun. Qavi had entered the house with Gharal and Deshmukh. Dilip Buwa was sitting on a chair with a revolver on the table next to him. As soon as he saw the trio, he picked up his weapon and began to fire. As they were not in uniform, and he mistook them for members of a rival gang. In the first round, Gharal was hit in the chest and as he was not wearing a bulletproof vest, he collapsed and began to bleed profusely. Qavi was injured in the arm but protected from graver injuries by his vest. Only Deshmukh and Qavi managed to return fire and began to withdraw, pulling Gharal to safety.

Outside, all wireless units were whipped out and news of the exchange of fire was conveyed. Never before had gangsters shot at the police to wilfully kill them. This was a first and it was an unbearable insult. Within minutes news of the injured cops spread like wildfire and several units of police from all over the city began to descend upon Lokhandwala, swearing the gangsters would not walk out alive from here. It was 1:30 pm.

By 1:15 pm, reinforcements were put in place and the complex was transformed into a fortress. All activity had ceased and people were cowering in their houses. But the police were being cautious, with two of their number already injured, they were not going to take any chances.

One crucial observation had been made by Qavi's team, in the meanwhile. They had seen Mahindra alias Maya Dolas in Buwa's flat. This was now a whole new ball game. Maya Dolas, once a small-time hoodlum, had shot to public attention when he escaped from judicial custody on 14 August earlier that year. He had attacked a constable and run away from Mazgaon court, and this was not a slight the police were going to forget in a hurry. Subsequently, he shot at Ashok Joshi, a member of Arun Gawli's gang, at a Ganpati pandal in Bhandup. This shootout had left five innocent bystanders dead. Lately, reports of his increasing closeness to Dawood Ibrahim had been trickling in. The police had come in looking for Buwa— Dolas was an added bonus. Additionally, they had spotted other gangsters, Gopal Pujari, Anil Khubchandani, Anil Pawar, and Raju Nadkarni, and one unidentified man inside the house. It was time to take action.

The police took their positions in the building compound, united in a full show of strength. Khan announced the necessity of surrender to the gangsters under siege, using a loudspeaker. In the meantime, Dilip Buwa, accompanied by an unknown man, emerged from the southern entrance and headed towards his Esteem, firing indiscriminately, in a bid to escape. But there were far too many cops around for them to take on. When the police returned fire, it came from so many directions that Buwa and the unknown man were reduced to a couple of bullet-ridden bodies. They collapsed a few metres from the front door and died on the spot. Now, there remained Maya Dolas and his henchmen. It was 1:40 pm.

The action now moved to the terrace, which connected the two wings of the building. One unit of the police reached the terrace of the A-wing through the B-wing. They wanted to ensure that no civilians were taken as hostages. No sooner did they reach the terrace than they heard Gopal Pujari and Raju Nadkarni rushing up the staircase. The team swooped down on the two gangsters. Raju Nadkarni was shot down on the second floor and Gopal Pujari on the first. Now Dolas and Pawar remained. Anil Khubchandani could not be seen anywhere.

Khan continued to demand surrender, all this while; there was no way these men could hope to escape alive. But finally, when Dolas and Pawar emerged from the exit near the staircase, they too appeared not in surrender, but rather with their AK-47 rifles. The police immediately opened fire. They could not afford more casualties. In a hail of bullets, Dolas and Pawar were seen going down. For a long time after they were dead, the sound of the bullets could be heard resounding through the compound. It was 4:30 pm.

The police stormed flat number 5, and found the flat in shambles, pockmarked with bullets. The TV screen was shattered, and nearby lay Anil Khubchandani, dead in a pool of bullet casings and blood. A framed picture of Sai Baba lay shattered, even the guru's image pierced by a bullet through his forehead. It had been a four-and-half-hour-long encounter and over 2,500 rounds had been fired. It had not been an encounter; it had been a war, a war where every shot was fired to kill. It was a warning, an open threat, and a death knell for the underworld stating in no uncertain terms that the blood of no policeman would flow at the hands of a gangster.

Subsequently Gharal, who had been rushed to the Hinduja Hospital in Khan's car, survived his injuries. Qavi also healed and continued to serve his entire term. A formal complaint was lodged at the D.N. Nagar Police Station by Sub-inspector Sunil Deshmukh. The complaint accused the deceased of unlawful assembly, attempting to commit murder of police officers and men by means of dangerous weapons, and deterring public servants from discharging their legal duties. The unknown man at the flat was later identified as Vijay Chakor, a 28-year-old constable from the Yerawada prison in Pune. It was never established what he was doing with the gangsters. However, it was alleged that he was a messenger for some gangster lodged in the Yerawada prison at the time. The matter was never conclusively investigated.

All the officers were recommended for gallantry awards. However, the awards never came. On that fateful day, a team from a news channel called Newstrack had recorded the entire incident. Questions about the veracity of the encounter and the genuineness of the threat from the gangsters were raised and the entire team was embroiled in a controversy, which later culminated into a petition filed by a social activist Vinod Mehta at the Bombay High Court. The court promptly dismissed this petition.

The most important consequence of this encounter was, however, the survival of S. Ramamurthy. Even though according to rumours, he was poised to be replaced by S. Parthasarthy, with this victory however, Ramamurthy's position was once again cemented. He would not be shunted out now, and all threats had been silenced. The position came in return for the shootout at Lokhandwala, the death of the seven gangsters and the blood of a few good men.

6

JJ Shootout

Chhota Rajan's clout was increasing within the D Company. He had slowly become the brain and brawn behind Dawood Ibrahim. And he had reached a stage where Dawood had begun to trust him with his life. There was not a single operation for which Dawood had to look beyond Rajan (also known as Nana) for its execution.

Rajan had given the corporate structure of the gang its finishing touches and had not only defined its various levels and complicated layers, but also monitored its evolution personally. This was something that neither Dawood nor any of his cronies had managed, with the exponential growth of the gang in terms of manpower and money.

Rajan had brought his own trusted men into the Dawood gang and made it look invincible. D Company now boasted of around 5,000 members. Sadhu Shetty, Mohan Kotian, Guru Satam, Rohit Verma, Bharat Nepali, O.P. Singh, Mama, and scores of others had pledged their allegiance to the Dawood gang courtesy Rajan. By now, at the beginning of the nineties, the Dawood gang could easily be called the most powerful gang in the world. None of the international mafia, except the Russian gangs like Dolgoprudnenskaya and the Solntsevskaya, could boast of the power that

Rajan had brought to the D Company. In fact, Rajan had modelled his gang after the Solntsevskaya, named after the Moscow suburb of Solntsevo from which it hails. The mafia in Italy, Mexico, Israel, and Chechnya looked like pygmies when compared to the D Syndicate.

Rajan had also forged new alliances. The Mohajir's mafia of the Karachi underworld and the Turkish Cypress underworld had also struck up a rapport with the D gang. With Dawood at the helm, the Muslim mafia across the world readily placed their allegiance with his gang, and now with Rajan calling the shots, the Maharashtrian boys began gravitating towards Dawood without any communal wariness.

Rajan's latest campaign involved a list of hoteliers, builders, contractors, money changers, and agents he had drawn up, and from whom he had begun extorting money. In fact, from government agencies like CIDCO alone, Rajan made an impressive 3 crore rupees in a year. It was a unique racket. CIDCO gave contracts on a tender system to contractors for road, drainage, sewage, filling, and other projects. They also sold open residential and commercial plots by tender. Rajan bulldozed the CIDCO officials in such a manner that only his contractors would get work orders from the agency. Other contractors were not even allowed to submit their tenders. Thus, Rajan managed to get a 3–5 per cent cut on these contracts.

Then hoteliers and bar owners were made to shell out 50,000 rupees per month. And whenever a builder started a new project, Rajan's men would contact him and ask him to call Rajan on his cell. After a brief consultation, the amount was fixed and swiftly delivered to the sister of Chhota Rajan aide Mohan Kotian in Chembur.

According to police records, the money collected in this manner amounted to 80 lakh rupees per month, while the same dossier states that Rajan himself owned 122 *benami* (illegal) hotels and pubs in Mumbai. A part of the money earned and collected by the gang was invested back into gang members. Some amount was spent on supplying food and daily essentials in jails and on court fees of jailed gang members, for example.

Rajan had also clearly allocated work responsibilities among all his men. Moreover, while he delegated carefully, he personally kept in touch with even the lowest rung shooter in the gang. Dawood was proud of Rajan and his skills as his manager. He realised that with Rajan around to look after the business, he could let up a bit and enjoy life, free to bed Indian starlets. Some slept with him out of compulsion, while most of them did it willingly, as it gave them a feeling of power over their producers and distributors. Plus, they always preferred to be exclusively available to Dawood than to several financiers and moneybags, every time they signed a project.

Dawood had begun to throw lavish parties for film units visiting Dubai. Almost all the top stars of the era attended his parties and shared drinks with him and made it a point to mention their revelry in their circles back in Mumbai.

Dawood's life was luxurious, opulent, and carefree. While Rajan was toiling for him and expanding the gang so it got bigger and bigger, Dawood could rest and he rewarded him for this. Soon, a few gang members grew jealous of Rajan's growing clout. Sharad Shetty, Chhota Shakeel, Sunil Sawant, and others did not like Rajan and the amount of trust Dawood placed on him, so implicitly. They also did not enjoy Rajan's independence and the power he held when it came to crucial decision making. They could not order a hit in Mumbai or oversee a business dealing anywhere in India unless Rajan sanctioned it. It was all proving to be quite irksome.

Festering frustration and simmering discontentment brought the gangsters together against their common enemy. Ganged up against Rajan, they decided to go to Dawood, but cleverly. Dawood was loath to listen to any gossip about Rajan as he was aware of the widespread jealousy he invoked among his boys. Dawood had to be convinced in a different manner.

The men all cornered Dawood at one of his drinking sessions. As Dawood had immense respect for Sharad Shetty and never rebuked or chided him, he took the initiative. 'Bhai, do you know Rajan is becoming a power centre within himself? He has such a grip over the gang that tomorrow he can orchestrate a coup and take over the gang.'

'*Kya anna*, when did you start believing such hearsay?' Dawood replied lightly.

'Bhai, tell me, do you know how many men he has? How many of his people are running hotels, how many there are in the construction business, who his jail punters are and how much money he spends on himself?' Sharad Shetty continued.

'Why should I, when he is the gang manager?' asked Dawood smugly.

'Bhai, his people have now started saying we are Nana's men. They are wiping out even your name slowly,' Sautya interjected.

'Every man has an ambition and wants to reach the top. Rajan wants to become the "Godfather" of India",' said Sharad, trying to hurt Dawood's massive ego. Sharad Shetty knew about Dawood's historic struggles with Baashu Dada, Haji Mastan, the Pathans, and the Gawli gang.

Dawood was quiet for a long time. He did not want to believe what Shetty and Sautya were saying. Rajan had worked hard for the gang but at the same time, it could not be denied that he held the keys to the gang. He was the power centre—he ran a syndicate within the syndicate. There was a chance he would get power hungry some day and run amok. But Dawood's other men were not as enterprising and shrewd, none of them could pull off the handling of operations in India like Rajan did. There was simply no one who could replace his managerial skills.

'We don't know how loyal he is,' the men continued, unchecked. 'What has he done so far to avenge Ibrahim Bhai's killing?' This was a sore point, and it proved to be the gangsters' victory. It had been several weeks since Dawood's brother-in-law Ibrahim Parkar had been killed and so far there had been no retaliation from Dawood's side. Ibrahim had been killed on 26 July and it was already the second week of September; the Gawli gang had not been punished. Why Rajan not seen to this?

Dawood immediately asked Shakeel to get Rajan on the phone. When Shakeel got through, he handed over the cordless. Without any prelude, Dawood immediately shot out his question—only it was couched as a matter-of-fact statement. 'You still have not gotten the people responsible for Ibrahim's death.'

Rajan, who was in the middle of a sexual orgy and not ready for serious talk, was initially baffled by Dawood's brusque manner; he had never heard his boss speak so directly. He said, '*Haan bhai*, my boys are still chasing them. Gawli's men who were responsible for the attack have been admitted to JJ Hospital and are under tight security. We were waiting for them to be discharged from the hospital. I will get an update and call you back.' Rajan felt a bit queasy as he disconnected the phone, wondering at Dawood's tone and tenor.

'Rajan's boys are after them. Two of them are admitted in the JJ Hospital, the security is quite tight for them,' Dawood was talking more to himself than to the people in the room.

'Bhai, give me one chance and I will prove it to you that Rajan is just not interested, he is giving lame excuses. I will get those boys killed in JJ Hospital itself and you will see how I can screw the tight security,' said Sautya, jumping at the opportunity to upstage Rajan.

Now, Dawood wanted to placate his widow sister Hasina. An audacious attack on JJ Hospital despite its challenging security set-up would serve the purpose. Also, it would be the litmus test for Sautya and his abilities as a leader of gangsters.

After one long searching look, he nodded at Sautya.

Sautya leaned forward, touched Dawood's feet and said, '*Bhai, aapka ashirwad chahiye* [Bhai, I need your blessings].'

✠

This was a big challenge for Sautya and Shakeel. It was their do-or-die moment. If they failed here, they would have to stop nursing their ambitions to be Dawood's right-hand men. But if they managed to pull this off, they could kiss Rajan a royal and permanent good bye.

Sautya had decided to lead from the front and participate actively in the operation. Apart from other top people like Brijesh Singh, two of the most dreaded sharpshooters in the Mumbai underworld were hired for the kill—Bacchi Pandey and Subhash Singh Thakur. All kinds of automatic weapons including 9 mm Star pistols, carbines, and .32 revolvers were given to the shooters. For the first time a Kalashnikov rifle AK–47 was used in a gang shootout. Preparation for the assault was made on a massive scale, leaving no margin for mistake and keeping Rajan in the dark.

Jamshedji Jijibhoy Hospital, otherwise known as JJ Hospital, is one of the largest state government-run hospitals in the city. Sprawled over 20 acres of land, the hospital had over 45 wards and 1, 500 beds. Over half a million patients were treated in the hospital every year. The serene precincts of the hospital not only provided succour to the patients who they soothed and the medical college students they housed but also to intimacy-starved couples, who used the cover of thick green bushes for the odd clandestine rendezvous. As the hospital was spread over a large area and had a constant stream of visitors to its various wards, it was not possible to monitor everyone who made an entrance and exit.

Sautya and Shakeel had readied their plan in a matter of days and were ready to strike. All the preparations were made in such haste that the most important element of a strike—the reconnaissance of quarry or 'recce' as it is also known—was skipped and was performed, at last, only hours before the planned assault.

Around 1:30 am on 12 September 1992, a couple sneaked into the hospital premises to conduct the recce. As men would have attracted suspicion at this late hour, a couple was sent in, as they would be relatively innocuous-looking.

The couple was briefed to move around the hospital and assess the strength of security arrangements, ward locations, and exit points. They took a solid hour and returned at 2:30 am to report that their targets were in ward number 18 of the general administrative building, guarded by only one officer and four constables.

What they had missed was that only Shailesh Haldankar was in this ward; Bipin Shere had been shifted to Ward 6 on the first floor the previous morning.

At 3:40 am the assault party struck with full force. Subhash Singh Thakur, Sunil Sawant, Shrikant Rai, Bacchi Pandey, Shyam Garikapatti, and Vijay Pradhan went into action.

The constables were dozing and inspector K.G. Thakur had just begun to think of lying down on a couch himself, when the assailants barged into the ward and began to fire indiscriminately.

Even as Haldankar's lifeless body slumped on the bed, riddled with bullets, the shooters began looking for Shere. Sub-inspector Krishnavtar Thakur, who had jumped off his couch and taken cover behind it, managed to remove his service revolver from its holster and fired back at them.

The dozing constables seized the moment as well. Police head constables P.G. Javsen and K.B. Bhanawat grabbed their .303 rifles and began shooting. This firing from two sides had stunned the shooters; they did not expect any resistance from the police. Normally, the underworld never targets the police because this could antagonise the police force, who could then seek out and get rid of the whole gang for vengeance.

A volley of bullets caught the rattled Shrikant Rai and Vijay Pradhan unawares and injured both of them. Sautya indicated they should all leave but before this, he decided to fire in such a manner that the police party would be scared to fire more bullets.

Turning the barrel of his AK-47 on the constables, he let forth a flurry of bullets which proved to be too much for them. Both Javsen and Bhanawat were hit and fatally injured. Another ricocheting bullet pierced the leg of constable Nagre.

While Subhash Singh and Inspector Thakur were exchanging fire, Sautya called out to Subhash and Shyam and gestured for them to leave. They obeyed, but not before firing a last volley of bullets from their carbine and automatic pistol. Thakur managed to duck and save himself, but the shower of bullets hit a patient, a nurse, and the relative of a patient in the ward.

The hit squad immediately retreated from the scene. In the final analysis, a handful of policemen who were seriously outnumbered and outmanoeuvred put up a courageous fight against the desperadoes. According to the police *panchnama*, over 500 rounds were fired. An AK-47 took its toll in the outcome of this violent skirmish which lasted barely five minutes yet claimed the lives of many policemen, while inflicting only minor injuries on the shooters.

The audacity of the attack shocked not just those on the hospital premises but the entire locality. Mumbaikars never forget the constant sound of shooting guns, something they had only seen and heard in the movies till now.

The incident also highlighted Dawood's political connections. The mayor of Bhiwandi-Nizampur Municipal Council Jaywant Suryarao was roped in for the operations; his official red beaconed car was used by Sautya as a getaway vehicle. Also, MLA Pappu Kalani of Ulhasnagar and Union Minister Kalpnath Rai's nephew Virendra Rai had provided logistical support to the hit squad. The most startling revelation came later when it was discovered that two of the dreaded shooters had travelled on the special plane of a union minister from Maharashtra.

However, despite the colossal amount of legwork and investigation the police and the prosecution undertook, the trial process was arduous. The case went to trial after eight years.

Ironically, Sub-inspector Thakur, the original complainant and key witness, whose heroics on the day made the police force proud of his achievements, could not back up the story of what had really happened during the trial and turned hostile.

Special public prosecutor Rohini Salian, who had implicated forty-one people as accused, could only bring nine of them to trial.

7

Communal Strokes

It was a pleasant September evening. A party was in full swing on the open lawns of Dawood Ibrahim's brother Anees' bungalow. The event: a celebration of the success of the JJ Hospital shootout.

The audacious shootout had sent the city into a tizzy. The story made it to the front page of all the national newspapers, not only in Mumbai but country wide. That Mumbai's mafia had a free run of the city's public institutions, extending even to health care facilities, was unnerving. People were concerned that Bombay, the commercial backbone of the country, would turn into yet another anarchic Indian state like Bihar. The logic was that if criminals could run amok in a state government-run hospital like JJ Hospital, it would not take them long to strike in the corridors of power. From bus stops to trains, in cafeterias and in parties, everybody everywhere was discussing the shootout.

The government and the bureaucracy set up a police outpost in the huge, sprawling hospital premises, in their typical, knee jerk style. This made little sense, as there were several gates which were operational at the time and manned by civic security personnel. Later the police checkpost gave way to a full-fledged police station known as the JJ Marg Police Station.

The JJ Hospital shootout was a watershed moment for Dawood Ibrahim. Before this, he had never been able to proclaim his stake in the city with such impact. Dawood had cemented his reputation from far afield, and with a bang. For this was not merely one gang taking revenge on the other, or extracting its pound of flesh: it was a daring daylight attack on the system itself. The killing and injuring of policemen was unheard of in Mumbai's chequered mafia history, and it seemed Mumbai was turning into another Sicily.

At the celebratory party, a puffed-up Dawood went about greeting friends and well-wishers who thought they were congratulating Dawood for getting even with his brother-in-law's killers. Dawood was celebrating on several counts, however. He knew he had not only gotten even with Arun Gawli's gang, but that he was now calling the shots once again.

'Sautya *ne achha kaam kiya* [Sautya has done a good job]', Dawood announced loudly, as the conversation inevitably veered towards the JJ Hospital shootout. Ever since their bloody victory, Dawood had been openly expressing his admiration of Sautya, who had personally led the JJ Hospital shootout. Subhash Singh Thakur, Manish Lala, and Chhota Shakeel, who had also contributed significantly, got equal footage.

One man sat quietly in the midst of all the fuss. By now, everybody knew that for once, the shootout was not the handiwork of Chhota Rajan. Earlier, Dawood would always stake claim for Rajan's work, giving his stamp of approval. This had suited Rajan perfectly at that time, as he took it as a compliment.

But today Rajan had discreetly withdrawn, preferring to drink alone. He felt humiliated because he had not figured anywhere in this big triumph. When he saw Dawood gushing over the 'JJ team', he seethed with frustration. He felt the operation was not a success, in real terms. So much firepower and human resources had been used for the operation and in the end only one gangster, Shailesh Haldankar, had been killed, while Bipin Shere had not been taken down.

Rajan felt it was ironic that his boss was acknowledging the bravery of these stupid men who had, to his mind, botched the entire operation. Rajan drank on, brooding, until he could take it no more and walked out of the party. But he decided to let this one go. He consoled himself with the thought of all those times Dawood had been kind and compassionate to him, lauding his enterprise and giving him unrestricted rights over his business and gang operations. Dawood had never humiliated him, insulted him, or rebuked him in public.

Meanwhile, the JJ Hospital celebration party continued unabated. The shootout was an excuse. Everybody wanted to hitch a ride on the Dawood bandwagon. He was growing bigger and bigger. Some 'friend' or 'well-wisher' organised a party every second day, as many businessmen had already realised the value of having Dawood Ibrahim as their ally.

Soon, the events of September were forgotten. Months passed and December came around, time for another round of celebrations. Dawood's sycophants were known to organise several parties to celebrate the don's birthday on 31 December. Like most dons, Dawood who personally never attached much importance to his birthday, made it a point to see how his friends celebrated his birthday—whether they cared to wish him, send him flowers and gifts, and throw parties. He, of course, never organised any parties. For a don, he was rather shy about celebrations of this nature. But among the mafia, a note is made of all the parties thrown in Big D's honour. The rival gangs also kept watch over these parties, making notes of those who attended and those who did not. But very rarely would Dawood himself attend other parties.

But even as grand plans to celebrate Dawood's birthday mounted, another political development which had been brewing for a while culminated in what Indian history was to remember as one of its blackest of black days: a day when India ceased to be an inclusive, pluralistic nation. On 6 December 1992, a mob of Hindu militants tore down a mosque in Ayodhya and in the process rent apart the communal fabric of the country.

On 6 December, a mob of 70, 000 comprising members of right wing political parties and believers converged around the Babri Masjid, a disputed structure since 1853. Hindus believed that this was actually the birthplace of Lord Ram and that a temple had once existed here, later demolished by Mughal emperor Babar's commander, Mir Baqi. A masjid was built on the spot and it was named Babri Masjid.

After 1983, the Sangh Parivar (the Rashtriya Seva Sangh and the Vishwa Hindu Parishad) realised that Ayodhya was a political goldmine. By October 1992, Lal Krishna Advani's rath yatra (a motorised chariot), which had been mobilising support for the construction of the Ram mandir in the disputed site, had gathered sufficient steam. When it was clear that their plans included the demolition of the Babri Masjid, Advani's rath yatra was stopped midway in Samastipur in Bihar on 23 October 1992. The next day the Sangh Parivar announced a Bharat Bandh.

Two months later on 6 December 1992, Advani finally reached his target. The *kar sevaks* (volunteer to a religious cause) eventually brought down the structure and the entire world saw the footage of this live on television: the falling domes of the masjid and the *kar sevaks* scrambling to climb atop the masjid and dancing with joy after the demolition. The communal riots post-Babri Masjid demolition left over 2,000 people dead across the country and a legacy of deeply-entrenched communal hatred.

This caused much pain and anguish among Muslims across the country and sparked nationwide communal riots. If northern India was shaken, the tremors were felt as far as Mumbai; Bal Thackeray's Shiv Sena owned up to the destruction of the Babri Masjid.

In Mumbai, the riots which were triggered due to the frenzied, impulsive response of the Muslims, caused more loss of lives and property to Muslims than the Hindus. It seemed like the Hindu groups had anticipated the Muslim reaction and were prepared for the onslaught. So when the Muslim youth came out on the streets and started stone pelting and violent protests, the Hindus gave it back to them in full measure. Thus the violence escalated and Mumbai witnessed its worst ever communal carnage.

Muslims in Mumbai became vulnerable in the December-January communal riots after the Babri Masjid demolition. They expected the police force to play a fair and judicious role, but the police were mute spectators as the mob went berserk. Later, the Sri Krishna Commission revealed the unfair and partisan role of the police in the Mumbai riots. When they witnessed the police bias and the government's callousness in handling the riots, even the most optimistic of Muslims found their belief in a pluralistic, secular India shattered. Even in upmarket areas like Bandra, Muslim homes were marked for an attack with a chalk mark.

The general feeling was of insecurity and fear. Muslim youth found that they were not only oppressed by the system, but felt widely alienated and isolated. This feeling generated a widespread antagonism among them and a sub-section began to seek out revenge.

The climate was ripe for Pakistan's ISI intervention, always awaiting just such an occasion. They saw this as the perfect opportunity to sow the seeds of terrorism in India.

The ISI generals activated all their handlers and gave them instructions to launch a massive attack on India. The brief was clear: unlike the Kashmir operations where they had followed the practice of 'prick and bleed', this time it would be a 'deep incision' into the psyche of the country.

The lack of effective and charismatic leaders always forced the Muslim youth to choose the wrong role models. They usually made their choices looking for somebody who could buck the system. Earlier they had looked at Haji Mastan as their messiah, who was later replaced by Dawood Ibrahim. Muslims from south Mumbai wanted Dawood, with his mighty arsenal, to settle scores with the Shiv Sena, who had gone on a rampage.

The ISI, meanwhile, called together Dawood Ibrahim, Anees Ibrahim, Mohammad Dossa, Tiger Memon, Tahir Merchant, and several other Indian Muslim dons based in Dubai and Europe. They managed to bring the rival Indian dons together under the aegis of their operation of 'tehreeke-inteqaam' (the initiative of revenge). In fact, this was the first ever ISI operation where help was also sought from further afield; other international terrorist groups, including the Palestinian Liberation Organisation, Afghan Mujahideen, and several Dubai-based financiers were enlisted.

Several conspiracy meetings and brainstorming sessions were held across Dubai, Abu Dhabi, London, Karachi, and other cities. The ISI wanted to strike at once so that their planned terrorist attack would be connected to the Babri Masjid demolition. They also wanted to use Mumbai Muslim youth for the task so that the operation could not be traced back to Pakistan.

Tiger Memon and Mohammad Dossa were chosen to spearhead the whole operation. Tiger Memon was a smuggler who was born and bred in Mumbai. His task was to induct Muslim youth from Mumbai, get them to Pakistan, and train them in handling explosives and sophisticated weapons.

Memon knew that he would not be able to execute the operation without the blessings of Dawood Ibrahim; at the earlier meetings Dawood had not really promised anything. This resulted in a further flurry of meetings.

Chhota Rajan, who was even otherwise sidelined, was surprised by the number of endless meetings Dawood was attending, with both known and unknown quantities. Rajan brooded over the fact that Dawood remained closeted in meetings for hours. Moreover, Shakeel always attended these meetings but Rajan was never asked to join them in the conference room.

Finally, Dawood acceded to Tiger Memon's request for logistical support for the operation. A month after the Babri demolition, thirty young Indian men were flown into Pakistan and trained in warfare, using sophisticated guns and making RDX bombs. They were brought to Dubai and sworn to secrecy. All the while they were brainwashed into jihad; they were shown videos of Muslim women gangraped in Surat during the riots in Gujarat. The young men promised to retaliate by launching a massive attack on Mumbai.

Memon, in the meanwhile, managed to smuggle over eight tons of RDX and thousands of grenades and Kalashnikov rifles from the coast of Raigad, Maharashtra, all into Bombay, in February 1993. The scene was set.

✠

On 12 March 1993, a series of ten bomb explosions disrupted the uneasy calm of Bombay. The city, wrecked by bloodshed, firings, and communal divide, was just returning to normalcy after two months of relative quiet. The explosions began at 1:28 pm at the Bombay Stock Exchange Building, ripped apart the Air India Tower, the grain market at Masjid Bunder, Plaza Cinema and Sena Bhavan at Dadar, Passport Office at Worli, and five star hotels in Bandra and Santa Cruz. Grenades were also hurled at the airport and the Mahim Fishermen's Colony.

Long before 11 September 2001, the Bombay attack was one of the most audacious attacks of its kind. The 12th March attack on Bombay was regarded as the biggest terrorist act on any city in the world at the time. While all such terrorist attacks are usually the handiwork of highly trained and seasoned men, police investigations revealed, ironically, that this attack was carried out by a handful of young men who were neither religious bigots nor highly motivated. The entire operation, which had resulted in 257 deaths and injured 700 people, was the result of indiscreetly and hurriedly placed bombs, planted more out of fear of Tiger Memon than out of any religious zeal.

On the morning of 12 March, hours before his men had began planting the bombs, Tiger Memon and his entire family—including his old parents, four brothers and their wives—left the country. The Bombay police were already on his trail. They had gotten lucky and had several breakthroughs in the first few hours after the blasts. This included a clumsily abandoned Maruti van at Worli and a carelessly parked scooter at Dadar. The van belonged to Tiger Memon's sister-in-law Rubina and the scooter belonged to his brother, Yaqub Memon.

While most of the perpetrators of the blasts and their accomplices were arrested, some of them who had managed to reach Pakistan, including the Memon clan, managed to evade the law. Yet, Deputy Commissioner of Police, traffic, Rakesh Maria, who had additional charge of Zone IV, was assigned the investigation and managed to gather evidence and arrest over 200 people. He chargesheeted them under the stringent Terrorist and Disruptive Activities (TADA) Act.

Meanwhile, the entire country blamed Dawood Ibrahim for the blasts. Everybody was convinced that it was he alone who had planned the attack. Only he had the power to bring Bombay to its knees like this.

When the Indian government clamoured for Dawood's deportation from Dubai and began exerting pressure on the United Arab Emirates government to launch a crackdown on the fugitive don, India's most powerful gangster was actually worried for a moment. For, the pressure was so considerable that the UAE's mighty sheikhs were shaken by it.

Barring its neighbours, the Indian government had always enjoyed smooth and harmonious relations with countries across the globe. The respect that the country had earned was by its sheer goodwill and over eagerness to help everyone; apart from China, Pakistan, and Bangladesh, India had never overly antagonised other countries. The Middle Eastern countries, which were at loggerheads with each other, had always been friendly with India.

However India, as usual, failed to capitalise on its clout. Post the 1993 blasts, a wave of sympathy for India had swept across the world. If India wished, she could have used the opportunity to bring Pakistan to its knees and get Dawood back to the country. But the opportunity was frittered away. The shrewd, wily rulers of UAE realised the pressure from India was weakening and immediately announced that Dawood was not on their soil. This was a baseless claim but the Indian establishment never pursued it aggressively, as reported widely in the media at the time.

However, India's outspoken media did not spare the government and its half-hearted effort. They launched a massive effort to expose Dawood Ibrahim. While the English media published reams of newsprint detailing the don's vast empire in Dubai and the Gulf region, the local Marathi press branded him as a 'traitor'—a *deshdrohi*.

But those who knew Dawood very well were certain that even though he had the resources to do orchestrate something of this scale, the Mumbai blasts were not his brainchild. His best friends were Hindus and he was not known as a religiously motivated person. Dawood Ibrahim's core group, which included several of his non-Muslim aides like Sunil Sawant, Manish Lala, Anil Parab, and above all Chhota Rajan, were sure that Dawood was not involved in the blasts.

In fact Dawood's close allies know that upstaging and exiling Tiger Memon from Mumbai was one of the don's masterstrokes. Memon was fast growing as a smuggler in the city, and clients in the Middle East had started to deal with him. Dawood never entertained a rival's growth and increasing influence lightly. But Memon had never even thought of Dawood as competition, instead actually wanting to be in his good books, so it was not easy to upstage him or stall his growth with direct intervention.

However, if Tiger Memon got entangled with the law in a messy manner, he would have to escape from the country and abandon all operations. He would thus not be able to expand his influence and Dawood could reign supreme. So, when the proposal for leading the attack and blasts in Mumbai came up, Dawood had cleverly asked the ISI to make Tiger Memon the hero. Memon bit the bait and was ousted from the city, and Dawood managed to outmanoeuvre his competitors without shedding a single drop of blood. This is why Indian agencies could never pin the whole operation onto Dawood and named Tiger Memon as the key accused and perpetrator.

The public was not fully convinced, however. And when Shiv Sena supremo Bal Thackeray wrote scathing editorials calling Dawood a 'deshdroshi' and dubbed Hindu dons like Arun Gawli and Amar Naik 'Aamchi muley' or our Maharashtrian boys, Chhota Rajan rose to Dawood's defence.

Rajan, also a Maharashtrian, was aware of the extent of Dawood's involvements in the blasts. He decided to prove his loyalty to his friend and boss. Rajan began calling up and sending faxes to newspaper offices, defending Dawood. He labelled the accusations of Dawood's involvements in the blasts as flimsy and religiously motivated.

In fact, Rajan went a step further and took on Bal Thackeray. He began sending faxes to English newspapers, where he wrote in Marathi that Thackeray should mind his business and focus on politics and stop commenting on the business of the underworld. Rajan went on to proclaim that Dawood was not a *deshdrohi* and that he did not need a certificate from Thackeray.

8

Surrender Offer

The events of 12 March 1993 had left the country, its citizens, and the government shell-shocked. They were not the only ones rattled; Dawood Ibrahim was seriously shaken by the events which unfolded on that fateful day. However, there is no real evidence to suggest why he was in that state of mind. His friends and associates believe that when he provided logistical support for Pakistan's ISI to smuggle in the RDX via the long coast of Maharashtra, he did not realise the magnitude of the act of terror they were to perpetrate on Indian soil, six years after he left.

Dawood believed that the plan was to conduct one of those 'prick and bleed' operations that had almost become an ISI calling card in the Kashmir region, where a small number of casualties and minimal infrastructural damage was regularly witnessed. The all-seeing and all-knowing don who sat atop his throne in the White Castle had no clue, say those close to him, that this operation would turn out to be the most heinous terror attacks that had ever been orchestrated anywhere in the world, until then.

A doleful Dawood now wanted to get out of the whole mess and come out clean. He wanted to assert his innocence and convince people he was not involved in the blasts. The irony was that the don, who was once near impossible to seek an audience with, now found no one willing to give him a patient hearing. A flood of hate mail had been steadily piling up in Dubai where he lived then. Epithets like 'Qaum gaddaar (traitor to the community)' and 'mulk gaddaar (traitor to the country)' were frequently hurled at him. Avalanched by all the ill-will, Dawood could barely bring himself to read a couple of bile-filled letters before returning to his despondent state.

It was shortly after this incident that it began to dawn on Dawood that the hate mail cut across communities, coming from those of every faith and allegiance, and among those leading the charge were his fellow Muslims. In fact the day after the blasts, he received a call from a Maharashtrian woman police officer of the Mumbai police then posted at the Mumbai airport. As one of his aides brought him the phone, Dawood was not prepared for her angry, accusatory speech. *'Besharam! Tujhe sharm nahi aati hai? Jis mitti par tune janm liye, ussi mitti ko badnaam kiya!* [Have you no shame? You have humiliated the same country where you were born!]' raged the officer on the phone. Dawood had nothing to say, silently hearing her out. The barrage left him so stunned that even when it was over he held the phone close to his ear until much later. As if it was not enough that his post box was full of such hate, it was now being delivered to him on the telephone.

The fact that Muslims were also so angry with him left him flummoxed. After all, it is a documented fact that when Hindu-Muslim violence broke out across Mumbai in 1992-93, Dawood categorically refused to be drawn into the mess of communally motivated action. It was then that he began receiving 'gifts' at his White House villa in Dubai. Some of these dubious presents included boxes of broken bangles with a note attached: *'Yeh us bhai ke liye jo apni behen ki hifazat na kar saka* [this is for that brother, who couldn't defend his sister]'.

Mocked and chastised for not taking up arms back then, he was now a traitor in the eyes of the entire world for allegedly taking action. This was a very sticky situation. Dawood sat for hours, mulling over each option. These options, he noticed, were slowly dwindling. Finally, he decided to make his move and called out to one of his aides for the telephone.

The period immediately after the blasts and months after that were difficult for Dawood in more ways than he could have imagined. He used his contacts in the police and found out the enormity of charges and the strength of the evidence against him. He realised that the Mumbai police, despite all their fancy investigation and sleuthing, had managed to only extract two confessions against him under the heinous TADA Act. (Later the Central Bureau of Investigation got one more confession that named Dawood in the conspiracy.) All the statements dwelled on the fact that Dawood was involved in the conspiracy and had agreed to provide logistical support to Tiger Memon for the execution of the serial blasts. But Dawood realised that this was hardly a watertight case and that he could easily defend himself in a court of law.

Dawood was aware of advocate Ram Jethmalani's reputation as one of the top lawyers in India. If there was anyone who could get him out of this mess, it was Jethmalani. So, the don decided to call the advocate at his London residence. Typically not wanting to waste time in small talk, Dawood kept it short and simple. 'Mr Jethmalani, I want to surrender,' he said, quietly and humbly.

Surprised that a fugitive don was calling him and that too for legal counsel, Jethmalani was not very keen on speaking to Dawood. But the don was insistent that he wanted to return to India and he persistently called the advocate, who at last relented. Dawood said he was willing to face the government and the charges against him in the blast case and that he would do so with total cooperation.

However, he had certain conditions which were to be fulfilled before he would turn himself in. Apart from the charges in the 1993 blasts case, he wanted all previous charges against him to be dropped. Additionally, for the duration of the blasts case, he was to be kept under house arrest and not in a jail. If these two conditions were accepted, he added that he would happily return to the country of his birth and surrender.

Dawood's offer sent ripples across India and created an uproar in Parliament and Mantralaya in Mumbai. A section of senior intelligence operatives did not want Dawood to come back as they felt he would go back on this deal. Yet senior leaders in Parliament wanted him to return and face the music, because having Dawood Ibrahim surrender to their government would be a historic achievement. Members of the ruling party could thump their chests in pride at what they had accomplished.

A spanner was, however, thrown into the works by the apprehensions of a few politicians from Maharashtra. They were concerned that if Dawood was to return and come clean, a lot of shady dealings by a number of people in the state and at the Centre would be revealed. As the man on trial, Dawood was ironically shaping up to be the executioner for a number of politicians. If he was brought back, information on all illegal meetings with him in Dubai and London would be out in the open. Every instance of Dawood coming to the aid of these politicos would be out in the open.

This particular lobby was up in arms about the conditions laid down by Dawood as part of his surrender deal. They told Jethmalani that India was a democracy and as such would not allow a fugitive don to dictate terms. He was still welcome to surrender and would be given a fair trial. However, none of his conditions would be complied with, the government said.

As eager as Dawood was to clear his name, he was not naive. He knew that if his conditions were not met with, the Indian government would take him to task.

Later that year, developments around the Memon family's surrender proved him right. He stood vindicated in his decision not to surrender unconditionally, when he saw what happened to Yakub Memon, who came back to India with a tonne of evidence against the various accused in the blasts case. But he was tried like a street thug and given the death penalty. There was no compassion for the man who had readily volunteered information and agreed to surrender.

Thus, the Indian government let one of the biggest fish in the underworld slip through its net. Experts believe he could have been brought back and then the government could have quickly reneged on the deal struck with him. The end result was that Dawood remained a free man and managed to wreak havoc on India later, from the secure palatial mansions of Karachi.

9

Maal, Moll, or Mole?

The infinite smoothness of her skin, her barely-clad bosom, a flimsy
white saree teasingly caressing her under a gushing waterfall: this was
how cinemagoers saw India's sexy new actress on screen. Mandakini, or
Yasmin Joṣeph, was a buxom, young girl who was originally from Meerut
and later grew up in the middle-class Antop Hill area in south central
Mumbai. Her father was an Anglo Indian, her mother a Muslim.

Mandakini's terrific complexion was as natural as her well-endowed
figure, and she soon attracted the attention of the film world. At the age
of 16, she got a break that any new actress would have died for. Veteran
filmmaker Raj Kapoor identified her as the new chosen one for his
youngest son Rajiv Kapoor's debut in *Ram Teri Ganga Maili*. The movie was
not the hit of the century, but Mandakini's breasts became the talk of the
town in direct proportion to her popularity. She was the stuff titillating
dreams were made of.

Mandakini has been touted as Raj Kapoor's hottest find. Raj Kapoor's
role in an actress' career was legendary. Although it was Dev Anand who
brought actress Zeenat Aman to Bollywood, it was Raj Kapoor who
uncovered Zeenat in full frontal glory in *Satyam Shivam Sundaram*; the

graceful Simi Garewal in nude and Padmini with open bosom both in *Mera Naam Joker*. Mandakini's daring drenched pose on the marquee became the stuff of unrealised wild fantasies. The cascading Ganga waters drenched her, and as her shy nipples peeped through the saree, the stringent Censor Board of India could do little to delete those scenes; Kapoor himself maintained that the scene had been shot tastefully.

Certainly Mandakini, or for that matter Zeenat Aman before her, could not bathe in the confines of their shanty and would not be fully draped from head to heel. The only way to do it was to shower in the open exposing their curves. In the movie, Raj Kapoor had gone a step further and had even showed Mandakini breastfeeding an infant. Even when the infant was through his feed, Mandakini's bare breast was exposed.

Months became years and after scores of flops or semi flops, Mandakini soon joined the bevy of young girls who were on their way to stardom. She bagged projects with successful co-stars like Mithun Chakravarty, Govinda, Sanjay Dutt, and Anil Kapoor. The filmmakers emulated the great Kapoor and made Mandakini expose in all her roles, whether it was *Param Dharam* with Mithun or a miniscule role with Anil Kapoor in *Tezaab,* where she appeared in a two-piece bikini.

In the early nineties, Bollywood was abuzz with photographs of popular stars posing with Dawood Ibrahim. However, close on the heels of the 1993 blasts, public sentiment was raging against these denizens for hobnobbing with the man who laid the city low. The air was thick with fear, intrigue, denials, and some brave admissions from a few who said they were pressured into socialising with Dawood. Not that the photographs evidenced it. But there was one picture that set tongues wagging.

In the late eighties and nineties, Bollywood films were full of young girls, starlets mostly, falling for the street thug or the loafer. The mafia's fascination with film bombshells was nothing short of a global phenomenon. Hollywood had set the precedent in the case of Chicago's big boss Sam Giancana, who had foisted himself on Marilyn Monroe. Giancana was soon besotted with Monroe and after a brief affair Monroe was found dead under mysterious circumstances. Another mobster, Bugsy Siegel, was crazy about not one but two Hollywood starlets, Ketti Gallian and Wendy Barrie.

Mumbai's big boys were not to be left behind. Their lust for glamour and weakness for flesh made them weak in the knees for the fair-skinned Bollywood 'would-be's. Haji Mastan, for example, married a Madhubala lookalike, Sona, whose flagging career was given a sudden boost after her marriage to Mastan.

The picture that made headlines was of the young starlet Mandakini posing cosily with Dawood Ibrahim at a cricket match in Sharjah. The year 1994 was a time when images of the Mumbai serial blasts were still raw, and when Dawood's links with Tiger Memon, the main accused, were bared. For Mandakini, the timing was all wrong.

She was a mysterious woman. Like most women who lived in the sulphuric golden shadows of Mumbai's mafia men, she witnessed the expected meteoric rise in popularity. But till then, to the public, with Mandakini, all her 'connections' were speculation and her expeditious success a matter of lucky coincidence. (If that exists!)

After her photographs with Dawood Ibrahim were released in 1994, there was no respite for Mandakini. She was labelled Dawood Ibrahim's moll, and hounded by journalists, photographers, and eventually the police. But when her film *Zordaar* released in 1995, no one was to know it would be her last performance in Hindi cinema.

The Mumbai Crime Branch had only just changed their strategy in chasing Dawood. Just as a mouse is baited with cheese, the police went after Dawood's mainstay in the country: his assets. Every apartment, bank account, farmhouse, money-laundering operation that had any inkling of a connection with Dawood Ibrahim was raided and sealed by the Mumbai police. They were hunting down his money with a vengeance. This same money, they believed, he had used to engineer an instant death for thousands of people. After all, they reasoned, what was a merchant without his money, even if he was the merchant of death?

The Mumbai police received a tip-off about a farmhouse on the outskirts of Bangalore that was purportedly built with Dawood's money and was one of his many illicit properties across the country. They passed on the lead to their counterparts in Bangalore who raided the property. But to their surprise, the property was registered in Mandakini's name. The news did not take long to leak out. The press had a field day with the prospect of establishing a connection between the fair lady and the dusky don.

So much did this romantic connection tickle the imagination of the readers that it became an almost permanent feature of page one news. There were so many questions. Why would someone like her get involved with an unsavoury criminal from Dongri? She came, after all, from the glitzy and glamorous world of Hindi cinema. Did she need a 'mentor' in the industry? Just how common was this phenomenon in Bollywood? Were more actresses/starlets involved? Where was Bollywood's cash flow coming from? Why was Mandakini keeping a low profile in Bangalore and almost living in seclusion? Why was she wearing a burkha when she went out? Who was Mandakini really? Was she an innocuous young girl trapped in something far bigger than her understanding or was she a conniving, manipulative woman who charmed her way to stardom using below-the-belt tactics?

The questions were innumerable and no answers were forthcoming. Mandakini refused to say anything but deny her connections with Dawood Ibrahim. She repeatedly said, 'I am not Dawood's moll.' She said she knew him but was never romantically involved with him. Perhaps by then she was just terrified. Perhaps she had not expected the uproar that would ensue. Perhaps she had underestimated the implications of the liaison. Perhaps she had not thought so much about it. Perhaps she momentarily forgot herself. Perhaps the man was just too charming to resist. Perhaps it never happened. Perhaps. The truth we may never know, as Dawood never really spoke much about her. The answer to that question is so fundamental. He may be a murderer, he may be a saint. But the clue to attraction between a man and a woman is more elemental than that. Could there ever be an answer to that question?

In the midst of this commotion, the Mumbai police gave the actress a surprising clean chit. They could not find enough evidence to link her with Dawood. No reasons were given and no further questions asked. Maybe now she could find some peace and return to work. However, Mandakini's career and personal life nose-dived from there on. Film offers dried up and she became a social exile in Bollywood. She was screaming from the rooftops for all to hear that she had no connection with Dawood Ibrahim. But no one was listening.

In 1995, it was revealed that she was pregnant. Her child had a middle and last name before he was born—one that the whole city ridiculed.

Like a woman scorned, she lashed out at everyone, saying the child was not Dawood's but was even less forthcoming about the identity of the father of the child. She dropped out of society, stopped returning phone calls, and retreated to a point, it seemed, of not return.

A few years later, reports turned up her quiet marriage to the unlikeliest of people, Buddhist monk and Dalai Lama follower, Dr Kagyur Rinpoche Thakur. Mandakini herself became a practising Buddhist, in desperate search of the meaning of her life. Popular imagination is fertile and suggested that the change was so she could atone for her sins. But popular interest is also short-lived and if left unstoked soon dies out. Mandakini was a has-been, a short-lived wonder, one of many in Bollywood. Bollywood too, keen to put its underworld connection firmly in the past, did not take a second look at her. And so it seemed her saga would end.

But there is a saying about bad pennies, women, and lost socks. They always turn up again. In 2000, Mandakini produced and acted in two music videos. Music videos were the rage of the season and maybe this was a fit of nostalgia speaking on her behalf. Both the videos, 'No Vacancy' and 'Shambala' bombed badly. No takers for an ageing starlet. Very few among the generation who watched the videos even remembered her name. Some of the older ones even said she resembled the old actress Mandakini. So much for a comeback. Some say she has found solace in teaching Tibetan yoga and she runs a centre for Tibetan medicine with her husband in Yari Road, Mumbai.

In her last known tryst with the Indian media, it was reported that she was working on an English language film with her husband. But ever since, only silence of the most unsettling kind. The quiet kills some people because they can not make peace with their thoughts. But with others, it is a way of life.

For Mandakini, a teenager from a small town, an upcoming Bollywood star, and an alleged moll of Mumbai's arch nemesis, this is also a way of escaping the goldfish bowl that is public attention, a way to live with the idea that although life has not been perfect, it certainly does not have to be led in accordance with the wishes of a billion people. A million girls would have killed to be her at the peak of her career. A million people would not be seen with her now. Fickle fame and its ways. Nevertheless, Mandakini's fair-skinned youth remains immortalised.

10

Developments in Dubai

Chhota Rajan's daring defense of Dawood and challenge to Sena chief Bal Thackeray had pleased the don but there was far too much coming for him from various quarters; this was too little, too late. Sitting in his White House, one day, Dawood decided that it was time to make a decision.

Dawood now realised that he had submitted to the ISI's designs and gotten initiated into Islamic terrorism on the pretext of avenging the Babri Masjid riots. Deep inside he had always known, of course, that the ISI was executing their own agenda. The gameplan was to frustrate the country and its countrymen to such an extent that they would finally cave in and allow India to hand over Kashmir to Pakistan. But Dawood knew it was naiveté to even dream of winning Kashmir.

Dawood was happy running his global business of real estate and restaurants in various international metros, financing movies, hobnobbing with Indian film stars, and courting Bollywood beauties. He did not want to become a pawn in the ISI's hands but he understood that the dice had already been cast, leaving him with almost no control over his destiny anymore.

On the other hand, his top lieutenants had been hankering for more power and clout. Dawood knew that Rajan was capable of handling his gang but if he allowed him to continue, he would be faced with widespread mutiny among his own ranks. Shakeel, Sautya, Sharad Anna, and others who seemed to have ganged up against Rajan would not allow him to rest in peace. While there was no way for him to find out if their notion that Rajan had become too powerful and might float his own outfit was accurate, Dawood dithered for a while, trying to avoid a decision.

Plumes of cigar smoke hung heavy in the air. Even the quietly efficient air conditioner could not clear the smoky environs of the room. After pacing endlessly and impatiently for a long time, Dawood reached a conclusion.

The decision was not a practical or a judicious one, rather it was a convenient one. He had decided he could not pay attention to supremacy disputes and so would call a meeting of all his men and instruct them to behave maturely. He also planned to make it clear he did not want them to occupy themselves with this self-perpetuating game of one-upmanship.

The meeting was called in the conference room at the White House in Dubai and the don ensured that all those men who mattered to his gang were present.

'I'm tired of seeing you guys using your power and strength to fight among yourselves and weaken the gang. Don't do this. Concentrate this power and strength on attacking your rivals and weakening them, not yourselves,' Dawood said, quiet, calm, deadly in his authority.

There was pin-drop silence in the room. People waited for him to continue, they thought he would use anecdotes and stories to clarify what he wanted to say, but nothing came.

'I'm warning all of you to finish any and all discord and dissension you have between yourselves and focus on business. *Aapas mein jhagra dhande ki maut hota hai* [fighting between ourselves means death for business]. To me, business is bigger than even my brother, and I want all of you also to understand this,' Dawood added, and fell silent again, waiting for his words to sink in.

Someone in the room tried to object, and started saying that it was Nana (Rajan) who was responsible for a lot of the bad blood among the senior members of the gang. Without saying it directly, he tried to tell the don to ensure that Rajan remained judicial and fair in his dealings.

But no, Dawood remained non-committal, and said, 'Nana *mere bure waqt ka dost hai. Main uski burai nahin sunna chahta hoon.* [Nana has been my friend in bad times. I don't want to listen to anything negative about him.]' From now on, I will ensure that everyone has equal power and flexibility in the gang, and everyone will report to me. All of you are equal, there are no favourites.'

The meeting was brief and Dawood thought that he had averted a major crisis by being decisive and forceful. Now it was the duty of his lieutenants to solve their problems and eliminate their grouses. But Dawood had acted with shortsightedness and did not pay attention to long-term repercussions.

Rajan was mighty pleased at Dawood's intervention; however, Sautya and Shakeel were not one bit satisfied. All this was doing was maintaining the status quo.

The period after the communal riots in Mumbai and before the serial blasts had seen a flurry of meetings. This series of long meetings continued even after the blasts. Shakeel had taken on the duty of meeting organisers, planners, financiers, strategisers, of the gang. People around Dawood knew how important Rajan was in the scheme of things; he was second-in-command. Yet Shakeel had deliberately kept Rajan out of the meetings. When people casually asked about the absence of Rajan, they were told that he was a 'kafir' (a disbeliever), non-Muslim, hence he did not belong at meetings, which were by and large attended by Muslim expatriate dons.

This exclusion from meetings and the 'kafir' rationale had hurt Rajan and the slight began to rankle. He desperately wanted to draw Dawood's attention towards this gross injustice. Dawood, on the other hand, continued to focus on efforts to consolidate his position as a don and global power player, rather than paying attention to the minor tiffs among his managers.

But the ill feeling soon turned into public arguments and brawls, with Rajan and Shakeel and their partisans virtually coming to blows. Over the few years of their association with each other, the enmity had grown intense and by 1993-94, both the groups were baying for each others' blood. Rajan had stopped handling the gang's business and was confined to his house most of the time. He was also contemplating returning to India but he did not have his passport.

As per Dubai laws, the visa sponsor, known as a *kafeel* in the local language, has to keep non-Emirati passports in his custody. In case his subject is found loafing in the streets or accused of a crime, the *kafeel* is held responsible. If the passport is in his custody, then he gets away lightly and his subject is summarily deported out of the country.

Dawood and his clan had relocated to Dubai ostensibly under the sponsorship of certain powerful Arab sheikhs. These sheikhs had kept all passports in their custody, which suited Dawood fine, as it helped keep his men on a leash. He was, of course, above all this, and never relinquished his passport to anyone. In fact, he even obtained a Dubai passport and a UAE citizenship under the names of Sheikh Dawood Hassan and Dawood Khan.

Rajan felt totally helpless. He did not know how to leave Dubai. He was sure that staying in Dubai any longer would get him killed.

Meanwhile, Dawood had announced a major bash on a cruiseliner. The who's who were invited and obviously Rajan was expected to attend as well, but he had some vague premonition about attending the party. He did not know why he felt the way he did, what it was that was holding him back from attending a party he was required to go for. Who skipped Bhai's dos? That too without a valid reason!

Reluctantly, Rajan began to prepare for the party, taking his time over it. Somehow he combed his hair, picked up his car keys, and decided to leave. But just as he was about to close the door behind him, the shrill sound of his telephone drew him inside again. Rajan took the phone and his face turned white. The call was from one of his close associates, who was already at the party. '*Nana, woh tumko tapkane ka planning kiye la hai* [Nana, they are planning to kill you],' whispered his friend nervously.

Just the thought of getting killed and dumped in this manner sent a shiver down Rajan's spine. Strangely, he had never felt anything while masterminding several killings. But the irony that someone else was meticulously planning to kill him in such a gruesome and heartless manner was too much for Rajan to swallow.

He replaced the phone, went to his garage and drove his car out, slowly and quietly. Rajan could not make up his mind: should he conjure up a subterfuge and avoid going to the party or should he go and take Dawood Bhai aside, informing him of Shakeel's treachery? More importantly, would Dawood Bhai listen to him? What if he dismissed it as Rajan's paranoia and insecurity? Worse, was he part of the gameplan to get rid of him in this manner?

Questions, questions, and more questions! Rajan's mind was a minefield. He was driving slowly but his mind was racing. The cruiseliner party was hardly a half an hour's drive from his residence but Rajan kept driving in circles; despite driving for over an hour and a half, he was nowhere near a conclusion.

The evening had turned into night and the night was getting only darker. Finally Rajan realised he had been driving for over three hours: he had to take a decision soon. He stepped hard on the brakes and brought the car to a screeching halt. His mental turmoil stopped with the impact; breathing heavily, Rajan knew he had made up his mind.

He turned the car towards the Indian embassy in Abu Dhabi. The Indian embassy in UAE had so far specialised in dealing with cases of fraudulent employers, stranded Indians, and stray passport cases. Rajan had taken it upon himself to make history there.

✠

The RAW officer looked at Rajan, seated across him in a soundproof room, intently. Matching his gaze, the seasoned RAW officer was trying to read the gangster's mind. They say that in intelligence operations half the success is achieved by getting the right guy and judging him accurately. Judging a mole or an operative is always the most difficult part of intelligence gathering.

The RAW man, after having gathering relevant answers from Rajan and satisfying his curiosity, asked him to wait while he excused himself to an ante chamber to make a call to his bosses in New Delhi.

Rajan had spent more than a couple of hours in the Indian embassy now. After facing initial hassles with the security man at the gate, the rest of the night had gone quite smoothly. Rajan had sought to see the officer on duty and mentioned the name of the intelligence officer he wanted to meet.

Across the world, all embassies and consulates have at least a few intelligence operatives. Depending on their ranks and profiles, they are given suitable designations that offer appropriate cover in the embassy, ranging from desk officer to a cultural attaché or even assistant or deputy consular. But they do not report to the consul general; they report to their respective intelligence heads in their country.

When the security officer informed the RAW man about Rajan's impatience to meet him and willingness to wait for him through the night at the embassy premises, the officer was quick to acquiesce, rushing to the embassy to meet the gangster.

Rajan then narrated the whole story to his newfound RAW contact, who had met him earlier in a five-star hotel in Dubai during one of the high profile parties thrown by the Shaikh family. Rajan wasted no time and told him that he wanted his help in escaping from Dubai. In return he was willing to provide them all information about Dawood and his business interests across the world—legitimate or otherwise.

The RAW agent had an hour-long session with Rajan but required approval from his bosses in New Delhi. For a third of the top honchos at the Ministry of Home Affairs (MHA), this was going to be a long night. The intelligence chiefs in Delhi and senior bureaucrats exchanged ideas and the whispers on the phones continued into the wee hours. It was a major coup for the beleaguered Indian government, whose efforts to lay their hands on Dawood had hitherto been like drawing designs on water.

Finally, the Indian government decided to provide tacit support to the renegade gangster. Papers were immediately drawn up and it was agreed that they would facilitate Rajan's exit from Dubai.

Rajan returned home, collected all his vital documents and account details, and within hours was on a plane out of Dubai. His first stop was at Kathmandu, where he met some more Indian officials and handlers. He was given a different identity and was flown to Kuala Lumpur in Malaysia. Rajan, with his wealth and the logistical support provided by the RAW agents, managed to blend into this new background afforded by the Indian diaspora in Southeast Asia. Now he had only one leit motif left: to finish off Dawood and destroy his ill-gotten empire.

Ignoring Rajan and his growing frustration turned out to be Dawood's most expensive mistake. Dawood had never dreamt Rajan would dare to cross lines and disengage from him, throwing down the gauntlet. Although Dawood, Rajan, the RAW handlers, and the MHA bureaucrats had different motives and intentions, they all might be said to agree on one truth: man's most dangerous enemy is the one he was once closest to.

Dawood had several enemies in his chequered career but none turned out be as lethal and wily as Raja, a fact which Dawood was still unaware of while he was partying on the cruiseliner that night, off the Dubai coast.

11

New D Company-HQ:
Karachi, New CEO: Shakeel

Rajan's disappearance from Dubai was not noticed until after a couple of days. And when it was, all hell broke loose. It was not the ensuing bloodshed that bothered the D Empire, but Rajan's access to the syndicate's soft underbelly. Rajan was privy to the goings on in Dawood's gang; he knew the range of his global network, the extent of the gang's operations, the location of bases across the world, their key personnel, Dawood's political friends in New Delhi and Maharashtra, his financial conduits in India, his nexus with top rung police officers in Mumbai and other cities, his wealth and assets and his association with various mafia organisations and intelligence agencies, as well as the various fronts that Dawood had floated. Rajan was the only one who could expose the whole gang, and the only one who knew the chinks in Dawood's armour.

As if in tandem with Rajan's escape, other related developments tied the D empire into knots. The Indian government began pressing for an extradition treaty with the UAE government. This spread panic and insecurity among the Indian expatriate fugitives who were holed up in this part of the Persian Gulf.

Dawood and his ISI masters realised that the UAE government would not be able to resist India's pressure for long. They had to relocate Dawood and his key associates before the Indian government could lay their hands on him. Therefore, towards the end of 1994, Dawood moved his base to Karachi, Pakistan. Karachi is known to be Mumbai's sister city, as it has similar features and character, the same look and feel, and like Mumbai, is a port city; in some areas it even smells like Mumbai.

Dawood moved into a villa at Clifton Beach. He also acquired properties in Khayabaane Shamsheer, which is like Mumbai's Malabar Hill and Shah Rahe Faisal, which is the arterial road in the heart of the city. Shah Rahe Faisal is a little similar to Mahim's Cadell Road in northwest Mumbai.

Once ensconced in Karachi, Dawood also trained his sights on other Pakistani cities like Lahore. He acquired properties in Madina Market in Lahore, which is similar to Mumbai's Manish Market, and in the Blue area in Islamabad, which is regarded as one of the prime locations in the Pakistani capital.

The ISI was very accommodating, and Dawood decided Pakistan would be his home until he could return to India. They were his best ally, in these times. In the meantime, he was making efforts to get adjusted to this new city, which was not proving to be too difficult. Karachi, in a lot of ways, was like the Mumbai Dawood had to leave, and was more accepting and familiar than Dubai; also, though he moved there out of compulsion rather than whim, he knew he would be safer there from the Indian authorities. However, he was aware of a seething distrust and ill feeling from the local mafia, who were predominantly Jats and Mohajirs.

Dawood's Clifton Beach villa was in the vicinity of the shrine of Sufi saint Shah Abdullah Ghazi. The shrine has an uncanny resemblance to Mahim's Makhdoom Shah dargah as the façade and the portico of the shrine looked exactly the same; Dawood felt at home. Especially as his father Ibrahim had been a devout Muslim and was a regular at the shrines of the Sufi saints; Dawood had inherited this trait from his father. Incidentally, most of the underworld dons had some kind of special affinity with Makhdoom Shah of Mahim. In fact, Makhdoom Shah Baba is also popular not just with the mafia but also with the Mumbai police; the Mahim Police Station led the annual convention or 'urs' of the saint and every year the senior police inspector is given the responsibility of leading the procession with the customary *thaal* on his head, which is why the shrine of Abdullah Ghazi made this feel like a homecoming.

Among the mafia, the Baba Bahauddin dargah in south Mumbai abutting Bombay Hospital also has a loyal fan following. The Baba is fondly referred to as the finance minister by the Muslim mafia. The Memons, Muslims from Gujarat considered a trader community, revere the Baba and most of them attribute their riches to him. Most Muslims in Mumbai genuflect before the Bahauddin Shah Baba near the Metro cinema in Mumbai 'to ask for money'. They still talk about the rags-to-riches story of Mustafa Dossa alias Majnun, a don from Mumbai whose father unfailingly sang praises of the Baba every Friday. Mustafa Majnun's brother, Haroon, a budding Sufi himself, still visits the dargah every day. It is said that if you ask the Bahauddin Shah Baba for money, he will shower it on you. '*Sab log yahan paise ke liye mannat mangte hain* [every devotee comes here wishing for money] and the Baba never disappoints. Hence he is known as the finance minister,' he says.

Dawood disposed of most of his properties in Dubai and wound up all his business interests in the Emirates so that the Indian agencies could never trace them back to him. By the end of 1994, Chhota Rajan had firmly ensconced himself in Kuala Lumpur, while Dawood and his tribesmen had found a safe haven in Karachi. The map had been rearranged, but the gangsters remained at large. After Chhota Rajan's exit from the scene, Chhota Shakeel had officially donned the mantle of Dawood's aide de camp and begun to handle the business of the D gang. Even though the gang's headquarters had been relocated from Dubai, Shakeel and his men outwardly maintained that they were still stationed in Dubai. In order to complete the deception that they were still working out of the emirate, Shakeel even used a Dubai SIM card, all the while safe in Pakistan.

New to this seat of power, Shakeel began to flex his muscles, asserting his might. Unlike Rajan, who believed in centralised command and checked even on the lowest rung operator in Mumbai, Shakeel followed the principles of decentralised management. Sharad Shetty was assigned the fiefdoms of horse racing, cricket betting, and dealing with hoteliers and builders in Mumbai. Sautya was responsible for weapon handling, mediation in disputes and looking after imprisoned men, Shakeel himself had begun to coordinate film funding and hawala. Apart from this, Shakeel also poked his nose into other business interests like real estate. In spite of this over-reaching, he managed to keep everyone happy and remained in the good books of Dawood and his old friends—something which Rajan, known to be a very blunt person, had failed to pull off and rubbed everyone wrongly.

Shakeel had learnt one thing from Dawood's friends in the Turkish mafia and their operations in Cyprus though he claimed it as his own brainchild. He had begun cultivating young Muslim boys barely in their teens to use guns and shoot to kill. These school dropouts were from predominantly Muslim localities like Dongri, Pydhonie, Bhendi Bazaar, and Antop Hill areas. These teenagers, disillusioned with society, shouldered the burden of supporting a family prematurely and were frustrated at the prejudices against their community in the job sector. They were quickly drawn towards the lure of easy money.

For them, 5, 000 rupees for one careful pulling of the trigger at point blank range was a lucrative offer. Of course this was risky but for a ruffian who had been loafing around the whole day and had to listen to a volley of abuses at home for not making a decent living, any risk that could boost his self-esteem was worth it.

Becoming a hitman for Shakeel Bhai not only gave these boys quick money but earned the appreciation and trust of the great Shakeel Bhai, who was a right-hand man of the legendary Dawood Bhai, and all this gave the young gangsters an aura of power.

Shakeel had started hiring and Arif Khan, Asif Shaikh, and Feroz Sarguroh became some of his boys, barely 17 or 18 years old when Shakeel hired them and gave them guns. The biggest surprise came in the form of Feroz Sarguroh, who became a dreaded sharpshooter in the underworld and was soon known as Feroz Konkani.

Hailing from a conservative Muslim family, the good-looking Konkani lad had begun his career at the age of 16. He had caught Shakeel's attention with his first crime: slitting the throats of two Mathadi workers at Masjid Bunder in January 1993. The gruesome killing of two Hindu labourers triggered the second round of rioting in Mumbai, which was also much more violent then the first wave of bloodshed soon after the demolition of Babri Masjid in December 1992.

Feroz joined the Shakeel gang and became the most daring and fearsome sharpshooter it had. After Feroz, other teenage Muslim shooters like Shakir Durbar and Ibrahim Shaikh joined the gang but Feroz's track record remained unsurpassed. Shakeel managed to wield terror and fear in the hearts of Mumbai's business community. And Feroz had earned the nickname of the 'youngest killing machine': here was the new generation of Mumbai gangsters.

The killing of BJP leader Ramdas Nayak, flanked by his security men, in broad daylight at a Bandra junction was one of the most gruesome murders recorded by the Mumbai police.

It was just another day on the busy Hill Road in Bandra on the morning of 25 August 1994. MLA Nayak left home in his Ambassador at 10 am, accompanied by police constable B.M. Tadvi, who had been supplied to him as protection by the Bombay police. As the car pulled into the main road and turned towards Bandra's SV Road, nobody noticed the two men walking towards them. At least, not until the shooting began. It was only then that people noticed that the two, later identified as Feroz Konkani and Javed Sayed alias Soni, had AK-47 rifles in their hands which were spewing bullets at Nayak's car. Even as the car's windshield shattered and people began screaming, Tadvi came rolling out of the car, armed and ready with a sten-gun, and returned fire. However, his gun was no match for the assault rifles used by militant organisations around the world, and he too was riddled with bullets.

'Gurnam, John, *bhaago!*' Feroz shouted to other accomplices who were standing across the street from Nayak's house. One of them escaped in a waiting Fiat, while another escaped on a motorcycle. He and Soni then hijacked a passing autorickshaw and fled the scene.

Investigations later revealed that gangster Chhota Shakeel had given the contract to kill Nayak to one Sajid Batliwala who, in turn, had given the assignment to Fero, the dreaded contract killer. Batliwala was also instrumental in supplying firearms to Konkani and his hit squad. Nayak was an elected councillor of the BMC and Shakeel felt that his activities were causing harm to the Muslim community.

Feroz had humiliated the police; they now had to get him to retrieve their lost prestige. With a string of murders to his name, Feroz was finally tracked down and arrested at the Blue Diamond hotel in Bangalore in

October 1995. However, in 1998, he escaped in a daring jailbreak, in broad daylight. His men opened fire at the police while Feroz was being brought out of the JJ Hospital to be taken back to the Thane Central Jail after a CT Scan. Police constable P.D. Kardile lost his life in the firing. Until his arrest, Feroz was involved in eighteen killings, of which sixteen were at the behest of Shakeel.

By then Shakeel had understood the success of finding young boys with no police records and training them to kill. As there was no dearth of unemployed Muslim boys willing to emulate Konkani, the business of bloodshed continued unabated and Shakeel seemed to have benefited by it the most.

Shakeel had managed to establish himself and consolidate his position in the gang. Within months of Rajan's exit, Shakeel had established an all-pervasive presence in the D Syndicate. Dawood, who initially doubted how capable Shakeel would be as second-in-command, was relieved that his business would not take a beating.

However, there was one man who did not like Shakeel's success and his being considered Dawood's alter ego. This was Dawood's brother Anees. Anees had often made snide remarks about Shakeel and tried to ridicule him, but Shakeel could not retaliate, as he knew that Dawood would not tolerate any action against his brother.

Anees liked Dawood's style of functioning—to take a back seat and delegate authority and choose someone as the CEO. You get your job done smoothly, without dirtying your hands. And if a particular job gets botched, it can easily be disowned; you blame it on some incompetent men in the gang hierarchy and placate the affected party, who readily buy the explanation, knowing the gang and the sub gangs within the gang.

Shakeel had several detractors and rivals within the gang. While Shakeel could stand up to his other competitors, he could not do much against Dawood's sibling, who himself nursed ambitions of heading the D Syndicate. He liked the idea of delegating to get the job done, sitting back while the dirty work was done, and Shakeel was only in his way, as far as this was concerned. Also, Anees never liked Shakeel and had had a good equation with Rajan. In fact, he was the only sibling or D gang member who kept in touch with Rajan for a couple of years after his escape from Dubai.

However, Anees also wanted a Man Friday, who could be his ace manager, keep his coffers flowing with cash and promote his name in India. He looked around amongst the members of the gang and did not find anyone who would fit the bill.

Meanwhile, Abu Salem Ansari, who had been on the run since the serial blasts in Mumbai, had landed in Dubai. Salem had been accused of delivering AK-47s and grenades to film star Sanjay Dutt at his residence at Ajanta in Pali Hill, Bandra, in what was to become an infamous takedown of the popular Bollywood star.

When the Mumbai police launched a crackdown on all the Dawood men, Salem too appeared on the police radar. He sped off from Mumbai and reached his village Sarai Mir in Azamgarh. After having spent some time in Lucknow, from where he kept calling Anees Bhai, he was called to Dubai. Once in Dubai he realised that he was on his own and needed someone powerful close to him. Perhaps it was Abu Salem's good fortune that Anees was trying to find a confidante. Since he had no godfather in Mumbai or Dubai, Salem thought he would adhere to Anees Bhai's diktats and make him his godfather, growing in the mafia hierarchy. Salem began kow-towing to Anees and bragging about his own exploits in Mumbai to impress him.

As Anees had no other option and Salem seemed sincere and loyal, he decided to give him a chance. Thus is many a collaboration born.

12

Rise of the Minions

Salem stood before a life-sized mirror. It was as if he was inexorably drawn to his reflection. He could not take his eyes off his face.

Salem had recently shaved off his moustache and beard and now sported a clean-shaven look. While in Mumbai, he had sported long tresses and a Muslim beard and moustache, a legacy from his Azamgarh days. His devout Muslim look was complete with a fez cap, giving him the aura of a highly religious Muslim youth.

But when he made an escape from Mumbai, on the run to Hyderabad, Lucknow, and Delhi before eventually landing up in Dubai, he kept changing his appearances. Once he shaved, he was transformed—and he had fallen in love with his new look.

Salem thought that his handsome face was now befitting that of a Bollywood hero. Thus was born Mumbai's most narcissistic, self-worshipping gangster, who loved his looks so much that he decided to earn the epithet of 'the handsome' ganglord.

Salem had seen lot of balding dons—Chhota Shakeel, Anees Bhai, Noora, Tiger Memon—and shuddered at how ugly and repulsive they were. He was not going to let himself go like that. Salem began to pay attention to the clothes he wore, colognes he used, and the branded leather belts and shoes completed the picture. Witnesses who lived with him for years say that he was obsessed with his looks to such an extent that he used to brush his hair every hour He was also extremely particular about his manicure and pedicure sessions—something perhaps no other mafia don had ever paid any attention to.

Abu Salem Abdul Qayyum Ansari belonged to a family of conservative Muslims, who hailed from a small hamlet of Sarai Mir some 30 km from Azamgarh in Uttar Pradesh. His father Abdul Qayyum Abdul Hafiz Ansari was a respectable lawyer in his village and wanted his children to study. Known as Qayyum Vakil, he had never been able to make it big in the legal circuit. After Qayyum's death, Salem's mother Jannatun Nisa began making beedis to make both the ends meet.

Salem, being the second eldest, had attended school until Class IX, but after his father's death in a road accident, he had dropped out and begun looking for work. Salem and his elder brother Abu Hakim both started working as bike mechanics as their two other brothers Abu Jaish and Abu Lais were still in their teens. Initially, he tried to work in Delhi for a few months but finally moved to Mumbai.

In Mumbai, his uncle gave him a small stall in Arasa Shopping Centre and allowed him to sell belts and moonlight as a real estate broker. It was during these stints as a broker that Salem came in touch with Anees Bhai. Once indoctrinated into the gang, he followed any instructions Anees gave him slavishly. After a few assignments, Anees began using him as a top confidante, and after the communal riots of 1993, assigned him the major task of delivering guns and grenades to Sanjay Dutt.

Salem almost fainted when he was told to pay a visit to Dutt at his bungalow at Pali Hill. Salem, like all the village youth, was star struck. He delivered the deadly package of weapons and explosives but did not lose the opportunity to hug the star several times. He could never forget his encounter with Dutt: it was his first meeting with a film star. What is more, Dutt was a reigning superstar and son of the legendary actor and member of Parliament Sunil Dutt. Back in his village, Salem could never have dreamt of such a moment. The sheer proximity to Dutt had boosted his ego. And Dutt had welcomed him warmly, like a friend and brother.

Much later, when he reached the shores of Dubai, the naive Salem realised, of course, that it was not his personality that had made Dutt warm to him; rather his connection with the Bhais or the dons. The man who has a gun owns the world, he thought to himself.

He thought that if he could become powerful, the whole of Bollywood would pay obeisance to him. Salem decided that if Shakeel could be the right-hand man for Dawood Bhai, he could acquire a similar status with Anees Bhai. All he had to do was handle this smartly.

Anees had told him once, '*Hamara dhanda, darr ka dhanda hai aur Dawood bhai ne sabke dil mein darr bitha diya hai* [our business is the business of fear and Dawood has planted fear in everyone's hearts].' Salem looked at him replied, '*Bhai, main samajh gaya, Dawood ke darr se yeh dhanda chalta hai* [Bhai, I've understood what you've said about Dawood and fear].'

Salem got down to work seriously. He knew that in Mumbai real estate builders and Bollywood were two money churners. If he kept them scared, he could fill his coffers for three generations.

The year 1995 began with a bang for the Anees-Salem combine. Just three years ago, Prime Minister Narasimha Rao with the help of the then Finance Minister Manmohan Singh had opened up India's economy, after years of permit raj. He had thus rendered India an open economy, after years of protectionist policies and regulatory constraints. The impact was far reaching as private players were allowed into many new spheres. The doing away of an over-bureaucratised system which inhibited competition, innovation, efficiency, and economic growth was appreciated everywhere, and the resultant free flow of capital brought with it tremendous opportunities. The first sector that saw plenty of activity was the building and construction industry.

And where could this increased activity be evidenced more than Mumbai? Mumbai, the commercial capital of India, was one of the first cities to show evidence of the effects of liberalisation. Construction activities began everywhere. To Salem, it was clear that the builders were minting money, not just in Mumbai but also in the city's outskirts. Western suburbs extended to as far as Mira Road, Nalla Sopara, Vasai, and Virar and the Central Exurbia stretched from Mumbai's neighbourhood city, Thane, to Mumbra, Dombivali, and Kalyan.

Salem asked his boys to do some scouting around the city and got hold of some builders' phone numbers. A string of calls were made to builders across the city and Salem, with his unpolished Mumbai lingo and a smattering of Urdu, spoke with a distinct Uttar Pradesh inflection, managed to frighten a lot of builders.

Salem had managed to instil fear in the hearts of the Mumbai's business community. Several builders began loosening their purse strings. The initial flow of cash from Mumbai boosted Salem's morale and he began to exult. Most of all, Anees was pleasantly shocked; he could never have anticipated that a man from the back and beyond of Azamgarh could fatten his kitty by actually shaking up Mumbai's rich and knocking some money out of them.

Intimidation thrives on violence and bloodshed. Yet Salem had not shed any blood so far; he had been milking the Dawood terror factor. He realised that he did not have any foot soldiers to execute his diktat, if some builder were to defy him. Salem's thoughts went to the rampant joblessness and poverty in his hometown, Azamgarh.

The north Indian provinces of Uttar Pradesh and Bihar are notorious for their lawlessness. There is hardly any development, corruption is rampant, and administration non-existent. Abject poverty has driven and continues to drive youngsters to crime.

In the wake of this convenient demand-supply situation, Salem hit on the idea of importing sharpshooters from his hometown, which though not ingenious was radically unconventional. Most of the village youth had used a country-made revolver, known as a *katta*, at some point of time. A *katta* is a handgun moulded in a small-scale iron-welding unit and is good for a single shot. After a bullet is fired, it cannot be reloaded and used again. The *katta* industry is a cottage industry in many Bihar and UP villages and the weapon comes in handy for village ruffians looking to intimidate lesser mortals.

Salem, who had grown up amongst street thugs, knew most of these youth could pull a trigger and run from the scene if required. Any of them could be hired for a paltry amount of 3,000 to 5,000 rupees. If the shooter were smart enough to duck the police, he would be paid his remuneration and if he got arrested, there was no liability for Salem.

Salem became the first ganglord to import shooters from Uttar Pradesh. These boys were told to fire at the door of the builder, shatter the glass pane, or just barge into the office, brandish the gun, and scare the manager. Filmmakers Subhash Ghai and Rajiv Rai were threatened in this manner. Later these boys were also assigned the task of shooting to kill. As the boys had no police records in Mumbai, the cops were totally taken aback by these new entrants in the world of crime.

A spate of shooting incidents was reported across the city and the cops were reduced to mere spectators. The only clue to these killings and shootouts were Salem's own claims to his victims, while boasting about his exploits.

Builder Pradeep Jain was one such victim who was targeted by Salem. Salem had wanted a share in a property that Jain was developing, but he refused to buckle under Salem's threats. On 7 March 1995, Pradeep Jain was shot dead by Salem's men outside his Juhu bungalow. Jain was regarded as a top builder in the city, and his killing established Salem as a ruthless don and announced his arrival on the crime scene.

The killing also had a suitable impact on the business community. Everyone began to pay up quietly. This attracted other lumpen elements towards the Salem gang. The two most dreaded shooters who joined Salem immediately were Salim Shaikh alias Salim Haddi (*haddi* means bone, and the nickname was used because of his reed-thin physique) and even a suspended police constable, Rajesh Igwe. Igwe was associated with the local arms division II of the Mumbai police and had been suspended on corruption charges. Igwe, who was proficient at handling all kinds of weapons, wanted a comfortable and lavish life. He joined the gang and began working for Salem. It was unprecedented in Mumbai's mafia history for a policeman to join a mafia gang and execute killings at the instance of a ganglord. But Salem now had this unlikely new gang member on his side.

Salem began to expand his circle of victims; the next person he chose was Omprakash Kukreja of Kukreja builders in Chembur. The police dossier describes Kukreja as a Rajan sympathiser and financier, while the newspaper reports claimed that Kukreja contributed 50 lakh rupees every year to the annual Ganeshotsav celebrations organised by Sahyadri Krida Mandal at Tilak Nagar. When Salem's men reported this to him, he began calling Kukreja for protection money.

However, Kukreja refused to pay up and increased the security cover at his Chembur office instead. Salem asked his two ace shooters Salim Haddi and Igwe to punish Kukreja for his impudence. The two stormed Kukreja's office on 18 September 1995 and not only killed the builder but also other employees who were present in the office, including Deepak Bilkiya and Mohammad Ansari.

But the Mumbai police also killed both the shooters, in the notorious 'encounter' style. Igwe's death was particularly important; other ex cops in this lawless city would get the message.

The police failed to detect the Kukreja murder case. After a yearlong investigation, they had to close the case on 11 November 1996 classifying it under 'A', meaning true but undetected.

Significantly, Kukreja became the first casualty of the inter-gang rivalry between Dawood and Rajan. Infuriated at Kukreja's murder, Rajan decided to retaliate.

13

Shocking Bollywood

The five-pound hammer hurled in the air came crashing down, reducing the windshield of a spanking new white Contessa to smithereens. The shattered windscreen and the accompanying deafening noise brought the car to a screeching halt.

The serene quiet of Perry Cross Road in Bandra West, known as the queen of Mumbai's suburbs, had been pierced by a few gun-toting men dressed in black. The quartet closed in on the car. One of them nudged at the shattered windscreen; the laminated polyvinyl acrylic sheet gave way easily, giving the gunmen an unhindered view of the people inside.

They pointed their guns towards a man wearing a black suit, comfortable in the rear seat. After pumping several bullets into him, the killers disappeared from the scene.

The incident was over in little more than a minute, enacted in full view of the street's bystanders. Shocked residents peeped out of their balconies. Perry Cross Road residents had never witnessed violence of such an inhuman, gruesome nature before.

The killers had left behind two things: a hammer and a dead man riddled with thirty bullets. The victim was airline tycoon, Thakiyuddin

Wahid, of East West Airlines. Wahid, an entrepreneur from Cochin in Kerala, came from a humble background. Initially, he had established a successful travel agency at Dadar, central Mumbai. Subsequently, in the post liberalisation era of Prime Minister P.V. Narasimha Rao's government, with Dr Manmohan Singh at the helm of the country's economy, Wahid became the first businessman to launch a private airline and compete with the government-run Indian Airlines and one fledgling airline, Vayudoot.

But one cruel stroke of fate killed not only the man behind the enterprise but the spirit behind it. Wahid's killing proved fatal for East West Airlines and its other businesses.

The high-profile murder pulled Police Commissioner R.D. Tyagi, Joint Commissioner of police, crime, R.S. Sharma and some top politicians to the spot immediately. The hammer lying on the bonnet of the car stumped them; an odd choice as a signature. But the hammer subsequently became the signature of Rohit Verma, Rajan's ace hitman.

Within two months, Rajan had decided to avenge the Kukreja killing and had not wasted any time before retaliating. He wanted the opposition to know he was giving it right back to them. Like the others, he had figured out that after every high-profile killing, the cops stepped up their security arrangements and rounded up the usual suspects from their respective gangs; thus ensuring that they beat a hasty retreat from the city. This kind of swooping crackdown was a dampener for the hired mafia killers and they resurfaced only when the police became a little more complacent. Rajan had waited a requisite two months before it was safe to strike and settle scores with Dawood.

Now, the killings of Kukreja and Wahid had not only shaken Mumbai's moneyed class but also rattled the top brass of the police force. When the mafia takes to the streets, it is always the Mumbai police who receive unremitting flak both from the public and the nervous politicians. The police tried to say that those killed had some connections with the mafia and that innocent people were not affected by these inter-gang tensions. The state administration and the politicians, however, were intent on proving that the police had failed, dealing a body blow to the law and order system in the state.

But no one, not the police, nor the administration nor the politicians had any clue of what was to come. They had no idea that what they had witnessed was just a preview.

✠

The murders of Kukreja and Wahid opened the floodgates to trigger-happy dons and uncontrollable bloodshed. Rajan, Shakeel, Gawli, and now the new entrant Salem had begun ordering the killings of gang loyalists or covert financiers. At times they were also gunned down because they refused to pay up the extortion money that the gangsters demanded. Builders like Manish Shah, Dilip Valecha, and Natwarlal Desai were killed in broad daylight, as were tycoons like Karim Maredia, Vallabh Thakkar, and Sunit Khatau.

While these killings were feathers in the caps of the warring dons, they also served as a warning bell for those who were dithering over whether they should loosen their purse strings.

Meanwhile, the list of murders was growing with each day. Months turned to years but there was no letting up. In four years, gang warfare became bloodier and violent. And the dons were safe, keeping their distance as their foot soldiers and loyalists paid with their lives.

Salem had decided to focus on the film industry, and after the aborted attempts on the lives of filmmakers Subash Ghai and Rajiv Rai, he got Riyaz Siddiqui killed. Shakeel did not want to be left behind and commissioned the killing of filmmaker Mukesh Duggal, claiming that his association with Rajan made him a target. Salem, for his part, set his eyes on a bigger and better target. After three years in Dubai, Salem finally closed in on his biggest quarry.

✠

Gulshan Kumar was a self-made man. As a son of a humble fruit juice seller on the streets of Daryaganj in New Delhi, Kumar had always aspired to make it big. At the age of 23, he founded the company Super Cassettes in Noida, which marketed cheaply priced audio cassettes. The low cost of the cassettes made Super Cassettes a super success. Subsequently Gulshan Kumar began promoting audio cassettes of Hindu religious songs. With his business flourishing, he ventured into producing video cassettes on

Hindu mythology and made every effort to promote Hinduism through his company in India.

In the late eighties, the film industry was controlled by powerful cartels, which promoted only select artistes. Gulshan, who had slowly managed to gain clout in the music world, introduced fresh new talents like Sonu Nigam, Anuradha Paudwal, and Kumar Sanu. He also brought new actors and directors into the industry. He promoted these new singers through a new brand in Mumbai called the T-Series. T-Series became the most popular brand in entertainment, not just in India but abroad, and Gulshan Kumar was hailed as a music baron with the Midas touch.

As a devout Hindu, Gulshan Kumar organised a free meal provision every year for the pilgrims of the shrine of Vaishno Devi known as Devi ka Bhandara. Slowly his popularity, wealth, and clout increased manifold; so much so that in 1992–93, he was said to be the highest taxpayer in the country.

During his hunt for a movie moghul between 1994 and 1997, Salem had thought of two other people: Subhash Ghai and Rajiv Rai. But when his plans failed with both, his shooters being caught both times, he began to focus on Gulshan Kumar. Salem had been threatening Kumar for a long time, demanding money from him, which the latter had adamantly refused to pay. This infuriated Salem to no end, and he soon hatched a master plot to eliminate the music baron.

On 5 August 1997, after the attack on Rajiv Rai, a reporter from the *Indian Express* called Salem on his Dubai number and tried to ferret out information from him about the attacks on film personalities.

Salem said at the time: 'I never wanted to kill Subhash Ghai or Rajiv Rai, the idea was to only scare them. But watch out next week when my men kill a film personality. This time the idea is not to scare anyone but to warn the entire industry.'

The reporter immediately hailed a cab for the Crime Branch police headquarters, near Crawford Market. He reproduced the entire conversation to the Crime Branch chief, Ranjit Singh Sharma who took a serious note of the whole episode and personally began calling the crime unit chiefs. Immediately, security was provided to several bigwigs of Bollywood, including Pahlaj Nihalani, who was the head of the Indian Motion Pictures Producers Association (IMPPA) at that time.

Sharma made one major mistake. He failed to cover Gulshan Kumar. To be fair to Sharma, no one in the police machinery anticipated that he might figure as a target.

Much later, during their investigations, the cops discovered that Salem had begun to demand 5 lakh rupees from Gulshan Kumar every month. Kumar defiantly told Salem that he would rather donate the money to Mata Vaishnodevi's *bhandara* (coffer) than to the Dawood gang. A vengeful Salem decided to kill him right in front of a mandir.

Every morning when Gulshan Kumar started for work, he visited the Jeeteshwar Mahadev Mandir in Andheri to pay obeisance. As a matter of precaution, he had hired a private security guard, who had reported sick for a couple of days. So on 12 August 1997, Salem's men reported that he was unguarded. Salem immediately instructed them to kill Kumar outside the temple, adding that they should call him from their cellphone when firing so he could hear Gulshan's screams of agony. As Gulshan Kumar emerged from the temple the killer, known as Raja, opened fire on him. Kumar was hit in his arm and waist and began bleeding profusely.

He tried to duck for cover and found a public urinal. The killer followed him and pumped some more bullets into him. Gulshan, who was writhing in pain, began to crawl out of the urinal. He spotted a shanty next to the urinal and, desperate to save his life, Gulshan crawled inside it. Blood and life were both slowly leaving him, when a breathless and panting Kumar pleaded with an old woman inhabitant to save him by shutting the door and not allowing the killers inside.

The old woman, too stunned by the sound of gunshots and the sight of so much blood on this badly wounded man, could not muster enough courage to close the door. The killers, who had all the while kept their cellphone switched on, made sure that Salem could hear everything on the other end. They finally decided to complete their assignment.

They entered the hut, pumped fifteen bullets into Gulshan Kumar, and left him dead. The whole sordid drama had continued for over 15 to 20 minutes in a busy bylane of Andheri in broad daylight, but none of the bystanders tried to help Gulshan Kumar or sought police help. The story of this rags-to-riches man who had helped countless people, ended with his dying alone, without any succour.

The cruel and heartless manner in which Kumar was killed shocked the entire nation. Mumbai had witnessed many mafia killings but this one simply surpassed all degrees of cruelty. It was beyond heinous, and Salem's monstrosity was discussed everywhere from Parliament to pubs.

The Prime Minister of the coalition government Inder Kumar Gujral reacted to the killing at once. 'This criminal act is totally out of place in a civilised society and particularly in a city known for its discipline and civic consciousness...' Gujral said, in the *Indian Express*. He added how Gulshan Kumar had 'carved a niche for himself in the world' of film music', concluding that 'his loss will be mourned by all music-loving people'.

The film fraternity was frozen with fear following this cold-blooded murder, which was so much worse than anything they had dreamt up in their movies. Director Mahesh Bhatt, who directed the hit film *Aashiqui* for Kumar, summed it up aptly when he said, 'When you kill Gulshan Kumar, you kill one of the biggest people in the entertainment industry. By killing Gulshan Kumar they are saying, 'We are calling the shots,' and they have proved it... The entire film fraternity is in a state of terror.'

The *Indian Express* reporter called Abu Salem again and enquired, 'Was this the murder you were talking about?' he asked. But this time the bluster was missing. His own gang members had quartered Salem. From Mumbai to New Delhi and from Delhi to Dubai, the mafia was getting hot under the collar with outrage; such a significant act perpetrated by a relative small-timer, yet to find his feet. The entire Dawood gang was scared with tails between their legs.

The reporter noticed that Salem was not the same authoritative, confident, boastful don he had been last week. Salem's tone and tenor was entirely different. He hesitated for a moment before he could speak and when he did, he said something highly incredulous. '*Yeh murder* Lal Krishna Advani *ne karvaya hain.* [Lal Krishna Advani had commissioned this murder.] Why don't you call and ask him?' (Advani was a senior leader of the BJP, the ruling party in the state at the time.)

Shocked, the reporter could not think of anything to say.

14

Peanuts That Proved Costly

Joint Commissioner of Police Ranjit Singh Sharma, despite his army background and his interactions with international police organisations, was finding it difficult to handle the intense media glare and political pressures following the Gulshan Kumar killing.

His overly hectic daily routine was such that even his worst detractors were pleased that he was at the helm of the Crime Branch; he was experiencing one of the most turbulent phases of his career.

His days after the killing comprised a series of calls from the Police Commissioner Subhash Malhotra and calls from several ministers from Mantralaya, including Chief Minister Manohar Joshi and Home Minister Gopinath Munde. Sharma also had to give a lot of explanations to several other bigwigs in the state and top leaders from the Bharatiya Janata Party. Each time a heavyweight called Sharma, he offered explanations and provided reasons for not being able to make a breakthrough in apprehending the killers.

Several days after the music magnate had been gunned down, the Crime Branch, which usually made a big show about getting a lot done, had not been able to produce any tangible results in this investigation.

Sharma and his deputy K.L. Prasad were constantly on their toes and worked round-the-clock to make some headway in the killing. But despite all their efforts, there was no progress.

Normally, after any criminal incident, the police pick up some informants at random. These informants, even if they are unable to provide any vital clues in the ongoing probe, can at least give the cops a line of investigation to follow that may eventually lead to cracking the case.

All the units of the Crime Branch were working on the brief to tap all their informers and ferret out important information relating to the case. Nizamuddin, who was close to the Abu Salem gang, was picked up. He was detained in the Crime Branch lock-up for days and subjected to intense interrogation, before being let go, but without the cops being any wiser.

The cops' failure to stem the escalating law and order situation in the city put immense pressure on the state government. Right-wing political party Shiv Sena's supremo Bal Thackeray was at his vitriolic best in the editorials that appeared in his party's mouthpiece *Saamana*. Every day, he took potshots at the city police and even branded the Police Commissioner Subhash Malhotra a scarecrow who had failed to scare anyone.

But even while the cops were still smarting from Gulshan Kumar's killing, the mafia struck again and gunned down builder Natwarlal Desai in the business district of Nariman Point, just below Tulsiani Chambers. The high rise is just across the road from the seat of the state government; newspapers screamed the next day: 'Murder under the nose of Mantralaya!'

The then Chief Minister Manohar Joshi and Home Minister Gopinath Munde were finding it difficult to put up a brave front continuously. They concluded that the police machinery was seriously failing them. Some heads had to roll if they were to survive. Munde decided that Malhotra was incompetent to lead the police team and so, two weeks after the killing, he was unceremoniously shunted off to the nondescript posting of police housing and welfare. Malhotra's name will go down in the police record book as the first police chief to have suffered the ignominy of transfer just because of one high-profile killing.

Among all the police commissionerates in the country, the job of the Mumbai police chief was the most fragile and insecure. The city police chief has to please many bosses and suck up to many power centres to retain his job. Whoever understood the essence of survival managed to stay put longer and whoever failed to impress all bloated egos, had to make a disastrous exit. Malhotra and his predecessor Ramdev Tyagi were both thrown out because they could not win Bhartiya Janata Party leader Munde's approval.

Ronald Hyacinth Mendonca was appointed as the police commissioner of the Mumbai police on 28 August, in Malhotra's place.

✠

Two weeks since the assassination, the cops had not been able to make any headway in the case, but they also avoided major goof ups: some respite. Next came the controversial encounter of one Javed Fawda, at Ballard Pier on 28 August, the day Mumbai got its new police chief. Assistant Police Inspector Vasant Dhobale headed this encounter, and soon Dhobale's men cleverly leaked news of this encounter to some of their friends in print media. 'Gulshan Kumar's shooter killed in encounter', 'Crime branch hits back in style, guns down Gulshan Kumar's killer', read the headlines. The press, especially the Marathi press, went gaga over Dhobale's perceived gallantry.

At other times, Deputy Commissioner of Police, K.L. Prasad and his chief, R.S. Sharma would have been in a celebratory mood. But a pall of gloom had descended on the Crime Branch headquarters. The officers brushed aside the queries of the reporters over whether Javed Fawda was the main shooter or the side shooter, with a generic response: 'We are still investigating'.

In underworld parlance, the man who pulls the trigger on his victim is the main shooter, while the one who gives cover to the shooter or is merely a sidekick, is known as the side shooter or second shooter, and both are clearly identified as such. The very fact that the cops were so noncommittal about Javed Fawda's role in the killing meant that there was something extremely fishy going on here.

As it turned out, Javed Fawda turned out to be the Crime Branch's nemesis in more ways than they ever fathomed. Javed Fawda was actually Abu Sayama Abu Talib Shaikh, also known as Javed, and as he had a bucktooth, had earned the nickname 'Fawda'. Unfortunately, he was not the shooter Javed Fawda, just a mere peanut vendor who happened to be known by the same name.

Javed's sister Rubina who lived in a slum in Bandra, now called up a storm. She claimed that her brother used to sell peanuts outside the Masjid near Bandra railway station west and had been missing since 26 August. Four men had taken him away on the night of 26 August, following which she had lodged a missing person complaint with the Bandra Police Station.

On 29 August, she was summoned to identify the badly mutilated body of her brother. The autopsy revealed that not only Javed had been riddled with bullets fired at close range, but he was also run over by a vehicle, as his ribs were crushed under the impact of a car's wheels. Discoveries like this had put the police back in a difficult spot.

Sharma and Prasad tried desperately to explain to the media and human rights watchers that they had actually killed a criminal and not an innocent peanut vendor, but the worse was yet to come.

✠

Every phone call that Sharma answered and every visitor he met exposed the Crime Branch chief to major embarrassment. The Crime Branch had no defense when questioned by the media about the total failure of intelligence. This Fawda encounter had become a massive fiasco for them. Sharma decided to launch an offensive. Three days after the encounter, while the media was still sharpening their swords, Sharma decided to unmask the dirty underbelly of the film industry, which had allowed for these eruptions of violence.

Sharma had so far managed to piece together various conspiracies of revenge and execution: the scattered pieces of the puzzle that made up a complicated investigation. Abu Salem had organised a musical extravaganza for famous Bollywood composers Nadeem-Shravan in Dubai which was to be attended by top film stars like Shah Rukh Khan, Salman Khan, Jackie Shroff, and Aditya Pancholi. Salem had hosted the party and was seen hobnobbing with prominent business rivals of Gulshan Kumar, which led to the suspicion that the conspiracy to kill Gulshan Kumar was hatched at this party.

That such big names in the industry had any association with Salem had rattled Mumbai's top cops. Should they initiate action against them and book them for their nexus with the underworld or make them witnesses and strengthen their case? Also, unlike the police top brass in developed countries, the Indian police bosses have to always reckon with a major factor whether the suspect is related to some top politician, film star, or a business baron.

Touching any film star without a watertight case could result in a severe backlash, which might result in these stars using their contacts in Delhi and putting pressure on the Mantralaya mandarins. In a set-up where the chief minister and home minister do not see eye-to-eye, the proverbial Damocles' sword always hung over the top cop's head.

The most recent example had been made of Deputy Commissioner of Police, Rakesh Maria. Maria had had a phenomenally successful stint at the Crime Branch when he had cracked the Mumbai serial blasts of 1993. But when his men visited the house of Shiv Sena supremo Bal Thackeray's estranged son Jaidev on a tip-off that he had some animals of endangered species in his private zoo at Kalina, Maria was unceremoniously shunted out of his office within days of the episode.

Suave and politically smart as he was, Sharma decided to think one step ahead of potential opponents. He would first seek the consent of his political masters in Mantralaya and New Delhi. The idea was that the stars would be questioned, even grilled, but that even if they came clean, they would not be able to pull strings and make life miserable for the harangued cops. What they were asking for was immunity of a kind.

Sharma began working on his campaign, meticulously laying it out. The aim was to slowly provide nuggets of information to whet the curiosity of the powers that be in Delhi while keeping his political bosses in Mumbai appraised of his every move and initiative during the investigation.

Sharma knew very well that this was a huge risk but his stint in Delhi and interactions with wily national-level politicians had honed his skills in taking calculated risks. Sharma took the consent of his political masters in Mantralaya and called for a mega press conference. Each and every member of the press fraternity was called, even if he represented a shady street-side rag.

The orderlies were instructed to call, send pager messages, or even personally inform everyone who had occasion to call the main police control room to be present. The Commissioner of Police, Ronald Mendonca, would be holding a huge press conference after all.

Rarely has the police commissioner's chamber become so crowded that even policemen find it difficult to move around the room. Normally press conferences are a cacophonous event and crime reporters are at their meanest while posing uncomfortable questions. But to everyone's chagrin, Sharma was smiling. The man even appeared to have slept well the previous night. When Sharma was ready, he raised his hand to silence the media. Quiet fell over the room; only the whirring of conditioners going at full blast was audible.

Sharma began. 'During the course of our investigation, we have come across some startling background information on the Gulshan Kumar murder case. The famous music director, Nadeem Saifi, gave the *supari* for Gulshan's killing. The plot was hatched at the Empire Hotel, owned by druglord Vicky Goswami, in June this year. It happened in the presence of several Bollywood personalities.'

Even after Sharma stopped talking, there was a full 30-second silence in the room; some of the reporters were busy taking notes while the others looked at Sharma, mouths agape.

Nadeem Saifi of Nadeem-Shravan fame, the flamboyant music director, was involved in the barbaric killing of fellow Bollywood member Gulshan Kumar! Unbelievable. There was a squeal of disbelief. Everyone began to shout questions at the same time.

Sharma answered each and every question patiently and calmly. When asked why they had not arrested Nadeem, he said that the man was abroad as his wife had suffered a miscarriage. But they were in touch with him and he had promised to return the following week.

When asked what about the top film personalities who were present when the conspiracy to kill Gulshan Kumar was hatched, Sharma made it clear that all the stars were to be summoned soon. The press conference made headlines across the globe. It became a hot topic of discussion on all fronts; corridors of power and courtrooms began debating the whole issue. The killing and conspiracy exposed India's film industry and its murky world and laid the operations of the mafia bare, to some extent.

Everyone wanted to get to the root of the conspiracy. No one wanted to seem like they were taking sides with the tainted lot, and this did not spare the best actors in the country either. Sharma was given carte blanche, with a rider to 'be discreet and not let the shit hit the fan'.

Thus began the biggest star parade of the world in the high security precincts of the Mumbai police headquarters. No police headquarters in any city has ever witnessed the kind of spectacle Mumbai recorded in its annals of crime history.

The first one to be summoned to the Crime Branch was Shah Rukh Khan. Dressed in a black jacket and denims, he tried hard not to look nervous and tense. Khan was ushered into the small cabin of Assistant Commissioner of Police (ACP), L.R. Rao. For the huge and bulky ACP it was his hour of glory: sitting across King Khan and quizzing him over his indiscreet presence at the wrong party.

Rao was deferential with Khan and questioned him for over an hour as he recorded his statement formally. Shah Rukh, in his two-page statement, admitted that he had gone to Dubai for a Bollywood show organised by Dubai locals, but that he did not know the organisers personally and had no inkling that Salem and Anees Ibrahim were actually managing the whole show from behind the scenes. When he heard of their involvement, he had made an excuse, saying he had slipped and injured his leg, rendering him unable to attend the Nadeem-Shravan party.

Shah Rukh was allowed to leave, but not before he was mobbed by the waiting hordes of media men and camerapersons. Shah Rukh, who was smoking constantly, was sweating when he stepped out of ACP Rao's cabin. When some reporters accosted him and asked him questions, he got livid and scolded them, in an unlikely display. 'Can you please at least let me light my cigarette before hounding me with your questions?' he snapped at me when I asked him. The superstar was visibly trembling though it is not clear whether this was due to rage or nervousness. Somehow he managed to get into his car and vanish from the scene.

Jackie Shroff and Aditya Pancholi were next to be summoned to the Crime Branch and they had to pass through a similar routine. Unlike Shah Rukh, at least Shroff tried to keep it amiable with the media men and he did not get into an altercation with them.

Salman Khan, who had heard of the media circus, outsmarted the reporters and requested the cops to talk to him in a smaller office to which the media did not have access. He was called to the Bandra unit office where he spent a couple of hours with Crime Branch investigators.

But he was let go after making his statement to the cops, and nothing much came of it any more.

Sharma had successfully managed to ward off the raging storm. But this was just a temporary reprieve. Sharma had not forgotten Fawda, and neither had his detractors.

15

Clandestine Coups

The Mumbai police is the most unique law enforcement agency in the world. One of its most fascinating methods of dealing with an escalating crime situation is the 'encounter'. The media dubs police encounters as 'extra-judicial killings' where criminals are purportedly killed in what is reported as encounters.

The Mumbai police has scripted hundreds of encounters since 1982, when Julio Ribeiro was at its helm. The narrative of a police encounter rarely has any variation. The police *vaarta patra* or a press communiqué generically reads: 'A police team had gone to arrest criminal X. When the cops asked him to surrender, he opened fire at the police. When the cops fired back in self-defense, X was fatally injured and was rushed to the hospital, where he succumbed to his injuries'.

Section 100 of the Indian Penal Code (IPC) clearly states that if during the course of a violent assault a victim ends up killing the assailant, the killing is not tantamount to murder. Using this particular section of the law, the cops always maintained that it was the criminal who had opened fire on the police. Claiming that this was life threatening, the police team would suggest that they had to fire in self-defence–even if they had initiated fire. Now if the assailant was killed in the exchange, the policemen who had actually 'gone with the intention only to arrest him' should not be held responsible.

No one knows how and when the idea of this extra-judicial killing was mooted, but certain police historians have tried to record the evolution of police encounters.

According to the history of the Mumbai police, the first ever encounter that took place at the hands of the Mumbai police was that of Manohar alias Manya Surve, in which Ishaq Bagwan was hailed as a hero and got his name into the police archives as the first encounter cop. Reams and reams of newsprint were devoted to the pontification that the encounters were the brainchild of the then police chief Julio Ribeiro. During his stint in Punjab, it was said, he had found this to be an effective method to handle anarchists. Later, when Khalistani separatist ultras tried to make Mumbai their base, Additional Commissioner of Police Aftab Ahmed Khan, who was the chief of the Anti-Terrorism Squad, had taken on the Sikh militants and ostensibly dubbed the whole skirmish as encounters.

However, encounters were brought into fashion and given respectability by Police Commissioner Ramdev Tyagi. During the course of weekly crime meetings, Tyagi clearly exhorted his people to chase down the criminals and, if need be, 'encounter' them.

His successor, Subhash Malhotra, continued with the tradition but had to be stopped in his tracks after the police goofed up the Javed Fawda killing.

As petition after petition was filed in the High Court, all of them insisted that encounters were actually cold blooded murders, as if the criminals were awarded the death penalty right there on the streets without a trial. The High Court then came down heavily on the police, forcing them to consign their guns to their holsters.

The embargo on police actions continued for several months. The petitions around the Fawda encounter and subsequently around Sada Pawle's encounters put the brakes on the Mumbai police' crime busting aspirations. And when a division bench of the Bombay High Court was appointed in 1997-98 to probe into the veracity of these controversial encounters, the cops were caught on sticky ground.

The sessions court judge Aloysius Stanislaus Aguiar was the head of the probe committee. Judge Aguiar was a maverick judge and known for his unyielding integrity and probity.

Aguiar was one of the few Catholics of Mumbai to be elevated to the position of judge, and then to the elevated position of High Court judge. In his acceptance speech, he said, 'Critics of the legal system, and not without justification, refer to the Law as an Ass, but let us not forget, that it was on an Ass that Jesus Christ, the Ultimate Judge, rode triumphantly into Jerusalem (http://spotlight.net.in).'

After several months of investigation, Judge Aguiar filed a 223-page report on the encounters and declared that the police encounters of Javed Fawda and Sada Pawle were fake and did not match with the version and explanation that the cops had given to describe proceedings.

The report was so scathing and critical that the cops under question began to twitch in their seats.

Meanwhile, Ronnie Mendonca took over as the police commissioner. Mendonca was known for his integrity but had the mild mannerisms of a college professor. His tenure had started off in a controversial manner; he had named Nadeem as the key accused in the Gulshan Kumar killing and stirred up a hornet's nest. This was no sleepy professor.

But Mendonca did not believe in the unconventional policing methods practised during encounters. For months, he tried to experiment with laws like Maharashtra Prevention of Dangerous People's Act, which was commonly known as MPDA. As sterner laws like TADA had been repealed by 1995, the criminals were emboldened.

The year 1998 recorded the highest number of shootouts: over 100 people were either killed or badly injured by the firing of underworld operatives. 'Shootout' in police parlance means a firing incident, where a gunman opens fire on the victim, with the intention to kill, but sometimes if the victim is fortunate he may survive.

The police registers recorded a shootout every third day. The Crime Branch was constantly on its toes and the morale of the police force hit an all-time low. The human rights activists, the courts, and the media had all lambasted the cops in their respective manners. Arguments over the genuineness of the encounters and the Judge Aguiar Committee report raged on in the Bombay High Court.

The cops realised that they had to retaliate. They could not allow the gangsters to run amok and cast aspersions on both their practices as well as their competence. Every shootout was like a mockery of Mendonca's three-decade long career. Media pundits and columnists were writing blistering reviews while Mantralaya mantris had begun to lose patience at the worsening law and order situation.

And then something unexpected happened. The division bench of High Court rejected the Aguiar report and declared that the encounters were not fake.

Fawda encounter was genuine, says HC
EXPRESS NEWS SERVICE

MUMBAI, FEBRUARY 24: In a major boost to the Mumbai Police, the Bombay High Court today rejected the findings of the Aguiar Committee while upholding the genuineness of the encounter in which dreaded gangster Jawed Fawda alias Abu Sayama was killed on the midnight of August 28, 1997 at Ballard Pier. Justice Aguiar, who was asked by the High Court to conduct a probe into the encounter killings of Jawed Fawda, Sada Pawle and Vijay Tandel, had indicted Mumbai police for staging encounters and had said that they had killed an innocent peanut vendor Abu Sayama mistaking him for Jawed Fawda.

The division bench of Justice N Arumugham and Justice Ranjana Samant-Desai while dictating their order in a series of public interest petitions filed by the Samajwadi Party, the Committee for Protection of Democratic Rights (CPDR) and the Peoples' Union for Civil Liberties (PUCL), said that the police had fired at Fawda in self-defence. The bench had said yesterday that there was no mistake on police's part and that person killed was indeed Jawed Fawda the gangster.

The Bombay High Court judgement came as a major shot in the arm for the Mumbai police. Their enthusiasm and self-confidence returned with full vigour and gusto. And now they wanted the top brass to help them formulate a strategy to take on the underworld.

Mendonca decided to shed his mild manners once and for all. He had roped in retired colonel Mahendra Pratap Choudhary of special operations to train the cops in gunbattles with the underworld and to meet any eventuality. One day, he called a press conference and announced his bullet for bullet plans for the underworld. The plan had two dimensions to it: one, psychological warfare and two, covert operations.

The next day, the media went to town with Mendonca's gameplan. The *Indian Express*, which had taken a serious anti-encounter stance earlier, appreciated that he was bravely challenging the underworld. Their front page report declared:

Mendonca's battle cry: We'll now retaliate in gangsters' lingo
S Hussain Zaidi

MUMBAI, May 12: After a lull of six months, Mumbai police is all set to renew its fight against the underworld. And the battle is going to be bloody. For, Police Commissioner Ronnie Mendonca has promised this time his men "will answer the gangsters in their language."

His pronouncement is as much a warning to the gangsters as it is a signal to his own men that the unofficial ban on use of arms against gangsters, that was imposed after human rights organisations raised a hue and cry against encounters, has been lifted.

Mendonca's bullet-for-bullet game plan is based on a strong conviction that any more dithering on his part would adversely affect the morale of his men and boost that of the gangsters. He has already taken steps to send the message across that he is serious -- a group of 100 policemen are currently undergoing advanced armed combat training at Ghatkopar under Col M P Chaudhary, an ex-serviceman. Apart from sophisticated arms, they are also taking lessons in guerrilla warfare. The first batch of 25 men is likely to be out next week and that's when the police intend to raise the battle cry.

The commando teams will work in tandem with the elite Anti-Extortion Cells (AECs). Besides one such cell in the Crime Branch, there are four more cells created under the command of each regional additional commissioner of police. As the officers in these AECs have not been trained in handling automatic firearms, setting up ambushes and chasing criminals, the commando combat teams will provide them with the required "muscle and fire power." While the first batch of commandos will be attached to the Crime Branch, the subsequent teams will go on to consolidate the regional AECs.

And though not a single bullet has been fired yet, the entire police force is crackling with enthusiasm. At a meeting to discuss the measures to tackle a resurgent underworld last Saturday, senior officers had unanimously supported Mendonca's aggressive posturing. An additional commissioner of police who attended the meeting said: "In a nutshell, the strategy that we discussed was attack." One of the deputy commissioners of police added: "We are already cleaning our guns."

But they have an uphill task ahead.

The covert aspect of operations had a much more aggressive gameplan. Additional Commissioner of Police Dr Satyapal Singh and Param Bir Singh were assigned the task of wiping out the underworld from the city. Both the Singhs had a superb rapport and a burning desire to rid the city of its pervasive mafia menace. The two stalwarts formed three elite encounters squads under the leadership of three daring officers, inspectors Pradeep Sharma, Praful Bhosale, and Vijay Salaskar. The three officers belonged to the same 1983 batch and had certain 'killing instincts' in them.

Also, they were known to have the best intelligence network in the city. While Sharma was a protégé of Satyapal, Bhosale, and Salaskar owed allegiance to Parambir. As Chhota Shakeel and Arun Gawli were the immediate priorities of the Mumbai police, the three encounter squads were working on a specific brief: 'Finish off the Shakeel and Gawli gangs'.

Salaskar and Bhosale went after Gawli, while Sharma decided to take on the Shakeel gang. Between the three of them, they eliminated over 300 gangsters, of which Sharma scalped the highest number. Sharma alone managed to eliminate over 110 gangsters, which also included three terrorists from the Lashkar-e-Tayyeba, while Bhosale managed to kill over ninety gangsters from both the Gawli and Chhota Rajan gangs.

Salaskar could only kill sixty gangsters but he managed to singlehandedly finish off the muscle power of Gawli gang. Almost all the top shooters of the Gawli gang met their fate at Salaskar's hands.

The police top brass believed that encounters would prove to be a major deterrent for the underworld as they would instill the fear of God in the minds of the reckless gangsters. It was a grim war. As rising unemployment continued to drive scores of youths to join Mumbai gangs, earning anything from 5,000 to 25,000 rupees, the cops had found it difficult to stem the growing number of sharpshooters. But encounters ensured one thing: the young men who had been inveigled into this life of crime realised that the underworld was a one-way street. The fate of joining the underworld could only be death.

This understanding seriously depleted the growing numbers of underworld recruits. The bullet-for-bullet and life-for-life credo the Mumbai police began to follow ensured that the mafia ran out of getting fresh blood. The ranks and files of the underworld were thrown out of gear.

Finally, the cops had something to smile about.

16

Tech That

The British must have had their reasons to shift the Mumbai Police Commissioner's office in 1896 to an Anglo-Gothic building, which faced a very busy thoroughfare and a wholesale fruit and vegetable market. Although the majestic Arthur Crawford Market building, an architectural marvel, overshadows all other British architecture in its vicinity, the Mumbai Police Commissioner's office which serves as the headquarters of the city police is no poor cousin. It too figures on the heritage list.

More than a hundred years later, the Mumbai police headquarters (HQ) is still sitting in the midst of the sprawling Crawford market and many other shopping plazas and markets that have mushroomed around it. For great bargains there are Mohatta Market and Lohar Chawl, Manish Market on the other side, Dava Bazaar on Princess Street, and Fashion Street if you walk a little further on the Metro Cinema side. While the entire stretch near the Mumbai police HQ is a shopper's delight, for traffic, pedestrians, and the police it is a nightmare junction. It is always throbbing with roadside vendors, the *mathadi* workers pushing handcarts and a sea of shoppers who spill over onto the roads jostling for space with the oncoming traffic.

Back in the early nineties, when the then Prime Minister P.V. Narasimha Rao and then Finance Minister Dr Manmohan Singh ushered in economic liberalisation, most of Mumbai's traders and businessmen quickly cashed in on the moment to import things that were once only smuggled in. It was a time of sweeping changes everywhere in India, more so near the Mumbai police HQ'S unofficial shopping district. Rundown old shops were giving way to swankier departmental stores with elegant facades and amazing window displays. While the wholesale markets were still doing business in small, stuffy shops, new stores like Roopam, Roop Milan, and Metro, bang opposite the police headquarters, were actually minting money as shoppers went berserk.

For the businessmen who set up shops here, it was bonanza time from day one, and they had the added bonus of having the Mumbai police as their neighbour. Yet, while genuine traders set up shop here, so did the dubious ones. Notorious drug baron Iqbal Memon alias Iqbal Mirchi acquired a cluster of shops across the pavement from the headquarters. The Mumbai mafia, much like the other organised gangs in the world, cocked a snook at the law enforcers. Dawood Ibrahim's gang managed to construct an illegal shopping complex on government land near the police headquarters. It was called the Sara-Sahara shopping centre and the police did not have a clue about this for a long time.

But the worst was yet to come. The perpetration of a violent crime in broad daylight, right across from the high security precincts of the Mumbai police HQ, was to prove an indelible blot of shame for cops who prided themselves as the second best after Scotland Yard. The Mumbai police would never recover from this embarrassment.

✠

The first shooter spotted his quarry dressed in a blue shirt and black trousers coming out of Roopam and walking towards a public telephone booth. He picked up his mobile phone, dialled a Karachi number, and called Chhota Shakeel who asked him to stand by for further instructions. The first shooter nodded at the second shooter, who discreetly began moving towards the same public telephone booth.

Bharat Shah was one of the top business tycoons in the city. He had several huge departmental stores. Often he was spotted at Page 3 parties, where his picture merited a mention in the tabloids. Of late, though, Shah had been a worried man. He was being forced to do the bidding of lowly riff raff, the likes of whom he would not even allow to stand in front of his store; the mafia had been giving him trouble. Today, on 8 October 1998, he was asked to call a Karachi number. He did not like to leave his work and walk towards the public booth designated to make the call.

Reluctantly, he went to the public booth and placed a call. He barely spoke a few words but a witness recalled later that he sounded agitated and non-compliant. He also got irritated midway and hurriedly finished the conversation, minutes after he was connected, exiting the booth. While Shah was making the payment for an international call, the first shooter got a call from Karachi.

'*Daal do behenchod ko* [kill the sister fucker]!' was all the caller from Karachi said.

The first shooter looked at the second shooter and gesticulated with two fingers across his jugular vein, indicating a symbolic slitting of the throat.

The second shooter, who was waiting for his cue, now moved with amazing agility, whipped out an automatic pistol from the small of his back, and accosted Shah, who had stepped out onto the pavement outside the public telephone booth. Shah, still irritated, had turned disdainfully towards the man, when the shooter began firing at him point blank. Shah's eyes had widened with fear and disbelief, but by then enough cordite had entered his blood to stun his voice and reflexes. Shah's lifeless body slumped to the ground.

The second shooter climbed onto the pillion of the bike behind the first shooter, fleeing the scene. The motorbike quickly disappeared into the swarm of vehicles at the Crawford Market junction.

Two more men, backup shooters, emerged from the woodwork and dialed the same Karachi number to report the killing.

'*Bhai, Shah ka kaam tamaam ho gaya* [Bhai, we've killed Shah].'

Shah, a billionaire, lay dead on the Mumbai pavement. He had been shot dead in the police's own backyard. The killing shook the city and left the reputation of the famed Mumbai police in tatters. The edifice called the Mumbai police HQ did not seem so formidable now.

✠

The 27th Police Commissioner of the Mumbai Police, Ronald Mendonca, now came under immense flak from all quarters. Any other police chief would have been punished for this slackness and given the marching orders for failing to prevent such a sensational crime. Another Police Commissioner Subhash Malhotra had been shunted out after the Gulshan Kumar murder. Mendonca survived because the de facto chief of the then Shiv Sena-BJP state government in Maharashtra was Bal Thackeray. For some reason, Mendonca was his favourite.

But one police officer took this personally: Assistant Commissioner of Police Pradeep Sawant. At the time, he was a handsome, strapping young police officer who brooked no nonsense. He was resourceful, diligent, and one of the smartest cops in the Mumbai police. Unlike those who belonged to the illustrious Indian Police Service (IPS) cadre, Sawant had been inducted into the service through the Maharashtra Police Service Commission (MPSC), which made him inferior to the so-called 'blue blooded' IPS. But Sawant decided to ignore this notional superiority of cadres and establish his worth through merit. Starting as an assistant commissioner of police (ACP) from the quiet division of Byculla, Sawant rose through the ranks. He managed to crack many sensational crimes in the Byculla division and won the annual award for the best detection officer. Sawant won accolades from his friends and grudging admiration from officers who had initially looked down upon him for being of state cadre. Unlike other DCPs of Crime, Sawant had been picked up purely on merit, as a man who deserved a place in the hallowed precincts of *patharwali* building (a building made of stone), another name for the Crime Branch building in the Mumbai police HQ.

At the Crime Branch, Sawant continued his lucky run. Mafia gangs had begun to recognise him and were often scared to take on an assignment, fearing his iron hand. They knew that if they were caught by Sawant, they were as good as dead or handicapped. Sawant reveled in their fear; if the mafia was afraid of him, he had really arrived.

But Shah's killing had come as a head-on punch to the face, leaving him with a black eye. Sawant was seething with frustration and anger. He wanted to retaliate and convey a lasting message to the mafia: that they could not get away this time.

However, Sawant realised that the mafia had all the means at their disposal and no rules to abide by—while the Crime Branch was shackled with so many antiquated laws.

Sawant's subsequent investigation revealed that Bharat Shah had received a call from Shakeel and was asked to return the call. While Shah had made the call, several communications were exchanged between Shakeel and his shooters and it seemed that it was decided that Shah had to be killed following the end of that brief phone call.

That half an hour between the first call to Shah to the first bullet that was shot was crucial to his eventual fate. If only the Crime Branch had been listening in, the killing could have been avoided.

Now, Sawant was not a technologically savvy man. He did not know much about wire tapping or telephonic surveillance. In fact, the whole of the Mumbai police were luddites when it came to technology. No police officer had ever actually tried using technology to his advantage. Indian communication systems and police surveillance were in their infancy until the turn of the century.

There was only one instance where the police had managed to beat the criminals with the help of technology. In 1995, Arun Gawli's men had killed Bal Thackeray's *manasputra* (adopted son), Jayant Jadhav, in Prabhadevi. The city police was totally clueless and had no inkling of who killed Jadhav and why, except that a boy had seen one of the shooters using a mobile phone right after the killing to inform someone that Jadhav had been eliminated.

Additional Commissioner of Police, central region, Sridhar Vagal, who was from an engineering background, used this clue and got in touch with mobile service providers to crack the case. Maxtouch services helped the cops in identifying the signals and the cell phones that were within the crucial range and at the spot of the killing. The cops began zeroing in on all identified numbers and got their first clue when it turned out that the number was registered in the name of a Dagdi Chawl resident. The case was cracked thanks to Vagal's quick thinking.

Sawant did not have an engineering background; he began reading books and summoned all service providers to the Crime Branch office.

Wire tapping was still carried out by means of the antiquated methods of parallel line, also called a dummy line. Whenever a call came in, the voice got recorded on a tape which could be used as evidence in a court of law during a trial.

Incidentally, the Indian Penal Code did not have many provisions for wire tapping except a century old law of the Telegraph Act of 1885, which was later updated and became the Indian Telegraph Act of 1975. The procedure was as such: if a particular number had to be tapped then the concerned officer would make a request to his senior, who could be an additional commissioner of police or joint commissioner of police. He in turn would seek a go-ahead from the police chief. The police commissioner would have to get the approval of the home department. By the time, the procedure was followed through, precious time was squandered and the quarry lost, most of the time.

'The first World War happened because of a stray telegraph. When Arch Duke Ferdinand was killed in Austria, a telegraph using Morse code alerted all the people concerned. Consequently, Germany moved swiftly and annexed Austria,' observed an additional commissioner of police. Such were the dangers that prompted the powers that be to realise the need for a controlling act for the telegraph during war.

Sawant learnt that off the air or illegal interception required just technological knowhow and no paperwork or extra time: it could be done by anyone with a briefcase-sized gizmo in his car. There was also a major issue in the conversation thus recorded; someone had to hear each and every word and build up a case as the cops never had access to advanced software, which could be used for automated content analysis.

In techno-surveillance of all kinds, the only privacy left is inside your head. The software of automated content analysis picks up chosen words and throws up that particular conversation after a random search. So, for the Mumbai police any conversation that had words like Dawood Bhai, Shakeel Bhai, paisa, wasooli (procurement), ghoda (gun), or other similar flagged terms would be picked up and brought to their attention.

The Mumbai police, accustomed to the old parallel line methods which involved hours and hours of listening, recording, and manual transcription, somehow failed to adopt and adapt to this new technology. One group of policemen from the Mumbai police, the controversial encounter specialists, managed to crack it. They got a mobile tower and started doing off the air interception.

After Sawant met the major service providers of the time, Maxtouch and BPL, he realised they had hit pay dirt. The cops realised they could tap whichever phone they wanted and in whatever manner they wanted.

At the time, the Crime Branch's human intelligence or what is also known as the informer's network was still strong. The cops found out that the murder was organised by none other than Chhota Shakeel and that his two men Mohammad Ali Kanjari and Yusuf Shaikh might be involved.

Necessary permissions were soon sought and the police began listening to the conversation of the duo. Soon after, they picked up Kanjari and Shaikh in the Bharat Shah murder case to salvage their lost pride. In the process, they outdid themselves, achieving a coup of sorts when they managed to crack Karachi-based Chhota Shakeel's SIM card. Now, they realised, they could even tap his Pakistani phone.

The Mumbai police to this day, rely on phone tapping for most of their intelligence. All this began way back then, when the Bharat Shah case gave them confidence that they could tap anyone's phone, even beyond the city or the country.

Once they began listening to Shakeel's phone, what they found was a goldmine of information. The cops were led to a trove of Shakeel's connections with politicians, senior cops, journalists, and above all most of the film stars, including some of the reigning Khans.

17

Close Shave

For six years, he had constantly been on the run. Running from the law of the land, running from Interpol, and above all running from arch fiends Chhota Shakeel and Dawood Ibrahim, his nemeses. Now, in 2000, he was tired of running.

Chhota Rajan was a classic example of the gangster who could not find a safe place to hide and live happily, despite having been on the move for six years. He was, however, never short of money or resources. The Intelligence Bureau was clearly giving him the required logistical and financial support, yet Rajan could not escape the hawkish eyes of his enemies.

Rajan spent several years on a yacht off the Kuala Lumpur coast in Malaysia. The waters there were usually safer than buildings; anyone approaching the yacht could be spotted from a distance, intercepted, and neutralised.

Rajan felt safer in Southeast Asian countries. With multiple Indian passports in his kitty, he kept shuttling between the various cities of Malaysia, Cambodia, and even Indonesia. Finally, Rajan realised that Thailand had the potential to become a safe haven. It was undoubtedly a more 'India-friendly' country than the others. Under the assumed identity of Vijay Daman, with an Indian passport issued from Chennai, Rajan rented a spacious flat in Charan Court in Bangkok's plush neighbourhood of Sukhumvit Soi, 26th street.

The idea was not to get a beautiful house but to ensure a location that was secure. It was a single-storeyed structure and had a massive wrought iron gate in front, with round-the-clock security arrangements. Rajan's current location was known only to a handful of his trusted aides, which included his right-hand man, Rohit Verma, who was living under the assumed name of Michael D'Souza.

Rajan had slowly begun to feel safe in the anonymity of Bangkok. He had begun to move around in Thailand and was exploring business opportunities that could legitimise his stay in the country. But on the advice of his controller in the Bureau, Rajan had not taken a Thai number. He was still using a Malaysian SIM card, but had managed to set up other logistics and a support system in Thailand. The hawala channel was organised, his local contacts from agencies were introduced, and he had received his instructions of do's and don'ts. He had also identified the popular Indian joints that he needed to avoid. Ironically, Indian ganglords never imagined that their paths would cross with the infamous mafia from other countries of the world. Rajan happened to know of some of the top bosses of the Triads in Bangkok, one of the world's most dreaded mafia, but he neither thought of collaborating with them, nor did he want to risk anything that would irk them. Things were fine the way they were.

But Rajan's feeling of peace and security was short lived. One fine day he got a tip-off from his controller that he should not be leaving the protection of his house. He was also told to restrict his movements within the country. Rajan was stunned when he realised that Shakeel's men were there on the lookout for him.

Apart from his wife Sujata and a couple of highly trusted lieutenants, Rajan had not disclosed to anyone that he had moved to Bangkok. In fact, he had not even changed his cellphone number. But his agency man was serious and had told him clearly that 8 to 10 men were trying to track him down and that their campaign had been on for the last couple of months. The threat to his life was really serious, Rajan was told.

Rajan and Verma had become alert and wary of people moving around Sukhumvit Soi. But it is human tendency to take any threat seriously when it is fresh. As days pass and no untoward movement is seen, people tend to become complacent. Rajan waited things out for days and then weeks, but when nothing happened and not even a suspicious movement was reported around his house, he presumed that the intelligence input was a hoax and the agency had raised a false alarm.

✠

There was no reason for Rajan to feel complacent, as he himself had been part of such long term missions. In a high stake game of assassination, sometimes one has to wait for the quarry not for months, but for years. Former French President Charles De Gaulle and late Libyan leader, Muammar Gaddafi, both had survived over thirty assassination attempts. Fidel Castro survived assassination attempts from his own relatives. And in several cases the assassins patiently waited for a year to strike, but still could not achieve what they set out to do.

In the case of Rajan, Shakeel had been working on the job for six months. His men had been scouring all the probable hideouts of Rajan. From Australia to Malaysia and from Hong Kong to Bangkok, they had hunted for him everywhere. But everywhere they drew a blank except for a small but significant kernel of information: that Rajan and Verma were together.

It was never known how Shakeel's men managed to trace Rajan's whereabouts down to the precise details of his Bangkok address. The hit team which was tracking him for months got lucky and found themselves with Rohit Verma's address. Shakeel, in one of his interviews, later revealed that he thought as Verma wanted to become a don himself and topple Rajan, he had tipped-off Shakeel's men. After getting the address, six sharpshooters from Mumbai led by Munna Jhingada were assigned the task of killing Rajan.

Jhingada, a Mumbai-based sharpshooter who reached Karachi via Kathmandu, met Shakeel, who briefed him about the plan, availability of the weapon, escape possibilities, and gave him access to endless supply of cash. Jhingada had never been given so much importance in his life. Money and proximity to his master made him feel heady. He agreed to kill Rajan even if it meant giving up his life.

Jhingada was given Pakistani citizenship through Shakeel's contacts. Travelling on a Pakistani passport, Jhingada became Mohammad Salim when he disembarked from a Pakistan International Airlines flight in Bangkok. On 31 August 2000, Jhingada made the first breakthrough when he discovered that Verma along with his wife Sangeeta and his 2-year-old daughter were staying in Charan Court on Sukhumvit Soi. Jhingada was instructed to rent a flat opposite Charan Court. Fortunately, with the help of a local businessman known as Cirrac (according to a police dossier), he rented a place in Amree Court. The location was such that Jhingada could keep a close watch on Rajan and Verma in Charan Court.

Now, the plan to strike was in its final stages. Shakeel sent more men from Karachi, who also moved into Amree Court along with Jhingada on 11 September. All the preparations were in place and the men were waiting for the final call from Karachi.

The call came on the morning of 14 September and the final briefing was given to Jhingada with the instructions that the attack had to be carried out on the same evening without fail. Jhingada in his earlier reconnaissance had discovered that the massive gate in the premises of Charan Court remained closed from inside and that it was guarded round-the-clock by two burly men.

It was easy to get rid of the men but any sign of violence at the gate would alert Rajan inside, giving him enough of a headstart to escape. There had to be a non-violent way of entering the building premise.

Finally, a way was found. Four Thai men dressed in black suits approached the gate. They were carrying a huge birthday cake. They told the guards at the gate that it was the birthday of Michael D'Souza's little daughter and his Indian friends wanted to surprise the family with the cake. The guard looked at them suspiciously but the cake and the men seemed harmless. Even as they were considering the pros and cons, when a 200-dollar bill was slipped into their palm, the decision was made easier. The gate was opened and the four men slowly drove their car inside the premises. As the guards moved to close the gates, four more Indians showed up out of nowhere and pounced on them. The guards were overpowered and trussed up. These four men who had roughed up the guards were now stationed at the gate.

Jhingada and his Thai aides stealthily entered the building and knocked at the door of Rajan and Verma's first floor flat. The door was opened by Verma, who was startled to see four men at the door. Even before Verma could get a gun or alert Rajan, a volley of bullets mowed him down. They stormed the house and began scouring for Rajan. Verma's wife was also injured in the firing, while his maid servant and daughter were locked inside a room. Rajan, who was in another room, heard the gunshots and was not prepared for this sudden attack at all.

Considering the choice between fight or flight, he chose the latter. He immediately locked the door and began looking for a way to reach the ground floor. The gunmen, after having searched the whole flat, including the washroom, finally realised that he was in the bedroom. They tried to push open the door but it did not give way. Without wasting any time, they started firing indiscriminately at the wooden door.

One bullet managed to pierce through the door and hit Rajan in his abdomen, as he searched for a rope with which to climb down the building. Rajan, in a state of panic, jumped out of the window and landed on the thick bushes below. A profusely bleeding and petrified Rajan crawled down and managed to hide himself amidst the thick foliage in the compound. Finally, when the assailants managed to break open the door, they found that the room was empty and splotches of blood were everywhere including the window. They thought Rajan had managed to escape. No one imagined, even for a moment, that he could be lying beneath the bushes barely a few feet away. The whole attack was over in less than five minutes.

But the non-stop gunshots were enough to alert the entire neighbourhood and the police. The cops rushed to the spot and apart from blood, gore and a dead Verma, they recovered sophisticated weapons from the spot left behind by the shooters.

Meanwhile, Rajan, through his contacts, had managed to contact the Thai police, who rushed him to the Intensive Care Unit of Smitivej Hospital. Eyewitnesses recount that Rajan was terrified after the attack and desperate for protection. He was also delirious and kept screaming 'they will bomb the hospital' through the night.

The once confident, cocksure don was now a scared, shattered man, hallucinating about the end of his days.

18

The Art of Survival

The news of the attack on Chhota Rajan trickled down to Mumbai on the afternoon of 15 September 2000. The television channels and news websites had reported the killing of an Indian gangster who was probably Chhota Rajan in Bangkok. It was widely speculated that Rajan had been killed by the Triads because they did not like an Indian gangster on their turf. The Indian media and the police, back then, could not have imagined that it was actually the Karachi-based Chhota Shakeel who had organised this killing from afar. Until Sheela Bhatt (from Rediff.com) and I (from eindia.com) spoke to Shakeel on the same day and carried his detailed interviews, details of the incident remained hazy. Shakeel, in an interview with Sheela, had boasted of his planning and his men's courage. This is also when Shakeel revealed that it was Rohit Verma, who wanted to take over the mantle of the gang, who had tipped him off about Rajan's whereabouts.

By evening the news of this death had spread across the corridors of power in New Delhi and Mumbai. The top brass of central intelligence were chiefly concerned about the shift of balance and the establishment of Dawood's hegemony, which would be the outcome of Rajan's elimination. The police, however, heaved a sigh of relief.

But when official channels got involved and the Ministry of External Affairs got in touch with the Thai government, they found out that Vijay Daman alias Chhota Rajan was quite alive and out of danger.

Whatever followed is beyond comprehension for most Indians who were following the news of the assault on Rajan in Bangkok, barring a few of the senior police officers of the Mumbai police who desperately made efforts to reach Rajan for interrogation and subsequently to get him extradited to India.

In fact, even the sharpest newshounds and analysts faced a wall of deafening silence when it came to the Rajan saga in Thailand. The events following the attack on Rajan unfolded in the most bizarre manner. It seemed more confounding and till date, there is no real clarity regarding what went down. Soon after the attack on Rajan, Shakeel had clearly bragged in his telephonic interviews to reporters in Mumbai that his men had docked a speedboat on the Bangkok coast to make a swift getaway after the killing.

But barely two days after the incident the ringleader Munna Jhingada, and his accomplice, Sher Khan, were arrested at Robinson Departmental Store in the Bang Rak area. Another shooter, Mohammad Yusuf, was arrested at Sukhumvit Soi and the local Thai shooter Chavalit was arrested at a flat in Intarnara Soi area. All four were purportedly those who had attacked Rajan.

While the arrests of these shooters were inexplicable, a confidential dossier of the Mumbai police explained they were part of a strategic move of Chhota Shakeel's, who let his men surrender and show them as cooperative so that he could score brownie points with the Royal Thai police.

A team of police officers led by Assistant Commissioner of Police Shankar Kamble was sent to Bangkok to interrogate and extradite Rajan. The team reached Bangkok and met Police Colonel Kriekpong, who was in charge there. They apprised him that Vijay Daman was none other than the Indian gangster Chhota Rajan living under an assumed identity.

A private jet parked at the Bangkok airport was hired by Rajan's men to whisk him away. But with Kriekpong's intervention, the plan was foiled and Rajan was detained for the offence of illegal entry into Thailand. However, Kriekpong, who until that day was cooperation personified, did an about turn soon after.

The dossier adds that Kriekpong told the Mumbai police team that as they never sought the assistance of the Mumbai police, there was no way that they could become part of the investigation. Also, as neither Interpol nor the Central Bureau of Investigation (CBI) had conveyed to them the impending visit of the Mumbai police, there could not be any official communication between them, Kriekpong told the Mumbai police team.

The Mumbai police was making desperate efforts to ensure that they got hold of Rajan, while the Royal Thai police expected communication through diplomatic channels, which was not forthcoming. Even as a series of requests and reminders were made to the First Secretary for an official draft to the Thai government, no such letter was issued by the Indian government. The Mumbai police soon understood that Colonel Kriekpong would not cooperate with them. He had not allowed them to have any meetings with Rajan or his assailants, who were also under detention.

The Mumbai police made a last ditch effort, proposing for Rajan's extradition from Bangkok. The documents were routed through CBI and Interpol in Delhi. But the papers never reached Bangkok.

Even as the Indian bureaucrats were procrastinating over the sending of these documents, formal extradition requests and such other important communication, Rajan's wound was healing fast.

Over seventy days had passed after the incident and the Mumbai police, despite a couple of visits, had not been able to make any headway in the case. Nor were they any closer in getting Rajan back on Indian soil.

And then, on 24 November, Rajan mysteriously disappeared from the Smitivej Hospital. His escape was next to impossible, situated as he was on the heavily guarded fourth floor room of the hospital. His escape was unanticipated especially as Rajan was not only physically unfit but also overweight and weakened by his wound.

Several theories were offered around his escape. The Thai police claimed that Rajan took the help of professional mountaineers to escape and climb down the four floors of the hospital. Thailand's scientific crime detection division found mountaineering rope and descender equipment along the wall of the hospital and found scratches and traces of cement on them, which confirm that they were used in Rajan's getaway, reported *Bangkok Post*.

According to the report, professionals helped Rajan slip down the 40-metre rope from the fourth floor of the hospital within minutes. The 13-mm rope had a breaking point of 200 kg. A man was also seen buying the rope and the equipment from a shop in a locality in Bangkok called Soi Rangnam, the paper reported. Deputy Commander of the Division Chuan Voravanich, had forwarded these findings to chief investigator of the Thonglor Police Station, Mantharn Abhaiwong.

According to other news reports, Rajan's Thai lawyer, Sirichai Piyaphichetkul had a simpler explanation: Rajan paid 25 million baht ($5,80,000) to Thai police major-general Kriekphong Phukprayoon—who later denied it—in exchange for his freedom. He simply walked out of Smitivej to a car waiting outside to drive him away to safety.

Rajan's escape and the police's fanciful account of what happened at Samitivej on 24 November have caused considerable embarrassment in Thailand. Nine non-commissioned police officers were sacked for 'grave negligence'.

The same paper also claimed that the commander of Metropolitan Police Division 5, Krisda Pankongchuen, had ordered investigations into a report that a number of police officers had visited Rajan at the hospital to receive money.

Thailand's Prime Minister Chuan Leekpai has said that he believed the Indian mafia figure could not have escaped without help. 'Obviously it would not have been possible for Rajan to escape if his helpers never stood to gain anything,' he said.

The Maharashtra state government was just as stupefied at this unprecedented vanishing act, that too from a secure hospital. The Maharashtra home minister, who was also the Deputy Chief Minister Chhagan Bhujbal, had vociferously alleged that the Centre allowed the gangster to escape. He reiterated the hurdles and obstacles that the Mumbai police faced at every juncture and how their efforts were sabotaged by lack of cooperation by the central government.

These allegations made by such an authority with so much conviction. stung the Union government. Silence on their part would have been only detrimental.

The then Minister of State for External Affairs Ajit Panja got into damage control mode and claimed that the Centre had done whatever the Thai government wanted it to do for Rajan's extradition. 'But, if they [the Maharashtra government] have said so it is absolutely wrong. Point to point action was taken and there was no delay on our part,' Mr Panja was quoted as saying. The Union Minister of State for Home Vidyasagar Rao said it was not proper for anybody to comment on this case till the government received full details of the incident.

The mystery of Rajan's disappearance had only deepened after such statements from the government. A certain section of the media reported it as a 'conspiracy of silence'.

However, Rajan's lawyer remained forthcoming with whatever details he could share with the media. Sirichai claimed that Rajan phoned him from 'abroad' to tell him about how he had bribed the Thai police officials. He said Rajan was in Cambodia and was intending to go to a third country, possibly in Europe. According to another version by Sirichai, Rajan was in a Southeast Asian country, planning to continue his journey to 'somewhere' in the Middle-East.

Speculation aside, it is obvious that Rajan had every reason to fear for his life in Bangkok and that his escape was carefully planned. The gunmen who were sent to kill him, identified as followers of rival mafia boss Dawood Ibrahim, had vowed to fulfill their mission as soon as they were released. It might be some time before the three gunmen who were apprehended after the shootout walked free, but other gunmen from Dawood's gang were suspected to have arrived in Bangkok, awaiting the chance to kill Rajan.

So where did Rajan go? It would have been foolish of him to try to leave via any of Thailand's airports, where the immigration authorities maintained computer records of everyone entering and leaving the country. The fastest and easiest overland escape route would be a five-hour drive from Bangkok to the Cambodian border. Cambodian immigration authorities issue visas on the spot to anyone for USD20. Rajan could then have continued by car to Phnom Penh, and from there left by air to any destination in Asia, the Middle-East, Europe, or Australia.

Another possibility would have been the more than 24-hour-long drive down to the Malaysian border. It is possible to sneak across undetected, as hordes of illegal immigrants and smugglers do all the time. Given that Rajan used to be based in Malaysia and had extensive contacts within the Indian community there, it would have been possible for him to hide there till the uproar over his escape died down. Then he could arrange for a passport and leave for a safer destination. Thailand's only other land borders are with Myanmar and Laos, which are not considered likely escape routes.

Regardless of how he escaped, Rajan's flight from Thailand meant that an important chapter in his criminal career had come to an end. Rajan, as Vijay Daman, had initially obtained a tourist visa, but in May 2001 he requested to have his visa status changed to that of a business visitor, which would have made it possible for him to obtain a permission to run a company, called Daman Import-Export. The company ostensibly exported dried fish from Thailand to Hong Kong, but it is suspected that it was a front for his illegal activities. A business visa simply enabled him to stay on in Thailand.

Rajan's near-perfect set-up in Bangkok went up in a burst of gunfire three months before the attack on him, and recreating such a set-up was not going to be that easy with Dawood's men hot on his tail.

19

Post 9/11

The promise of a virginal, green-eyed hourie in the garden of paradise, where streams of honey and milk have been abundantly flowing, has been the most powerful motivation for crazy men since time immemorial. But none can beat what a few insane pilots did on the historic morning of 9/11. In a series of coordinated suicide attacks by Al Qaeda upon the United States on 11 September 2001, a group of jihadis launched one of the most heinous attacks in modern history.

Early on the morning of 11 September, nineteen hijackers took control of four commercial airliners en route to San Francisco and Los Angeles from Boston, Newark, and Washington D.C. (Washington Dulles International Airport). At 8:46 am, American Airlines Flight 11 was flown into the World Trade Center's North Tower, followed by United Airlines Flight 175, which hit the South Tower at 9:03 am.

Another group of hijackers flew American Airlines Flight 77 into the Pentagon at 9:37 am. A fourth flight, United Airlines Flight 93 crashed near Shanksville, Pennsylvania, at 9:57 am, after the passengers on board engaged in a fight with the hijackers. Its ultimate target was thought to be either the Capitol (the meeting place of the United States Congress) or the White House (http://news.bbc.co.uk).

It is reported that the suicide attack resulted in the death of 2, 973 victims, apart from the hijackers. The overwhelming majority of casualties were civilians, including nationals of over seventy countries.

These men had learnt that the attack would give them a quick death and an equally rapid meeting with a seductress in heaven. For them, jihad was the quickest means to reach heaven, regardless of any insanity that they may have to perpetrate in the process.

Muslims across the world reacted to the incident in different manners. While some were jubilant that the mighty United States of America had been brought to its knees, others had to hang their head in shame, feeling that the attack was orchestrated in the name of Islam by a few self-appointed guardians of Islam. The attack thus blemished a religion of peace forever. The 9/11 attacks became a watershed incident, one that changed the world forever.

The incident also had far reaching repercussions for Dawood Ibrahim. One of the famous euphemisms that Dawood cited while giving instructions to his men to kill his detractors was, '*Duniya uske liye choti kardo* [make his world smaller than it is now]' — implying that the movement of his enemies be restricted so as to not let them roam around the world freely. Let them be cocooned in their shells with fear of getting caught or killed.

Ironically, the 9/11 attacks made the world a smaller place for Dawood. In fact, he had been on the US radar for a long time, but as terror had not hit Uncle Sam earlier, they did not get serious about apprehending him.

Way back in 1995, US President Bill Clinton, by presidential decision directive number 42, designated the activities of organised crime groups a major threat to national security and made it a priority for American intelligence agencies to apprehend such groups. A similar decision was taken by John Major's government in the United Kingdom on the recommendation of Stella Rimington, the then director-general of MI5, and by other European Union governments.

Since then, the Dawood gang was amongst the organised crime groups being closely monitored by various Western intelligence agencies, thereby keeping him largely confined to Karachi, where he is a privileged guest of the ISI.

Over the years, Pakistan premiers and later its military dictator General Pervez Musharraf and the ISI have fine-tuned the art of hoodwinking the international community and particularly the US Administration—be it with respect to its assistance in supplying clandestine weapons of mass destruction to North Korea and Iran, its sponsorship of cross-border terrorism into India and Afghanistan, or evasion of action against terrorists and other organisations.

At the request of the Government of India, Interpol, based in Lyons, France, issued many lookout notices for Dawood's arrest and deportation to India if he was found in the territory of any member-country. The lookout notices also gave his Karachi address.

In response to these notices, the Pakistani authorities kept denying the presence of Dawood in their territory. Earlier, the matter was taken up by Atal Behari Vajpayee with President Pervez Musharraf during their meeting in Agra in July 2001 (which was reiterated during their meeting in Islamabad in January 2004). Dawood's name also figured in the list of twenty terrorists wanted for trial in India, which was handed over by the Government of India to Islamabad. The stock response from Musharraf was, of course, that Dawood Ibrahim was not in Pakistan.

During the Agra Summit, Musharraf was not lying because as an astute military leader he knew that if the RAW sleuths decided to call his bluff and expose Dawood on Pakistani soil, it would be an international embarrassment for him. So Dawood was shifted from Pakistan for a temporary period, just like Tiger Memon's family was shifted to Bangkok when the Indian government had turned the heat on Pakistan in 1993.

It was widely speculated that Dawood was shifted to Waziristan near the Federally Administered Tribal Areas (FATA), northwest Pakistan, bordering Afghanistan.

However, the Intelligence Bureau later gathered that before Musharraf visited India in 2001 for the Agra Summit, the ISI secretly sent Dawood away to Malaysia through Singapore with the help of one Rakesh Tulshiyan and Shahid Sohail. He stayed in Malaysia as a guest of billionaire Mohammad Tahir's family and returned to Karachi later. Dawood is believed to have extensive mining interests in Malaysia, from where he and his group indulge in the smuggling of silver into India via Nepal.

Many Caribbean and South Pacific countries offer fugitives from justice what is called 'economic citizenship' to enable them to evade arrest and deportation to countries where they are wanted for crimes. This citizenship is sold in return for a minimum deposit in foreign currency kept safely in local banks.

Pakistan does not have any laws providing for such 'economic citizenship', but its government, on the ISI's advice, informally awarded economic citizenship to Dawood, who was issued a Pakistani passport under a different name. Similarly, his brothers, including Anees Ibrahim and his aides, including Chhota Shakeel, were given Pakistani passports under pseudonyms.

It is believed that in the nineties, Dawood had offered Pakistan financial aid in the clandestine procurement of nuclear and missile technology and components and that this factor too probably influenced Islamabad's decision to grant him economic citizenship.

All of this had helped Dawood in developing thick contacts with the Lashkar-e-Tayyeba (LeT) and Al Qaeda elements such as Ramzi Binalshibh (a top LeT operative who was later arrested by the Pakistani authorities and handed over to the US), who had been given sanctuary in Karachi by the LeT.

Over the years, somehow Dawood and Musharraf had become indispensable to each other. In fact, Dawood had reportedly hired several retired Musharraf loyalist officers of the Pakistani intelligence community as his security officers.

And according to an IB dossier, Dawood Ibrahim also played an active role in organising the referendum campaign of Musharraf in Karachi by bringing in voters to the polling booths in trucks to vote for Musharraf.

But even as Musharraf was on his denial spree, the Pakistani press went ahead and exposed him. Then there were two simultaneous developments, which not only nailed the fragile lies of Musharraf but also made the world a smaller place for Dawood.

Newsline, a prestigious Pakistani monthly, in its September 2001 issue, carried a detailed article on the presence of Dawood and his men in Karachi and their activities here. The Pakistani media reported that the journalist who wrote this article, Ghulam Hasnain, was detained and harassed by the Pakistani authorities.

The article stated as follows: 'Dawood Ibrahim and his team, Mumbai's notorious underworld clan, including his right-hand man Chota Shakeel and Jamal Memon [Tiger Memon], are on India's most wanted list for a series of bomb blasts in Mumbai and other criminal activities. After the 1993 Mumbai bomb blasts, the gang have made Karachi their new home and operating base. Living under fake names and IDs (identities), and given protection by government agencies, they have built up their underworld operations in Karachi employing local talent like Shoaib and Bholoo.

'In Pakistan, Dawood managed to establish another huge empire, comprising both legitimate and illegitimate businesses. In fact, the last few years have witnessed Dawood emerge as the don of Karachi. Dawood and his men have made heavy investments in prime properties in Karachi and Islamabad and are major players in the Karachi bourse and in the parallel credit system business—*hundi*. Dawood is also said to have rescued Pakistan's Central Bank, which was in crisis at one point, by providing a huge dollar loan. His businesses include gold and drug smuggling. The gang is also allegedly heavily involved in (cricket) match-fixing.

'Not only have the Pakistani authorities turned a blind eye to the gang's activities within Pakistan, but many in the corridors of power have partaken of Dawood's hospitality... He is said to have the protection of assorted intelligence agencies. In fact, Dawood and his men move around the city guarded by heavy escorts of armed men in civies believed to be personnel of a top Pakistani security agency. A number of government undercover agents, who came into contact with Dawood because of their official duties, are now, in fact, working for him. Nearly all the men, who surround him for security reasons, are either retired or serving officers, claims an MQM (Muttahida Qaumi Movement) activist.

'According to informed sources, Dawood is Pakistan's number one espionage operative. His men in Mumbai help him get whatever information he needs for Pakistan. Rumour has it that sometimes his men in Karachi accompany Pakistani intelligence agents to the airports to scan arriving passengers and identify RAW (Indian external intelligence) agents.'

Ghulam Hasnain was so harassed and tormented by the government that he had to flee Pakistan and take refuge in the US.

The fallout of the 9/11 attacks was that the US had begun to realise the proportions of the menace that is dirty money as it floats around the world, ploughed for terror operations and the despicable aspect of the global brotherhood of Muslim terrorists. They realised that they would have to cut both the jugular vein of slush funds, money for multifarious activities, and the umbilical cord of the Muslim terrorists.

Shortly after 9/11, US President George Bush signed Executive Order (EO) No.13224 on 23 September 2001, declaring a national emergency to deal with terrorist threats to the US. He said in his EO: 'I also find that because of the pervasiveness and expansiveness of the financial foundation of foreign terrorists, financial sanctions may be appropriate for those foreign persons that support or otherwise associate with these foreign terrorists. I also find that a need exists for further consultation and cooperation with, and sharing of information by, United States and foreign financial institutions as an additional tool to enable the United States to combat the financing of terrorism.'

The annual report on the Patterns of Global Terrorism during 2001 submitted to the US Congress in May 2002, by General Colin Powell, US Secretary of State, described the significance of this EO as: 'EO 13224 enables the US Government to block designees' assets in any financial institution in the US or held by any US person. It also expands US government's authority to permit the designation of individuals and organisations that provide support or financial or other services to or associate with, designated terrorists. EO 13224 designations allowed the US government, as well as coalition partners acting in concert, to block tens of millions of dollars intended to bankroll the murderous activities of Al Qaeda and other terrorist groups.'

Unlike the Indian government, the US government moved swiftly and under this EO, has so far designated 322 individuals of different nationalities and organisations as terrorists and terrorist supporters, and frozen over $136.8 million in terrorist assets by acting in concert with other member-nations of the UN. Apart from terrorist organisations such as the Al Qaeda, the Jemaah Islamiya, the Harkat-ul-Mujahideen (HUM), the Lashkar-e-Tayyeba (LeT), the Jaish-e-Mohammad (JeM), etc., which have been so designated under this EO, a number of individual terrorists wanted for acts of terrorism in different countries have also been so designated. The most important among them are Ayman Al-Zawahiri and other leaders of the Al Qaeda.

While the US government has designated the HUM, the LeT, and the JeM as Foreign Terrorist Organisations, none of their leaders has so far been designated as global terrorists. The only individuals living openly in Pakistan and brought under the purview of this EO till 15 October 2003, were Sultan Bashir-ud-din Mahmood, Abdul Majeed, and Mahammed Tufail, who were suspected of trying to help bin Laden in the clandestine acquisition of Weapons of Mass Destruction (WMD). They were so designated on 20 December 2001, and their bank accounts, wherever found, were ordered to be frozen.

A press release of the US Department along with the Presidents' EO (available on the website) said: h'Dawood Ibrahim, an Indian crime lord, has found common cause with Al Qaeda, sharing his smuggling routes with the terror syndicate and funding attacks by Islamic extremists aimed at destabilising the Indian government. He is wanted in India for the 1993 Bombay Stock Exchange bombings and is known to have financed the activities of Lashkar-e-Tayyiba (Army of the Righteous), a group designated by the United States in October 2001 and banned by the Pakistani Government—who also froze their assets—in January 2002.'

A fact sheet attached to the press release said: 'Ibrahim's syndicate is involved in large-scale shipments of narcotics in the UK and Western Europe. The syndicate's smuggling routes from South Asia, the Middle East and Africa are shared with Osama bin Laden and his terrorist network. Successful routes established over recent years by Ibrahim's syndicate have been subsequently utilised by bin Laden. A financial arrangement was reportedly brokered to facilitate the latter's usage of these routes. In the late 1990s, Ibrahim travelled in Afghanistan under the protection of the Taliban.'

It added: 'Ibrahim's syndicate has consistently aimed to destabilise the Indian government through inciting riots, acts of terrorism and civil disobedience. He is currently wanted by India for the March 12, 1993, Bombay Exchange bombings, which killed hundreds of Indians and injured over a thousand more.

'Information from as recent as Fall 2002, indicates that Ibrahim has financially supported Islamic militant groups working against India, such as Lashkar-e-Tayyiba (LeT). For example, this information indicates that Ibrahim has been helping finance increasing attacks in Gujarat by LeT. '

The statement and the attached fact sheet, however, do not say how the US government came to know of Dawood's links with the Al Qaeda, bin Laden, and the LeT.

The Executive Order and the tightening of the noose by the US had rattled the Pakistani government. Dawood Ibrahim and his cohorts had clearly been asked to shut up, as it was obvious that Indian agencies would now be waiting to pounce on any opportunity to establish that Dawood was in Pakistan.

20

Not so *Chori Chori, Chupke Chupke*

Chhota Shakeel, for time immemorial, had always harboured aspirations of being the one holding the reins of Bollywood. Highly enamoured as he was by the glitz and glamour of India's tinseltown, he had always been left with a bitter taste in his mouth when he was told by the powers-that-be to quietly focus on his designated area of work or 'beat', which was extortion. He was left gritting his teeth whenever he was reminded that it was Abu Salem and Anees Ibrahim who were in control of the coveted Bollywood end of things.

Additionally, it did not help Shakeel's cause that Salem was tremendously ambitious and wanted to procure international distribution rights for films, in addition to a number of other plans to secure control of Bollywood at home and overseas. Shakeel was sunk in a private pit of gloom, until suddenly out of the blue, the unimaginable occurred. Sometime around 1999, Anees had parted ways with Salem, something Shakeel had never imagined would happen. There were several reasons for the fallout, including Anees suspecting Salem of embezzling his money and not giving a clear account. It was not just that. The fear that

Anees might get him killed had forced Salem out of Dubai. Shakeel could scarcely believe his luck.

Unopposed, Shakeel decided to try his hand at the kind of work he had been salivating over for years. One of the first things he did was to start hunting for a frontman, a face of the operation. Someone to play big boss and keep Shakeel's role in the scheme of things under wraps. The polished, stylish, and suave Nazeem Rizvi (also referred to as Raja saab) was identified for this purpose. His job was to contact the biggest names and get them to sign up for films that would be made as per Shakeel's designs. Moreover, Rizvi would have to get them to agree to work on the film on the designated days of the year. In Bollywood parlance, this is referred to as the slightly misleading phrase 'getting dates'.

Rizvi got down to business immediately and set about assembling a team that included director duo Abbas and Mustan Burmawalla, referred to commonly as Abbas-Mustan. Shakeel was specific about his demands for what would be his first film. He wanted a big star. That was non-negotiable. The biggest open secret about Bollywood, as Shakeel had realised, was that star power sells more than any other element of a film, be it a brilliant plot, excellent direction, or fancy foreign locales. In other words, even a potential dud of a film could be a box office hit if it was packed with enough stars.

Getting Shah Rukh Khan or Salman Khan for the film was Shakeel's topmost priority. Accordingly, Rizvi began to make rounds of various studios in an effort to hobnob with the stars and get them to sign on for the film. Coincidentally, the police's Crime Branch had been keeping tabs on phone calls made by Chhota Shakeel from 14 October to 14 November 2000. This was when the police unearthed some horrifying details that helped establish the seedy links between Bollywood and the underworld as the latter was making massive inroads into Bollywood.

For the film that Abbas-Mustan were attached to direct, which later came to be known as *Chori Chori Chupke Chupke*, Rizvi had secured the services of Salman, Rani Mukherji, and Preity Zinta. The Crime Branch had discovered, through monitoring telephone conversations, that Rizvi was a mere pawn in the whole game. The rationale for having a frontman was basically that Shakeel could play it safe, especially as this was his first foray into Bollywood. If the film was a hit at the box office, the cash registers would start ringing and stars would want to come and work on the next film Rizvi was working on. But if it was a flop, it was merely a case of Shakeel having to cut his losses and finding a new frontman; his own reputation in the film business would remain untarnished.

Rizvi's modus operandi was not very complicated at all. His job was to visit the sets on which Salman and Shah Rukh were working at the time and meet them. After a few threats in the past from Salem, Shahrukh strictly avoided meeting any shady strangers. Consequently, whenever Rizvi tried to approach him or turned up on the set, Shahrukh avoided him like the plague. A frustrated Rizvi complained to Shakeel about how he had tried his best to approach Shah Rukh but was thwarted every time. There was even an instance when Shahrukh fled to Rani's vanity van and sat there for over an hour before inexplicably disappearing from the set. When Rizvi complained to Shakeel on the phone, the Crime Branch cops were listening. They were soon to become familiar with a new set of nicknames for Bollywood's stars.

In the course of keeping tabs on the developments in this Bollywood-underworld nexus, the police realised that the underworld had a unique set of code names for members of the film fraternity. Just as the underworld had its own lingo for a gun, a car, or money, there was now a list of names used to refer to certain big names inconspicuously to avoid detection. The names ranged from the obvious *Jodi* (pair) for Abbas-Mustan, BS for diamond merchant and film financier Bharat Shah and *Pehelwan* (muscular man) for Salman, to the amusing *Chikna* (chocolate-faced) for Hrithik Roshan and *Takla* (baldy) for his father Rakesh, right to the offensive *Hakla* (the stutterer) for Shah Rukh.

A transcript of several conversations between Chhota Shakeel and Rizvi, which later became part of the chargesheet against Nazim Rizvi, Bharat Shah, Chhota Shakeel, and other aides, became a gold mine of information for the Mumbai police. One such transcript is produced below.

Rizvi: *Chikne ka show hai. Yeh Hakla hai apna, usmein jaa raha hai.* [Hrithik has a show and Shah Rukh is going for it].

Shakeel: *Achha.* [Okay].

Rizvi: *Kyonki kya hua tha, aaj mujhe pata lagaa ki apne yahaan jo hai na Rani?* [Do you know what happened today? You know Rani Mukherjee right?]

Shakeel: *Haan, haan.* [Yes, yes].

Rizvi: *Aaj yeh apna Hakla aayaa aur uski van mein ghusa raha. Dedh ghante tak. Toh main usko bola ki jaate time zara mujhko milke jaana, meri van mein.* [Today Shah Rukh came and sat in her van for around an hour and a half. I told him to come and meet me in my van before he left the set.]

Shakeel: *Haan.* [Yes].

Rizvi: *Bola aata hoon lekin yeh chupke se nikal gaya vahaan se, maine maloom kiya.* [After telling me he would come and meet me, I found out later that he had quietly slipped away].

Shakeel tried to reassure Rizvi that he would take care of Shah Rukh because the don could see that Rizvi was beginning to get desperate, losing whatever little composure he had left.

In Rizvi's moments of anxiety, he would regularly visit Salman and say politely, 'Excuse me, Salman Khan. Could you please speak to Shakeel bhai?' The muscular movie star did not take him seriously at all and snubbed him regularly. Rizvi was very often dragged kicking and screaming to the gates and kicked off the set by the security guards there.

Fed up with Rizvi's incompetence, Shakeel sent his henchman Anjum Fazlani to the set one day, armed with nothing but a mobile phone and the tangible air of confidence a life of violence affords. Fazlani walked in and handed the phone over to Salman, telling him that Shakeel was on the line and wished to speak with the actor. Salman took the phone and found himself backed into a corner, with no possible way to deny Shakeel his demands. Salman was forced to work in the film. Shakeel funded it, pumping 15 crore rupees into this first venture, and people like the Morani brothers were strong-armed into contributing to the film as well.

Buoyed by the early takings of the film, Rizvi and Shakeel were now discussing the marketing of the film. Talks revolved around details such as the selection of television channels that would air promos of the film and the way in which the soundtrack should be released. Rizvi told his boss that he estimated that the film would net a profit of at least 6 crore rupees and thereafter, no one would refuse to work with him. A content and calm Shakeel went on to tell Rizvi not to worry about people coming to work with him; if push came to shove, the don would create such havoc in the industry that no one would dream of saying no.

To cover their own tracks and keep up a facade of respectability, lastly, Rizvi and Shakeel also discussed putting the names of one of their wives down as producer. This, they reasoned, would keep them out of harm's way.

> Shakeel: *Apni* cassette release *kab hai?* [When is our cassette set to be released?]
>
> Rizvi: 1 November. 7 *mein* market *mein aa jaayegi aur 9 ko hamaari* party *ho jaayegi.* [Release is on November 1. It'll be in stores by November 7 and our party will be held on the 9th.]
>
> Shakeel: Opening *woh* cassette *ke gaanon ki kis se kar rahe hain?* [Whom are we getting for the music launch?]
>
> Rizvi: *Is.. Is... Is.... Pehelwaan se. Isise maine* phone *kiya tha. Munasib rahega aur ismein bhi achha* value *hai.* [We'll get Salman to do it. I've spoken to him on the phone. It'll be appropriate and good value if he does it.]
>
> [On the topic of promotion.]
>
> Shakeel: SAB TV *hai.* STAR *hai. Yeh na* public *aaj kal* SAB TV, STAR TV *bahut dekh rahe hain.* [There's SAB TV. There's STAR. The public these days watches a lot of SAB TV and STAR TV.]
>
> Rizvi: SAB *mein toh shuroo hua na.* [Promotion has already begun on SAB.]
>
> Shakeel: SAB *mein kahaan shuroo hua?* [Where has it already started on SAB?]
>
> Rizvi: *Haan ho gaya.* SAB *waalon ne bola tha ki* programme *mein daalaa gaya. Toh* Monday *se ya aaj se ho gaya shaayad.* [Yes, it's begun. The SAB people told me that they would introduce our promos in their programmes. So, from Monday onwards, or perhaps they've already started from today.]
>
> Shakeel: *Nahi. Nahi. Daala nahi hai.* SAB *mein* Blockbuster *mein aata hai na?* [No. No. They haven't done anything. On SAB, it should appear on 'Blockbuster', right?]

Rizvi: *Haan daalenge. Abhi* coming week *mein aapka* SAB *mein bhi shuroo ho jaayega.* STAR *mein bhi shuroo ho jaayega.* [Yes, they'll put it. Now in the coming week, it'll start on SAB and STAR as well.]

Shakeel: *Nahi nahi. Asal kya hai na* publicity *bhi sabse ahmiyat rakhti hai na.* Publicity *toh bahut zaroori hai kyunki aadmiyon ko samajh mein aata hai. Abhi dekho, doosre* picture SAB *mein aate hain. Sab* channel *mein aate hain. Khaali apna jo hai na* Zee *mein aur* ETS *mein* slowly *bajta hai. Kisko diya* music? [No no. The reality is that publicity is the most important thing, right? Look, other films are on SAB and they find a way to appear on all channels. Only ours is slowly gathering steam on Zee and ETS. Whom have you given the music to?]

Rizvi: Universal. *Woh* London *ki* company *hai.* [Universal. It's that company from London.]

Shakeel: *Bewakoof woh* SAB mein *nahi daala? Do-teen* channel *mein daal.* [You fool, why didn't you put it on SAB? Put it on two or three channels.]

Rizvi: *Nahi. Uska chakkar aur hai, bhai. Apne jo yeh daalte hain na.* Publicity *jab* start *karte hain toh pehle* A-Class channels *mein daalte hain, phir* B, *phir* C. *Toh yeh jo* Sony *aur yeh* Zee *hai na, woh* A *mein aate hain. Purane hain.* [No. There's another issue with that. When we start the publicity campaign, we first target the A-Class channels, then B, and then C. So this Sony and Zee, they fall under the A category, because they're old, established channels)

Shakeel: *Achha.* [Okay.]

Rizvi: *Yeh iske baad* second *aata hai* STAR *aur* SAB *ka* number. Third *aata hai* ETS *vagera aur jitne* channel *hain.* [After that in the second list are STAR and SAB and then finally are ETC and all the other such channels.]

[On the topic of rival films.]

Shakeel: *Maine suna hai ki woh Mohabbatein achhi rahi.* [I heard *Mohabbatein* did well.]

Rizvi: *Nahi. Nahi achhi hai. Matlab paone chaar ghante ki. Aap samajh lijiye. Woh kya achhi hogi?* [No, it's not doing well. I mean it's three and three-quarter hours long. You can imagine what it's like. How could it possibly be good?]

Shakeel: *Aur uski?* Mission [*Mission Kashmir*] *ki?* [And what about *Mission Kashmir?*]

Rizvi: *Nahi woh bhi koi khaas nahi hai.* Mission *se thodi behtar hai Mohabbatein.* [*Mohabbatein* is a little better than *Mission Kashmir.*]

Shakeel: *Maine suna Sanju ki tareef ki hai logon ne.* [I've heard people have praised Sanjay Dutt's work in *Mission Kashmir.*]

Rizvi: *Uski tareef hai. Baaki picture mein dum nahi hai.* [His work is good. But the rest of the film is poor.]

Shakeel: *Aur Chikna? Woh gaandu jaana chahiye. Woh bhadwa.* [And Hrithik? That arse should really get it. That pimp.]

Rizvi: *Woh Chikne ki to apne dostne hi uski buraai likh di hai Times mein. Hu hu hu. Fiza waale ne. Likha kuchh khaas nahi kar paaya.* [Hrithik's own friend wrote some really bad stuff about him in the *Times*. Hu hu hu. The *Fiza* guy—referring to critic and filmmaker Khalid Mohammed. He wrote that Hrithik wasn't able to do anything.]

The case was filed under the Maharashtra Control of Organised Crime Act (MCOCA), one of the most stringent crime enforcement laws ever. When the case came up in the MCOCA court, the police presented thirty-one witnesses and demonstrated how Rizvi was taking instructions from Shakeel and then squealing on people who were uncooperative. So, if Shahrukh was unwilling to speak to Rizvi, the latter would complain to Shakeel. Similarly, when Hrithik—who on seeing the pre-release response to *Chori Chori Chupke Chupke* considered working on Rizvi's next project—was told by his father not to work with these people from the underworld, Rizvi complained to Shakeel and the don assured his frontman that he would threaten Rakesh in such a way that he would never say or do anything against the underworld's wishes again.

Rizvi: *Yeh Takla apna. Jodi ke paas kahaani bhi* complete *hai aur* hero *ne* toh final *kiya hai, uske bete ne. Aur usne market mein bolna shuroo kiya hai ki main Rizvi sahab ke liye kaam kar raha hoon, jodi ki next* film *kar raha hoon.* [This Rakesh... Abbas-Mustan have already completed the story and finalised the hero—Rakesh's son who has already started talking about how he's working in my project, Abbas-Mustan's next film.]

Shakeel: *Toh ek kaam karo na.* Monday *ya* Tuesday site *pe uske chale jaana, Chikne ke. Bolna apne baap ko samjha chutiya, bolna teri* life *kharab ho jaayegi.*

[Then do as I tell you. On Monday or Tuesday go to the site where Hrithik is presently filming and tell him to explain to his fucking father that his life will be ruined if Rakesh keeps interfering.]

Rizvi: *Bilkul bilkul.* [Absolutely.]

Shakeel: *Bolna bhai ne bola tera baap teri* life *kharab kar dega.* [Tell him that I said that his dad will end up ruining his life.]

The conversation was a little worrisome and the cops had now become edgy with Shakeel's designs on the film industry.

In January 2001, Shakeel decided to make Rakesh Roshan an example for the industry and sent his men to open fire on him just to scare him. Subsequent investigations revealed that the shooter wanted to shoot at the car, but unfortunately a bullet grazed Rakesh's arm. The bald filmmaker, already under a lot of pressure, had put up a brave front in the face of the intimidation of Mumbai's underworld. He had defied Shakeel one time too many.

When Shakeel's men ambushed Rakesh as he was getting into his car outside his office, he was taken by surprise as they opened fire on him. Despite the bullet injuries, Roshan drove off himself and reached Cooper Hospital safely. Calm in the face of this unexpected adversity, he saw a doctor and called his family members to tell them what had happened.

The shooting incident spread panic waves in the film industry. A pall of fear and terror descended on its glamorous denizens.

There was widespread panic and an atmosphere of intense paranoia within the film fraternity; most of its members began to fear for their safety. While cops were listening they found that during the course of one of the conversations Shakeel had wanted Ajay Devgn to shift the dates of his film *Raju Chacha*, so that they did not clash with those of *Chori Chori Chupke Chupke*. As a result, Kumar Mangal (Ajay's secretary) was threatened.

Moreover, Shakeel had said in one of his conversations that if Shah Rukh continued to be non-compliant, shots should be fired at his car; Shakeel had claimed boastfully that within half an hour, the star would call back and humbly say that he was ready to work. But the plan was, for some inexplicable reason, never acted upon. Perhaps he was merely boasting, and actually had no intention of doing this.

It was around this point that the police realised that they could not wait any longer and would have to move in on the targets. Rizvi was arrested under the MCOCA on 13 November and subsequently, the man known to the underworld as BS was also picked up. Realising that a whopping eighty-four witnesses were needed to convict Rizvi, the police was on the warpath. No less than sixty-six police officers had been put on surveillance and in investigating teams in order to create an airtight case against Rizvi, identifying him as Shakeel's henchman.

Shakeel's henchman and Rizvi's assistant Abdul Rahim Allah Baksh and later Anjum Fazlani were also arrested for their complicity. It was the first time that anyone had seen a police commissioner (Mahesh Narayan Singh) take such severe action against the film fraternity. He demanded that everyone associated with the film be quizzed at length, irrespective of whether it was a big name like Salman or a simple spot boy on the set. It was later established that Salman, Rani, Abbas-Mustan, and the others had participated in the film under duress as their lives were in danger and so, they were not detained further, nor were charges filed against them.

Unfortunately for Shah, he was unable to provide this sort of information and he was subsequently booked under the MCOCA by Singh. Shah, who was well-connected and knew some senior Shiv Sena leaders in Mumbai—and even senior politician L.K. Advani, among his close contacts in Delhi—was unable to wriggle out of this mess. After appealing against the verdict in the Supreme Court, however, Shah was able to get out of jail after only a year. There was no such luck for Rizvi, who was convicted and spent five years in jail. Needless to say, Shakeel got away scot free.

The rights to *Chori Chori Chupke Chupke* were later taken over by the government. Realising that the film was an underworld venture, filmgoers began to give it the cold shoulder and the film tanked horribly in the box office. Far from Rizvi's projections of 6 crore rupees and above, the film managed to make only a paltry 25 lakh rupees. Sensing this rapidly deteriorating situation, Shakeel realised that he had one last throw of the dice left. To try and stymie the rapidly declining ticket sales, Shakeel called up a number of top English dailies to put out stories that *Chori Chori Chupke Chupke* was not *his* film, but Shah's film. He claimed that people were just spreading rumours against him to try and make him seem like a villain trying to take over Bollywood.

Unfortunately, the horse had already bolted and no matter how securely he tried to lock the stable door, there was no escaping the fact that it was too late. Besides, the police had ample transcripts of phone conversations linking Shakeel to the film. *Chori Chori Chupke Chupke* had flopped massively, as had the don's short stint in Bollywood.

21

'Judge' Dawood

The people of Pakistan are not only enthusiastic about Indian films and actors, but they also seem to be taking to Indian eating habits —eating vices, to be specific—like ducks to water. The highly addictive and equally carcinogenic gutkha is as popular among Pakistanis as it is among Indians. To put it very simply, it is a mixture of crushed betel nut, tobacco, *katha* (catechu, an astringent), *choona* (lime), and sweet or savoury flavourings. This mixture is packed in individual serving-size pouches and gives consumers a kick or a buzz that is thought to be far more intoxicating than tobacco. Unsurprisingly, given the composition of gutkha, it is also majorly responsible for oral cancer.

Due to the discreet nature of gutkha consumption (it can be kept in the mouth completely inconspicuously, as opposed to the more obvious vice of smoking), this blight is a rage among children and adults alike. In the mid-1990s and early 2000s, it was being smuggled illegally into Pakistan across the border and being imported to Pakistan via Dubai. Among the gutkha brands that were the most well-liked were Goa, 1000, RMD, etc. As a result of the expenses associated with smuggling or 'importing' gutkha, it gradually became too expensive for the common man and the poor (who had been the biggest consumers of gutkha due to its inexpensiveness and easy availability).

According to a Pakistani commercial survey that was carried out in 2000, the illicit gutkha trade was worth 300 crore in Pakistan. Despite its increasing price, the demand for gutkha did not abate, and predictably, this burgeoning business did not go unnoticed by the expatriated Pakistani mafia in Dubai, who decided to cash in and capitalise on it. The major obstacle in their path, however, was the fact that it was impossible to obtain gutkha legally from India, as there were hardly any trade relations, and there was no way to manufacture it locally.

During this time, Anees was creating cheap imitations of well-known Indian brands to sell in Pakistan. He had kept an eye on the gutkha trade and began considering manufacturing it himself. Accordingly, he started doing a bit of research to learn more about gutkha, its manufacturing methods, and the biggest players in the gutkha field.

At the same time, back in India, two of the gutkha world's biggest players were in the midst of a long-running feud. Jagdish Joshi of the Goa brand and Rasiklal Manikchand Dhariwal of RMD had been waging a hotly-contested business battle for some years. Ironically, it was not all that long ago that these two arch-nemeses had worked on the same team. Joshi started off as a manager and a know-how expert working for RMD in 1990. He is believed to be responsible for the meteoric rise of the brand and for taking the business to new heights.

However, he was apparently unhappy with the money he was making for the sort of work he was putting in and the results he produced. Ultimately in 1997, he parted ways with RMD and started his own gutkha-manufacturing firm. The feud between these two gutkha barons, one which had raged for around four years, allegedly began with Joshi's claim that he was owed a whopping sum of 70 crore rupees by Dhariwal, something the latter refuted vehemently.

When Anees heard about the Joshi-Dhariwal dispute, it brought a smile to his face; he realised that he could make the most of the situation. Joshi allegedly sought out Anees in Dubai and requested his assistance in resolving this dispute and getting for him the money he was apparently owed. And Anees is believed to have assured Joshi that he would do his bit to help and lay the feud to rest once and for all.

Incidentally, both Joshi and Dhariwal are non-resident Indians (NRIs) and in order to maintain that status, they were required to have been out of India for at least 181 days a year. In order to bring his tally up to 181 days, Dhariwal decided to go to Dubai for a while. While he was there, he was allegedly approached by Anees, who said that he wished to intervene in the dispute in the capacity of an arbitrator. The RMD head honcho is said to have been comfortable with that arrangement—with just one proposed change in plan.

Dhariwal allegedly wanted to have the meeting in the presence of Dawood, and so, Anees decided that the meeting would take place in Karachi. A few days later, both Dhariwal and Joshi made the trip to Karachi and arrived at Dawood's palatial residence. After lengthy discussions, deliberations, and debate, Dawood announced that he had come up with a solution that would be acceptable to all parties. He is believed to have said that Dhariwal would have to cough up 11 crore rupees in total. Of this amount, 7 crore rupees would be given to Joshi and the remaining amount to Dawood as a negotiation fee.

Just as Joshi and Dhariwal seemed to be accepting the solution, Anees saw a window of opportunity and pounced on it. Interrupting the meeting, he said that in exchange for having settled a dispute that had been raging for a long time, he wanted Joshi to provide Anees with gutkha production know-how and manufacturing machinery. Wanting a piece of the gutkha pie, Anees had long sought to set up a manufacturing plant in Pakistan, but had neither the equipment nor the expertise to do so. Finally, in Joshi, he found the perfect way to get both.

Joshi seemed extremely pleased with Anees for his intervention in the dispute and so, readily agreed to help out. Very soon, fifteen manufacturing machines and four pouch-making machines were exported to Dubai and then sent to Karachi in 2001-02. The machinery was exported from Nhava Sheva to Dubai under the name of the 'Ali Asgar Company' and Joshi had one of his associates, Raju Pacharia, oversee the export. Magnanimous as Joshi was feeling at the time, he also sent one of his senior employees, Biju George (aka Babu), to go to Karachi and train the workers at the manufacturing unit.

Within a few months, Anees launched the hugely successful Fire brand of gutkha that is still very much in vogue in Pakistan. Anees and his aide

Aftab Batki oversaw the entire operation and made sure everything went according to plan and that they, the top players, remained incognito. The whole operation would have remained anonymous, had it not been for what can best be described as serendipity.

In 2004, the police was trying to monitor calls between Dawood aide Salim Chiplun and Anees. At one point in the conversation, the topic changed to the purchase of some spare parts for the gutkha-making machines, and Chor Bazaar was decided upon as the best place to buy them. The spare parts were then supposed to be sent to Dubai, from where they would be sent to Karachi. Finding the whole deal quite suspicious, the police began its investigations. As part of their inquiries, the cops called in Salim Ibrahim Kashmiri (Dawood's father-in-law) for questioning. After he was interrogated, he allegedly spilled the beans on the set-up and the arrangement with the gutkha barons, tipping off an astonished police force. Whatever next!

Subsequently, the then Commissioner of Police A.N. Roy quickly swung into action and ordered the Crime Branch to conduct deeper investigations. Joshi and Dhariwal were then charged under the MCOCA for forming a nexus with the underworld. After having such grave charges levelled against them, both businessmen were understandably reluctant to return to India. If the ignominy of being charged with working with Dawood and Anees was not bad enough, the extremely severe MCOCA would destroy their reputations and those of their companies. Their respective empires now potentially lay in ruins. And what was more, the country would be shocked to hear that two top businessmen had required the help of the underworld.

The CBI was soon handed charge of the case and began to exert pressure on Dhariwal and Joshi to return to India and face the music. When they continued to abscond, Interpol launched the dreaded red corner notice against the businessmen, Dawood and Anees. The red corner notice is an alert sounded by Interpol and circulated to all countries, and is a request for arrest of wanted persons with a view to extradition. After a number of months had passed, both Joshi and Dhariwal were left with no other option but to return to India. Joshi returned first and Dhariwal followed a little while later. Needless to say, they were immediately taken into custody. Both gutkha barons made trips to the high court to try and have the case dismissed, but their efforts were in vain.

They initially insisted that they had never been to Karachi and that they had never supplied any equipment to Anees or Dawood. However, Pacharia's statements to the Crime Branch and the CBI contradicted their claims. Among other incriminating statements, Pacharia had spoken at length about how the duo had gone for the meeting and met the Ansaris and struck a deal with them. The case against them is still in court.

Additionally, while the police discovered the links between the gutkha barons and the underworld through the statements of Jamiruddin Ansari alias Jumbo, who used to handle hawala operations for Anees, it also made another major and startling discovery.

Jumbo stated that he had made a trip to actress Nagma's flat on Carter Road in Bandra recently to deliver 10 lakh rupees to her from Anees. Jumbo insisted that Anees and Nagma were 'close' friends.

Nagma had made her debut in Bollywood opposite Salman Khan in *Baghi*, where she had played the role of a girl forced into prostitution. She subsequently worked with Sanjay Dutt and other Bollywood stars. The revelation of her apparent closeness with Anees, which made headlines in all the major dailies, upset her and could not have been more ill-timed.

As the revelation had come at the time of parliamentary elections and she was trying to get a ticket to contest for the Congress party, Nagma dubbed the whole disclosure as a conspiracy engineered by the Opposition and dismissed these claims as a smear attempt designed to derail her election campaign. But, just as had been the case with all other controversies, this too quietly disappeared from the media's attention.

The footnote that no one missed was that Dawood was still ruling the roost and involved in arbitration among top business people who would approach him for redressal of their grievances instead of going to a court of law.

22

Carnival of Spies

One of the most loathed Pakistani figures in India is the former cricketer, Javed Miandad.

Quoting *India Today's* Deputy Editor Sharda Ugra, 'If Sachin Tendulkar was like Superman for India, Miandad was like his villainous counterpart, perhaps dressed in a black uniform. He was one person whose career was built on making Indians miserable.' His last-ball six off Chetan Sharma in the final of the 1986 edition of the Australasia Cup traumatised a generation of Indian cricket lovers almost as much as (and perhaps even more than) it thrilled their Pakistani counterparts.

In fact the hate was so widespread that Bollywood even started naming their villains after Miandad. For instance, the Dharmendra and Rati Agnihotri-starrer *Hukumat*, released in 1987 had a corrupt cop named after Javed Miandad. Every time Dharmendra bellowed his name on screen, the audience broke into thunderous applause.

India would never forgive him, as was evidenced by the reaction of spectators (laughter at his expense) at Bangalore's Chinnaswamy Stadium during the World Cup quarter-finals in 1996 when he was run out in what would be his last international match. But what Miandad did nearly two decades later turned him into a far greater recipient of Indian resentment and scorn.

Miandad announced the wedding of his son Junaid—a student of business administration at Oxford University—to Dawood Ibrahim's daughter Mahrukh, who was a student in London. While the engagement was a complete hush-hush affair, news that the two were to be married broke out in January 2005. When asked about it, Miandad reacted angrily, telling people to respect his privacy. However, in June 2005, it was he who confirmed the news and famously claimed that according to Muslims, marriages were made in heaven and as such, he was in no position to challenge the union.

Later, in an interview to an Indian sports magazine, Miandad said that the marriage had been mooted by his wife, Zubeen Zareen, and Dawood's wife Mehjabeen in December 2004. And soon after, an expensive invitation card was published in a Dubai daily that read, 'Mr and Mrs Dawood Hassan Sheikh Ibrahim announce the wedding ceremony of their daughter Mahrukh to Junaid Miandad, son of Mr and Mrs Javed Miandad, Inshahallah on 23 July 2005'.

✠

A few days earlier, soon after the wedding was announced, the Intelligence Bureau (IB) officers had decided to activate their vigilance machinery just to ensure that they could gather enough fodder around Dawood's attendance of the wedding. Any substantial evidence of his participation in the wedding would become part of primary ammo for the Indian government to launch an I-told-you-so campaign against Pakistan. The intelligence think tank was working overtime to try and find a way to make use of this golden opportunity. After all, it was not every day that one had information about exactly where Dawood was going to be at a particular time. The IB knew that this was a chance they could ill afford to waste and it was going to require something a little different this time. The nikah had already been solemnised in Mecca on 9 July and the mehendi and other rituals were to be carried out in Karachi. The stage was set.

✠

On 23 July, the Grand Hyatt in Dubai would be the venue for the *walimah*, a post-wedding feast that is hosted by the bridegroom's father. Before the *walimah,* however, events took an interesting and strange turn. According to observers and members of Indian intelligence agencies, the post-wedding feast was one of the most closely monitored events the world had ever seen. Intelligence agencies from across the world were crawling all over the Grand Hyatt.

It seemed almost like a global confluence of all the important espionage networks. The CIA's field agents were in position and watching events carefully, MI6 sleuths surrounded the hotel and in their midst were operatives from Mossad, RAW, IB, and a number of unidentified intelligence agents from numerous countries. As expected, the ISI was also managing protective surveillance of the proceedings.

What was most interesting was that most agents were disguised as door attendants, chauffeurs, page boys, mediapersons, and waiters. Normally, a wedding in Dubai would not attract this sort of attention, but this was no normal wedding. The CIA and its allies were interested in monitoring proceedings because in 2004, Dawood had been declared a global terrorist by the United States. MI6 was there to gather information about the possible perpetrators and planners of the 7 July 2005 blasts in London. They figured that there would definitely be a number of people present at the *walimah* who would be useful to the investigation. RAW and IB officials were there to find out more about what Dawood was plotting next, as India's enemy number one.

✠

The Indian government was well aware that it was not possible to extradite or get Dawood deported as he was no more Dawood Ibrahim. Pakistan had already given him a totally new identity. The only option that was left for them was to eliminate Dawood without any fingers pointing towards them. The IB had no intention of sending its own men to do the job. They also needed to ensure that they had plausible deniability if their plans led to some sort of international incident. They would need guns-for-hire. How could they outsource such an important task without causing an international embarrassment for themselves?

'Lucky Luciano,' said a senior officer.

When others looked at him inquisitively, he explained, 'We have so far used Chhota Rajan's services in so many projects where we cannot exercise our jurisdiction. Why not give him something which he would love to do? He would be willing to give his left arm for the job.'

The older officer walked towards the window and after pulling in a deep swig from his cigarette said, '*Sholay* will never go out of style.'

And everyone laughed at the joke.

'But who will be our Thakur Baldev Singh?' asked a young officer.

'It has to be someone who is really a Baldev Singh,' the senior officer replied, emphatically crushing the butt of his cigarette.

The two officers looked at their senior for a long time. Their eyes met and realisation dawned on them. This meant that the handler of this operation should ideally be a retired officer from the IB with proven credentials and heroic track record.

It was decided to assign the elimination of Dawood to Rajan and his shooters. It was to be remotely choreographed by a senior IB officer, who was by then retired from the service.

Word was sent to Chhota Rajan. They believed that as Rajan also had a score to settle against Dawood and was still smarting from the almost fatal attack on him in Bangkok in 2000, he would be keen to kill Dawood. Even if he did not have resources, a coup of sorts could be pulled off together.

✠

Deputy Commissioner of Police, Detection, Crime Branch of Mumbai police, Dhananjay Kamlakar, was a young and enthusiastic officer. Driven by his recent successes of crackdown on the organised crime syndicates, he was hungry for more. Kamlakar had clearly instructed his men to ensure that no gangsters should be allowed to have a free reign. 'They should be either behind bars or in their graves,' he used to say.

When the Crime Branch received a tip-off that two top sharpshooters of the Chhota Rajan gang, Farid Tanasha and Vicky Malhotra, had entered India through 24 Parganas in West Bengal, they were raring to go. Both Tanasha and Malhotra were absconding for a long time and were known to be holed up in an undisclosed location in some Southeast Asian country. If they themselves had walked in, they should not be allowed to escape this time.

The Crime Branch sleuths immediately got on their trail. Tanasha and Malhotra were totally unaware of the remote surveillance on their movements by the Crime Branch sleuths. They were following instructions from their handler, who was a friend of their *seth* or master. In this context, the *seth* was Chhota Rajan.

After visiting a few of the north Indian locations, Tanasha and Malhotra were told to meet their handler in Delhi. The Crime Branch had been tapping Tanasha's phone line after a few extortion calls he had made, recently. This latest conversation of his with someone who was clearly giving him instructions seemed extremely suspicious. And so, Kamlakar's men kept tabs on his movements, following him like a second shadow. All the while, the IB was providing Tanasha, Malhotra, and a few other shooters with the training required for the upcoming operation.

DCP Kamlakar thought that the duo was on its way to Delhi to eliminate some top businessman or politician. After seeking consent from his superiors, Kamlakar and his crack team of Crime Branch officers left for Delhi.

✠

Grand Hyatt is one of the most luxurious addresses of Dubai located in Bur Dubai area. Sprawled across thiry-seven acres, the hotel seemed to be the perfect venue for the post nuptial feast for Dawood's daughter; just seven kilometres away from Dubai's international airport. It was widely believed that the hotel's proximity to the airport was a clue that Dawood would definitely attend the feast, as it would be convenient for Dawood to flit in and out without any complication; if any untoward incident at all were to take place.

The D-day was approaching. And veteran field agents from various agencies had begun trickling in to Dubai. Some had managed to station themselves outside the periphery of the hotel. Enterprising journalists from India and Pakistan had booked rooms in the hotel days in advance so that they could move around the hotel without raising any suspicions.

At the *walimah*, mediapersons from various news agencies swarmed around the Grand Hyatt, but most of the Indian media was forced to stay outside the hotel. To the untrained eye, the hotel did not seem to have a huge security set-up, but it was actually an invisible fortress. A phalanx of security units remained incognito, but there were no visible signs of surveillance like CCTV cameras or metal detectors.

✠

Time was fast running out for New Delhi. This was one of the most daring operations ever planned by the Indian intelligence agencies and it just had to go right. Dawood, who had given them sleepless nights for over two decades now, might be put to rest, conveniently, at his own daughter's wedding.

The IB officers had now given final shape to their grand strategy. Travel arrangements were made and fake documents for Tanasha and Malhotra were prepared. They just need to be briefed and sent to Dubai. A meeting was arranged between the shooters and the former IB director. All details had been chalked out and planned to the minutest detail. All three of them were poring over a set of schematics—blueprints of a sort—of the Grand Hyatt, to evaluate the best positions at which to install shooters. They needed to have every angle covered and the importance of getting those details right was not lost on any of the trio.

The meeting was about to conclude, when Kamlakar and his officers showed up at the door. The IB officer lost his cool and began screaming at Kamlakar. But Kamlakar himself was not new to political bluster; he was a seasoned police officer who had seen such histrionics earlier. He refused to back off.

Finally, when some calls were made and Kamlakar heard from his superiors in Mumbai, he backed off. But still, he was left with Tanasha and Malhotra, both wanted men. With no other alternative, Kamlakar hauled the two to Mumbai. The bespectacled officer had to beat a retreat. A major operation had to be abandoned because of turf war; because two agencies remained in the dark about each other's move. If only the IB had warned the Mumbai police, this embarrassing and wasteful scenario could have been averted.

The incident earned a front page mention in the *Times of India* the next day, followed by reports several language dailies the next day. The officer who was handling Tanasha and Malhotra was identified as Ajit Doval. Doval had recently retired as IB chief. Known to be the hero of Operation Blue Star in Punjab, Doval was also known to be an astute negotiator, as he had handled the hijackers of IC 814. Perhaps he was the only IPS to have received the Kirti Chakra, an award reserved for military honours.

The police and media circles were shocked at the disclosure made by the *Times of India* report. It was the first such instance of intelligence officers' open involvement with gangsters that has come out in public. However, when *Mumbai Mirror* did a detailed follow-up of the story and got in touch with Doval for his version, he flatly denied the whole incident. 'I was watching a football match at home,' was all he said.

But the cat was out of the bag. That the Indian government tried to outsource the killing of Dawood and their plans had been exposed.

✠

Finally, the most anticipated day at the Grand Hyatt had arrived. Five hundred guests had been invited to the hotel's regal Baniyas Grand Ballroom, where they were served a sumptuous 12-course dinner. According to an IB operative, who was disguised as a chauffeur, the whole ballroom was decorated with red roses and white tulips.

The centre stage for the bride and groom was draped in white and embellished with white orchids. A luxurious green sofa sat in the middle. The most intriguing element of the feast was that guests were served piping hot *jalebis*, a uniquely Indian delicacy that is not available outside India and Pakistan, and certainly not in a hotel in Dubai.

Most of Dawood's Mumbai-based relatives who were desirous of attending the wedding could not make it. Even his sister Haseena Parkar was denied a visa.

But there was simply no way Dawood could miss what would be one of the happiest days of his life. For the days leading up to the *walimah*, all Dawood could do was to weigh the pros and cons of attending the function. His men advised him to stay away, but he was not convinced. How could the father of the bride miss D-day?

It is unclear how and when Dawood got a whiff of IB's plans, but he realised that attending the *walimah* could prove to be extremely risky.

Dawood, who had been present at the nikah and all the other rituals, finally decided that he would not be at the *walimah* in person and was conspicuous by his physical absence. However, in reality, he enjoyed a somewhat omniscient presence as he watched the whole function and monitored the goings-on around the Grand Hyatt via an array of video cameras. These had been installed all over the hotel and with the help of those, he was able to identify people whose agenda clearly looked like they entailed something other than conveying their best wishes to the newlywed couple.

Miandad welcomed each and every one of the 500 guests and when people pointedly asked him if Dawood was present at the *walimah*, he only said two words, '*Sab aaye* [everyone's come]'.

23

Detained in Lisbon

Abu Salem had almost been chased out of Dubai and realised in no uncertain terms that Pakistan was no longer hospitable to him. Dawood had after all made it his own backyard. For the best part of three years, since that fateful night in Dubai when Salem decided to flee, he had been on the run. These three years had seen him running from country to country, across six continents. He had been to the US and then found himself travelling through Europe, eventually ending up in Southeast Asia.

Over these three years, he saw the world with his paramour Monica Bedi, spending a massive chunk of his time with her. Back then, Monica was a Bollywood starlet, a struggling actress from Hoshiarpur in Punjab. The rest of Salem's time was spent with his first wife Samira Jumani in the US. Monica and Salem looked at a number of cities as potential safe havens for them to settle down in. Sadly for them, it seemed like there was no place on earth that they could go to and escape from Dawood and his associates or the police.

Salem and Monica gave due consideration to the idea of Laos as a base of operations, but quickly changed their mind when they remembered that Chhota Rajan's base was in Cambodia, which was not all that far away. Being located that close to Rajan would not have been a smart move. Discussions about a new place to call home continued and while Europe was a heavily favoured location, Switzerland was discarded as an option. The duo would not be able to stay incognito there for too long, they decided, as it was the favourite foreign location for Bollywood shootings.

Monica was no stranger to Europe, considering the fact that she had been born and brought up in Europe and considered it her second home, if not indeed, her home. She decided that they would have to stay in a country where English was not very commonly spoken. It would also need to be a place where Salem and she could slip into the local fabric seamlessly and inconspicuously. But the question was, where?

The duo finally zeroed in on Portugal and decided to live in the picturesque capital city of Lisbon. The Mediterranean nation's largest city would be a perfect location, they reasoned, partly due to the fact that they would not attract attention and partly because the climate was so pleasant.

Monica and Salem moved into their new home in Lisbon and for the first time in three years, had the luxury of being able to relax. After a quest that had seemed never-ending, they had finally found their ideal new home. A few blissful weeks later, Salem got a call from Karachi that turned his blood icy cold. 'Anees *bhai ne abhi tak tera peechha nahi chhoda hai* [Anees has not stopped chasing you],' said an emotionless, anonymous voice on the other end. Salem was very shaken by the call. Just as things had started to look up for him, his whole world had been turned upside down once again by his relentless arch enemies.

There were only two choices left before him, at this point. He could either pack his bags and continue running, thereby leaving Portugal, or he could call Anees, talk things out with him man-to-man and try to negotiate a truce. With the first option, the idea of returning to the US seemed like a good idea, but after the September 11 attacks on the World Trade Centre and Pentagon, the US was no longer safe for Indians with dubious passports.

The next idea that occurred to him was that of talking to Dawood to request Anees to let bygones be bygones and bury the hatchet. But that plan, he realised would probably lead to both Dawood and Anees trying to hunt him down, which needless to say, was not a desirable option. Just how had things got so bad with Anees, Salem wondered. There was a time when he and Salem had been almost like brothers. But now Anees was after Salem with great vengeance.

On one seemingly uneventful day, there was a knock on the door of Salem and Monica's Lisbon apartment. The events that unfolded after this completely changed the course of their lives. The Portugal police was found standing at their doorstep and the couple was informed that they were under arrest.

It was September 2002. Salem was thrown into a jail near Lisbon. Fortunately for Monica and Salem, they were in the same jail facility for a few weeks and got to meet each other once in a while. When he was not with Monica, he was wondering how the police had gotten wind of his location. Had Anees tipped the Portuguese police off? There was a very strong possibility that this was the case, thought Salem. Soon, the rumour mill began working overtime and word got out to Salem that both he and Monica would be getting transferred. After several weeks of depression, this was the first thing to bring a smile to his face.

He was hopeful of getting transferred to Pakistan or Dubai because he had citizenship for both those places and would be able to survive in the jails there. But as luck would have it, he did not get shifted to any of those places: the CBI had set the wheels into motion to have him extradited to India, the scene of most of his illegal activities.

Salem realised that his extradition to India would certainly be the road to perdition. Desperately, he began to make efforts to scuttle his return to India.

24

The White Kaskar

D awood Ibrahim and, to a slightly lesser extent Anees, are the
best known of the Kaskar siblings and indisputably the most
active in the underworld. Their sister Saeeda was killed in an accident
in their village in 1980, elder brother Sabir had fallen to gangland
bullets in 1981, and another brother Noorul Haq alias Noora
had succumbed to cancer in 2010. Noora was a bit-member of the
D Company who harboured aspirations of writing for Bollywood.
He is believed to have written a number of songs for Hindi films
under a pseudonym.

Dawood now had seven surviving siblings—four brothers and three
sisters; all the sisters were living in Mumbai, while the brothers continued
to live in Dubai and Pakistan with Dawood. Anees was the only notorious
sibling, while Humayun, Mustakeem, and Iqbal Kaskar, Dawood's other
brothers, who did not have any profession per se and sat at home living
off Dawood's money, boasted of a clean slate, with no police record
whatsoever. Iqbal had always been someone who was unequivocal in
his decision to keep away from all underworld dealings, and wanted to
maintain his clean record. However, years of being antagonised by the

Mumbai police, harassed by the Crime Branch, and frequently summoned to courts became a bit too much to handle for the three brothers.

It was at that point, sometime in 1988-89, years after Dawood had set up his empire, that the three brothers relocated to Dubai and joined brother Dawood. They would never have considered this but for the fact that authorities in Mumbai had turned their lives into a living hell. Moving to Dubai seemed like a much better idea at the time. And when Dawood shifted base to Pakistan, Humayun and Mustakeem were more than happy to follow suit. Iqbal though was a different kettle of fish altogether.

Constantly being on the run and hopping from one place to another seemed to have taken its toll on Iqbal. He introspected at length and decided that this time, he would not accompany his brothers. He knew that he had a spotless record and that the police had absolutely no dirt on him. These facts would work in his favour, he believed, and he felt he would get justice if he decided to return to India.

The only thing that held Iqbal back and cast a doubt on his decision was that he knew of the Mumbai police's reputation for carrying out encounters and making people 'disappear'. He knew they would not hesitate to shoot a man dead right outside the airport as soon as he arrived. With these worries in mind, Iqbal began making calls to some influential people he knew in Mumbai. He had been an informant for the police at one point in time and knew some of the top IPS officers in Mumbai. Apart from them, he also called some Muslim politician friends in India.

Finally, he got in touch with one of his old contacts in the Crime Branch, a junior-level officer, a police inspector by the name of Aslam Momin. Aslam and Iqbal were similar in a lot of ways and yet had found themselves (inadvertently, as it was, in Iqbal's case) on opposite sides of the law. Iqbal was from Ratnagiri and Aslam from Kolhapur, and as Marathi-speaking Muslims, they shared a very good rapport. This was what had actually been instrumental in Aslam roping Iqbal in to be an informant for the Crime Branch.

Ever since Iqbal decided to leave behind the problems in Mumbai and move on to Dubai, he had been in regular touch with Aslam. And naturally, when he wanted to make his return to the country where he was born, Iqbal called Aslam from a landline. Aslam was not overly surprised to receive the call and traded the customary salaams with Iqbal. The exchange of polite pleasantries quickly came to a close as Iqbal got to his point. 'Sahab, I want to come back. Are there any cases against me in Mumbai?'

Aslam, with his voice exuding a calming sense of reassurance, said, 'Don't worry, Iqbal.' Encouraging Iqbal to return to Mumbai, he added, 'There are no cases against you. There will be no fake cases filed against you and you will definitely not be "encountered". You have nothing to worry about.' After mulling over the pros and cons for a few months, Iqbal Kaskar finally returned to his homeland in May 2003. Expectedly, there was no red carpet welcome for him and he was taken straight into custody because officially, he had been deported from Dubai. As per procedure, being taken into custody was inevitable.

Now normally, it would be quite natural for someone to be a little anxious about being taken into custody, but Iqbal was not perturbed in the least. He was confident that he would be out of prison and free as a bird in a couple of weeks, at the very most. After all, he *had* just voluntarily returned. It was not as if he was a fugitive who had been captured and brought back. The Mumbai police, unfortunately, did not see things this way, and was on hand to throw a spanner into the works. To the police officers, it was a matter of reputation and pride that they had Dawood's sibling in their custody. The fact that he had no cases against him was dismissed summarily, as when it came to Dawood's brother, the bottom line was that there was no way on earth that he could possibly be clean.

The cops began working overtime and scoured high and low for cases against Iqbal. After burning the midnight oil going over old records, they finally found an age-old murder case that had been filed against him. Victorious, the police threatened to book him for those charges. And yet, Iqbal was still cool and collected. He knew that the case had been filed on very weak grounds because a co-accused had testified that the victim and Iqbal were on bad terms. This, Iqbal thought, would never stand scrutiny in a court of law, and so, he felt he would be discharged in no time.

Iqbal was guilty beyond doubt of counting his chickens much too prematurely. He underestimated the Mumbai police's fervour to see him locked up and put away for good. Even as the enthusiastic cops were looking for a case to supplement the weak murder case, by a blinding stroke of luck, they struck gold. A large plot of land that measured around 20, 000 square metres and was located right next to Crawford Market was owned by the Public Works Department, had been usurped by Dawood's men. Two shopping complexes had appeared there, the Sara Shopping Complex and the Sahara Shopping Complex (referred to collectively as the Sara-Sahara Shopping Complex).

Each of these complexes housed around fifty retail shops, and every single one was doing brisk business. In fact, the twin shopping complexes became so infamous after a while that they were called 'Dawood Mall'. The Mumbai police uncovered a veritable treasure trove of incriminating evidence comprising fifty-six tapes of telephonic conversation between Dawood or his men and people from the BMC and other government departments. The cops realised that they could probably book Iqbal and did exactly that. Iqbal was swiftly booked under the extremely stringent MCOCA for conspiracy and aiding and abetment of organised crime's effort to usurp government property.

Iqbal was now left with little recourse, other than fighting the charges in court, and his case went on for several years in the court of special judge A.P. Bhangale. During the course of the trial, the police discovered that Iqbal's voice had also been recorded on the tapes. Although there was no concrete evidence on the tapes to incriminate Iqbal, the Mumbai police nevertheless decided that some action, whatever it was, had to be taken. The then Commissioner of Police A.N. Roy, using the police chief's prerogative under Section 311 of the Indian Penal Code (IPC), decided to sack Aslam Momin for what was described as his 'alleged involvement with the underworld'. Three years after Iqbal's fateful call to Aslam, the latter was unceremoniously booted out of his job by Roy. Naturally, Aslam was distraught and went to the tribunal to see if he could clear his name. The Mumbai police did not make this task any easier and took their own sweet time to provide the requisite affidavits. The entire process took an excruciating fifteen months, but Aslam was finally given a clean chit.

Unfortunately for the former inspector, the Mumbai police quickly went to the high court to appeal against his clean chit and Aslam had to wage yet another long drawn-out battle against his own former bosses with no immediate reprieve in sight.

In 2004, inspired by the example set by Arun Gawli, who was then a member of the legislative assembly despite the significant handicap of being lodged at Arthur Road Jail, Iqbal decided to contest the elections as an Independent candidate from the Umerkhadi constituency. With everything in place, he filed his nominations and was all set to go head-to-head with the Nationalist Congress Party's Bashir Patel. It was then that something went awry and Iqbal had to withdraw his nominations.

It is widely believed and was reported in the *Times of India* on 28 September 2004 that a high-ranking IPS officer who enjoyed a close proximity with an NCP politician, was responsible for getting Iqbal to withdraw his nomination. The story goes that Iqbal was threatened that 'the cops would not spare him if he contested' the elections.

Over three years later, in the MCOCA court, where Iqbal was still fighting his case, Bhangale was no longer the judge and was replaced by Judge M.A. Bhatkar. She found that there was insufficient evidence against Iqbal, his voice did not match the one on the tape, and there was not a shred of information linking him to the Sara-Sahara Shopping Complex. Finally, it was then, four years since his return to India, that Iqbal could walk away a free man.

The case, however, was not totally unfruitful for the police as they saw three people from the BMC and other government agencies suspended for their involvement in the shopping complexes. The entire 'Dawood Mall' was also ordered to be torn down to the ground. The shopkeepers saw their cash cows slowly slipping from their grip and were naturally, up in arms. They went to the high court and managed to get a stay order against the demolition. Undeterred, the state went to the Supreme Court and managed to get the final orders for demolition.

While the only remnants of the Sara-Sahara Complex today are in the memories of the shopkeepers, for Aslam, the nightmare has refused to end. Even today, he is still under suspicion and continues to wage his lone struggle, contesting his case. There does not seem to be any relief in sight for him because he believes that he will still be fighting his case well into his retirement.

Iqbal seemed to have learnt his lessons albeit the hard way. The surname of Kaskar had been a stigma and he realised that the name would keep getting him into trouble. He decided to approach the Bombay High Court and asked to change his name to Shaikh Iqbal Hasan instead of Iqbal Hasan Kaskar.

25

Global Terrorist

After a struggle of over a decade, the Indian government finally managed to convince the mighty United States that Dawood Ibrahim was now a crucial cog in the wheel for terror activities perpetrated internationally.

The Indian government had launched intensive efforts to convince Uncle Sam that Dawood, who organised the serial blasts of 1993 in Mumbai, was capable of attacking the US interests anywhere in the world because of his liaisons with Osama Bin Laden. The initiative finally worked with Capitol Hill though it took over 10 years and 6 months to achieve their desired objective.

The US Treasury Department on 16 October 2003 announced that it was designating Dawood Ibrahim as a Specially Designated Global Terrorist under Executive Order 13224 and would be requesting the United Nations to list him as well. The global terrorist designation froze any assets belonging to Dawood within the US and prohibited transactions with US nationals. The UN listing required that all UN members take similar actions.

While proclaiming him a global terrorist, the US government declared, 'This designation signals our commitment to identifying and attacking the financial ties between the criminal underworld and terrorism,' stated Juan Zarate, Deputy Assistant Secretary for Terrorist Financing and Financial Crimes. He added, 'We are calling on the international community to stop the flow of dirty money that kills. For the Ibrahim syndicate, the business of terrorism forms part of their larger criminal enterprise, which must be dismantled.'

The executive order clearly describes Dawood Ibrahim as an Indian crime lord who has found common cause with Al Qaeda, sharing his smuggling routes with the terror syndicate and funding attacks by Islamic extremists aimed at destabilising the Indian government. He was wanted in India for the 1993 Bombay Stock Exchange bombings, it stated, and is known to have financed the activities of the LeT, a group designated by the United States in October 2001 and ostensibly banned by the Pakistani Government—which also froze their assets—in January 2002.

Another US Congressional report released simultaneously identified the D Company as a '5,000-member criminal syndicate operating mostly in Pakistan, India, and the United Arab Emirates,' which has a 'strategic alliance' with the ISI and has 'forged relationships with Islamists, including Lashkar-e-Tayyaba and Al Qaida'.

The report, prepared by the Congressional Research Service (CRS), the research wing of Congress, was aimed at priming US lawmakers on various issues, and had no immediate policy implications. The US Department of Treasury had already designated Dawood as a Specially Designated Global Terrorist (SDGT) and subsequently President George W. Bush designated him, as well as his D Company organisation, a Significant Foreign Narcotics Trafficker under the Foreign Narcotics Kingpin Designation Act.

According to the report, Dawood began his foray in terrorism as a 'criminal specialist' in Bombay, first as a low-level smuggler in the seventies and later as the leader of a poly-crime syndicate. He formed a thriving criminal enterprise throughout the eighties and became radicalised in the nineties, forging relationships with Islamists, including LeT and Al Qaeda. D Company's evolution into a true criminal-terrorist group began in response to the destruction of the Babri Masjid and the subsequent riots that killed hundreds of Muslims, the report said, clearly indicating the lack of research and shallow observations of the American research group.

'Outraged by the attacks on fellow Muslims and believing the Indian government acted indifferently to their plight, Ibrahim decided to retaliate. Reportedly with assistance of the ISI, D-Company launched a series of bombing attacks on March 12, 1993, killing 257 people. Following the attacks, Ibrahim moved his organization's headquarters to Karachi, Pakistan,' the report added, mincing no words about the terrorist don's Pakistani location and patronage.

The US Treasury Department's website gives his location as Karachi and identifies him by his Pakistani passport bearing number G869537, and his telephone number as 021-5892038.

Certainly, Dawood has not been sighted in Karachi or Dubai for some time, but while he kept travelling between these two cities, his activities must have been well-known to the CIA hawks, but they never decided to designate Dawood a global terrorist until trouble landed on their doorstep.

And it was not as if Dawood made much effort to keep a low profile. Whether in Dubai or Karachi, he was courted by top South Asian cricketers for his cricket betting activities. Similarly, with regard to Bollywood, hardly a film could be produced in India without investment from Dawood. Dawood's guests were always lavishly entertained, and the best Scotch flowed, even in a dry country.

Dawood's underworld connections are extensive, and he 'sublets' his name in Pakistan, Thailand, South Africa, Indonesia, Malaysia, and the United Arab Emirates, among other countries, to 'franchises' in the fields of drug trafficking and gambling dens.

At the time of the declaration, India's Deputy Prime Minister L.K. Advani, who also looked after the Home Affairs Ministry, said the US designation of Dawood as a global terrorist vindicated India's stand. Since its inception, the Bharatiya Janata Party (BJP)-led coalition government was stridently parlaying for Dawood's extradition to India and seeking US help in keeping a check on Pakistan's nefarious activities.

The government had demanded that Pakistan hand over Dawood, who figures in India's twenty most wanted men from Pakistan. Advani said

Dawood's handing over to New Delhi would improve relations between the two countries. But the Pakistan spokesman retorted, 'This is a false premise. Relations cannot improve on the basis of such premises.'

The BJP had cleverly begun collating details on Dawood's network across the world. The D Dossier, as it had become known in the core group of the government, clearly mentioned that Dawood had travelled through Afghanistan in the nineties under Taliban protection, which was later corroborated by the US Treasury Department statement, and it had now been confirmed that his routes and networks converge at many significant points with those of none other than the late Osama Bin Laden, the D Dossier said. This is the reason why the US has suddenly become alert about Dawood's importance. Some analysts, however, speculate that Dawood's handlers in the Pakistani intelligence apparatus, especially the ISI, may have forced him to surrender his network and his smuggling routes to the Al Qaeda.

It was on the basis of inputs by Indian intelligence that the US went hammer and tongs after Dawood. Advani had shared reams of 'top secret' information with top officials of the Bush administration during his visit to the US. Advani's trump card during his US visit was that he focused on Dawood's links with the LeT and Al Qaeda, knowing fully well that Washington was not interested in Dawood's anti-India operations. Advani gave plenty of evidence to the US of how Dawood was no longer an underworld don but a shipping magnate, media baron, drug trafficker, arms trafficker, and the CEO of a huge corporate called D Company, all rolled into one.

Advani's masterstroke lay in the presentation that how Dawood's operations had lately turned against Israeli interests and that of the US. The Americans would have never acted on Dawood had it not been for the double attack by suspected Al Qaeda cadres in Mombassa (Kenya) in November 2002. The terrorists attacked a hotel where Israeli tourists were staying and almost simultaneously made an abortive attempt to blow up an airliner packed with Israelis. Shortly after the Mombassa incidents, Dawood's main operations man, Anees Ibrahim, was picked up in Dubai. The IB officials and RAW operatives emphatically tried to prove how Dawood had contributed in the Mombassa incidents. The D Company had a warehouse in Mombassa and Anees Ibrahim was its chief operator. It is understood that Advani educated the US on this particular aspect of the D Company's operations. India already had a lot of information available on this subject in the wake of the arrest of another D Company operative, Madad Chatur, who was picked up in Kenya and jailed there some four years ago.

Pakistan's claim that Dawood was not on its soil was demolished when the Treasury Department's Office of Foreign Assets Control determined that he had a Pakistani passport and a Karachi telephone number. Indian intelligence agencies were well aware that Dawood's residence was an ISI-protected house in Peshawar. Islamabad protested its innocence at the most authoritative level when its then President Pervez Musharraf denied any knowledge about Dawood's whereabouts during the July 2001 Agra Summit.

This position was not changed after the Pakistani media reported that Dawood was operating in the country with official patronage. The de facto Home Minister of Sindh, Aftab Sheikh, sprang a surprise when he announced that Dawood was running his network from the capital of the province. But Sheikh and the US were contradicted by a spokesman of the Pakistan government, proving that Dawood was protected by powerful elements in that country.

The mafioso from Mumbai had been so useful to Pakistan's intelligence services and in return had learnt so much about the activities of the ISI that they could never be handed over to the US, let alone to India. Dawood was accorded Pakistani citizenship so that he could save himself from the clutches of law in India for his role in the 1993 Mumbai serial bomb blasts and other cases registered against him. India has been asking Pakistan to hand him over to New Delhi along with the others whose names figure on the most wanted list of twenty fugitives submitted to Islamabad, but the stock reply from the other side is that Dawood is not in Pakistan. This was what Islamabad said again after the American admission of the Indian viewpoint.

After his cover was blown, Dawood reportedly shifted his headquarters to Peshawar. When General Musharraf had visited India in July 2001, the Pakistan government knew he would be confronted with the demand for his custody, and so Dawood was sent out to Singapore so that Musharraf could say that he was not on Pakistani soil.

Dawood, Shakeel, and Ibrahim alias Tiger Memon, all three listed among the twenty most wanted men by India from Pakistan, were granted Pakistani citizenship in June 2003. Dawood has also undergone a name change and his new identity is Iqbal Seth alias Amer Sahib, while Chhota Shakeel is known as Haji Mohammad and Tiger Memon as Ahmed Jamil. The underworld don had been issued his first Pakistani passport number G866537 at Rawalpindi on 12 August 1991.

Soon after the US Treasury Department declared Dawood a specially designated global terrorist, the Pakistan Deputy High Commissioner in New Delhi was summoned to the Foreign Office to convey India's demand that Dawood Ibrahim be handed over to New Delhi to face charges pending against him in connection with widespread extortions and the serial bomb blasts in Mumbai in 1993. But, given the flat denial of Pakistan, there is a big question mark over the US action's making any difference to the Pakistan Government's stand.

For India, however, this is a big shot in the arm and a long overdue success in making the world a smaller place for their bê te noire Dawood Ibrahim.

26

Salem's Extradition

As a fallout of Anees' vengeful attitude towards him, Salem was arrested in Lisbon along with Monica Bedi one fine day in 2002 when he was at her apartment. Locked up in a jail just outside Lisbon, Salem knew that the CBI was exploring all diplomatic and legal channels to have him extradited to India so that they could take custody of him. Fortunately for Salem, the legal battle between Portugal and India was a protracted one, as the two countries have no extradition treaty between them. Besides, the Indian government's track record with securing extradition was less than average, to put it politely.

In 1995, the government attempted to have drug lord Iqbal Memon (known in some circles as Iqbal Mirchi) extradited from London. Years later, the government tried to have music composer Nadeem Saifi extradited for allegedly paying for the murder of music magnate Gulshan Kumar, which was carried out by Salem's shooter. Both these efforts were in vain. Despite spending a truckload of money and lawyers and cops making scores of trips to London, the Indian government failed to extradite any of the accused.

The CBI's legal eagles were arriving in droves to secure Salem's extradition after Portugal refused to deport him. The Government of India then invoked a special treaty with its Portuguese counterpart and extradition was quickly back on the cards. However, the Portuguese government sought several assurances from India. The CBI, which originally had twenty-four cases against Salem, began paring down the list of charges, which resulted in his escaping charges of having murdered Gulshan Kumar.

Meanwhile, Salem's dream relationship with Monica Bedi was slowly beginning to deteriorate. From the perky, love-filled and optimistic letters that she used to send him in the past, the tone of her latest communiqués was turning frustrated, confused, scared, and increasingly cryptic. Lines like 'Babu, tumhe Khudaa bula rahe hain [God is calling you]' were confusing him to no end. After all, it was the occasional meetings with Monica and the thought of being with her that kept him going throughout his time behind bars.

In a letter to Salem, she wrote that her new faith seemed to have given her a new way to deal with problems. She added that she was shattered by the verdict that the Supreme Court had delivered against Salem and her and so, in her hour of need, she decided to reach out to Jesus Christ and turn Christian. Finally, in January 2005, the CBI began preparing to bring Salem back, but it was only in the month of November that year that Salem was sent back to India via Cairo on a special aircraft. A team comprising CBI Deputy Inspector General Omprakash Chatwal, Deputy Superintendent of Police Devendra Pardesi, and two inspectors, including a woman inspector, was rushed across to Portugal from Mumbai to take charge of Salem and Monica.

Salem had served a three-year sentence in Portugal and was extradited on the conditions that there would be no death sentence, he would not be ill-treated and he could be given no sentence longer than twenty-five years. Communications broke down further between the former lovers and their strained relationship truly reached its nadir when the CBI team brought Salem and Monica back to Mumbai from Lisbon. All through both legs of the journey (Lisbon to Cairo and Cairo to Mumbai), Monica refused to even glance at Salem, choosing instead to sit quietly, clutching her Bible. They had landed in Portugal as man and wife, but were leaving as strangers.

And so, Salem began his stay at Arthur Road Jail as a resident of the *anda* cell—10 x 10 feet, oval-shaped, high security cell, where one is in solitary confinement and has no contact with the outside world. The government did not want to risk Salem being attacked or worse yet, killed in jail and so, he was kept in this cell for around a month or so. Once the authorities were satisfied that Salem's life was in no immediate peril, he was moved to Barrack No. 10.

This particular barrack has been home to a number of major gangsters and others accused in high-profile cases and is considered to be among the most luxurious of barracks. Inmates had access to a few amenities and things that would be considered a massive luxury in any other barrack. Being moved to Barrack No. 10 saw Salem reunited with his old friends from the underworld and life was good again.

His nephew ensured that the procurement of branded goods and restaurant-made food was delivered to Salem. Apart from regular trips to the court for hearings of the cases in which he was an accused, life was good for Salem until the day the 1993 Mumbai blast accused were handed their sentences. With most of the convicts being sent to Thane Jail and Yerawada Jail, Anees's one-time right-hand-man saw his set of friends dwindling. The only person left with him at Arthur Road was Mustafa Dossa.

Very soon, two sensational murder cases saw navymen Manish Thakur (accused of killing his girlfriend) and Emile Jerome Matthew (accused of killing media executive Neeraj Grover) being arrested and Salem had new companions. But they too could not protect the vain Salem from the famous 'sharpened spoon attack' at the hands of Dossa in 2010, one which left his face partially scarred.

27

Boucher's Botched Attempt

It has been over three years since the Treasury Department of the United States has declared Dawood Ibrahim as a global terrorist. Despite the branding, albeit after much chest-thumping by India, it does not translate into: 'We are going to bring him to book and get Pakistan to send him back to India'. For the US, Dawood is simply not in their scheme of things.

The executive order entails that his properties should be seized and bank accounts frozen, but Dawood continues to live in Pakistan, unhurt, untouched, and unaffected by the declaration.

I always felt US and their agencies were aware of Dawood Ibrahim's whereabouts and his contribution to terror activities across India, but they do not want to bring him back or hand him over to India deliberately. Notwithstanding the US belief that Dawood is actually a collaborator of Osama Bin Laden, he can still live a luxurious life in Pakistan.

In a bid to defend their South Asian ally Pakistan, who has provided safe sanctuary to several of India's absconding terrorists, the US State Department officials prefer to simply beat about the bush.

It took a personal experience with the US authorities to realise that this declaration is just eyewash. The US prefers to play the part it is traditionally known to play in matters that are actually of some consequence—being fence-sitters. They want to keep the Indians happy with petty official documentation but support Pakistan in whatever way they can.

It was May 2007. East West Center of Honolulu, Hawaii as per their annual routine, had invited Asian journalists for a cultural exchange programme. There were eight participants from various Asian countries including Pakistan, Afghanistan, Indonesia, Bangladesh, Philippines, Malaysia, and India. India was the only country to have two participants: Shahid Khan, Bureau Chief of Press Trust of India, Kolkata, and me, working as Senior Editor in the Mumbai bureau of the *Indian Express*.

The East West Centre wanted to invite Asian journalists to give them an insight into the US policies towards Asian Muslims. They had also invited some senior journalists from American newspapers for discussions and debates.

The gamut of public relations exercise also included a tour of various US cities and government offices in those cities like a visit to Pentagon, Capitol Hill, and the state department office in Washington.

In the round table conference with the journalists, the East West Center representative Ms Susan Kreiffels introduced us to Assistant Secretary for South and Central Asian Affairs, Richard Boucher, a senior US diplomat.

Boucher was assigned the task of being a troubleshooter for the long standing dispute between Pakistan and India but suffers from the Henry Kissinger syndrome of being anti-India and pro-Pakistan. It may be noted that Kissinger is the only US diplomat to call the late Indira Gandhi 'a witch' and that 'Indians are bastards'.

Similarly, Richard Boucher is known to be sympathetic to Pakistan in keeping in line with his country's policy of turning a blind eye to Pakistan's follies.

Reproduced below is an excerpt from the verbatim transcript of the discussion with Boucher.

Roundtable with East-West Center Journalists Tour
May 14, 2007
Washington, D.C.
Assistant Secretary Boucher: Good to see you all. Welcome. When did you all arrive? This weekend?

Shahid Khan: Friday.

Assistant Secretary Boucher: Friday. So you probably feel the way I do. I came in Friday, not too late in the morning, from Sri Lanka and Maldives. All I can tell you is it's a long way. You guys know that. I handle—I work on a region from India—actually, Maldives is the farthest south, to Kazakhstan. You might call it a backbone of stability—from India to Kazakhstan.

Shahid Khan: Are you comfortable with what the Pakistani Government is doing with you?

Assistant Secretary Boucher: I'm comfortable [that] the Pakistani Government has done a lot to keep the pressure up and to actually impose more pressure on the foreign fighters and the Taliban and the others who are out there.

Bangladeshi reporter: Sir, it's known, well known that the Bangladeshi... Bangladesh is now, you know, is run by a quasi-military government, kind of, and there is a popular perception that they're enjoying American blessings out there, because America is interested to...you know, in our coal mine and gas line and, you know, the sea port and—

Assistant Secretary Boucher: That's silly, actually. I mean, if that's what people think, I'm afraid they're just wrong.

Bangladeshi journalist: A statement of people—

Assistant Secretary Boucher: We're interested in stability in Bangladesh. We're interested in having a good partner in Bangladesh. We're interested in the two things we've always worked on in Bangladesh: One is promoting democracy, and the second is helping them fight terrorism. I'd say the third one is developing the nation. Bangladesh has done pretty well economically in the past few years, but they've had a lot of political trouble and political turmoil. This government is a caretaker government. It's important to remember that because the role of the caretaker government is to have an election, is to get to an election, a fair, free, open election that gives the people of Bangladesh a choice.

[I raised my hand.]

Hussain Zaidi: Sir.

Hussain Zaidi: Are you aware that Pakistani soil has been used to create terrorism not only in India and Kashmir, but also in cities like Bombay? Karachi in Pakistan has been a safe haven for at least 30 terrorists wanted by Indian Government in Mumbai blasts of '93 and subsequently other bombings?

Assistant Secretary Boucher: Well, if you're going to accuse every country—I mean, there are terrorists in India. Look at the Mumbai bombings. Look at the train bombings.

Hussain Zaidi: Yeah, but—

Assistant Secretary Boucher: They were local people and there were people with connections to other places, including Pakistan.

Question: Yeah, but the kingpin is always Pakistan.

Assistant Secretary Boucher: No, I..I don't think that's completely true, frankly.

Hussain Zaidi: India has always been a victim of terrorists who were remotely controlled by Pakistan and they have always produced evidence to the US, you still maintain that—

[Boucher once again switches to a defensive mode.]

Assistant Secretary Boucher: I'm not here to have an argument. If you want to ask me a question, I'll give you the answer, okay? There are terrorist groups that originated in Pakistan that are operating throughout the region. Some of those groups are now banned in Pakistan. Some of those groups have tried to assassinate President Musharraf as well as other people throughout the region. The fact is, you know, this is not a gang from one country to another. This is not an accusation from one country to another. These terrorists are operating and attacking governments throughout the region and particularly India and Pakistan. India and Pakistan have recognised that they have a common problem. They need to find common solutions. That's why they have a mechanism to work together against terrorism. We think that's good development. We're against terrorists. We're with India against terrorists. We're with Pakistan against terrorists, and we all have to work together if we're going to stop it. That's our view of the situation.

[I was absolutely shocked by Boucher's partisan attitude but now I have to directly ask about Dawood Ibrahim and the hypocrisy of the US in turning a blind eye towards him.]

Question: Just one last thing. Dawood Ibrahim is declared global terrorist by the US. I think the US has also declared that Dawood is an ally of Al Qaida. So I think even the US appears to have in their possession, evidence of his being in Pakistan.

Assistant Secretary Boucher: I don't know if that's true. I mean, I do know that Dawood Ibrahim is a bad guy, and we deserve to get him, but we all have to work together. Yes?

[By now Boucher was thoroughly miffed with my persistent line of questioning and wanted to address other journalists.]

Shahid Khan: How far are you confident that that India will be able to complete the nuclear deal, the US nuclear deal?

Assistant Secretary Boucher: I'm pretty confident. We had some good talks a couple of weeks ago when Foreign Secretary Menon was here. I think we went through things quite thoroughly and made some real significant progress. We're trying to get back together as soon as we know we have a good basis for the next round to take it the next step forward. And so we're waiting to hear back from the Indian side right now, but I'm pretty confident that we're making the progress now that we had hoped to make, and that we'll be able to conclude this deal the way both sides want to.

Question: Does the position of India Government, the Manmohan Singh government and [inaudible] minority is there view [inaudible] the parliament deliberate?

Assistant Secretary Boucher: I think, you know, we've done this from the beginning with the Prime Minister. The President and the Prime Minister reached an agreement a long time ago. What we're trying to do is carry out what they've already agreed. Their political situation hasn't changed. The Prime Minister has been leading this process throughout. So I think the record so far shows that he can do this, and that he has been doing this successfully, and we're going to continue to work with him to achieve it.

[The discussion continued for another 40 minutes where Boucher patiently answered questions about Afghanistan, Bangladesh, and, of course, Pakistan and how they have convinced President Musharraf to hold elections in Pakistan.]

The transcripts of the round table conference was made available to me by a State Department Official Ms Jennifer L. Viau on 9 June 2007.

28

The Big D Makes the *Forbes* Cut

On his 55th birthday on 26 December 2010, Dawood Ibrahim could not have asked for a better gift. In his chequered career as a mafia head, he added another bullet to his belt when the *Forbes* magazine listed him as the 50th most powerful man on the planet in its first annual 'World's Most Powerful People' list of 2009. The list was topped by US President Barack Obama. The most recent list, when this book was in production, ranks him at 57, with Obama still at the top, and Joaquin Guzman Loera, the Mexican druglord still ahead of Dawood at 55. Interestingly, ISI chief Ahmed Shuja Pasha is the one separating the two of the most wanted criminals in the world.

Incidentally, India's most wanted fugitive ganglord is thirty-eight ranks behind Prime Minister Manmohan Singh, who is currently at no. 19. Incidentally, in 2009, Al Qaeda leader, Osama bin Laden was just one step behind Manmohan Singh, who was then at 36, on the *Forbes* list of sixty-seven politicians, businessmen, religious figures, media heads, and one drug trafficker. Now though, with his death, Osama for obvious reasons does not feature on the list anymore.

Forbes editors say they went by four broad parameters to make their list: Does the person have influence over lots of other people, financial resources controlled by these individuals, if they are powerful in multiple spheres, and do they actively use their power.

To quote from the article 'The World's Most Powerful People' by Michael Noer and Nicole Perlroth in *Forbes* (11 November 2009, www. Forbes.com), 'Power has been called many things. The ultimate aphrodisiac. An absolute corrupter. A mistress. A violin. But its true nature remains elusive. After all, a head of state wields a very different sort of power than a religious figure. Can one really compare the influence of a journalist to that of a terrorist? And is power unexercised, power at all?' *Forbes* asked.

Based on these parameters, Obama is followed by Russian Prime Minister Vladimir Putin with Chinese President Hu Jintao coming next.

Former President George W. Bush did not come close to making the final cut, while his predecessor in the Oval Office, Bill Clinton, currently ranks 50th, ahead of a number of sitting heads of government. Pope Benedict XVI, ranked 7th on our list, is the spiritual leader of more than a billion souls, or about one-sixth of the world's population.

The only other notorious top criminal to figure on the list is billionaire Mexican drug lord Joaquin Guzmán. His family's profile and rise in crime is strikingly similar to Dawood's. Guzmán had over half a dozen siblings and had a hand-to-mouth existence in his childhood, though his father, unlike Dawood's, was well-connected. Dawood's father was a constable with a limited sphere of influence in the Muslim pockets of south Mumbai.

Again like Dawood, Guzmán made his mark at the age of 20 and then kept rising. He is the most notorious and feared drug trafficker of Mexico and his assets are valued at US $1 billion. There is no account of Dawood's tangible or intangible wealth.

Dawood, the US business magazine says, runs an international drug trafficking, counterfeiting and weapons smuggling empire and is suspected to have links with the Al Qaeda, which seems to have more shades of powerplay than Guzmán, but the latter still remains higher on the list. Incidentally, Guzmán also celebrated his 55th birthday recently.

Reliance Industries Ltd chief Mukesh Ambani is ranked No. 35, while Lakshmi Mittal is at No. 47. To those who know of Dawood Ibrahim's might, power, and reach, it is no surprise that he has managed to upstage so many heads of state and business tycoons in the power list. Dawood Ibrahim is more cunning and smarter than most heads of state put together and has the business acumen of several Dhirubhai Ambanis rolled into one. For example, if you examined even one aspect of his business and survival skills, you would be convinced that he thinks as fast as lightning. Mumbai's Anti-Terrorism Squad chief, Rakesh Maria, explained the fine nuances and intricacies of Dawood's empire in an exclusive interview with me,

'When you are declared a global terrorist, survival is difficult. Seven years ago, Pakistan used the opportunity to tighten the screws on him after the global terrorist tag by America. Dawood, of course, knew that was his death knell and soon he would become expendable. But this is where his astuteness came into play. He knew long before anybody else in Pakistan that the country was going to be outrun by fundamentalists and that the Lashkar-e-Tayyeba and Talibanic elements were busy making inroads into Pakistan's polity and framework. When terrorists like Maulana Masood Azhar, who was released in exchange for the IC 814 hijacked passengers, were treated with kid-gloves instead of being handed over back to India, he realised that he too had to become integral and indispensable to Pakistan's scheme of things and that alone would ensure his survival.

'And the best way to achieve this status was to fund the biggest power brokers in Pakistan which included ISI, Jaish-e-Mohammad and Lashkar-e-Tayyeba, or its parent organisation Markazud Dawa,' said Maria.

Dawood thus began offering huge donations to these rogue outfits and fuelling their gargantuan growth. The money donated actually emboldened these organisations' jehadi activities and changed the dynamics of Pakistan's politics and the power equations between the ISI and the jehadi organisations.

The Markazud Dawa, which was trying to ostensibly be a legitimate organisation, began using Dawood's services for international money laundering. For Dawood, cleansing the Markaz funds from his bases in Europe and Southeast Asia was a cakewalk.

Maria adds, 'Dawood managed to do all these through video piracy, which he managed to remotely choreograph using the hidden cubby holes in the labyrinthine alleys and basements of the Lahore's Madina Market. These piracy centres sold Bollywood movies to Pakistan's Bollywood-crazy audiences, who loved to devour Indian cinema in any format.

'It was a quid pro quo situation. While Dawood managed to strengthen his clout in Pakistan and built a virtually impregnable wall around himself, Lashkar and other such groups became affluent because of his generous donations,' Maria said.

Until the Rand Corporation declared in March 2009 that film piracy was funding Islamic terrorism across the world, and that the Dawood Ibrahim syndicate was the biggest player in South Asia, the Indian enforcement agencies always believed that drug trafficking and weapon smuggling were bolstering the size of the terrorists' coffers.

'The piracy industry in India is 1,500 crore rupees and much of it goes into funding terror,' said Moser Baer India Chief Executive Harish Dayani during the Confederation of Indian Industry (CII) conference in Panaji in 2010. A cabinet minister from Maharashtra, meanwhile, pegged the figure at 4,000 crore rupees.

Dawood through his well-oiled network in Dubai and Pakistan has managed to generate a massive turnover only through film piracy. According to a dossier accessed from the CBI Special Task Force, 'The D-Company was readily able to transition to film piracy through its well-established hold and influence in the Bollywood movie industry. Beginning with humble King's Video, the D-company's film piracy business became a business empire in itself, a very profitable one. The syndicate's Al-Mansoor and SADAF brands acquired extraordinary market power in the distribution of pirated films throughout the South Asia region and also spread to European and American markets. Still, SADAF's biggest exports were to India, which, due to lax anti-piracy enforcement on the part of Indian authorities, remained an open channel.'

Bollywood and Hollywood products duplicated at SADAF's plant were readily smuggled into India via Nepal. The D Company gained control of the SADAF Trading Company based in Karachi, which allowed the gang to better organise distribution in Pakistan and, more important, acquire the infrastructure to manufacture pirated movies. Indian authorities had been aware of D-Company's film piracy operations in Pakistan since the nineties but were practically powerless to intervene. Only after 2005, when US Customs seized a large shipment of SADAF brand counterfeit discs in Virginia, did Pakistani authorities, under a threat of trade sanctions, begin raiding D-Company's duplicating facilities in Dubai and Karachi.

Piracy funds generated through such massive operations were diverted for funding of jehadi activities. Millions of dollars that went into the coffers of these radical organisations made Dawood their financial artery. There was no way that they could allow any government or a politician to extradite their golden goose and cripple them financially.

Ironically, Dawood himself is a Konkani Muslim who believes in Sunni Islam and does not adhere to the Wahabi idealogy. Tiger Memon who triggered the serial blasts in Mumbai in 1993, on the other hand, keeps shuttling to various Pakistani cities, like Muzaffarabad and Jalalabad, talking about jehad and exhorting the youth of PoK (Pakistan-occupied Kashmir) to fight for the Kashmir cause. Dawood does no such thing. Dawood is not even a practising Muslim.

It was easier for him to buy his freedom by donating funds to these organisations and remain invincible and unassailable.

'So Dawood is not doling out funds to these fundamentalist organisations out of his religious zeal or jehadi fervour but he is doing it for his own vested interests of survival and endless clout,' Maria explains.

In India, he used the Mumbai police and influential politicians, while he is using the jehadi elements of Pakistan for his survival.

It appears for Dawood that the show should never stop, even if the players change.

Epilogue

The sprawling compound was completely quiet, the silence broken only by footfalls of the patrolling guards. Boots crunched on gravel as they strolled along the high-walled perimeter and inside it, their hands resting casually on the assault rifles slung over their shoulders. It seemed just like any other night.

This was the hiding place of Osama bin Laden in Waziristan Haveli, literally meaning a 'mansion in Waziristan', located at the end of a dirt road in Abbottabad, Pakistan, just off a major highway. Not even a mile away lay the Pakistan Military Academy in Bilal Town, the suburbs of which hosted retired military officers. The mansion was like a mini fortress with 12 x 18 foot high walls, no telephone to prevent any signal being traced, and with guards patrolling 24x7.

Bin Laden was not hiding in some obscure cave in Afghanistan then, he was right here in Pakistan under the nose of the Pakistani military despite Pakistan's vehement denials. His location was revealed after the CIA tracked down one of the Al Qaeda chief's trusted couriers. After a long debate, US President Barack Obama gave his approval to invade the mansion and kill Osama if need be even though Bin Laden was never actually seen in the compound. And so, at 1 am on the night of 2 May 2011, a team of US Navy SEAL commandoes landed from two helicopters to execute the operation with the code name Operation Neptune Spear.

The objective of the mission was simple and unambiguous. Storm the mansion, remove all perceived threats, eliminate public enemy number one, Osama bin Laden, then scour the compound to retrieve any and all important documents.

The commandoes had all the practice they could possibly get. In preparation for the mission, the CIA had built a replica of the mansion, where the commandoes had spent days practising and maneuvering through the maze of rooms of the three-storey building. They were on edge, and were ready to carry out what would definitely be the most important mission of their lives. The dangers were many, as not only was the operation to be carried out so close to a military base and the target was the most wanted man in the world, but the Pakistan government had been kept completely in the dark about the entire mission. So, if anything went wrong, the commandoes knew they would probably not make it out alive.

The stage was set. A couple of US Navy SEALs planted the explosives on a wall, and waited for the right moment. It was not long in coming.

Precisely at 1 am, the US commandoes breached the boundary wall. The deafening explosion took out a few guards nearby, who fell down stunned, and it dawned on the others that the unthinkable had happened: the safe house had outlasted its safety. The guards immediately began firing at the commandoes, who had, however, come armed with heavy firepower. All guards on the outside were quickly overpowered, and the fight moved into the building with the Navy SEALs team hardly stopping for breath.

The next gun battle ensued inside the building on the first floor, where two adult males lived. They were ready for the onslaught, but gave way under the relentless determination of the team. One of them even tried to use a woman as a human shield, resulting in her death as well.

The commandoes fought their way to the second and third floors where Bin Laden's family used to live. One by one, the family members were all overpowered, and Bin Laden was shot dead. One of his adult sons perished in the battle, so did two couriers and the unfortunate woman.

The intensive training in the replica mansion had prepared the commandoes well. The entire firefight was over in just a few minutes.

The men then spent the next few minutes scouring the headquarters, gathering any computers and documents they could find.

The only glitch in the well-oiled plan was that one of the helicopters reportedly failed due to a mechanical failure. So, the commandoes loaded Bin Laden's body into the other one, along with all the retrieved items, and left behind a smoking compound, flames licking at the building, a safe house that ultimately could not keep the terrorist safe.

Earlier, the CIA had devised another plan, one where the compound would be bombed with a dozen 2000-lb pound bombs dropped from two B2 stealth bombers. However, the drawback was that in such an event, it would have been impossible to actually determine if Bin Laden was indeed among the dead, and eventually, it was dropped for the far more risky, but ultimately successful Operation Neptune Spear.

Later, it was confirmed that the body recovered by the US Navy SEALs commandoes was indeed that of Bin Laden. A DNA test was carried out, and his DNA matched that of his sister, who had died of cancer earlier in Boston, and whose brain was taken into custody and preserved for that very reason, that some day, it would aid in identifying the dreaded terrorist.

After the Raymond Allen Davis incident in early 2011, the ties between the United States and Pakistan had already become strained. The killing of Bin Laden by the CIA, sanctioned by the US, on Pakistan soil and without any knowledge of Pakistani authorities, served to further alienate the two from each other. The world was now pointing fingers at Pakistan and the ISI because contrary to Pakistan's claim that Osama bin Laden was not on its soil but was in fact hiding in Afghanistan. Operation Neptune Spear proved otherwise. This in turn implied one of two things, either that the Pakistani authorities there had no idea about the fact, something that could be extremely embarrassing for the government or that the ISI knew Bin Laden was hiding in Pakistan and had chosen to turn a blind eye, or worse, kept him as a guest. For a country that received billions of dollars in aid from the US, this was a precarious situation to be in.

Either way, the then ISI's Director General Ahmad Shuja Pasha found himself in a difficult situation on 2 May. Not only had he to contend with the bold and audacious operation of the CIA, he now had a liability on his hands—Dawood Ibrahim, whom the ISI itself had welcomed into the country. The brazen killing of Bin Laden the CIA carried out right under

Pasha's nose was proof that Dawood too could be targeted and just as easily bumped off as Bin Laden.

Dawood himself had yet another worry on his mind. He had been welcomed into Pakistan by the ISI, and was well settled in his home in Karachi. But the local mafia had always been hostile toward him. If the CIA could take out Bin Laden so easily, how would long would it be before the local gangs were emboldened enough to attack him? But Dawood need not have worried. After Dubai, Karachi had become his second home; the ISI and the Pakistan administration had taken pains to ensure that he felt completely at home. They would never let him be captured, let alone killed. He was far too valuable an asset to them to neglect.

The ISI set about strategising how to get the don safely out of their country without falling into the US's hands. Had it been anyone else, the ISI would simply have sent them away and hid them somewhere in Federally Administered Tribal Areas (FATA) or in Pakistan Occupied Kashmir (PoK). But these places had caves as hideouts, and here, they had a thoroughly urban man on their hands who used the latest technology and was used to a life of luxury and opulence, someone whom they simply could not send to hide in caves in a remote corner of the country. Something else would have to be done.

And something else was indeed done to ensure the don's safety. It would have to be either Jeddah or Riyadh in Saudi Arabia, the ISI decided. If executed well, the plan was foolproof. Dawood would be out of the country and out of the US's clutches, and as India did not have an extradition treaty with Saudi Arabia, out of India's grasp too.

In fact, Dawood's exact location and whereabouts were not known even to most of the ISI's top echelon. It was a closely guarded secret, shared only on a need-to-know basis. Dawood's right-hand man, Chhota Shakeel had set up base in Jeddah, something that the Mumbai Crime Branch already knew. Jeddah, therefore, seemed to be the safest hideout for Dawood.

Within hours of Operation Neptune Spear, the ISI had everything ready. A passport was prepared for Dawood, and an entire escort of Pakistani Rangers were deputed. Their orders: guard Dawood with your life. Air routes were out of the question, as the CIA was watching every single airport, and nothing would escape them. However well they planned, trying to board a flight out of Karachi would be suicidal both for Dawood and for the ISI, especially on such short notice.

It was decided to take the road route. On the night of 2 May, a cohort of Pakistani Rangers arrived at Dawood's villa in armoured vehicles, on orders to escort Dawood out of the country in top secrecy.

Throughout the day, Dawood had received a flurry of calls from top men in the ISI and the Pakistani government. Interestingly, they all spoke chaste Urdu but betrayed varying accents, from Lahori Punjabi to Karachi Sindhi to the polished and suave sophisticated Urdu. But there was one thing in common in all the calls—all of them expressed the desperate urgency that Dawood be moved to a safer hideout without delay.

As Dawood stood in front of the mirror, he saw a man with a dark complexion, fast receding hairline, a hint of gray on his eyebrow, and a hardened, ruthless face staring back. The man, who was codenamed as 'Muchchad' (moustachioed man) by his enemies, is better known as Amir Sahab these days. The only thing he still carried with him through the years was the pair of pensive eyes.

Although his mind was in turmoil, he revealed no signs of stress or pressure, exuding instead a serene calmness. It was completely at odds with his highly strung aides around him, whose faces were creased with worry and anxiety.

He gave one last long look at the man in the mirror in the impeccable suit, before striding out to the portico of his palatial mansion towards his spanking new golden BMW X3. The car, recently imported, with Dawood's finance managers having had to shell out over a crore in Pakistani rupees, was among the don's latest acquisitions. He still loved fancy cars and fast women.

As he walked towards his car, he was assailed by a feeling of déjà vu. Memories kept coming back to him, flashbacks, and he tried to ignore them. Exactly twenty-seven years ago, Dawood had escaped from Mumbai. Now, he was making an exit from Karachi, a port city and financial hub of Pakistan. Then a call from Mantralaya, the seat of the Maharashtra government, had alerted him just in time and warned him to relocate from Mumbai. This time, the call came from Islamabad from an aide of Shuja Pasha, the epicentre of power in Pakistan. When he had left Mumbai, he was grieving the loss of his brother Sabir; this time, the wound of losing his brother Noorul Haque alias Noora was still fresh.

As the door of the luxury sedan was held open by an agile, gun-toting Pakistan Ranger, Dawood threw a longing glance back at his mansion. He then sank into the rear seat. Immediately, the convoy drove out, armoured cars in front of and behind the bulletproof BMW.

But there was something different this time. When he had left Mumbai, he had known that he would never be able to return to India. But Karachi was different, it had become almost routine for him to leave Karachi for a while when things became a little too hot to handle, and then return when the dust had settled.

The car flanked by several military vehicles and Pakistani Rangers hit the Karachi National Highway. The world's second most wanted man, after Mexican drug lord Joaquin 'El Chapo' Guzman was on his way out of Pakistan, en route to Jeddah.

But Dawood was not too worried. He would be back soon.

And as anticipated, he was back indeed, within a few months. It took just over three months for the US heat to blow over, and the world had accepted the US's operation to kill Bin Laden; Pakistan's outrage had become old news.

So in September, Dawood was back in Karachi to celebrate and host his eldest son Moin's wedding to a London girl. On 28 September, his son's palatial bungalow, named Moin Villa after him, was filled with all the powerful people affiliated to the don, from politicians and businessmen to those at the highest levels of the ISI. The wedding itself was an extravaganza in pomp and grandeur, underlining Dawood's power and unwavering presence in his adoptive country.

The don was back on the throne.

Sources

M ost of the information in the book about the history of crime in Mumbai has been primarily sourced from former Mumbai Police Commissioner Mahesh Narain Singh's compilation, 'The Growth of Gangsterism in the City'. Singh had compiled it when he was the joint commissioner of police, crime, between 1993 and 1995. The book was written for the police department so that the policemen could get an orientation about organised crime in the city.

Veteran crime reporter and author Sharafat Khan's self-published book *Underworld King Dawood Ibrahim and Gang War* written in Urdu was another important source of information.

Text regarding gangland killings and shootouts was procured extensively from the dossiers prepared by the Mumbai Crime Branch.

The article entitled 'Manya Shot Dead' (dated 23 January 1982) in the tabloid *Current* and my interview with Assistant Commissioner of Police Ishaq Bagwan formed the base for information about Manya Surve's killing.

The details about the tussle between the Pathan mafia and Dawood Ibrahim and insights into the lives of Haji Mastan and Karim Lala were obtained from the cover story entitled 'The Clan, Bombay's Brotherhood of Crime' of *The IllustratedWeekly of India* (April 14–20, 1985) written by

Amrita Shah. Several editions (from 1980 to 1995) of the now defunct Urdu weekly *Akhbare Aalam* were also consulted with the consent of Mr Khaleel Zahid, the editor and publisher.

Information about Dawood Ibrahim and his empire in Dubai and Pakistan was mostly culled from several dossiers prepared by the Central Bureau of Investigations (CBI) and Interpol.

The book, *The Mumbai Police* by Deepak Rao has also been a valuable source of information.

Index

Acknowledgements

*D*ongri to Dubai: Six Decades of the Mumbai Mafia has taken me over six years of research, compilation, verification, corroboration, writing, rewriting, tweaking, and all that goes into the making of a book of this scale. At the end of it, all I can say, without sounding immodest, is that this is a complete chronicle of the Mumbai mafia—something like this has never been published before.

On my own, I would have plodded along for a good fifteen years to accomplish this colossal task. If I have managed to finish this book in much less time, the credit goes to the scores of my friends, coworkers, police, journalists, and experts on the Mumbai mafia.

When I began in 2004–05, I realised that burning the candle at both ends—holding a full time job as a journalist and writing a book — was hara-kiri. While the job pretty much sucked the marrow out of my life, the book simply lay on the backburner.

When I finally got around to starting work on the book, Meenal Baghel delivered *Mumbai Mirror* and roped me in to handle the newspaper's birth pangs. This proved a setback for *Dongri to Dubai*, though I kept researching. The more people I met and the more I worked on the book, my heart sank at the knowledge of the enormous task at hand.

Once again I approached my go-to-guy, Vikram-the-great-Chandra. He came to my rescue with a must-have bible for all struggling writers, a book called *Bird by Bird: Some Instructions on Writing and Life* by Anne Lamott, which helped me overcome my writer's block and the problem of processing such humongous amount of information.

Every time Vikram returned from the US, he would unfailingly bring me several books on various topics, which facilitated the task of simplifying the narration. He also gave me email tutorials on the art of story telling. Vikram, I could have never imagined authoring a book and I continue to write because of you. My most exclusive thanks are reserved for you.

So I began rewriting the chapters, which I believe is one of the most daunting tasks for any writer — to write something, trash it, and begin writing all over again.

In the meanwhile, I quit *Mumbai Mirror* and joined *Indian Express* before eventually going back to the *Asian Age* where I had first cut my teeth in journalism way back in 1995.

Here I met Lakshmi Govindrajan and Megha Moorthy, two fabulous women who decided that they would not spare the rod if I succumbed to laziness while writing the book. They kept pushing me to set smaller goals for the book. With their help and despotic compassion, I managed to finish the first draft in 2010.

In fact it was Lakshmi who kept a yellow diary to log the progress of chapters and discussed the flow and placements of the content. She did not ease up on the pressure until I finished the book. Thank you very much, Lakshmi.

Subsequently, Aditya Iengar, a sub editor at the *Asian Age*, took over from where they had left. He sat with a fine-tooth comb to look for gaps in editing. My profound gratitude to the two Tam-Brahm girls and the half south-Indian but fully Bengali Adi for making this book a reality.

Many thanks go to my publishers Pramod Kapoor sahab and Priya Kapoor for being so patient for over six years and putting up my with eccentricities and idiosyncrasies. I immensely appreciate the way they never gave up on me. *Shukriya*, to both of you for being so kind and accommodating. I am also thankful to the editors at Roli Books, Rajni George and Jyotsna Mehta.

In the process of writing the book, I relied heavily on the investigative skills of some of the finest journalists in this country like Usman Gani Muqadam, Pradeep Shinde, and Jyoti Dey, all of whom are no more with us. Their contribution to the book is immense.

Muqadam helped me with information on old mafia dons like Haji Mastan, Karim Lala, Bakhiya, and others who were active between 1947 and the 1970s. Shinde's insight into Varadarajan Mudaliar's gang was very helpful, while Dey generously discussed his perspective about the Kanjurmarg company and the Byculla company of the Gawli gang and the Nana company of Chhota Rajan.

I would like to profusely thank Misha Glenny, the celebrated author of *McMafia: A Journey Through the Global Underworld*, for his generous and insightful inputs on Dubai as the world capital and a burgeoning Mafiosi hub. Thanks a zillion, Misha.

Among other journalists of today who helped me is Jigna Vora, one of the best crime journalists in our country after the late Jyoti Dey. There is none like her, a woman of unimpeachable integrity, in contemporary crime reporting, while most of the crime reporters, I am sorry to say, are merely 'police-stenographers'. Thanks, Jigna, for your insights into the ways of the Mumbai mafia post 2006. A big thank you is also due to Josy Joseph of the *Times of India*, who plied me with reams of secret dossiers from the intelligence agencies.

Mateen Hafeez, special correspondent with the *Times of India*, who took pains to travel to Nalla Sopara, the far end of Mumbai's burgeoning western suburbs, and boarded a crowded bus from there, which took another hour of tedious journey, to interview exhaustively the late Usman Gani, deserves a special mention here. While two such trips took its toll on my mood, Mateen undertook over ten such rickety rides and did not flinch even once. He also pored over the archives of Urdu newspapers like the *Inquilab*, *Urdu Times*, and *Akhbare Alam* and translated the stories into English for me. There are few good men like him.

Danish Khan, my former colleague at *Mumbai Mirror*, who is presently in London, helped me unravel Dawood's teenage life from various cops and contacts. He also shared information and photographs of Abu Salem's house in Sarai Mir, Azamgarh, Uttar Pradesh. It is people like Danish and Mateen who have reinforced my faith in humanity.

My profound thanks to Smita Nair, the principal correspondent at the *Indian Express*, and one of the most underrated journalists in Mumbai, for digging out some unknown details about Varadarajan's empire in the city, interviewing Varda's daughter, Gomathi and also veteran journalist Pradeep Shinde.

Gautam Mengle from the *Asian Age* helped me with details on the Manya Surve encounter. Gautam is a promising reporter and, simply put, really good at his job.

Suhas Bhivankar is an encyclopedia on the Mumbai underworld. He is in his early seventies and is indefatigable. You would have to walk with Bhivankar for miles before he agrees to let you in on a glimpse of the past. He was the chief reporter of the Urdu daily *Urdu Times*, and must have been the first Maharashtrian to have held this job. He knows the Mumbai underworld like the back of his hand, as well as the various ranks of cops across the city.

My protégés — Menaka Rao of *Hindustan Times* who dug out old court documents and Rashmi Rajput of NDTV who procured a whole lot of old newspaper clippings and photographs of dons have been of great help to me. Rashmi especially has made me very proud with her sharp investigative skills and unfailing hardwork. A big thank you to both these girls.

Rehana Bastiwala of the BBC Urdu news service conducted several interviews on my behalf while Sandra Almeida, news editor of *Hindustan Times*, helped me immensely during my initial research. Thanks Rehana and Sandra for your valuable contribution.

Pranoti Surve, who interned with *Indian Express*, helped me with the initial ten chapters of the book. She was also my sounding board during the initial years when I started writing. Unfortunately for me but most fortuitously for her, she zipped off to London when she got a scholarship to study at the prestigious School of Oriental and African Studies in London. By the time she returned, I was wrapping up the book. Thank you Pranoti, for your time and dedication.

The other group of friends who were generous in their help was from the Mumbai police department. My profound thanks to Deputy Inspector General of Police, Anti-Terrorism Squad (ATS), Pradeep Sawant. When I started the book way back in 2005, Sawant was the deputy commissioner of police, Crime Branch. At my first request for help, he made several important files and documents available to me, which proved to be invaluable.

The legendary Rakesh Maria, chief of the Anti-Terrorism Squad, has been always forthcoming with information on the Mumbai mafia despite his hectic schedule. Thank you, Maria saab.

Additional Commissioner of Police, Traffic, Brijesh Singh's insights into techno surveillance is unparalleled. Every time I met him, I came back wi-fied and enriched!

Among the retired cops, Assistant Commissioner of Police (ACP) Ishaq Bagwan was of invaluable help. He gave me extensive interviews lasting several hours, which provided deep insights into the gruesome underbelly of the Mumbai mafia, especially the Pathans and their Machiavellian ways.

Retired ACP Madhukar Zende was amazing with his excellent recall of crimes that occurred forty years ago. We need many more like him.

Assistant Commissioner of Police Iqbal Shaikh and ACP Sunil Deshmukh helped me with the reconstruction of the 1991 Lokhandwala encounter, which, two decades later, is still the Mumbai police's most sensational run-in with the mafia.

I am also grateful to family members of Dawood Ibrahim, including his sister Haseena Parkar, who spoke to me at length. Ahmed chacha was also helpful as always.

The late Abdur Rahim alias Rahim chacha, the childhood friend of Baashu Dada, Ibrahim Parkar, and elder to Dawood, was generous in talking about Dawood and helped me reconstruct several scenes narrated in this book. Rahim chacha, who lived in Behrampada in Bandra east, called me to his home several times and spoke for several hours despite his ill health and infirmity.

Dawood's other Konkani relatives also helped and spoke to me extensively on the condition of anonymity.

This acknowledgement would be incomplete until I express my thanks to some of the unnamed members of the Mumbai mafia. The intimate, tiny details about Dawood's personal and early life came from them. These men were his childhood friends who played *gilli-danda* with him and some of them have still kept in touch with him even after he relocated to Dubai and Pakistan.

The scenes and dialogues in the book have been recreated and written with the help of these men who have sworn me to secrecy. The scenes are as close to accurate as it can get with some creative licence. It is needless to add that the accuracies in the book belong to these benefactors and the friends mentioned earlier, while the errors are solely mine.

Before I sign off, I have to mention my ferociously loyal friend Anuradha Tandon, who keeps me firmly planted on terra firma, and deserves a special thanks for always asking me to raise the bar.